Oral Performance and the Veil of Text

Oral Performance and the Veil of Text

Detextification, Paul's Letters, and the Test Case of Galatians 2–3

Ben F. van Veen

Foreword by Arie W. Zwiep

PICKWICK Publications · Eugene, Oregon

ORAL PERFORMANCE AND THE VEIL OF TEXT
Detextification, Paul's Letters, and the Test Case of Galatians 2–3

Copyright © 2024 Ben F. van Veen. All rights reserved. Except for brief quotations in critical publications or reviews, no part of this book may be reproduced in any manner without prior written permission from the publisher. Write: Permissions, Wipf and Stock Publishers, 199 W. 8th Ave., Suite 3, Eugene, OR 97401.

Pickwick Publications
An Imprint of Wipf and Stock Publishers
199 W. 8th Ave., Suite 3
Eugene, OR 97401

www.wipfandstock.com

PAPERBACK ISBN: 978-1-6667-6295-2
HARDCOVER ISBN: 978-1-6667-6296-9
EBOOK ISBN: 978-1-6667-6297-6

Cataloguing-in-Publication data:

Names: Veen, Ben F. van, author. | Zwiep, Arie W., foreword.

Title: Oral performance and the veil of text : detextification, Paul's letters, and the test case of Galatians 2–3 / Ben F. van Veen ; foreword by Arie Zwiep.

Description: Eugene, OR: Pickwick Publications, 2024. | Includes bibliographical references.

Identifiers: ISBN 978-1-6667-6295-2 (paperback). | ISBN 978-1-6667-6296-9 (hardcover). | ISBN 978-1-6667-6297-6 (ebook).

Subjects: LSCH: Bible.—Epistles of Paul—Criticism, interpretation, etc. | Bible.—Galatians 2–3—Criticism, interpretation, etc. | Oral tradition. | Detextification.

Classification: BS2655 V21 2024 (print). | BS2655 (ebook).

VERSION NUMBER 01/24/24

Unless otherwise noted, Scripture quotations are from the New Revised Standard Version Bible, copyright © 1989 National Council of the Churches of Christ in the United States of America. Used by permission. All rights reserved worldwide.

Contents

Foreword by Arie W. Zwiep | vii
Preface | ix

Introduction | 1

1. The Study of Oral Tradition: Getting before Homer as Text | 38
2. Pauline Scholarship and Oral Performance, but What about "Text"? | 73
3. Detextifying Paul's Letters | 154
4. Detextification: Test Cases in Galatians 2 and 3 | 195

Conclusions | 276

Bibliography | 295

Foreword

THAT THE BIBLICAL WRITINGS originated in a predominantly oral setting, is not a very revolutionary insight. Its implications, however, have dawned only very recently. The pioneering work of such scholars as Walter Ong, Werner Kelber, and David Rhoads has caused a revolution—a reluctant revolution, I'm inclined to say—in the study of texts from antiquity, including the biblical writings. Their work is innovative, promising, challenging, and to some a serious threat to the guild of biblical scholars, exegetes and theologians.

Of course, biblical scholars have always known that the New Testament writings, such as the gospels and the writings of Paul, were not normally read in silence but read aloud in early Christian gatherings, that is, in the presence of a live audience. In the first centuries, physical copies of the early Christian texts were unevenly distributed. The complete Bible as we now have it, is a relatively late development. Physical copies were not always and everywhere available, either because of the high illiteracy rate or because of the high expenses of a manuscript. One can thus easily imagine a local community in Asia Minor that was in the fortunate position of having one copy of the Gospel of Matthew, one of John, and perhaps some of the letters of Paul. And then someone had to do the reading, the public reading, that is. Yet the question how the communicative process between text and reader exactly worked (and works) in practice is not very often asked or problematized. In general, the invention of the printing press, the mass distribution of written documents, and the digitalization, were rightly seen as revolutionary stages in the communication process, yet seldom was it realized that this had a massive impact on how texts were perceived and misperceived. It was seldom realized that the "chirographic bias" (Walter Ong) was a real hindrance in understanding the communicative process from start to finish.

It is at this point that Ben van Veen takes his point of departure. Taking the example of a modern biblical scholar doing research in the New Testament writings—surrounded by all the technical tools at his disposal in an academic library stocked with all the literature available, including the most advanced digital resources—Van Veen is intrigued by the completely different mindset of this model modern scholar compared to the original audience present in an early Christian community gathering in which, say, a letter of Paul or a passage from the gospels, was read aloud and performed. This study, which is a revised version of the author's PhD at the Vrije Universiteit Amsterdam, is an attempt to come to an understanding of what is going on between the first oral performance then-and-there and the reading of the text here-and-now, and how the different mindsets complicate (facilitate or obstruct) the interpretive processes. In a sense, it is an exercise in the archaeology of the mind, analyzing how a highly literate reader in the present and someone living in a predominantly oral context in the past structure their thoughts in completely different ways: what does that mean for the interpretation of the New Testament writings? It is not about how the original documents came into being or were composed but about how their first (and subsequent) performance(s) worked out in practice, as autonomous text, to use a term of the author.

This book is no easy reading. The author has a habit of feasting the reader on complex thought structures, he is not afraid to bombard his readers frequently with Latin and German terms, and he enjoys neologisms, "detextification" being the most prominent one. One might regret such use of language, but it may be indicative of the complexity and the novelty of the domain explored.

As a prison chaplain, Van Veen has had ample opportunity to test his theory in practice in a specific professional domain and develop his ideas into a method. The application of his method to other professional fields, such as health care, education, and pastoral ministry, may yield additional insights in how to come (hermeneutically speaking) to a better understanding of both ancient text and modern reader. But that's for the reader here-and-now (*hic et nunc*) to discover!

Arie Zwiep
Vrije Universiteit Amsterdam

Preface

"Ben makes Paul even more complicated than he already is." A colleague minister made this remark in her speech at my leave-taking from the Protestantse Gemeente Heeze c.a. Ten years later, I will defend the present thesis and hope to present *detextification* as an approach that will clarify our understanding of the letters of Paul. However, experiences with co-readers throughout the years has made it clear to me that it takes time before the argument starts making sense. So, I feel urged in this preface to forewarn you: as highly trained reader, please, do not underestimate how much your way of thinking is based on the media of and fused with the mindset behind text.

The biblical text as *text* is a given. That is the starting point of this book. For that reason, the argumentation centres on detextifying "text" and "reader"/"to read"/"reading." Nonetheless, several incentives to other forms of detextification are provided as well. Related to the functioning of text, suggestions are provided for detextifying "meaning," "interpretation," "hermeneutics," and "media." Apparently more severed from text, detextification also sheds light on notions such as "tradition" or "theology" and schemes such as "text-context" and "subject-object." As a next project, I would be interested in labouring a detextification of Scripture. More personally, in my work as prison chaplain, I have detextified my own practice of preaching. More than just working without text as physical artefact in preparing and performing church services, it has radically changed my view of the Bible and the Gospel of Jesus Christ in relation to the inmates, who often have a low level of literacy.

This book is indebted to so many people. I hold invaluable memories of the time as a visiting scholar at the Duke Divinity School, in Durham, NC. Prof. Dr Richard Hays supervised me there in a cordial and inspiring way. These conversations led to the first test case as presented in Chapter 4. In a later stage, Prof. Dr Samuel Byrskog was willing to read through the manuscript several times. In particular, he has helped me in coming to terms with the roots of the term text itself. Throughout the years at the Vrije Universiteit, Prof. Dr. Martin de Boer has put his mark on my approach to Paul and his letters due to his perception of the apostle, his Letter to the Galatians, and, in particular, apocalyptic. I want to mention Prof. Dr. Jan Willem van Henten here, because he was right when he taught me that there is a difference between "gelijk hebben" and "gelijk krijgen." I also would like to thank Prof. Dr. David Rhoads, who read parts of the manuscript, also the discussion of his own proposal for performance criticism, with several critical questions on it, and reacted in a constructive, open and friendly way. As friends, who were interested and willing to read parts of the developing manuscript, I think of, among others, the late Dr. Janneke Raaijmakers, Dr. Jan Bor, and Dr. Daniel Timmerman. My head of the Protestant prison chaplaincy allowed me to take time off to finish this project and also challenged me to provide training for colleagues in detextifying church services in prison. My brother-in-law, Theo van den Heuvel, was willing to apply his professional qualities to create the Infographic and to help me design the cover (Studio Uitzien). Helen Pears did a great job in editing and at the same time teaching me how to improve my writing on an academic level (The Better Writing Service). I also want to thank the members of the reading committee, who were willing to read my manuscript and also helped me with their comments to further clarify aspects in the line of my argumentation. In this respect, I want to especially thank my promotors, Prof. Dr. Arie Zwiep and Prof. Dr. Bert Jan Lietaert Peerbolte. With professional guidance, sincere interest, and patience, Arie Zwiep has led me through many rewritings of my manuscript. In this way, the argumentation became clearer not only to him but also to myself. Bert Jan Lietaert Peerbolte has convinced me to insert the special Cautions to the reader #1–4 in the Introduction.

I am grateful for the financial support I received from Prins Bernhard Cultuur Fonds, Stichting Aanpakken, Stichting Zonneweelde, and Vicariefonds Ridderlijke Duitsche Orde Balije van Utrecht.

My parents and parents-in-law were supportive. It is incredible to have people around me who believe in me. Stefan Dijkhuizen and Giel Schormans have supported me in the moment of defence as paranymphen. Most important in this process and in my life, I want to thank my wife, Helene. She has been of great support and guidance in finding a way through all the barriers accompanying this project. Thank you for your belief in me, letting me grow, and enabling me to come this far. Also, my lovely children: Sarah, Noa, Tijs, and Jonas, you are the joys of my life! *SDG*.

Utrecht, 9 December 2023

Introduction

BIBLICAL SCHOLARS READ AND write texts.[1] They study the Bible. This normally leads to publications in books and journals. These texts again evoke reactions in writing. Beginning and end then are dominated by "text." In the words of Werner Kelber: "The methods that we deploy in biblical studies have instilled in us the idea of autonomous textual entities, which grew out of texts, linked up directly with other texts, and in turn generated new texts."[2] For centuries, this practice of going back and forth between texts has been common in academia. In this way, we relate to the world around us—it becomes abstracted "world" which is represented in text.[3] This dynamic prompts Paul Ricoeur to claim that "[t]his relation of text to text, within the effacement of the world about which we speak, engenders the quasi-world of texts or *literature*."[4] Metaphorically speaking, the biblical scholar exists in an ever-expanding universe of texts.

---

1. The writer of the present text comes from a Protestant background. As a characteristic feature of this tradition, one is urged to read and study the Bible for oneself, individually. In the Catholic tradition one encounters, as a rule, the Scriptures at the moment of hearing/reading them aloud in the liturgy. Traditionally speaking, individual engagement with the Bible is less familiar there. The same pertains to Orthodox communities. Characteristically, passages from Scripture are taken up here in the liturgy without being explicated as such. These differences came to me in a conversation with Prof. Dr. Jens Schröter, Prof. Dr. Arie Zwiep, and Prof. Dr. Bart Koet at a symposium in Utrecht in 2017.

2. Kelber, "Jesus and Tradition," 141. See also, Rodríguez, "Reading and Hearing," 151: "The various disciplines comprising biblical studies have at their heart literary agenda, a fact consonant with the etymology of *Bible*."

3. In the present study, by "us" I refer to you as reader and myself as writer of the current text. As reader, I presuppose that you live in the twenty-first century, have a basic knowledge of the discipline and history of biblical studies, and are trained or able to read on an academic level of literacy.

4. See Ricoeur, "What Is a Text?," 149 (emphasis original). I thank Prof. Dr. Arie

TEXT AND AN EMERGING *COMMUNIS OPINIO* IN BIBLICAL SCHOLARSHIP

In biblical scholarship there is, however, another perspective on the Christian Old and New Testaments to be found as well: these ancient documents functioned in a cultural context in which speech and sound dominated communication.[5] In the history of research, we find indications that a *communis opinio* is emerging in New Testament scholarship on the important role of the spoken word in the Roman era (Chapter 2).[6] Originally, lectors and emissaries mediated the New Testament gospels and letters to live audiences. So, the intended addressees did not read themselves, but they were exposed to someone embodying the message to them.

The present study seeks to carefully examine this approach to engaging with biblical material. In order to bring a clearer focus for this, the so-called authentic letters of Paul, and in particular, the letter to the Galatians will be considered specifically.[7] This restriction will lead to a clearer focus. The rather high degree of specificity in the case of the Galatian converts, their rhetorical situation (for example, other teachers[8]), and the tense relationship with the apostle will help shed light on the originally intended communicative process or media functioning of this letter there-and-then.[9]

Zwiep for drawing my attention to this article.

5. As a classic publication with regard to the Old Testament, see Niditch, *Oral World and Written Word*. For the New Testament, see Kelber, *The Oral and the Written Gospel*.

6. For the emergence of a *communis opinio* in New Testament scholarship, we can refer inter alia to the polemical and critical essay by Hurtado, "Oral Fixation," 321–40. Given Kelber's study, Hurtado explicitly affirms that the appreciation of the spoken word in the Roman era "may be taken now as widely accepted and not under dispute here" ("Oral Fixation," 323). He explicates this point of view in detail (Chapter 2).

7. Regarding the related genre, the present study prefers the designation "letter" over "epistle." This distinction was introduced by Deissmann; see his *Bibelstudien: Beiträge*, 1–59. Based on his explanation, we prefer the designation "letter," despite the confusing homonym, because it is framed in line with "mündliche Zwiesprache" and expresses the actuality and oral-aural aspect of this communicative event. "Epistle" refers to a piece of composed literature meant to be disseminated to a wider and more abstracted public of trained readers.

8. Most commentators and studies reconstruct the realm of history there-and-then in terms of "teachers" who arrived from outside these communities. An alternative view is provided by Oestreich, *Performanzkritik*. On pages 230–43 he argues that the opponents, with which Paul has to deal, are a minority of influential Jewish members in these communities themselves.

9. It is important to make a distinction between the rather simple compositional process behind Paul's letters and the rather complicated and layered ones underlying the gospels. Regarding the letters of Paul, we are dealing with the apostle as the composer (assisted by his co-workers), the emissary, one artefact (autograph), and the

Confusion of Roles: Reader and/or Historian?

In the above, two different situations are discernible: as physical artefacts, we as present-day readers are dealing with the gospels and letters as *text*. We see the characters of the Greek or English alphabet in specific combinations with spaces between them; these letters appear to us in black, ordered in straight lines, and by margins against the background of a white page or screen—that is, the so-called "text area" (to which you also relate right now). In this way, the available biblical text forces us to the familiar activity of reading. In principle, this engagement with text is repeatable and elicits intellectual labour: "What does the text say?"[10] or "What does it mean?"[11]

---

community that Paul wanted to reach in the event of delivery. Not to mention that the nature of the communication is direct speech, since the emissary represented Paul in person. In this historical trajectory, there are only a few identifiable links in the chain; the speech of the apostle is directly relatable to the specific rhetorical situations of these communities. Regarding the Gospel of Mark, Matthew, Luke, and John, the communicative trajectory is rather different and more diffuse. For their emergence, one has to start with the performances and reperformances of the *ipsissima verba* of Jesus himself. Subsequently, one has to consider how his friends and followers spread these *logia* and simultaneously how their experiences with Jesus turned into stories about him. The study of memory makes clear that one has to consider in this respect the role of appropriation and reappropriation of the past to the circumstances of the ever-changing present (see Kirk, "Social and Cultural Memory," 7). In that light, the stage in the Jesus movement comes to mind that is determined by a growing need to write down. Information about the circumstances of and the participants in these processes that led to the available gospels is sparse (Who are Mark, Matthew, Luke, and John and did they actually write these gospels themselves or were they even involved in this process?); their becoming and original functioning is open to many reconstructions. In this light, the question of composition of the gospels is different from the one of the letters of Paul. Therefore, the argumentation of the present study is in a more general way applicable to the genre of the gospels. For the role of memory, scribality, and textuality in the making of the gospels, see Byrskog, *Story as History*; Werner H. Kelber, "The Case of the Gospels"; Dunn, "Altering the Default Setting"; Kirk and Thatcher, "Jesus Tradition as Social Memory"; Schwartz, "Christian Origins"; Horsley, "Prominent Patterns"; Hearon, "The Story of 'the Woman Who Anointed Jesus'"; Kelber, "The Works of Memory—A Response"; Schwartz, "Jesus in First-Century Memory—A Response"; Dunn, *Jesus Remembered, Volume 1*; Rodríquez, "Reading and Hearing"; Kelber, "The Generative Force of Memory".

10. In an earlier stage of this research project, I was invited to present my work at the Amsterdam New Testament Colloquium. *Éminence grice*, the late Prof. Dr. Tjitze Baarda attended this meeting. He ended his response to my presentation with the statement that as a biblical scholar he was taught to ask the question: "What does the text say?"

11. In the opening chapter "What is Exegesis?" in *Handbook to Exegesis*, Porter and Clarke describe the existing ambiguity between words as "exegesis," "interpretation," and "hermeneutics" to arrive at the following clarification: "Broadly speaking, all three terms fall under the discipline of 'heuristics' (. . .) that is, the study and development of

Vis-à-vis text, we are determined to find some sort of meaning for ourselves and for the communities we serve—such as academia, biblical or Pauline scholarship, Christian churches or society at large.[12]

This relation to the letters in the present can be distinguished—especially when centring upon the Letter to the Galatians—from an unrepeatable, envisioned, and trenchant moment of oral delivery in the past. We can imagine someone standing amid the gathered assembly and addressing them. Not only aspects such as the raising of the voice, pausing at certain moments, and the role of gesticulation should be thought of, but also what went before (conversion, baptism, the appearance of other teachers, and their call to circumcision), the sphere of the gathering (anxiety, agitation, or anger?), factions and interests (Jewish and Gentile members, different social classes), power relations ([Jewish] teachers, leaders in the local congregations) and the authority of the sender (Paul) bestowed on the emissary. However, this past historical moment has vanished. Critical reconstruction and imagination are needed to come to an adequate description—as a rule, in text—of that historical context.

---

methods or principles that aid one in discovering *the sense and meaning of a text*" (4/5; emphasis mine). Subsequently, they state: "[T]he word interpretation is often used interchangeably with the words hermeneutics and exegesis" (5). At the end, they draw the following conclusion "The fact is that there are various aspects of a texts meaning and different types of exegesis can address these various aspects" ("What is exegesis?," 5) Thus, in this given and crucial question, the main focus and activity in biblical scholarship seem somehow condensed: the reader is exposed to the text looking for meaning, that is, what it meant and/or what it means.

12. This stance sheds light on how the objective of the present study relates to theories and approaches on "intertextuality." Julia Kristeva introduced this term ("Le mot," 85). Inspired by Michail Bachtin and Jacques Derrida, she wanted to break open the dominant structuralist view in literary criticism on "text." Instead of defining text as a set of linguistic structures in need of decoding, she advocates "the 'literary word' as *an intersection of textual surfaces* instead of a *point* (fixed meaning), as a dialogue among several writings: that of the writer, the addressee (or the character), and the contemporary or earlier cultural context" ("Word," 65). Although widening the scope of writing as far as the historical and social dimensions of the writer and reader involved, her theory emerges from literature functioning as text and/or writing. Next to this rather broad and open definition, more limited approaches were also developed. In this respect, the intertextual approach by Hays in *Echoes* and *Conversion* is highly relevant. In *Echoes*, regarding the broad matrix of intertextuality as used by Kristeva, Hays "propose[s] instead to discuss the phenomenon of intertextuality in Paul's letters in a more limited sense, focusing on his actual citations of and allusions to specific texts" (*Echoes*, 15). For discussion and an example on Hab 2.4/Gal 3.11, see footnotes 479 and 548. For the present study, the following observation is important: in an open as well as a limited intertextual approach, the biblical text functioning as text here-and-now-to-us forms the starting point. Therefore, the presented approach of detextification can also be relevant and applied to intertextual approaches of the biblical documents.

Self-evidently, a physical artefact was constitutive of this past event. The letter as thing (autograph) has been transmitted (apographs) and studied throughout the ages (manuscripts). In this process of transmission, the appearance of these documents has transformed into the printed or digital versions to which we are now accustomed. Thus, the transmitted documents constituting the corpus Paulinum here-and-now-to-us witness to these somehow lost and highly specific moments there-and-then-to-them. Paradoxically, however, as witnesses, these letters—that is, the physically transmitted and transformed artefact[s] here-and-now—did not yet function as "text" to the original addressees in the way they do to us. Put differently, there are two perspectives on the letters as written documents/"texts." First, and most familiar to us because of the relation to the available version as text, one is placed in the role of *reader* to ask, What does it mean? In this typical question, the fundamental, though implicit and intricate relation between "text," "reading," and "meaning" becomes visible to us. Second, the original addressees were exposed to someone who performed the documented wordings to them on behalf of Paul. More precisely, in the process of composition, the apostle must have envisioned and anticipated how his addressees would hear or react to the utterings of the one who read the letter aloud in his name.[13] So, in line with this second perspective, we become reconstructive *historians* in a sense and ask, What is happening, more specifically, What is happening there-and-then in the envisioned oral delivery between performer and his audience?

The purpose of the following investigation is to clarify the relation between our roles as historians and as readers: representation of the oral performance there-and-then is the role of the reconstructive historian, while the actual reading of the biblical text as text here-and-now is done by the present-day reader.[14]

---

13. In *Performanzkritik*, Oestreich argues that, instead of an emissary, local members function as public readers (146–51). This reconstruction of the realm of history there-and-then becomes more layered when he depicts the Galatian communities as existing of different and even partially opposed factions. Who will preside the meeting? Who will read the letter? Oestreich remarks: "He [Paul] had to expect that some performers might be on his opponents' side" (*Performanzkritik*, 150).

14. As we indicated in the footnote before the previous, with "text," "writing," and "literature" as bases, it is plausible to state that participants in theories in intertextuality will tend towards the role of reader.

Caution to the Reader #1: To Give Priority to the Historian

Pursuing this purpose necessarily involves much complexity. To present a clearer path, the exploration of the approach of *detextification* lies at the centre of this study. As it may seem counter-intuitive to speak of detextifying with regard to the study of "text," four "cautions" are noted in the Introduction with the intention of setting out some context for this approach from the outset.

As historians, we are in a fundamental way confronted with the hermeneutical gap between there-and-then and here-and-now.[15] In the present study, this gap is concretized by these two communicative situations of oral performance there-and-then and text here-and-now. However, this distinction becomes somewhat blurred: the operational way (textual) in which we argue for a distinctive media culture there-and-then (oral performance) turns the historian necessarily into a reader. Put simply, "history" is dealt with on the level of text (this actual text in front of you). Thus in the very nature of this thesis itself we find tension. We are engaged in one of the two media functionings involved (reading text *in actu*), while we want to do justice—in and through that same process—to that other communicative process (historicizing oral performance). In this imbalanced endeavour, one could ask whether we, instead of bridging a gap, resemble Baron Munchausen who tried to pull himself out of the mire by his own hair.

In doing justice to this analysis, the present research project takes on a philosophical dimension. How to proceed in this respect? When we speak of *history* (or to historicize) in this research project, we do not necessarily and solely relate to the "past" (there-and-then) in distinction from the "present" (here-and-now). Another dichotomy will structure the present argumentation. The terms past and present refer to a perspective on "reality" that is dominated by the human body or our senses: in this way, we relate primarily in real time/*in actu*, or uncritically, to the world around us. Put differently, the dimensions of time and place are constitutive of the realm of history.[16] Importantly, this applies to those "there-and-then" (Paul, the Galatians, and other teachers) as well as to ourselves "here-and-now"

---

15. In "What is Exegesis?," Porter and Clarke phrase the consequences regarding the exegetical task as follows: "Exegesis that seeks to answer what the text *means* at present is usually based upon the synchronic condition of the text, that is, *what it is*. On the other hand, exegesis that concerns itself with what the text *meant* relies more heavily upon the diachronic condition of the text, that is, *how it came to be what it is*" ("What Is Exegesis?," 11–12; emphasis original).

16. In Chapter 3, Section A.1. Textualizing text *hic et nunc pro nobis*, we will argue that another dimension is involved next to those of time and place, namely, the knowing subject *in actu*.

(biblical scholar, present-day reader, and in academia). So, instead of being applied pejoratively, the adjective *uncritical* is used in a descriptive way. A key characteristic of Western philosophical tradition, especially vis-à-vis text, is that the reader is enabled to create a distance between themselves (their participation/being present) and the object of study (their observation/representation of). This typical relation to the world around enables *critical* thought. The movement is from being uncritically present in to critical representation of the world. For that reason, we explicitly distinguish, in the present study, the *realm of history* (presence/uncritical) and the *realm of extra-historical thought* (representation/critical). The reader, text, and the typical way of relating to the world aligns with the latter realm, the historian focuses on the former realm. We will give priority to the historian and, therefore, the realm of extra-historical thought will be subject to the realm of history. That is to say, the way we are used to formulate and argue will be critically and systematically examined against the background of the realm of history. (This will be worked out in the subsequent Cautions to the reader.) For now, we will conclude this caution with four remarks. First, this distinction or dichotomy is itself highly critical in nature: to formulate the "realm of history" is not possible without and somehow takes place in the "realm of extra-historical thought." Thus, the intellectual endeavour of detextification should not be seen as a disqualification of or as being in opposition to text. It is important to state clearly that *we need text to detextify*. Second, this systematic approach of the "realm of history" and to giving this realm and its laws priority—in distinction from the "realm of extra-historical thought"—will constitute a critical structure in the argumentation as a whole. Third, because of this presuppositional level, the present study can be valued as a contribution to the philosophy of biblical studies in a sense. Fourth, the traditional hermeneutical gap is transformed from the separation between here-and-now and there-and-then to the distinction between the realm of history and *freischwebendes Denken*. In the second and fourth Chapters, several examples will illuminate the working of this structure. In this way, like Baron Munchausen, we will get hold of our own hair to begin pulling ourselves up.

The Communication Model: Sender, Message, and Addressee

These communicative processes of participating in oral performance and reading text overlap to some extent. When we take the standard communication model (singular) which is constituted by the elements of sender (singular), message (singular), and addressee (singular) as a starting-point, we do not immediately find substantial differences.[17] Such a model, however, presents as highly abstract and reductive—as witnessed in the typical formulation in the singular—where attention to the dimension of the media is virtually absent. These three elements represent "worlds" in themselves. Regarding the Letter to the Galatians, we answer the questions of sender, message, and addressees without much difficulty; the answers are as concise as the elements themselves: Paul, the letter or text, and his Galatian converts.

In line with the purpose of the present study though, the answer to the last question (addressee) needs to be refined. From the perspective of technology, one could argue that when we read the letter as text, we ourselves have become in a sense the addressees. The communicative dynamic implied in text is that the one who actually reads (in the present) is the one who comes to understanding (represent in the present). Against the background of the realm of history in which the biblical scholar participates in real time, it becomes clear that when the letter is functioning as text, the reader becomes the addressee. Inevitably, I emphasize here the media functioning of text. The role of what Hans-Georg Gadamer terms our *Vorverständnis* (prior understanding), or, in the words of Umberto Eco, our encyclopaedia of knowledge, is not to be denied. This should explain, for example, why a biblical scholar will say that not they themselves but the Galatians are the addressees—for they know that already on the basis of basic knowledge. And, as the practice of current biblical scholarship demonstrates, it is clear that different readings are certainly possible; they can even be in line with the originally intended communicative process (as we will see later on in the discussion of Chapter 4). The following point is important, however: It is the *actual reader of the text* who arrives, in the process of reading, at some sort of understanding; how *the originally intended addressees in the event of delivery* would have come to understand—and whether there are possible differences in their way of structuring thought—is a different matter. For the present study, this is an important distinction or plurality to explore further.

Umberto Eco: "What One Calls 'Message' Is Usually a Text"

We must also pay attention to the second element in the standard communication model, that is, the message. In his study *The Role of the Reader*, Umberto Eco comments on the above mentioned basic communicative

---

17. This model is based on the so-called Organon model developed by Bühler in his *Sprachtheorie*. He influenced Roman Jakobson to formulate his six communication functions, see the latter's "Closing Statements: Linguistics and Poetics," in Sebeok, *Style in Language*, 350–77.

model that it "does not describe the actual functioning of communicative discourse."[18] He concretizes the model and distinguishes the following layers: various codes and subcodes regarding sender and addressee, variety in socio-cultural circumstances—which can differ between the former and latter—and the rate of initiative displayed by the addressee in making presuppositions and abductions. He also makes an important distinction between "text as expression" (text as object) and "interpreted text as content" (the moment that the reading subject is relating to it to explicate an understanding). On this basis, Eco presents his famous distinction between "closed" and "open texts." Based on clichés, the former pull the reader along a predetermined path, "carefully displaying their effects so as to arouse pity or fear, excitement or depression at the due place and at the right moment."[19] These closed texts are 'open' to "any possible 'aberrant' decoding."[20] On the contrary, the open texts cannot be used as the reader wants, "but only as the text wants you to use it."[21] Here the real-time process of interpretation is a structural element of the generative process of the text. The layers in his theory of semiotics lead him to state that "[i]t is just by playing upon the prerequisites of such a general process that a text can succeed in being more or less open or closed." In a more general way then, Eco comments: "Moreover, what one calls 'message' is usually a *text*" (emphasis original).[22] First, his remark suggests that a message can be sent by more than one media. Second and important for the purport of this Introduction, in real time we "usually" and uncritically tend to funnel "message"—in our argumentations—into a single and implied media, that of "text." So, in the standard communicative model of sender, message, and addressee, Eco puts the finger on the suppressed role of media and he identifies this mechanism of implicit equation as a blind spot. This subliminal inclination requires systematic explication—which is the concern of the present study.

18. Eco, *Role of the Reader*, 5.

19. Eco, *Role of the Reader*, 8.

20. In Chapter 3, we will see that, according to Eco, the discourse in the letters of Paul resembles "closed text."

21. Eco, *Role of the Reader*, 9.

22. Eco, *Role of the Reader*, 5. When we ask how Eco defines "text," his preface provides an answer: Notwithstanding one essay dealing with "various sorts of texts," all the others deal with "verbal text" (*Role of the Reader*, vii). This limitation is underscored by his consistent use of terms such as "text," "reader," and "author" in his book.

Media Muddle: The Implicit Equation of "Letter" and "Text"

Above, we discussed the issue of the subordination of the reader to the historian (Caution to the reader #1). The semiotics of Eco turns our attention to text as media—to which we relate primarily as reader. With regard to this, Thomas Boomershine's article "Peter's Denial as Polemic or Confession: The Implications of Media Criticism for Biblical Hermeneutics" is a key work with which to engage.[23] As an important leader in the Biblical Storytellers Network, he criticizes the usage of "literature" as reference to the New Testament as anachronistic. In this article, he argues that in using this term, an anomalous media, which emerged only later, is brought into the New Testament documents in an uncritical way. He calls this "media eisegesis."[24] In this respect, one of the central arguments of this thesis is that regarding the corpus Paulinum, there tends to be an implicit equation of "letter" and "text." So, like Eco, Boomershine asks attention for the fact that distinctive media are mingled. Instead of a *communis opinio*—wrought in debate—we could speak of the functioning of "literature" and "text" in biblical scholarship as a questionable though given *communis practica* through mere repetition. In this way, the biblical scholar gets in a *media muddle*: In a formal way, the scholar can acknowledge or even advocate that the letters were meant to be embodied by the lector in the oral performance there-and-then, recall the emerging *communis opinio*, and the related question What is happening? Operationally however, by relating themselves in their real-time praxis to the letter as text-to-be-read (*communis practica*), the scholar overrules here-and-now the performance as the intended media *in actu*. The problem of the media muddle is that conclusions and insights on the formal level (representation) are made ineffective by, or do not reach into, the operational situation or praxis of the biblical scholar (presence). In still reading the letter as text in real time, the governing question will remain: What does it mean? As Chapter 2 will show, we even have to draw this conclusion regarding advocates of actual performances here-and-now of the New Testament documents.

HYPOTHESIS (1): TWO DIFFERENT MEDIA FUNCTIONINGS AT ISSUE

This equation of message and text (Eco) must be problematized, in light of the *communis opinio* on the originally intended functioning of Paul's letters.

---

23. Boomershine, "Peter's Denial," 48–50.
24. Boomershine, "Peter's Denial," 48.

When we do not make any fundamental distinction between the two, the functioning of "text" takes over in real time—to us—regarding the message of the letters. Now we can make a firm step to the hypothesis of the present study: *Regarding the letters of Paul, it is of the utmost importance to identify distinctive media; that is to say, we have to look for differences in the functioning of (the letters as) text to a present-day reader and the letter as oral performance/public reading to the originally intended addressees.* (In section E. of this Introduction, another dimension inherent in this hypothesis is set out.)

Caution to the Reader #2: The Level of Text and Textualization

In the present study, we refer to the way in which we are used in academia to come to an understanding of the world around us as the *level of text*. On and by means of this level, we are able to represent. What we represent is what we term "reality," "history," that which was/is "present" or the "concrete lifeworld." The latter, however, exists per se beyond the level of text. In this way, we are like a dog chasing its own tail. The conundrum is as follows: on and via the level of text, we understand that which is beyond that same level. We can recognize here the contours of the earlier presented dichotomy between the realm of history and the realm of extra-historical thought. Giving priority to the perspective of the historian, *we have to critically and continuously push our formulations at the level of text* (extra-historical thought) *beyond that level* (into the realm of the history involved)—although this intellectual endeavour takes place by means of that same level. The aim is to break through uncritical constraints inherent in the level of text or the realm of extra-historical thought. In particular, we will engage critically with and challenge the use of terms related to the crucial matrix of "text," and in dealing with "text" the terms "to read"/"reading"/"reader" and "to mean"/"meaning." In addition, "oral performance," "media," "interpretation," "hermeneutics," "composition" (Chapter 3), "syllogism," "theology," and so on (Chapter 4), but also the text-context and subject-object schemes (Chapter 3), will similarly be pushed beyond that level.[25] They will be placed against the background of the realm of history there-and-then and also the realm of history here-and-now. Without explication or explanation, we will

---

25. For a comparable though different endeavor in Homeric studies, see Powell, "Text, Orality". In this article, Powell wants to come to a redefinition of these terms by zooming in on relevant historical praxes, whether as described in ancient sources as retrieved by experiments, such as performed by Milman Parry and Albert Lord (see Chapter 1). On the one hand, he acts as a historian and pushes these terms as far as possible beyond the level of text, while on the other hand, he leaves the term "text" as such unchanged on the level of text.

see that these terms are used as a given—that is, on the level of text. Therefore, they will be framed by the actual reader *in actu* of that text beyond that level—that is uncritically in line with his own mindset and concrete lifeworld (see the exploration of "reading" in distinction from "public reading" below). Once we are aware of this tension between on and beyond the level of text, we will find a way out of the media muddle. In Chapters 2 and 4, we critically engage in this way studies on the distinctive media culture regarding the New Testament.

In the present study, we refer to the procedure to push concepts and notions beyond the level of text as *textualization*. This form of historicization or description will lead to a broadening of the level of text. In distinction to reasoning which is isolated in the realm of extra-historical thought, one can textualize history (see below). The framing of this intellectual movement is intentionally based on a verb, more precisely, a participle: to textualize/textualizing/textualization. It implies that a process is taking place or that an activity is in progress. In line with the distinction between the realm of extra-historical thought and the realm of history, this particular formulation of "textualizing" gives priority to the latter. In textualizing history, we do not only explicate and explain what we mean by certain familiar notions and words, but we also have to structure our reasoning as far as possible in line with the dynamics or laws of the realm of history (*becoming*). So, by reframing the overly familiar noun ("text") as an activity in progress ("to textualize"), the fixedness which comes with *being* should be loosened. Textualization is, therefore, a process which takes place through the level of text (means), yet on that level, we can continually move deeper into the realm of history (end). We do so by asking and describing what is happening or how it functions. It will never be finished, fixed, completed, or perfect (being). So, although, to follow the metaphor of Baron Munchausen, we may never fully get out of the mire, we can pull ourselves by our own hair always higher.

"ORAL PERFORMANCE": PRELIMINARY CONSIDERATIONS

To textualize differences between the functionings of the letter, we must start by first explicating the parameters of "oral performance" in the realm of history. Regarding the originally intended media functioning of the letters, we can take the example of Gal 3.1. Here Paul cries out: "You foolish Galatians! Who has bewitched you?"[26] For us, as present-day readers, this is an odd experience. When we process the text by reading and encounter

---

26. All quotations will be from the NRSV unless otherwise stated.

an exclamation like this, all of a sudden, our relationship to the letter changes. From thinking we turn to experiencing—as if we hear the apostle cry out himself! Several senses become activated and we ask: What is going on? What has happened to make Paul cry out like this? Similarly, we can experience Gal 4.20: "I wish I were present with you now and could change my tone, for I am perplexed about you." Here we sense a mixture of indignation and concern over his spiritual children. A different understanding is the result. In these passages of the letter, Paul comes very near to us. For a moment, the text becomes living or direct speech. At the same time, we realize that this exclamation is not meant for us as twenty-first-century readers. Needless to say, it was directed to the historical Galatians as persons of flesh and blood. Its intended effect was related to their specific situation (realm of history).

Parlance: "Public Reading" and "Reading"

As a consequence, "public reading" and/or "oral performance" cannot and will not be treated as opposites in the present study.[27] The goal of both activities is the same: to influence how the intended hearers grasp and act in their concrete situation. Hence, on the level of text, we will critically distinguish, in the present study, "reading" and "public reading" there-and-then-to-them. The use of notions such as "reading," "to read," and "reader" involves an abstracting tendency. We sense the consequence when we formulate, regarding the "original addressees," that they—or the "emissary"—would "read" the letter. Any form of explication or explanation is lacking in such a formulation as to the kind of reading we are dealing with. As a consequence, we will fill in—technically speaking—the kind of "reading" with which we are familiar ourselves in real time: namely that a particular individual is silently relating to a written physical record.[28] Since biblical scholars do this all the time in their own real-time realm of history, it is a subliminal or uncritical process. As a result, "reading" in the first-century Mediterranean world comes to imply—once more, technically speaking—the same practice as in the twenty-first-century Western academic world.[29] Thus the frame

27. In Chapter 2, we will see that Hurtado drives a wedge between them in his essay "Oral Fixation."

28. In the words of sociologist and psychoanalyst Jeffrey Prager, "[I]t becomes nearly impossible to parse out memories of the past from the categories of experience available in the present" (*Presenting the Past*, 5).

29. Note that this does not imply one and the same actual understanding, but technically speaking the approach is the same; the structuring of thought is comparable (Chapter 3).

of reference implied in the singular concept of "reading" is also bound to singularity. It will be everywhere, every time, and for everyone somehow the same.[30] This structuring of thought veils other possible practices of reading. In this way, the simple and singular mentioning of "reading" at the level of text presses us all the more into the real-time and uncritical role of "reader" looking for the meaning. Typically, the reader then takes over from the historian. So, in this functioning of text to us, we lack critical differentiation between the realm of history there-and-then ("oral performance/public reading") and here-and-now ("reading").

In public reading, the adjective binds the one who is reading first and foremost to other human beings. The problem here is when we limit our scope—on the level of the text—to the lector as "reader" and the letter as "text," we overlook the end of this communicative process, that is, the intended hearers; the lector is reading *to them*. The activity of public reading is a means to an end: the lector vocalizes these soundbites so that *the audience* can come to some sort of understanding and that they will be influenced in that way.

A distinctive structure in the presumed communicative process comes to the fore. The small extension of "public" enables us to structure our thoughts into the concrete situation of that act. The historian can stand up to ask, What is happening to the public there-and-then? As a result, the level of text more adequately resembles what is beyond that level.

Public Reading and the Crucial Role of the Body

We can deepen the difference between "reading" and "public reading" on the level of text, when we concentrate on the human body. In "reading text," our concrete lifeworld becomes concentrated in the visual exposure to the text area. Put simply, we should not look around—that is, beyond the boundaries of the text area—when we want to read effectively. Moreover, the (bodily) presence of the writer plays no role. We could describe this as the movement from "eye to text area." In this way, we see how text area and the level of text resemble each other (this is discussed in Chapter 3).

---

30. Beyond the level of text, that is in the concrete lifeworld of the Biblical scholar, there are of course several possible outcomes from our readings of one and the same text. However, we argue here in the main text consistently on and regarding the level of text as such. The relatedness of these different readings is seen as being related to the structuring of the propositions.

In regard to public reading, Robert Funk's "The Apostolic Parousia: Form and Significance" is highly relevant.[31] He states that Paul sent an emissary to represent himself amid his gathered addressees. This emissary communicated bodily Paul's message (verbal), intentions, and agenda (meta-verbal) as if they were relating to the apostle himself—in all sensorial aspects—at that moment. In this case, the human body is a crucial constituent of the intended communicative process involved. So, we can comprehend public reading as "body to body." Per se, it takes place beyond the level of text.

The differences between the given formulation of "reading" and the explication of "public reading" thus drives a wedge between rather highly abstracted reasoning (reading) on the one hand, and concretizing a specific realm of history with the human body (emissary, gathered addressees, and other teachers) within it as the focal point on the other hand (historicizing). In the latter, our imagination comes alive. When the emissary uses the registers of direct speech and sensorially based communication, we can differentiate between such an embodied experience—even in our lives now—and the intellectual or disembodying effect of reading prosaic and academic "text."

This stance also sheds light on "scribality" and "textuality"—both relate to the emergence and role of the written piece in the presupposed realm of history. Since Paul's concern is directed to his hearers (not his emissary who would be exposed to the documented wording), the implied structure might be summarized as the apostle trying to regain influence over his former converts in the envisioned event of delivery (Letter to the Galatians). On the one hand, the emissary or public reader related to the written words by a form of reading and this to some degree touches on our practice and the presence of text(s). On the other hand, there is no necessity to deal with the technical relationship between the emissary and the physical artefact, because that issue is valued as subservient to the earlier described goal of delivery. This is not to deny that the process of composition has led via dictation or documentation to the emergence of the physical artefact, which formed the basis of the performance and reperformances (Col 3.16) and is transmitted up to the present day as text, but the emphasis and focus of the exploration is upon the fact that the original addressees experience the

---

31. Funk, "The Apostolic Parousia." Margaret Mitchell nuances the generalizing argument of Funk. Regarding the first Letter to Timothy and Titus, she argues that Paul preferred communication through the letter to his presence there. She argues, "it is quite possible that we have a Pauline corpus in the first place because of the relative ineffectiveness of Paul's personal presence and his own creative recognition of that limitation" ("New Testament Envoys," 642).

words being embodied. This is the direction of travel intended when we speak of "oral performance" or "public reading."[32]

The Importance of the Study of Oral Tradition

The incentive behind the present study is found in the work of Milman Parry (1902–1935).[33] As a young American scholar in classical studies, he devoted his career to the study of the Homeric epics. His interest was directed towards the technique of composition behind these lengthy stories. He began studying Homer as literature. Later on, he was able to experience performances of similar extended stories in real time in the former Yugoslavia. He interviewed several bards who were used to performing their epics over and over without the aid of written versions. This research took place in a sociocultural context practically void of the influence of text-as-known-to-us, let alone academic training. Throughout the history of this discipline, other scholars such as Albert Lord and John Miles Foley addressed other aspects of this process (see Chapter 1). In several scholarly disciplines, a debate emerged not only on orality but also on literacy, scribality, and textuality.

To a certain extent, we can recognize here the contours of the same two media functionings in contemporary biblical scholarship. Parry's colleagues related to Homer solely through text—study based on printed versions without any mention of the possible impact of this specific media on their understanding. Parry was able to observe comparable epics performed in real time. These communicative events between non-literate though highly skilled bards, and similarly non-literate live audiences who were used to participating in this kind of occasion were *sui generis*. He started to relate to the Homeric epics as a historian, asking the question What is happening between the performer and his audience? Above, we suggested that oral performance is all about presence. Parry moved from the level of representation, that is, Homer functioning as text to him, into the situation of being present himself and observing bards and their audiences *in actu* (see Chapter 1). For the present study, this movement from representation to presence is the crucial transition that we seek to fruitfully employ for our understanding of the corpus Paulinum in its original functioning.

---

32. As set out in footnote 8, it is important to mark once more the distinction between the intended addressees of Paul's letters and the gospels.

33. See Parry, *The Making of Homeric Verse*. For a short biography and overview, see the introduction on pages ix–lxii.

Ancient Literacy in the First-Century Mediterranean World

There are differences between preliterate Homeric and early twentieth-century non-literate Slavic bards on the one hand, and Paul, his co-workers, emissaries, converts, opponents, and letters as physical artefacts on the other. It is well-known that the Judaism of Paul's day was especially a culture of studying and arguing with Scripture.[34] Paul participates in this praxis; one can point to the seven quotations from the Jewish scriptures as found in the short range of Gal 3.1–20—"for it is written." At the same time, it is telling that the kind of studying in Judaism as recorded in the Mishna and Talmud is categorized as "oral Torah," in contrast to the documents studied as "written Torah."[35] So, there is substantial evidence of writing, as well as indications of differing types and higher degrees of literacy with respect to Paul himself,[36] his socio-cultural (Jewish) context, his letters and, therefore, the realm of history in which we locate his original addressees. This train of thought might prompt the following argument on the level of text: since there is abundant evidence of "literacy," the role of "orality" can only be peripheral to the "literature" or "texts" of the New Testament.[37]

Hence, in the present study, "ancient literacy" is approached in the following way: while types, levels, rates, and activities in "literacy" in the realm of history there-and-then are acknowledged, subsequently, "literacy" needs to be extended beyond the level of text. This then, serves to guard against the implicit equation of our deeply ingrained way of structuring thought vis-à-vis the letters as text and text in general—that is, our kind of "literacy"

---

34. Mladen Popović describes certain groups in the Dead Sea Scrolls textual community as consisting of "intellectual" or "scholarly readers" ("Reading, Writing, and Memorizing," 447). In his article though, the question how these scholarly or intellectual readers came to structure their thoughts vis-à-vis these scrolls—possibly in distinction from the contemporary academic ("scholarly?") reader—remains open. A profound textualization could provide answers.

35. The distinction between "oral" and "written Torah" is seen as originating from the Second Temple period. However, it is only attested in rabbinic literature. In his article "The Origins of Oral Torah," Yael Fisch argues, in view of Rom 3.19–31 and 10.5–13, that Paul already presents a twofold torah.

36. Consider especially Keith, "'In My Own Hand.'" In this article, he explicates spectrums and kinds of literacies. In this historicization of "literate competencies," he states that Paul was—in his words—"grapho-literate": The apostle was not only able to read, but also—which added to his status—to write himself. Regarding Gal 6.11, "See with what big letters I write to you in my own hand," he, therefore argues that these words have rhetorical force, since Paul, on the one hand, demonstrates that he can write, but, on the other, is in a position that he can use an amanuensis.

37. In an exemplary way, we will encounter this reasoning in the essay by Hurtado, "Oral Fixation" (see Chapter 2 of this thesis).

in the twenty-first-century academia—with the construal of knowledge by the original addressees in the intended oral performances.

Contemporary Orality and a Predominantly Oral Mindset There-and-Then

Regarding the mindset in biblical scholarship, we intentionally continue to explicate the operational and real-time context, that is, "vis-à-vis text." When we, as highly trained readers, move away from the text area and are exposed bodily to situations of performance ourselves, we also deal with a different experience. A captivating sermon in church or lecture at the university, a political speech in times of election,[38] a TED Talk on YouTube, or an appealing call at a rally of some sort are perhaps cases in point. Regarding the present research project, these experiences are identified as distinct (body-to-body) from reading prosaic or academic text in silence and solitude (eye-to-text-area). We consume and do not produce these moments of performance as a rule. Traditional academic training is not directed towards this practice. When we keep these activities in mind though, we can relate ourselves better to the presupposed original functioning of the biblical documents. As we will see, we also structure our thoughts in a different way in such moments (Chapters 1 and 3). In this way, neither an "oral mindset" on their side nor a "literate" one on ours is absolutized. This acknowledgment prevents us from some sort of Great Divide thesis.[39] In this scheme,

---

38. In his article "Reading and Hearing," Rodríguez uses this same example to argue the opposite. Responding to another biblical scholar who introduces Walter Ong's oral psychodynamic "agonistic tone" as typical of oral thought and on the basis of a spectrum between primal orality up to high literacy, Rodríguez argues: "If we assume that twenty-first-century American political discourse properly resides nearer the literate pole of [the] spectrum bridging primary oral and literate cultures, what explains the agonistic tone of American politics?" ("Reading and Hearing," 153). Note that, in the present study, this specific example should illustrate our own (uncritical?) proximity to some sort of an oral-aurally determined mindset.

39. In his essay, "Creating a New 'Great Divide,'" Paul Evans notices that certain criticisms of the Great Divide thesis set up an artificial great divide of their own. Instead of a chasm between orality and literacy, he advocates an understanding of the relation between them as a continuum (750). In his third and fourth issue, he tackles the assumption that ancient scribes would have had an "oral mindset." In this mindset, the ancient scribe would be "more comfortable with variation and less concerned with exact detail than is the case with a literate mindset" (758). Based on research by Lord and Ong, he rejects the suggestion of Raymond Person of "non-literate scribes" (759). He argues that "caution must be taken in attributing a non-literate mindset to a highly literate individual such as, for example, the author(s) of Chronicles" (760). From the perspective of scribality, he explores the extent to which ancient scribes can

"literacy" and related "literate" societies are positioned over against "non-" or "preliterate" ones. Fixed dichotomies like these can preclude openness— on and because of the level of text—to kinds of continua between oralities and literacies (plural) in specific realms of history.⁴⁰

Nevertheless, since the intention is to compare the earlier hypothesized two media in which Paul's letters function[-ed], contrasts may help us to identify differences. We ourselves are familiar with and operationally caught up in one of them (text). The physical artefact, however, also plays a constitutive role in the oral performance there-and-then. Contrariwise, oral performance does not play such a role in our own processing of the letters as text. Heuristically speaking, we need a nuanced form of contrast.⁴¹

---

have an "oral mindset." Did they variate in the wording of repeated poems or narratives or did they tend to exact repetition? Based on ethnographic research, he comments, "If non-literate people . . . did in fact care about correct repetition—even verbatim repetition—we should be cautious in ascribing to literate scribes a mindset that was *not* concerned with verbatim repetition" (763). He concludes, "While the theory of a great divide between oral and literate cultures has rightly been questioned, we must be cautious not to put in its place a new great divide that exoticizes ancient cultures and exaggerates differences between ancient and modern literate cultures" (764). He adds, "As fieldwork has shown, literacy does have a powerful effect on non-literates; therefore caution needs to be exercised before an oral mindset is ascribed to a literate scribe" ("Creating a New 'Great Divide,'" 764). First, the present study underscores Evans's intent to advocate a continuum and not a chasm between orality and literacy. Second, his formulations such as "oral" and "literate mindset," "literacy" and "non-literates" can be deepened through this same continuum. The present study proposes framing the first-century Mediterranean world as a predominantly oral culture with varying types and high degrees of literacy and a similarly predominantly oral mindset—especially in terms of exposure to oral performances. In a similar way, readers in the socio-cultural context of academia here-and-now—also involving various sorts and degrees of orality and aurality—are understood as having a predominantly literate mindset, especially vis-à-vis text.

40. In this respect, we can turn, once more, to Rodríguez. He critiques an evolutionary paradigm regarding "orality" and "literacy": "the language of '*from* oral *to* written tradition' is . . . inappropriate because the earliest communities understood themselves, from the very earliest surviving evidence, with respect to (written) Hebrew biblical traditions" ("Reading and Hearing," 170).

41. Rodríguez takes a critical stance: "Nevertheless, we find compelling reasons to demur at the concept of an 'oral mentality,' and especially at the hopelessly vague 'oral culture,' both of which continue to be influential within NT research" (157). In another section, he adds, "we have to avoid idealizing so-called 'oral cultures' (primary, residual or otherwise)" (160). He wants to move beyond the opposition between "literacy" and "orality"; not only because they exclude each other, but also because of the inherent "universalizing" or "essentializing" tendency in defining them in this scheme (158): "We cannot reduce writing to frozen speech; it does not merely displace or replace orality, and it is not simply 'in service of' orality. Though writing can be any of these things, we are trying to avoid just these reductionist tendencies" ("Reading and Hearing," 161). It is important to notice that Rodríguez studies the gospels and the communities in

Therefore, in the present study, the distinctive cultural background of Paul's original addressees—especially in the exposure to oral performances—will be referred to as predominantly oral.[42]

Recapitulation: Oral Performance

A communicative act is framed as "oral performance" in the present study when someone addresses another/others by words which are either composed and documented to be read aloud or vocalized in the specific situation of those listening. The aim of this body-to-body communication is to affect these addressees in real time, so that they will change (or affirm) their grasp of and stance in their concrete situation. Thus, the goal of "oral performance" is inextricably bound to being present (live) in that specific realm of history. Relevant to us, as readers vis-à-vis text, "oral performance" in essence takes place beyond the level of text or representation. Therefore, regarding the letters of Paul, this study emphasizes that the originally intended participants have a predominantly oral mindset.

"TEXT": PRELIMINARY CONSIDERATIONS

We turn to the other media constitutive of the present study, that is "text." The aim is similarly, in explicating the parameters in the realm of history, we push the concept beyond the designation of the level of text.

It could be argued that the contemporary function of text is largely due to the educational culture of the West. This culture is driven by the capacity to read and write. The first evidences of writing systems in Western history go back as far as 1800 BCE (Cretan, linear A, linear B). Throughout the ages, the development of literacy has been both qualitative and quantitative.[43] In *The Universal Declaration of Human Rights* (1948), the right to education is structurally interpreted as "literacy" (article 26). From a young age, one

---

which they ("texts" [sic]) functioned. Note, in line with the earlier remarks in footnote 8, that the central role of the gospels as "texts" provides a different structure than, for example, the Galatian communities who are envisioned to be exposed to the unrepeatable and trenchant moments of body-to-body communication (oral deliverances of the letter by the emissary).

42. Chapter 2 discusses comparable stances in the following publications: Kelber, *The Oral and the Written Gospel*; Achtemeier, "*OMNE VERBUM*"; Botha, "Letter Writing"; Johnson, "Toward a Sociology"; Dewey, "Textuality"; Dewey, "Re-Hearing"; Davis, *Oral Biblical Criticism*; Rhoads, "Performance Criticism"; Oestreich, *Performanzkritik*; Hurtado, "Oral Fixation."

43. Goody, *Logic of Writing*; Fischer, *History of Writing*; Powell, *Writing*.

becomes acquainted with this ancient technology.[44] Levels and kinds of literacy are related to lower and higher degrees of education based on the capacity to read and write; it is more appropriate, then, to speak of literacies (plural). The academic community worldwide represents and sustains a culture of high literacy. Here text leads to more texts that describe, interpret, react, inquire, counter, comment, summarize, categorize, prescribe and so forth. The present study will be no exception and is only possible due to this tradition—namely, we need text to detextify. The actual reader of this specific text is seen as a product of this socio-cultural context. The pervasiveness of this tradition and training defines us as readers *par excellence*. Therefore, in search of differences, in this study we frame the socio-cultural context of biblical scholarship—especially vis-à-vis text—as predominantly literate.

Corpus Paulinum: Some Text from the Start

As already mentioned, in everyday life in biblical scholarship and beyond, one also speaks of the New Testament as "text." Let us now narrow the focus to the corpus Paulinum. Earlier we presupposed a trail throughout history: from the autograph, via apographs to the products of the printing press and the possibilities of the current digital revolution. This trail is in some way materialized in the artifacts with which we deal ourselves here-and-now, in the editions available to us. We can identify radical differences in matter and also between available editions; differences, for example, between *scriptio continua* then and word dividers now, iron-gall and carbon ink then and chemical ink and pixels now, or parchment and papyrus then and paper and screens now. The point to make here is that, despite all these differences, we often frame these letters as physical artefacts or things. This specific perspective on the documented word makes the letter a part of the so-called world of objects (being). Our thoughts become structured in line with the letter as a product. The result is that the letter as process—or how it functions in reality, in which particular realm of history it belongs (becoming)—is not reflected upon. The implicit equation in our parlance of "text" and "New Testament" or "Paul's letters" somehow strengthens this imbalance of objectification (being). The framing of the Bible as "text" on that level is ubiquitous. In line with this, we can conclude that we—as actual readers—are used to thinking that there has been (some) "text" from the very start.

44. As formulated in *Hamburg Declaration*: "Literacy, broadly conceived as the basic knowledge and skills needed by all in a rapidly changing world, is a fundamental right" (resolution 11). See also, *Persepolis Declaration*, 24: "Literacy is not an end in itself. It is a fundamental human right."

Illustrations: The "Text" of the "New Testament"

Many publications affirm this analysis. In literature in general and in commentaries, monographs, and articles within biblical studies, we can see that—on the level of text—the Bible is interwoven with the monograph or essay involved. Quotation marks, indentation, and referencing indicate the differing origins of the biblical text. Besides this familiar codification, there is no indication on that level of any fundamental difference—in nature and/or functioning—between the biblical text as "text" and the text that includes it. In the ever-expanding universe of text, we travel back and forth between biblical text and other texts.

In this light, we can scrutinize the discipline of biblical hermeneutics. In the introduction to the *Lexikon der Bibelhermeneutik*, editor Oda Wischmeyer explains,

> Die *textbezogene Hermeneutik der Bibel* stellt ein neues hermeneutisches Paradigma dar, in dem die kanonische Fassung der Bibel nicht primär binnentheologisch als 'Evangelium' und 'Heilige Schrift' verstanden wird und damit den nicht-theologischen textbezogenen Disziplinen hermeneutisch und methodisch weitgehend entzogen ist (. . .) Zum Verstehen dieser Texte bzw. dieses Textes werde *alle* gegenwärtige texterklärenden wissenschaftlichen Disziplinen mit ihren Theorien, Methoden, Konzeptionen und Begriffen herangezogen. (emphasis original)[45]

Wischmeyer's proposal here for a text-oriented approach of the Bible seeks to overcome an exclusively theological one. We see an enormous broadening of the horizon against which one wants to come to an understanding of these ancient documents.[46] At the same time, the presupposition and parlance is that the Bible exists of and as "text(s)" (singular and plural).

In a similar vein, we can turn to the commentaries on Galatians that are used in the discussion of Chapter 4. In his introduction, commentator Hans Dieter Betz opines on the "textual history" of this letter: "The text of Galatians must be discussed in conjunction with the tradition of the entire corpus Paulinum."[47] The way he expresses this thus gives the impression that the old manuscripts provide us with the "text" of the "letter." In the editorial preface to the *World Biblical Commentary* volume on Galatians by Richard Longenecker,[48] we read that "our commentators were asked to prepare their

---

45. Wischmeyer, *Lexikon der Bibelhermeneutik*, xiv–xv.
46. Wischmeyer, "Texte, Text und Rezeption."
47. Betz, *Galatians*, 13.
48. Longenecker, *Galatians*, ix.

own rendering of the original biblical text." In a note on the translation in his commentary, Martinus de Boer writes, "The aim of the commentary requires a translation that seeks to be as faithful as possible to the Greek text that Paul wrote and the Galatians actually heard."[49] In his commentary on Galatians, Louis Martyn speaks consistently of "letter" and "document"—not "text": "If the letter were literally presented to us today in dramatic form, we would see an actor seated and reading aloud from an epistolary scroll he holds in his hands."[50] Thus, Martyn suggests that the letter qualifies as "oral communication" and an "oral" and "highly situational sermon."[51] Nonetheless, he uses the term "text" consistently when it comes to Paul's quotations from the LXX; these documents equal "text."[52] So these commentaries illustrate the widespread idea that there is "text" from the start.

Textual Criticism: *Ausgangstext* and "Text"

Now we turn to textual criticism in New Testament scholarship.[53] This discipline provides us with, to use the typical parlance, the "text" of the "Greek New Testament." In its study of the Greek witnesses (papyri, majuscules, and minuscules), lectionaries, quotations from patristic literature, and early Latin, Syriac, Coptic, and other versions, this field of scholarship is dedicated to understand the creation and historical transmission of the documents which constitute the New Testament.[54] It is the concern of textual critics to establish a base text by the many snippets, parts, and complete old manuscript texts available to us. In the introduction of the twenty-eighth edition of the Nestle-Aland *Novum Testamentum Graece*, we read concerning the use of the *Editio Critica Maior*[55] for the Catholic Letters that "[i]t marks a new state of scientific research into the text of the Greek New Testament and offers a new constitution of the text created on this basis."[56] So the *Novum Testamentum Graece*—with which the fifth edition of *The Greek New*

49. Boer, *Galatians*, 2.
50. Martyn, *Galatians*, 13.
51. Martyn, *Galatians*, 22, 23.
52. See, for example, Martyn, *Galatians*, 299–300.
53. Prof. Dr. Bert Jan Lietaert Peerbolte urged me to include a section on detextification and the *Ausgangstext* in the present study. In this way, I came to the insights as presented in the next section, Section D.4. Text: The necessary media to transmit a dead language.
54. See the introductions to Aland et al., *Novum Testamentum*, and Aland et al., *Greek New Testament*.
55. Aland et al., *Editio Critica Maior: IV/I*.
56. Aland et. al, *Novum Testamentum*, xv.

Testament shares "an identical text"[57]—represents the most recent results of textual criticism. To do justice to the notion of "text" as used here ("a new constitution of the text"), exploration of the so-called *Ausgangstext* is necessary.[58] Textual critical research of the last century has led to establishing an initial text that is continuously improved.[59] This eclectic text is hypothesized as the initial version of which the available manuscript traditions originate. Important to note is that the stages in the process of transmission between the autograph and this *Ausgangstext* are not accessible to textual criticism.

This sketch allows us to draw some conclusions. First, in the present study, there is no intent to claim alternatives or offer improvements on the level of the documented wording as proposed by textual criticism. So, the edited documented Greek wording of the New Testament as presented in *Editio Critica Maior*, *Novum Testamentum Graece*, and *The Greek New Testament* is valued as the best representation of the verbal constitution of the autograph. Second, although we acknowledge the inaccessibility of the stages prior to the *Ausgangstext* on the level of the documented wording, we focus on textualizing the moment in which the autographs of Paul were orally delivered and on asking how the apostle would have envisioned the way his intended addressees would structure their thoughts in this process. One could even ponder whether the available old manuscripts and lectionaries that now operationally function in textual criticism as "manuscript texts" (plural) to establish the "initial text" (singular), would not once have functioned in a comparable (oral-aural) process. Third, we note that the biblical scholar relates in his everyday praxis (realm of history) to the editions of textual critical research as "text," that is, the initial text as the "Greek *text* of the New Testament" (emphasis mine), that is, eye-to-text-area communication. Not without reason, this discipline is named "*tex*tual criticism." It is this specific, singular, and restrained media perspective that makes that this different original functioning of autographs and apographs falls outside the scope of textual criticism.

Text: The Necessary Media to Transmit a Dead Language

It would be odd to speak of the "Greek letters" or the "Greek gospel." Intuitively, we feel that the language of the documents (koinè Greek) is not relevant to categorizing the different genres, but determines the text underlying them. All the New Testament documents are composed in the *lingua*

57. Aland et. al, *Greek New Testament*, ix.
58. Mink, "Genealogie."
59. Aland and Aland, *Text of the New Testament*.

franca of the first-century Mediterranean world. For centuries, however, this language has been regarded as being dead. That is to say, nobody speaks this language anymore as their native tongue or in a natural or everyday manner. It has become disembodied regarding living and regenerating communities. So, for us, "koinè Greek" and "living speech" go not together. Once more, the distinctive media, the focus of the present study, come to the fore: since this language is not spoken anymore, the sole media by which koinè Greek has been transmitted—and thereby survives—is that of writing and/or text. Per se, dead language is conserved in text; it needs text so that one can relate to it, namely by reading (not to mention the painstaking academic training and the lasting necessity of printed or digitalized grammars, concordances, and dictionaries to do so).[60] One cannot underestimate the impact of this dynamic on the community of biblical scholarship. Once caught up in this tunnel, one can only project some "Greek text" from the start. What else could we imagine from that perspective?

Etymology of Text: Between *Textum* and Text-as-Known-to-Us

In the attempt to establish the historical parameters of "text," it is beneficial to explore the etymological roots of "text." Derived from the Latin verb *texere* and related to the participle *textum*, the term carries connotations such as "to weave" and "that which is woven."[61] As readers, we might be inclined to fill that idea with the supposition that this exposure to text is primarily visual, text appears as a tapestry. The text area is woven of words, interpunction, lines, and margins. Should we take this solely and singularly visual view, however, we would be misled. The historical origin is dominated by a different sensorially based experience.

For example, we find the verb *texere* in Quintilian's *Institutio Oratoria* Book 9 4.13.[62] The art of oratory prompts him to comment here on Cicero. He argues that oratory involves the structural art of weaving (*texere*) together rhythm and melody as well as eloquence. He identifies how the inherent powers of the spoken word should be woven together. The technical role of writing is subservient to this end. So we get an indication that *textum* and

---

60. Dead languages can be attempted to be brought to life again. See, for example, Long and Halcomb, *Speak Koinè Greek*. Michael Halcomb has also started the *Koinè Conversational Institute*. On another scale, and already highly developed, we can think of how biblical Hebrew has been brought to life again throughout the nineteenth and twentieth centuries. Nowadays, this modern Hebrew forms the official language of the state of Israel.

61. Lewis and Short, *Latin Dictionary*, 1865.

62. Quintilian, *Orator's Education*.

texere originally point to the procedure of composing powerful oratory. We see this affirmed in the world of ancient Greece where writing was also seen as a form of weaving. In *The Craft of Zeus: Myths of Weaving and Fabric*, John Scheid and Jesper Svenbro point out that the metaphor of weaving resembles the functioning of writing there-and-then.[63] They distinguish woof and warp: the documented words (warp) ask for one to vocalise them in a specific moment to an explicit other (woof). So the combination of warp and woof constitutes the intended "weaving." In the present study, we attempt to relate the "letter" in the media of "text" and "oral performance" to each other. The inclination here might be to frame warp as "text" or the physical artefact and woof as the real-time "oral performance" experienced by original addressees. As a result, "text" as warp was only complete through the woof. When exposed to the oral performance (woof), though, the intended audience was, technically speaking, not in contact with the warp itself (exposed to the text area). In the actual experience of the hearer(s), the woof dominated and structured the warp. It is clear though important to observe that this weaving of warp and woof has ceased to be the standard practice today. In biblical scholarship, the woof is lost and the warp is what has remained—transmitted through history and transformed into "text."[64] The etymology of "text" indicates the aforementioned lack of clarity: throughout the long history of the biblical documents the functioning of "text" moves from *textum* to text-as-known-to-us, and sometimes (arbitrarily/confusingly or justifiably) back.

Paul Ricoeur: The Emancipation of Text

We now turn the focus upon how the notion of "text" is used in the present study. In his essay "What is a text? Explanation and understanding,"[65] Paul Ricoeur provides the following train of thought: he says "that a text is any discourse fixed by writing."[66] This fixedness of speech in writing has "provoked a radical change in our relation to the very statements of discourse."[67] Thus he situates "discourse" between speech and writing. Although a discourse could be orally expressed, it "is written precisely because it is not said." Speech discourse has to be differentiated from text discourse. So

63. Scheid and Svenbro, *Craft of Zeus*, 111–56.

64. I was introduced to this etymology and historical perspective in a personal conversation with Prof. Dr. Samuel Byrskog. See also Byrskog, "History and Story in Acts."

65. Ricoeur, "What Is a Text?"

66. Ricoeur, "What Is a Text?," 145.

67. Ricoeur, "What Is a Text?," 146.

"fixation by writing takes the very place of speech." This changed relation to discourse "suggests that a text is really a text only when it is not restricted to transcribing an anterior speech, when instead it inscribes directly in written letters what the discourse means." In conclusion, real text has to be different from (an anterior) speech.

Then Ricoeur compares dialogue—"an exchange of questions and answers"—with the writing-reading relation. Contrary to dialogue, "the writer does not respond to the reader" and "the book divides the act of writing and reading into two sides, between which there is no communication." Text provides monologue. Thus, we will suggest in the present study that text-as-known-to-us has to speak for itself.

The comparison to dialogue "confirms our hypothesis that writing is a realisation which takes the place of it [the act of dialogue] and, as it were, intercepts it." This interception is related to the reversal "that what comes to writing is discourse as intention-to-say and that writing is a direct inscription of this intention, even if . . . writing began with the graphic transcription of the signs of speech." The related discourse in text becomes abstracted from the circumstantial milieu. At the end of this section, we read that "[t]his emancipation of writing . . . is the birth of text."[68] So Ricoeur provides a historical understanding of how text-as-we-know-it developed and how it functions now. His train of thought commences with the situation in which writing is subservient to, defined by, and not more than the inscription of living speech in reciprocity to the actual circumstantial milieu of that specific speech. We can recognize here not only what has been said before on *textum* and the ancient Greek metaphor of warp and woof, but also the body-to-body communication which was originally related to the letters of Paul. His explanation culminates in the description of "text" as an idiosyncratic and independently functioning media. For reasons of clarity, in the present study, this specific media is framed as *autonomous text*, that is, autonomously functioning text. The historical analysis by Ricoeur prompts the conclusion that (autonomous) text emerges from the documentation of the spoken word, but cannot implicitly or self-evidently be equated with it or the documentation thereof (*textum*). In this light, explication or differentiation is imperative when we encounter or use the notion of "text" on the level of text.

In distinction from text-as-known-to-us, we will approach the corpus Paulinum in line with Ricoeur's "inscription of living speech." In search of forms of contrast, we will take into account the two distinctive contexts

---

68. Ricoeur, "What Is a Text?," 147.

mentioned, namely, the *circumstantial milieu of living speech* and the *quasi-world of texts* (Chapter 3).

Ricoeur draws a crucial conclusion from the emancipation of text. As we will see, this differentiation between "text" and "living speech" penetrates the mental dimension—which is of particular interest to this study:

> The eclipse of the circumstantial world by the quasi-world of texts can be so complete that, in a civilisation of writing, the world itself is no longer what can be shown in speaking but is reduced to a kind of 'aura' which written works unfold. Thus we speak of the Greek world or the Byzantine world. This world can be called 'imaginary', in the sense that it is *represented* by writing in lieu of the world *presented* by speech; by this imaginary world is itself a creation of literature (emphasis original).[69]

Living speech *presents*, whereas text *represents* the world. We can now add to the earlier argument that text has to speak for itself, that this monologue is structured on another level as well, namely, the level of representation. We can also refer to this dynamic as abstraction, formalization, or critical knowledge. As we saw in the introduction to section D. "Text": Preliminary considerations, this way of structuring thought is framed as the predominantly literate state of mind. Because of text, we can make the intellectual movement from the uncritical participation in a concrete situation (presence) to the formal and externalized knowledge of that same realm of history (representation). Due to this possibility, we do not need to be present ourselves per se in a particular realm of history to represent it. In this typical way, we relate to past events; this pertains, for example, to the earlier mentioned "Greek" and "Byzantine world" but also, as we will see in Chapter 3, to the originally intended delivery of the Letter to the Galatians.[70]

In line with Ricoeur, we observe that the emancipation of writing into text has created a new and fundamentally different relation to the world around us. Representation has brought a structuring of thought of its own. For this reason, we define "text" to be autonomous: *Autonomous text functions independently from the circumstantial milieu* (presence), *while it can represent—according to its own rules—reality in total* (representation/representing presence). Ricoeur's historical overview of "text," therefore,

---

69. Ricoeur, "What Is a Text?," 149.

70. Although we are not present ourselves, we will basically always fall back on and fill in uncritically this distant past "world" from our presently experienced world, unless we come explicitly and critically to another textualization. As was noted, for example, in the discussion on the parlance of "reading" and "public reading" regarding the original functioning of the New Testament (see above).

underscores the intent to take two distinct mindsets into account, that is, a predominantly oral mindset and a predominantly literate one.[71]

71. In this respect, we allow ourselves a detour to Jacques Derrida and "the question of the text" as addressed by him in his *Of Grammatology*. We do this in an extended footnote because the argumentation in the present study is not directed by his answer. As explained in his preface, this question is related to the "historical status" and/or "proper time and place" of "*text*" (lxxxix, emphasis original). In the first chapter, he concentrates on "writing." He distinguishes between a "secondary" and "primary" form of writing. The former is "writing in the narrow sense," that is, the common perception of writing as the "simple 'supplement to the spoken word'" (7). He explains this approach to "writing" on the basis of a scheme of Aristotle (*De Interpr.* 1.16a): knowledge starts with "mental experiences" which are symbolized in the "spoken word" which are symbolized and exteriorized in the "written word" (11). In this hierarchical structure, the written word is exterior and secondary to the *phonè* (voice) and, in particular, the *Logos*. Based on a dichotomy between "the non-worldly and worldly, the inside and outside, ideality and non-ideality, ... transcendental and empirical etc." (8)—which can be extended to the "signified" (thought-sense) and "signifier" (concept)—the Logos, as well as the *phonè*, belong to the first part of these oppositions. In different formulations, we can glimpse the Logos as follows: it is "full speech, that was fully *present* (present to itself, to its signified, to the other very condition of the theme of presence in general)" (8). This "logocentrism"—being closely related or even synonymous to "phonocentrism"—means that "[t]he privilege of the *phonè* does not depend upon a choice that could have been avoided (. . .) The system of 'hearing (understanding)-oneself-speak' through the phonic substance—which presents *itself* as the non-exterior, nonmundane, therefore nonempirical or noncontingent signifier—has necessarily dominated the history of the world during an entire epoch" (7/8). "All the metaphysical determinations of truth . . . are . . . inseparable from the instance of the logos . . . understood . . . in the sense of God's infinite understanding" (10, 11). He argues that the Logos is related to the metaphor of the "book"—for example, the "book of Nature and God's writing" (15) or "God's book (natural or law, indeed natural law)" (16). In this light, another quotation is helpful: "The idea of the book is the idea of a totality . . . of the signifier; this totality of the signifier cannot be a totality, unless a totality constituted by the signified pre-exists it, supervises its inscriptions and its signs, and is independent of it in its ideality" (18). For that reason and in line with his deconstructive agenda, he declares the "death of the book"—similar to "a death of . . . full speech" (8). In this way, we touch on his definition of "text": "[T]he destruction of the book . . . denudes the surface of text" (18). Destructing the totality of the Logos makes to shift the relation between the "signified" and "signifier" or the nature of the "sign." Here he introduces the thought of the signifier as "*trace*" (18). Beyond the instituting question of philosophy "What is . . . ?" (19), we move towards "the liberation of the signifier from its dependence or derivation with respect to the logos and the related concept of truth or the primary signified, in whatever sense that is understood" (19). Referring to Friedrich Nietzsche, he argues that at the moment that "writing" or the "text" does not any longer have "to transcribe or discover . . . the . . . presence of the logos" (19), we do not have to "restore . . . some originary truth" (19). The fundamental and repetitive distinction between "non-worldly and worldly," "transcendental and empirical," and "signified and signifier" does not have to be bridged anymore (9). Beyond this system of oppositions, he poses the *grammè* as the element which precedes the origin of meaning in general (9). Instead of a "secondary," he speaks of a "primary writing." This activity entails a deconstruction of the traditional and deeply ingrained perception of text. In the words of the translator,

With regard to the present study, there are two important implications in terms of doing justice to the different communicative processes behind the common "text" parlance in biblical scholarship. First, when we refer to "text" in the present study, we mean the independent media of autonomous text as we are used to in academia, not *textum* or the inscription of living speech. In Chapter 3, the textualization of "text here-and-now to us" will grant more depth to this framing. Second, the opacity in the phraseology makes clear that a radical path should be pursued to create more clarity on the status of "text" in biblical scholarship (concept and/or physical artefact and the implicit equation with letter). The present study is concerned to contribute to this debate. In a heuristic manner or "on the level of text," we posit, as a consequence, that the realm of history there-and-then is void of "text." This is not so much a claim on the factual or objective level, but, in this way, we force ourselves to critically reconsider our vocabulary and explore alternative formulations of the intended communicative act. In this respect, we will use terms on the original functioning such as "to compose/composition," "oral performance," "aural event," "oral delivery," or "embodiment by the emissary." Regarding the object, we will speak of "documented wording," "*textum*," "inscription of living speech," "scroll," "token," or "ancient document."

Caution to the Reader #3: The Galatians as Knowing Subjects *in Actu*—not the Reader

Now we bring together a number of lines of thinking mentioned in the previous Cautions to the reader. In accordance with the earlier sketched historical parameters of oral performance, not only a distinctive media is at stake (oral performance) but also a different subject *in actu* is at stake (Galatian converts). Next to "time" and "place," we get hold of another constituent of the realm of history, that is, the "knowing subject *in actu*." So not only the way in which present-day readers participate (reading text) is different than in oral delivery, but—put radically—in the originally intended realm of history they have no place. Paul related to his Galatian converts as the knowing

---

Spivak, one can formulate that this perception "is inadequate yet necessary to say" (xiii; see also 13) and "the 'text' is a preface to the next" (*Of Grammatology*, xii). This primary writing entails a continuously repeating though constantly deepening of what is expressed. From the perspective of the approach of detextification, two questions come to the fore. First, is this effect, in the end, restricted to the realm of text[s] or does it penetrate the participatory realm of history as such? The second question is related to the distinction between mindsets as applied in the present study: Does deconstruction and the "death of the book" affect and change the way in which we structure thought?

subjects *in actu*. This presupposition has the following crucial implication: as long as we, as present-day readers, remain in an uncritical or operational way the knowing subject vis-à-vis the biblical text as "text," we exclude the originally intended addressees from the process of coming to understand. So, instead of labouring to come to some understanding ourselves—What does it mean?—or debating differences in given meanings (what), *we have to come to understand the way in which these original hearers would have understood*, that is, differences in how thoughts are organized. Thus, when we explicate the Galatian converts as the knowing subjects *in actu*, on their own terms in the realm of history there-and-then, in distinction to ourselves vis-à-vis the biblical text in our realm here-and-now, we get sight of the mental dimension in the realm of history. That is to say, we are forced to do justice to their specific way of structuring thought in distinction from as well as by means of our (highly literate and dominant) way of doing so—we need text to detextify. Once more, we see in this way that the historian has to be given priority over the reader by asking what is happening, or how does it function.

Caution to the Reader #4: Detextification and Textification

In the preceding Caution to the reader, we touched on the most important insight of the present study: *detextification* means that the dimension of the knowing subjects *in actu* (plural)—that lies per se beyond the level of text—has to be included on the level of text. The problem is that the manner in which the original addressees of Paul's letters structured their thoughts is not intrinsically in line with the level of text or the realm of extra-historical thought. Now the dichotomy noted earlier will prove to be crucial (Caution to the reader #1): the letter functioning as oral performance there-and-then-*to-them* will be distinguished from the functioning as autonomous text here-and-now-*to-us*. In light of this, the study explicitly and systematically textualizes from the perspective of the different knowing subjects in these distinctive realms of history. These additions of the distinctive knowing subjects *in actu* have an important consequence: it breaks open the tight relation between the reader and their text—that is, the mechanism that at the moment that the biblical scholar turns in real time to the text area in the edition (Bible) before them, that they, by reading, will construe meaning themselves. Put differently, including and distinguishing the subjects *in actu* (plural) will problematize our search for the meaning of the text and will break open some inherent limitations of the level of text or the realm of extra-historical thought. This becomes apparent when we critically examine the question that governs reading: What does it mean? The knowing subject *in actu* implicitly determines the following dimensions of the realm of history in which that subject participates; that is to say, we have to add to the question, What does it mean, "to me/us," "here-and-now," "vis-à-vis text," and in a "predominantly literate mindset"? When we detextify the letters of Paul, we will ask, How does it function, to whom, in what state of mind, and from whose perspective? (Chapter 3).

Since the given object (*text* as noun) causes the reader to be the knowing subject *in actu*, the term *de-text-i-fication* enables to overcome this intellectual dynamic. Through this approach we can unmake (*de* and *facere*) the process that the reader vis-à-vis the given object (*text* as noun) takes over as knowing subject *in actu* in the process of reading and focus on and textualize the original addressees in their specific processes of understanding in the oral delivery.

We will refer to the opposite dynamic as *textification*. This movement implies that the distinctive functioning of the New Testament documents in the realm of history there-and-then is explicitly acknowledged (oral performance/public reading). However, in one and the same argumentation, the nature or essence of these documents is also defined as text in an absolute way: as we will see in Chapter 2, in several studies one refers to "the *text*" (emphasis original) of the Bible. In this way, we move alongside the realm of history (process) especially on the one of extra-historical thought (product); the originally intended and represented functioning cannot infringe on this status and the present availability of the New Testament. As a consequence, the biblical scholar—in the actual process of reading the biblical text—will always remain the single and uncritical knowing subject *in actu*. Textification is, therefore, the process in which the biblical text is declared to be *text* in an absolute manner, that is, on and beyond the level of text; the use of the *nomen* and related physically available artefact ("text") is placed beyond critical questioning.

Recapitulation: Text

In the present study, the notion "text" is only used to frame a distinct and independently functioning media. That is to say, on the level of this actual text, "text" consistently means "autonomously functioning text." This media can and has to speak for itself. This monologue is different from everyday speaking in that it re-presents the "world," "reality," or the "realm of history" according to its own rules. In this representation, it facilitates the realm of extra-historical thought.[72] The realm of history is characterized by flux and *becoming*, text resembles fixedness and *being*. This abstracted relation to the "world" is possible due to the eye-to-text-area communication. In academia, we not only have a predominantly literate mindset, but we also have internalized this media beyond critical awareness, that is, we live in an ever-expanding universe of text.

HYPOTHESIS (2): MEDIA AND MINDSETS— TO UNDERSTAND HOW THEY UNDERSTOOD

It is now time to turn to some preliminary considerations about the Letter to the Galatians. Notwithstanding the somewhat odd and exceptional passages of Gal 3.1 and 4.20 (see above), we normally deal with familiar kinds of reading experiences. We mean those passages that constitute the essential and theological core of Galatians. In these cases, reading often is taken as an intellectual labour. Take, for example, Gal 2.19–20—a passage we will investigate in Chapter 4:

> For through the law I died to the law, so that I might live to God. I have been crucified with Christ; and it is no longer I who live, but it is Christ who lives in me. And the life I now live in the flesh I live by faith in the Son of God, who loved me and gave himself for me.

Another example is 3.10–12, which will also be discussed later:

> All who rely on observing the law are under a curse, for it is written: "Cursed is everyone who does not continue to do everything written in the Book of the Law." Clearly no one is justified before God by the law, because, "The righteous will live by faith." The law is not based on faith; on the contrary, "The man who does these things will live by them."

---

72. This perspective has to be differentiated from "text" as used by Rodrìquez, In his article "Reading and Hearing," referring to Brian Street and "textuality," he wants to do justice to the fact "that Jesus traditions could enter written media without becoming 'frozen' or being severed from cultural milieu that incorporated but transcended written texts" (163). According to him, in these communities, "texts . . . emerge as a reference system for behaviour and orientation, they become central points round which group identities develop and cohere" (163); "the emphasis on oral performative dynamics and the decentring of written texts that I am proposing requires us to rethink the role written texts played in the production of other written texts in the ancient world" ("Reading and Hearing," 170). In line with this agenda, the contribution of the present study is to offer alternatives for the given use of concepts such as "text" on the level of our own texts.

Contrary to Gal 3.1, when we asked What is happening?, in this instance we are captivated ourselves by these complex reasonings. Vis-à-vis these passages, we are determined to understand the text: What does Paul mean? How does he reason? How does he use these Scripture proofs? What are his presuppositions? What is his theology? What do others write about this passage? The role of the reader seems to usurp that of the historian.

When we ponder over the different nature of this reading experience, compared to Gal 3.1, we realize that we do not hear him personally cry out to his Galatian converts anymore. These words are not self-evidently identifiable for us as direct speech. Neither the role of the emissary, nor the question of what had happened to cause Paul to reason in this (perhaps complicated) way comes naturally to mind. We are caught up in the zone (level) of text. In the role of historian, however, the central question is, What is happening to the Galatian converts in the moment of delivery of this passage—as envisioned by Paul in the process of composition? Therefore, as an antidote to the implicit equation of "message" (Eco) or "letter" and "text"— through which our reading of it could eclipse the original functioning in which the Galatian converts would have participated—we propose *to explicitly differentiate between not only media but also mindset*. This is the second step to come to the hypothesis of the present study (see earlier, Section B.).

DETEXTIFICATION: HOW TO GET BEFORE THE LETTER FUNCTIONING AS TEXT TO US?

On this basis, we can formulate the leading question of the present study: *How can a biblical scholar here-and-now relate to the text of the letters of Paul in such a way that one can understand how the apostle envisioned his original addressees to understand the documented words in the event of delivery?* In this way, we bring together in one question the two hypothesized media functionings, the related distinctive mindsets or knowing subjects *in actu*, and the roles of and hierarchy between reader and historian.

We can divide this overarching question into smaller units and turn to the Letter to the Galatians. Three governing questions come to the fore. The first two are related and concern the mode of communication. First, the question is asked, What does oral performance do to the participating hearer? How will the hearer structure their thoughts in this body-to-body communication? In our answering, we will concentrate on the Galatian converts. Second, we ask, What does eye-to-text-area communication, that is, processing autonomous text, do to the academically trained reader (including the letter as text)? How will they structure their thoughts? The present study is, however, constituted in real time by one of these media, that is, text. Since the predominantly oral culture of the first-century Mediterranean world has been studied extensively, we will pay attention in particular to the ramifications of the functioning of text here-and-now-to-us for our understanding of the functioning of oral performance there-and-then-to-them. Thus, we need to ask a third question that is more fundamental in nature and adds to the idea of the present study as philosophy of biblical studies: How does the real-time media and mindset in biblical scholarship (second question) influence how we answer the first question? Answers to this question should penetrate the technology of autonomous text. In this way, the approach of detextification will become clear (Chapter 3). So, the reader of the current text should be warned once more: the approach of detextification can impinge on how we are used to structuring our thoughts. The aim is to find guidelines to identify and overcome possible effects of the media muddle and to correct and/or deepen in certain aspects our representation of the original functioning of the Letter to the Galatians. The answers to this more fundamental question will help us to develop an approach in line with the leading question of the present study (see above).

To address these subquestions, we review in the first Chapter a selection of publications in the field of oral studies. Starting with the founding fathers of the modern study of oral tradition, Milman Parry and Albert Lord, we will turn to John Miles Foley, who was able to deepen their grasp of the oral traditions under scrutiny. In his Theory of Metonymical or Traditional Referentiality, Foley has described how structural elements—recorded in ancient documents—relate to the collective memory of the intended participants. Subsequently, we will pay attention to Eric Havelock and Walter Ong, who participated in a revolutionary exploration of, broadly speaking, orality as well as literacy.[73] They enable us to explore mental transformations in Western culture based on the technology of writing, that is, the typical way in which knowledge is construed (mindsets).

In the second Chapter, we provide a history of the research of biblical studies that relate the corpus Paulinum to the predominantly oral culture of the first-century Mediterranean world. Here the introduced implicit equation between "letter" and "text" becomes relevant. The following subquestions will govern the discussion of this Chapter: How do these studies relate the different media functionings or communicative processes involved to each other? What kind of critical attention is paid to the terminology—the

---

73. Despite valid critique on the autonomy as ascribed to literacy by Havelock and Ong and the allegation of the so-called Great Divide theory, we seek to demonstrate that several of their insights can help us to understand ourselves as present-day readers in the specific socio-cultural context of academia or high literacy (Chapter 1).

use of "text" and related concepts on the level of text (see Caution to the reader #2: The level of text and textualization)? What can we learn in this respect from these studies?

In the third Chapter, we present the approach of *detextification*. The Chapter contends that we can overcome an implicit equation of "letter" and "text" in real time by two intellectual movements. In both, we relate the totality of history to the particular artefact of the physically available letter. On the one hand, we argue that the realm of history (totality) is the background against which the intended exposure of the original audience to the oral delivery had to take place (there-and-then-to-them). On the other, our actual reading of the letter as text here-and-now also takes place in the realm of history as well. First, text *hic et nunc pro nobis* is textualized. Second, we provide a textualization of oral performance *illic et tunc pro eis*. In the terminology of our study, this intellectual endeavour is referred to as *textualizing history*. The Chapter goes on to argue that another intellectual movement is similarly needed. Next to the emerging *communis opinio* on the original oral delivery of the biblical documents, it was noted above that the presupposition and parlance in biblical scholarship is that there has been "text" from the start. This product is at the same time a given; it is physically available to us here-and-now. Thus, we have to deal with the crucial moment in which we ourselves turn in real time from the formal level of critical representation to the operational realm in which we are uncritically present. This transition is emphasised because the functioning of the rather unfamiliar *textum* has to penetrate the overly familiar one of text-as-known-to-us (that is actually operative right now!). We call this movement *historicizing text*. These two complementary movements will pave the way to the detextification of Paul's letters: through textualizing history and historicizing text, we can detextify our understanding of Paul's letters.[74]

In the fourth Chapter, we approach two specific passages from Paul's Letter to the Galatians, Gal 3.10–12 and 2.18–21. In comparison with existing perceptions of some contemporary scholars, the detextification of both passages will hone in upon differences in the structuring of thought by the intended addressees. In the first example, we will provide an enthymematical perspective on the reasoning in Gal 3.10–12. As a result, one simple and historically self-evident syllogistic structure will be identified as governing the whole reasoning in chapters 2 and 3 of the letter. In this *logos*,

---

[74] This is stated with the reserve that we will never bridge the gap between abstract and concrete, extra- and inner-historical and formal and operational. However, we can scrutinize degrees of abstraction in our structuring of thought. Although never fully, we can pull ourselves—like the Baron—more and more out of the mire. Though, the moment will never come that we are out of the mire and can walk away.

we encounter one of the means of power on the part of Paul's opponents, which the apostle attempts to counter. In a similar vein, we will concretize our grasp of Gal 2.18–21. The rhetorical strategy is inextricably related to the sensorially based memories of the Galatian converts. When we detextify our grasp of this passage, in particular we see—as affirmation but also deepening of the commentaries by Louis Martyn and Martinus de Boer—that the power struggle between Paul and his opponents is determined by the body. By recalling and reframing the baptismal experiences of his hearers, the apostle wants to counter the call to circumcision of these teachers. The concern of these examples is to validate the hypothesis of the present study.

1

The Study of Oral Tradition
Getting before Homer as Text

THIS CHAPTER EXPLORES NOT only the rather unknown world of preliteracy, the predominantly oral mindset, and the practice of oral performance, but also the interfaces with literacy and textuality, by engaging with the work of Milman Parry, Albert Bates Lord, and John Miles Foley as the founding fathers of this field.[1] The Chapter also examines Eric Havelock and Walter Ong as influential scholars in orality studies, acknowledging that in the contemporary debate, however, their contributions are partially regarded as outdated.[2] One reason is that their approach tends to be governed by an ideological presupposition. The critique is that they ascribe an autonomous status to "literacy" (singular): although operating within the realm of history, it is not affected or transformed by it.[3] In his *Literacy in Theory and*

---

1. The main forum in orality studies is the journal *Oral Tradition*.

2. In the field of ancient literacy, see Johnson, "Toward a Sociology." Given the debate on ancient reading hitherto—whether reading was aloud or in silence—he comments that how the question is formulated is decisive. He warns against an oversimplified approach. In his own words: "it will not do to focus narrowly, as in the recent debate, on a single mode of inquiry such as cognitive analysis. Similarly, the analysis . . . of scholars like Goody, Havelock, Ong, and their followers—who find in writing and in its reflex, reading, a 'technology' with (various) determinative consequences for the society—will, from this point of view, be seen as too simplistic, even reductionist, and too inattentive to the particulars of the specific cultures under study" ("Toward a Sociology," 604/5).

3. Another point of critique is related to the alleged Great Divide. For advocates of this standpoint, the presence, influence, and development of literacy entails a pejorative stance towards the preceding time and/or influence of primal orality. In Chapter 2 of

Practice, Brian Street states that Havelock and Ong argue that literacy does something to people, but they forget that people also do things to literacy.[4] Here a change of perspective is involved. Instead of a monolithic and *freischwebende* "literacy," Street frames these human activities as *literacy practices* (plural).[5] In the field of ancient literacy, the alternative title of a volume on the subject is illustrative: *Ancient Literacies: The Culture of Reading in Greece and Rome*.[6] The plural of "literacies" should correct the title of William Harris's seminal monograph *Ancient Literacy*.[7] In comparison to Havelock and Ong, scholars from the 1980s onward have a historical and/or sociological perspective and draw conclusions in a more tentative way as to what people do to literacy.

Nonetheless, there is still another valid perspective. In the Introduction, the long history of Western literacy is outlined, culminating in academia as our socio-cultural context. Especially in the Humanities, text is the dominant media. We postulated a predominantly literate mindset. Since the predominantly oral mindset of Paul and his original addressees in the moment of delivery has to be taken into account as well, these contexts are decisively different. Regarding the contemporary study of ancient literacies, we must, therefore, ask: What role does the "literacy" of these scholars, that is, the tradition of institutionalized research, autonomous text as dominant media, and the related socio-cultural mindset, play in their grasp of these distinct "ancient literacies" (see the third governing question in the Introduction)?

---

the present study, this viewpoint and critique will become clearer in the discussion of the seminal book by Kelber, *Oral and Written Gospel*.

4. Street, *Literacy*, 13. In his explanation of the problem of this approach, two alleged functions of oral language have to be distinguished. One function is directed towards "imparting meaning," that is, "statements . . . assigning a set of truth conditions." The second function is the one of "regulating and maintaining social or interpersonal relations between people." The pivotal and, as a result, debated effect of writing is that the latter enabled the separation of these two functions. The second one remained unchanged, whereas the first function could develop into "autonomous text" (*Literacy*, 20).

5. Street, *Literacy*, 1–2. The value of this perspective is that it is not dogmatic or—in terms of the present study—extra-historical in nature. "Literacy practices" have to be located in the realm of history and differentiated according to kinds of practices and several cultural contexts in which they take place.

6. Johnson and Parker, *Ancient Literacies*. This title is derived from the first contribution by Rosalind Thomas, "Writing, Reading, Public and Private 'Literacies': Functional Literacy and Democratic Literacy in Greece."

7. Harris, *Ancient Literacy*; see also Johnson's Introduction to *Ancient Literacies*, 3–13. Note that the plural is not extended to the key concepts of the subtitle, "culture," and "reading." As argued in the Introduction, we encounter here the extra-historical tendency to the one, unchangeable, and absolute (being). We could ask, therefore, whether it is not more logical to speak of "cultures" and "ways of reading" (plural).

As argued before, we use this contrast as a heuristic lever. So, the aim of the present study is not so much to isolate and study a historical practice (oral delivery of Paul's letters), but to explore the different ways in which the different subjects *in actu* arrive at understanding (original participants there-and-then and ourselves as present-day readers in academia). In view of this contrast, we will scrutinize these seminal studies by Havelock and Ong.

MILMAN PARRY: HOMERIC EPICS— BREAKING THE SPELL OF TEXT

Despite his early death and limited number of publications, Milman Parry (1902–1935) has changed Homeric studies. More so, he initiated with his research a new academic discipline, the study of oral tradition. At the age of twenty-three, Parry left America for France to study at the Sorbonne in Paris. There he studied under the supervision of the linguist Antoine Meillet. Not hindered by any convention in classical studies, this professor provided him with a rather unconventional perspective on Homer's epics: Meillet was convinced that the *Iliad* and *Odyssey* were not the product of a single literate genius,[8] but the residue of refined oral traditional techniques of several generations of singers. The Master of Arts thesis which Parry wrote in Paris, already adumbrated the outlines of his revolutionary approach to Homer.[9] Though the lasting impact of his research came as a result of fieldwork among bards in present-day Serbia and Croatia. His approach to Homer became decisively framed by a rigid historical or operational matrix. He was able to frame his understanding, not in the standard manner vis-à-vis text, but by getting before these epics functioning as "text" to him: he was present at and participated in live performances of comparable stories. Thus, Homer as text for highly trained readers, such as Parry's colleagues in academia, became distinguished from Homer as live oral performance. In short, he forged a way out of the media muddle in the study of Homer.

It is important to note at this point that, in terms of the methodology of this study, it is not possible to engage in fieldwork in the same way; we cannot personally witness processes comparable to the apostle *in actu*—in the sense of composing letters and instructing emissaries who will deliver them in real time, or gain personal experience of the influence of the predominantly oral mindset on this process.

---

8. The search for this kind of genius is characteristic of cultures deeply formed by literacy.

9. Parry, "Traditional Epithet."

Parry lived in the days in which historical criticism was on the rise. Contrary to the given traditional opinions, modern humankind felt obliged to comprehend reality by a radical application of reason. This movement—which gained influence in Homeric studies and in the approach to the Christian Bible—represented the modern era *in optima forma*. Regarding the *Iliad* and *Odyssey*, the Homeric question had come to the fore anew in a different way: Who was Homer? Were the epics written by one or several authors? By whom, when, and where were the poems composed? Under what circumstances were they composed? This historical-critical approach changed the debate. The conviction was that there existed different layers in the text of the Homeric epics. These layers—found in the text itself—represented different stages of composition throughout history. In addition to historical (higher) criticism, textual (lower) criticism became important; this discipline aimed at reconstructing the most original form of the text of the Homeric epics. In the early decades of the 1900s, it was assumed that the Homeric epics were memorized verbatim; they must have been recited word by word every time in the same fixed manner before the process of writing down. So, the highly literate academy approached Homer under its own conditions of media and mindset.

In comparison to his contemporaries in classical studies, Parry pursued his own path. It is in the last three years of his short life that he conducted fieldwork. On two trips in 1933 and 1934–35, he researched bardic culture *in actu*. Together with his assistant Albert Lord, he studied the complex communicative dynamics of traditional poetry as encountered in oral live performances. In the words of Milman Parry himself, "Its method was to observe singers working in a thriving tradition of unlettered song and see how the form of their songs hangs upon their having to learn and practice their art without reading and writing."[10]

In his fieldwork, Parry was able to study and describe the practice of bards in line with the question What is happening to them? (see the Introduction). The most fundamental insight was that, instead of verbatim rehearsals, these singers could (re)perform their epics time and again without the aid of writing. Dependent on the specific situation of the audience, in every performance, they created these same stories anew. Every time the same stories, but never verbatim the same. A distinctive perspective on the epics was the result. As phrased by John Miles Foley, "From unmatched philological scrutiny through innovative fieldwork that was as careful and thorough as it was creative, he fashioned the foundation for what has since

---

10. A quote taken from a manuscript for a book titled *The Singer of Tales*, which Parry started to write after his return from the former Yugoslavia and was unable to finish because of his untimely death. See the second edition of Lord's *Singer of Tales*, 3.

become an entire new discipline in its own right."[11] His work has generated a still growing and broadening stream of research and publications.

To break this new ground, Parry paid focused attention to the details of the Homeric epics down to their ornamental and minute elements. Due to literate biases, these components were not regarded then as being constitutive for the epics as such. In his Master of Arts thesis, his first step was to describe the *formula*. This formulaic structure—also referred to as the noun epithet—is a recurring fixed expression:

> The epic poets fashioned and preserved in the course of generations a complex technique of formulae, a technique designed in its smallest details for the twofold purpose of expressing ideas appropriate to epic in a suitable manner, and of attenuating the difficulties of versification.

The epics were sung in hexameter, a line of verse consisting of six metrical dactyls (one stressed syllable followed by two unstressed ones). These *formulae* occupied fixed places in the hexameter line. Their place was determined by audible pauses in the performance of the line (*caesura*).[12] These fixed elements were stitched together in various though recurring ways. The rhythm of the wording governed the choice and structuring of the *formulae*. In this way, the performer was able to capture the attention of his hearers. Here we gain an interesting perspective. Meter has to do with the activated senses (bodies) of a live audience. The rhythm takes hold of the body and via the body the heart is reached. In a similar vein, Parry studied in his subsequent doctoral thesis in Paris the ornamental adjective or *epithet*.[13] As with the formula, the ornamental adjective served meter as well. However, more was at issue, since he discovered a mechanism of *pars pro toto*. By mentioning a single epithet, the poet could evoke a matrix of associations in the minds of his audience.[14] Thus, the activated senses govern the communicative process in the realm of history there-and-then-to-them, whereas in the textual transmission of these stories this dimension is lost. So Parry disclosed a function of words that is not exclusively determined

---

11. Foley, *Comparative Research*, 19.

12. See Parry, "Traditional Epithet," 9.

13. A well-known example is the recurring fixed expression, "the swift-footed Achilleus" (ποδάρκης δῖος Ἀχιλλεύς). See "Homeric Formulae."

14. Parry, *Making of Homeric Verse*, xxix–xxx, and Parry, "The Homeric Gloss." This outlook necessitates postulating an original audience in distinction from ourselves. In their anticipated participation, we touch on the notions of collective memory and imagination (see the Introduction). We will see that Foley takes this aspect further.

by abstracted or free-standing "meaning"—as seems to be the case in text here-and-now-for-us.[15]

Although the specific role of meter cannot be transposed to Paul's letters, we can take a step in grasping the impact of oral performance on originally intended audiences.[16] The performer is called to capture and influence the hearts of his hearers. He does so via their bodily presence at and sensorial experience of the performance. Therefore, regarding the first governing question, we will stress the importance or dominance of context over text or—in line with the Introduction—the role of the body in distinction from a *freischwebende cognitio*. As a result, we are warned about an approach to these documents which is exclusively determined by "meaning" with which the present-day reader is acquainted.

We conclude that the major contribution of Milman Parry is the distinction between the overly familiar realm of literacy and the unknown one of orality.[17] In view of the Homeric epics, he left the quasi-world of texts (Ricoeur) and entered the forgotten world of preliteracy. Approaching Homer as oral performance or bard *in actu*, he broke the spell of text. That is, he got before Homer mediated by text and could thereby grasp these epics in a historically more adequate way by understanding the functioning of them as real-time oral performances. We emphasize, in the present study, that for understanding participation in oral performance the "body" is a focal point. In the terminology of the present study, Parry is the one who detextified the Homeric epics.

ALBERT BATES LORD: PRELITERATE BARDS AND THEIR RATHER UNKNOWN WORLD

Albert Bates Lord was a student of Milman Parry and accompanied him on his field trips to the former Yugoslavia. By his continuing research, Lord moulded their observations in the field into the Oral-Formulaic Theory or the Parry-Lord Thesis. As he states himself in the foreword to his *The Singer of Tales*, "a theory of composition must be based not on another

15. Parry, *The Making of Homeric Verse*, xx.

16. In this respect, we can refer to the study by Dan Nässelqvist, *Public Reading*. In this monograph, he describes and exemplifies a method of sound analysis regarding the Gospel of John.

17. See Parry, *The Making of Homeric Verse*, xxxiv: "What has made him best known, and has most aroused interest in his writing, is his sense that all poetry is divided into two great and distinct realms, the literary and the oral, that each of these realms has its own laws of operation and its own values, so that each is almost a way of looking at the world."

theory but on the facts of the practice of the poetry."[18] He made Parry's concern his own—to know how oral poets continuously compose and recompose their songs. Here we recognize the emphasis on the operational dimension of the process.

Their fieldwork in the former Yugoslavia and later by Lord also in Albania was originally intended to serve the needs of Homeric scholarship. This becomes clear in the structure of *The Singer of Tales*, which in 1949 Lord defended as his doctoral thesis.[19] In the first part, he develops a fully-formed version of the Oral-Formulaic Theory. In the second part, the observations on the Balkan bards are applied to the *Iliad* and *Odyssey*. The last chapter is entitled "Some Notes on Medieval Epic." Despite the brevity of these notes, the Parry-Lord legacy has extended far beyond the disciplines of classical and Slavic studies and even comparative literature.[20]

Contrary to the assumption that bards would have memorized a poem verbatim to recall it in the moment of public performance, Parry and Lord demonstrated that through development over generations and painstaking training of the individual singers, "[a]n oral poem is not composed *for* but *in* performance."[21] Here the modern reader has to embark upon a journey into the unknown:

> Since, as we shall see, he has not memorized his song, we must conclude either that he is a phenomenal virtuoso or that he has a special technique of composition *outside our field of experience* (emphasis mine).[22]

> Our proper understanding of these procedures is hindered by our lack of a suitable vocabulary for defining the steps of the process. The singers themselves cannot help us in this regard because they do not think in terms of form as we think of it; their descriptions are too vague, at least for academic preciseness.

Lord elaborates extensively on the differences between the primary oral singer and the predominantly literate reader. In particular, he deconstructs the basic unit in which modern man thinks—that is, "the word":

---

18. Lord, *Singer of Tales*, xxxvi.
19. Lord, *Singer of Tales*.
20. *The Singer of Tales* has become a standard work in several disciplines. See the introduction to the second edition.
21. Lord, *Singer of Tales*, 13.
22. Lord, *Singer of Tales*, 17.

> Man without writing thinks in terms of sound groups and not in words, and the two do not necessarily coincide. When asked what a word is, he will reply that he does not know, or he will give a sound group which may vary in length from what we call a word to an entire line of poetry, or even an entire song.[23]

Illustrated by the word-on-the-level-of-text over against continuously changing sound groups, it becomes clear how great the differences are. Put in a simple and abstract dichotomy, it is the ear versus the eye. "Word" dominates our field of visual experience in academia. In academic discourse, words-as-records help us to critically distance ourselves from the flux and complexity of reality: words fixate aspects of reality and become visible as externalization on physical surfaces (text area). In this socio-cultural context, the role of speech (sound) is subservient to the technology of reading and writing.

At the same time, we should note that when we as twenty-first-century persons speak, no interruption or pause between words can be distinguished—contrary to writing or typing. The natural way of conversation is a stream of sounds governed by breathing, and interrupted for emphasis or by others with whom we speak. In this respect, we can also think of pre-school children when they are learning to speak. As parents, we teach them objects "word" by "word." For them, however, at that stage they are mediated as sound only. Clearly, our training in literacy, dependent on the level, governs our processing of words-as-sound (talking). The important point is that the concrete lifeworld of the present-day reader resembles to a certain extent the one of the preliterate bard; there is no absolute dichotomy for us between "orality" and "literacy" or the "predominantly oral" and "predominantly literate state of mind."[24] So the formal framing of "word," or word as implicitly equated with appearance on the level of text, in the predominantly literate state of mind is severed from the real-time practice of talking—including ourselves. In the participatory realm of history, the basic unit is not fixed and does not function as w-o-r-d.[25] We conclude that, historically speaking, "the word" is not the basic unit—not even to us. In the realm of extra-historical thought, however, this is the case. More so, it forms the foundation and structure of our predominantly literate mindset.

---

23. Lord, *Singer of Tales*, 25.

24. For that reason, we prefer to qualify the world of preliteracy as "rather unknown" instead of "lost" (Adam Parry).

25. The letters are separated here to emphasize the nature of the word "word" as existing at the level of text. At the moment that you read this word ("word") in the line above, you experience or are exposed yourself to this specific media.

In this way, we find an answer to the third governing question: as present-day readers, we have to be aware that the basic unit of the word—which we discern on the level of text and which constitutes our default mode of understanding in the realm of history—does not coincide with that of (predominantly) oral humanity, nor with that of ourselves when we are caught up in talking or listening. This is the fallacy of the earlier mentioned assumption that all oral performance was verbatim. We cannot take for granted that they structured their thoughts through "words," in the manner that we do in this present study for example.

Notwithstanding the enormity of this critical step of Lord—exploring preliterate bards *in actu*—what was not fully addressed was the decisive role of the audience and how this might be incorporated into the Oral-Formulaic Theory. This step was made by John Miles Foley.

JOHN MILES FOLEY: PRELITERACY— GOING INTO THE METHODOLOGICAL DEEP

For the deepening of the study of oral tradition, John Miles Foley (1947–2012) has been decisive.[26] As a scholar in comparative oral tradition, he was at home in different academic disciplines such as ancient Greek (Homer), medieval and Old English literature, and Serbian epic.[27] Foley founded the academic journal *Oral Tradition* and the Centre for Studies in Oral Tradition at the University of Missouri. In the last phase of his career, he broadened his scope to studying the role of the Internet. He became convinced that the communicative dynamics in the Internet show parallels with those of primary oral communication. He brought the study of these communicative technologies together in the Centre for eResearch[28] and, in particular, The Pathways Project.[29]

---

26. John Miles Foley (1947–2012) was Curators's Professor of classical studies and English and occupied the W. H. Byler Endowed Chair in the Humanities at the University of Missouri until his retirement in 2011.

27. Garner, "Bibliography," 677.

28. Centre for eResearch, http://www.e-researchcentre.org/main/index.

29. Foley, *Pathways*. Centre for eResearch, http://www.pathwaysproject.org: "The major purpose of the Pathways Project is to illustrate and explain the fundamental similarities and correspondences between humankind's oldest and newest thought-technologies: oral tradition and the Internet."

What Does It Mean? Over against How Does It Mean?

Although Milman Parry and Albert Lord broke new ground with respect to oral tradition, Foley leads us into the methodological deep of this world void of text-as-known-to-us. Due to his efforts, the Oral-Formulaic Theory transformed into the much broader Oral Theory. Like Parry and Lord, he commenced his scholarly career by fieldwork in the former Yugoslavia. In line with their focus, his first area of interest was matters of composition. This resulted in *The Theory of Oral Composition: History and Methodology*.[30] Herein, he describes the history of the Oral-Formulaic Theory and its application to a myriad of ethnolinguistic areas (Hispanic, Old French, Medieval German, Irish, African, Arabic, Indian amongst others). Because of the diversity in ethnolinguistic research, the status of the *formula* as described by Parry required broadening. In his book *Immanent Art: From Structure to Meaning in Traditional Oral Epic*,[31] Foley did just this. The result was his Theory of Traditional or Metonymical Referentiality. For the present study, this theory will prove to be crucial.

In understanding oral traditional works, Foley's step forward is his rephrasing of the fundamental question "What does it mean?" As argued in the Introduction, we readers in the highly literate socio-cultural context of academia are trained to relate through this question to a transmitted epic or the Bible as text. An underlying, though silently assumed framing of understanding is, however, at issue here:

> Instead of asking "what" is meant by a work of art and its constituent parts, we should begin by asking "how" that work or part conveys whatever meaning can be or is communicated. Indeed, we are so imbued with the "literate and literary way of meaning," with our set of proscriptive rules for negotiating aesthetic content, that we customarily start the inquiry with "what," assuming silently and even unconsciously that we already know the "how."[32]

In short, he asks the question "How does it mean?" before and instead of "What does it mean?" We can relate this line of reasoning to the earlier described media muddle in biblical scholarship. When we ask "what?" while processing by reading a passage in Paul's letters, the media dimension ("how") is already implied. In the given versions within biblical scholarship,

---

30. Foley, *Oral Composition*. See also Foley, "Introduction"; Foley, *Oral Formulaic Theory*.
31. Foley, *Immanent Art*.
32. Foley, *Immanent Art*, 5.

the letter means as "text"—recalling the statement of Umberto Eco that "what one calls 'message' is usually a *text*" (Introduction).[33] Thus Foley also puts his finger on the media dimension in the praxis (realm of history) of scholarship.[34]

Structural Elements: Broadening the "Formula"

In developing this theory of verbal art, Foley broadens the *formulae* to *structural elements*. These structural elements constitute an "oral" or "orally-derived work" and function as *metonymy*. Metonymy refers to the communicative dynamic of *pars pro toto*. This is reminiscent of Parry and his study on the epithet. In the moment that the performer uses a sound group—being vocalized in real time and with which his implied audience is apparently familiar—this explicit part (*pars*) is substituted for the implicit traditional whole (*totum*) for which it stands for both orator and audience. We can add that this process is governed by their imagination.

Regarding the dynamic of the structural element in this kind of oral communication, Foley opines,

> Traditional elements reach out of the immediate instance in which they appear to the fecund totality of the entire tradition, defined synchronically and diachronically, and they bear meanings as wide and deep as the tradition they encode.[35]

This is clearly a subliminal or participatory process—something that happens by just doing. It puts into words the fundamental relation of an

---

33. In Chapter 3, Section A. Textualizing history, we will also involve the matrix of "meaning"/"to mean" in our effort to textualize history, because the question of how is also applicable in this respect.

34. Note that Foley's "literate way of meaning" is, in the present study, similar to thinking within the predominantly literate state of mind.

35. Foley, *Immanent Art*, 7.

audience to its specific collective memory,[36, 37] Notwithstanding Foley's fo-

36. This term has an academic history. Generally, Maurice Halbwachs has been recognized as the father of memory research. In the beginnings of the twentieth century, he claimed that individual memories can only be understood in the context of a group. These shared memories (collective memory) unify the group and create some sort of collective identity. He developed his theory on *mémoire collective* in his *Les cadres*, and *La topographie légendaire*; for an English translation, see *Collective Memory*. Debate and research are still ongoing. Over time, different perspectives and additions have been proposed. For example, in his book *Religion and Cultural Memory*, Jan Assmann introduces the term "cultural memory." Social or collective memory comprises knowledge of a certain group in a specific time span (canon). Cultural memory, which he defines with literate societies in view, however, comprises also a material archive that might be discovered and studied in later times. In view of his professorship in Egyptology, this perspective may not be surprising. Another perspective is suggested by Dunn. In *Jesus Remembered, Volume 1*, he speaks of "communal memory." In his research into the gospel and the historical Jesus, he pays attention to questions on memory and oral tradition. He speaks of communal memory in view of the situation that Jesus himself is not present anymore to the communities involved, but the narratives on him must have persisted and have been recorded. Dunn deals with the question of reliability of these biographical stories in the light of memory. In this perspective, communal memory is structured by and limited to specifically shared traditions on Jesus's ministry. In this respect, we can refer to a concise and insightful treatment of these different kinds of memories regarding the Markan community in Zwiep, *Jairus's Daughter*, 193–94. In the present study, we prefer the more general term collective memory, since the focus is on the rather recent experiences of the Galatian converts in view of their conversion to Paul's gospel, their communal life afterwards in his absence, and, finally, the presence and performances of these other teachers who call them to live out of the law.

37. In Chapter 2, we will discuss Bernhard Oestreich's *Performanzkritik der Paulusbriefe*, that is a performance criticism of Paul's letters. He incorporates Foley's Oral Theory: "Performance criticism will *also* take into consideration the places where traditional elements are evoked by the use of formulaic language (*Immanent Art*) as described by Foley" (94; emphasis mine). The section, in which he discusses formulaic language, is called "References to content." Next to the used adverb "also," we note the plural in "references." So, Oestreich strengthens the impression that formulaic language is for him one among several kinds of references to the "*content* of a performance." He elaborates on formulaic language as follows: "[S]imple phrases and characteristic wording stand *pars pro toto* for complex concepts that are part of the prevailing tradition of those who are at home in the performance.... for example, "ἐν Χριστῷ ['Ιησοῦ] ... or also διὰ Χριστῷ ... εὐαγγέλιον or χάρις θεοῦ and many other phrases" (94–95). Explicitly, he relates these "traditional elements" to the collective memory of the participants in the performance. We see this affirmed in another statement later on: "The presence of maxims and proverbs, which draw on knowledge stored in the collective memory, is a typical feature of discourses in orally oriented societies" (*Performanzkritik*, 221–22). Also here, Oestreich confines the metonymical perspective to outstanding and isolated elements such as maxims and proverbs. In this way, a difference between this appraisal of Foley's Oral Theory and the one in detextification comes to the fore. In the latter, because of the emerging *communis opinio* on the originally intended media functioning of the letters, all identifiable units of sound (nouns, adjectives, verbs; terms, theme's, narrative, or logical fragments, etc.) will be regarded as metonymical in nature. In detextification, the question is whether there is in essence conceptual or abstract

cus on traditional oral works, this applies also to ourselves here-and-now. For example, when someone utters "9/11" (*pars*), this date will evoke the related matrix (*totum*), for example, from the dreadful images of one of the Twin Towers burning and an aeroplane crashing into the other up to themes as the war on terror and Muslim fundamentalism. Contrarily, we could also argue that speeches, lectures, or sermons can be experienced as tiresome when an appeal to our concrete lifeworld is missing. Crucial for the present research project is that, regarding the originally intended operational matrix of ancient documents, the intended audience *in actu* and their memory cannot be equated with the situation in which we process them as autonomous text in the context of the quasi-world of texts. The role of the collective memory of the original addressees urges us to estrangement. Explicit historical reconstruction of the metonymical way in which the original addressees would have understood those specific structural elements is necessary.

In comparison to *formulae*, these structural elements are an important broadening of the Parry-Lord thesis. Since the focus in our study is on the Letter to the Galatians, the question of the collective memory of these converts of Paul comes to the fore.[38] In line with the first governing question, we can ask, How did they frame the structural elements (documented wording of the letter) by the implied whole (their collective memory)? In Chapter 4, the examples discussed there are structured by metonymical referentiality. In the first example, the syllogistic reasoning of Gal 3.10–12 will be identified as enthymematic in nature. Instead of complete formal syllogisms on the level of text, we will look for structural elements in the documented wording, that is, premises or conclusions (*partes*). In this way, we will provide a single and historically adequate syllogistic reasoning (*totum*). Hand in hand with synonymous and antonymous terms and themes we will discern up to twenty-one parts of this *totum*. We will then argue that Paul presupposes this syllogistic reasoning as constitutive of the collective memory of his Galatian audience. In the second example, we will contextualize Gal 2.19–20 as a rhetorical strategy of Paul. In this passage, we will identify structural elements such as "co-crucifixion" and the specific sequence of "to die"/"to live." On the basis of metonymic referentiality, we will argue that these specific terms recall and evoke their experience of baptism, as an event

---

referencing in intended moments of performance—especially for the originally intended addressees of Paul's letters with a predominantly oral state of mind.

38. In the present study, the concept of "collective memory" is preferred above the notion of "tradition." The latter can be fleshed out in all kinds of aspects on the level of text. As a result, it remains rather abstract, whereas "collective memory" urges taking the specific bearers of it into account.

having taken place in their concrete lifeworld and being constitutive of their collective memory. So, with his Theory of Metonymical Referentiality, Foley will enable us to detextify this letter.

ERIC HAVELOCK: BIRTH PANGS OF A NEW STATE OF MIND

Over time, the insights of Milman Parry and Albert Lord started to be picked up by other scholars. In classical studies, one such notable scholar is Eric Havelock, who examined how such insights on orality might inform and re-shape understanding on Greek philosophy. In this section, we engage in particular with his monograph *Preface to Plato*, in order to inform the discussion around the relationship between media and mindset.[39]

Homeric and Platonic States of Mind

At the beginning of his academic career, Havelock engaged with the earliest forms of Greek philosophy, the Pre-Socratics. The earliest history of Greek philosophy had been studied hitherto within the given intellectual framework of Western philosophy. Havelock was convinced that the highly developed literacy of his contemporaries influenced their understanding of these Pre-Socratics. In his early publication *The Liberal Temper in Greek Politics*,[40] he therefore stressed the distinctiveness of the vocabulary and syntax of these documents:

> [E]pigraphy pointed to the conclusion that the Greek culture was maintained on a wholly oral basis until about 700 B.C. and if this were true, the first so-called philosophers were living and speaking in a period which was still adjusting to the conditions of a possible future literacy, conditions which I concluded would be slow of realisation, for they depend on the mastery not of the art of writing by a few, but of fluent reading by the many.[41]

---

39. Havelock, *Preface*.

40. Havelock, *Liberal Temper*. On the Pre-Socratics, see also in his *Preface*, the section "The Supreme Music is Philosophy," 280: "Are they [Plato, Parmenides, Empedocles, Anaxagoras, Democritus] not equally committed to the assertion that a different state of mind must be created in Greece, one which they seek to link with knowledge or science, and that the problem of energising this mind is one of energising a new language?"

41. Havelock, *Liberal Temper*, ix.

Although these transmitted documents have been transformed into "text," his intuitive insight was that distinctive organizations of *litterae* indicated a different way of structuring thought. So, in this way, we touch on the mental dimension of phenomena categorized as "literacy" and "orality" (mindset). As a rule, this mental dimension is reckoned to be somewhat vague or even invisible.

Havelock discerned a continuum between primary orality and high(er) literacy. He wanted to do justice to the historical dynamic of development. He differentiated between a preliterate time and later periods in which growing masses were able to process by forms of reading. The vocabulary and syntax of the transmitted documents of these Pre-Socratics reflect a transitory stage, in which they attempted to come to a different way of thinking. In the words of some of his commentators, "Havelock's claim is that a major task of the Pre-Socratics was to depart from the mythos of the Homeric mode of orally structured thought to a more literal, prosaic logos. To accomplish this end—Havelock argues—the Pre-Socratics created an abstract vocabulary."[42]

Tracing the origins of abstract thinking, Havelock became interested in the work of Parry which resulted in the book *Preface to Plato*. Here he fleshes out the vocabulary and syntax of the transmitted Homeric epics.[43] "Homer, so far from being 'special,' embodies the ruling state of mind."[44] The transition that took place in Greece was from an oral (Homeric) to a more literate state of mind.[45] He designates the latter as the "Platonic state of mind." In this monograph, he sketches this transition and argues that Plato is both the product of and the advocate for this process of change.

Episteme versus Mimesis, Truth versus Experience

Havelock's book deals with Plato's *Republic*, in particular with the philosopher's attack on the poet and his poetry.[46] Given the prominent role ascribed to poetry, he is one of the first to conclude that the *Republic* is not

---

42. Havelock, Review of *Preface*, by Neeley et al, 201.

43. Havelock, *Preface*, part one "the Image-Thinkers," in particular, 61–86, 87–96, and 115–33.

44. Havelock, *Preface*, 135.

45. Havelock, *Preface*, vii: "Between Homer and Plato, the method of storage began to alter, as the information became alphabetized, and correspondingly the eye supplanted the ear as the chief organ employed for this purpose."

46. Havelock, *Preface*, 4–5.

about politics but about education.[47] The perspective of education in this treatise explains the crucial role of the poet—who should not be equated with his "literate" equivalent. The poet embodies the whole educational system of Plato's time. More so, "Plato's target seems to be precisely the poetic experience as such."[48] Instead of concentrating on the "poet" and his "works of verbal art," Plato locates the danger in the *interaction* between the poet and his audience, that is, the experience which the performer brings to the hearer:

> Thus the poet, he [Plato] says, contrives to colour his statement by the use of words and phrases and to embellish it by exploiting the resources of meter, rhythm and harmony. These are like cosmetics applied as an outward appearance which conceal the poverty of statement behind them.

This poetic experience is a threat. Plato wanted to separate "truth" from experience.[49] Enhanced by the Homeric state of mind, this aesthetic experience is a kind of psychic poison. Poetry "confuses a man's values and renders him characterless and it robs him of any insight into the truth."[50] The Homeric state of mind leads to a cynical and hypocritical attitude:

> What Greece has hitherto enjoyed . . . is a tradition of a half-morality . . . according to which the younger generation is continually indoctrinated in the view that what is vital is not so much morality as social prestige and material reward which may flow from a moral reputation whether or not this is deserved. Or else (and this is not inconsistent) the young are insensibly warned that virtue is the ideal, of course, but it is difficult and often unprofitable. Do not the gods so often reward the unrighteous?

47. Havelock, Review of *Preface*, by Hoerber, 70–71: "first complimenting Prof. Havelock on his keen observation that the theme of the Republic is educational instead of political."

48. Havelock, *Preface*, 6.

49. At another point in the same book, Havelock comments more extensively: "Plato was correctly concerned with the emotional pathology of the poetic performance, and it explains also why he chose the term mimesis to describe several aspects of the poetic experience which we today feel should be distinguished . . . But the minstrel recited effectively only as he re-enacted the doings and sayings of heroes and made them his own, a process which can be described in reverse as making himself 'resemble' them in endless succession. He sank his personality in his performance. His audience, in turn, would remember only as they entered effectively and sympathetically into what he was saying and this, in turn, meant that they became his servants and submitted to his spell . . . The pattern of behaviour in artist and audience was therefore in some important respects identical" (*Preface*, 159).

50. Havelock, *Preface*, 6.

And immoral conduct in any case can be expiated quite easily by religious rites. The over-all result is that the Greek adolescent is continually conditioned to an attitude which at bottom is cynical.[51]

Plato opposes the influences of poetry by the founding of his Academy. There the philosopher kings are educated and formed. Over against *mimesis*—as dramatic impersonation of the poet hypnotizing the audience by meter, rhythm, and wording—Plato places *episteme* as universal knowledge. The former is based on human beings as sensoria and determined by the relation to the poet, the latter becomes severed from the body as well as hierarchical relationships.

The intellectual distraction involved with poetry necessitated Plato's renowned Theory of Forms. Over against the sensual experience of poetry, he put the form as "the abstracted object per se which is the only possible object of thought."[52] As opposed to the concrete, Plato advocates the abstract. The knower becomes separated from the known. The Theory of Forms resembles the method of abstraction. The operational or real-time praxis is minimized or even rejected in favour of the formal or theory. The experience of the spoken word by skilled poets, rhetoricians, and performers is superseded by a search for unshakable and absolute Truth. This truth is not dependent on or mediated by meter, rhythm, and harmony. This knowledge seems to have an existence of its own, severed from time and place, bodies, senses and relationships it has become free-floating and extra-historical in nature.

In this context, Havelock also refers to the famous Allegory of the Cave as contained in book VII of the *Republic*. In this allegory, Plato explains the ignorance in which humankind lives. All their lives long, a group of people are chained to a wall in a cave. In this condition, they are not able to see each other, but they can hear and converse with each other. On the wall in the cave they see shadows projected. These shadows are formed by things passing in front of a fire behind them. These prisoners give names to these projections of unclear shadows. Plato's suggestion is that those who are ignorant view reality in this way. This procedure is comparable to the poetic experience. Human beings must liberate themselves from the chains to find a way out of the cave. In the first instance, when they get rid of the chains, the light of the sun will be overwhelmingly disturbing. Acquainted with reality outside of the cave though, they will become philosophers who know the truth. When they want to return to the cave to liberate and tell their fellow prisoners about the truth, however, they will encounter disbelief

---

51. Havelock, *Preface*, 12.
52. Havelock, *Preface*, 254.

and even hostility. The ignorant are not able to grasp pure reality. This parable "shall suggest to us the ascent of man through education from the life of the senses towards the life of the reasoned intelligence."[53] Plato juxtaposes the immediate sensorial stance in the participatory realm of history or human beings as sensoria—chained in the cave (becoming)—with the abstracted representation of that reality—liberated outside in the sunlight (being). From within the realm of history, he wants humankind to be able to observe what is really true without being sensorially, bodily, or historically determined or—more importantly—without being misled. Thus the realm of history is the cave, and Truth (extra-historical thought) emerges as the origin of a new realm.[54] This separation of the known from the knower inaugurates not only a new realm but is based on a new state of mind. In conclusion, according to Havelock, Plato has forced a way out of the realm of history. The realm of Plato's Forms—unleashing unequivocal mental powers—has caused Western humanity to be an inhabitant of two worlds.

Regarding the governing questions of the present Chapter, we can now begin to formulate some answers. In Havelock's treatise, we touch on a rough, though clear distinction between two states of mind. According to Plato, in Havelock's representation, the Homeric is inferior to the Platonic mindset, because it "deals with becoming rather than being, and with the many rather than the one and with the visible rather with the invisible and thinkable."[55] The key words in Plato's new language on thought are, therefore, "'itself per se', which is 'one', and which is 'unseen'."[56] This terminology is a shift from "the image-world of the epic to the abstract world of scientific description and from the vocabulary and syntax of narrativized events in time towards the syntax and vocabulary of equations and laws and formulas and topics which are outside time."[57] Imagination and narrative become juxtaposed with abstraction, the scientific description of laws and formulas. It is not hard to recognize in the latter the contours of prosaic text and contemporary academia.

---

53. Havelock, *Preface*, 205.

54. This extra-historical status or existence in se can and will be disputed in the present study. We do this because specific or socio-culturally contextualized groups of human beings are the bearers and advocates of this kind of knowledge and they are as such subject to the laws and values of the realm of history in general. In the end, this alleged independent realm has to be located somehow in the former. We will point to autonomous text as the most important and prominent bearer of this kind of thought.

55. Havelock, *Preface*, 189.

56. Havelock, *Preface*, 256.

57. Havelock, *Preface*, 259.

The Platonic State of Mind and Text

In Havelock's discussion, we can relate the different mindsets to the activity of writing and text. He compares the strengths of dialectic with those of the written word. In this respect, he defines dialectic as a way of critically questioning the one who is speaking so that the speaker can clarify, deepen, and develop their thoughts. Dialectic is a means to an end, namely, to grasp reality by elaborate reflection. Contrary to the hypnotic trance of performances, the recorded word offers the possibility of taking a critical stance. Since this new technology of communication muted the emotional identification with the poet, rational autonomy could be gained:

> Refreshment of memory through written signs enabled a reader to dispense with most of that emotional identification . . . This could release psychic energy, for a review and rearrangement of what had now been written down and of what could be seen as an object and not just heard and felt.[58]

Writing fills out what is "just heard and felt" so that the "object" can be perceived. Paul Ricoeur echoes this idea when he states that there is no communication between writer and reader. It is all about reader and text. To the reader, the author is an abstraction and vice versa. As we argued in the Introduction, the text has to speak for itself and live a communicative life of its own. In line with Plato's pursuit for *episteme* beyond the realm of history, text would then diminish bodily experience so that truth remains.[59] We touch here on the second governing question—What does processing text do to us in terms of the structuring of our thoughts? Texts ask for objectifying or abstracting thought, and diminish emotions or dampen sensorial stimuli.

While Havelock's clear-cut distinction between the Platonic and Homeric mindsets enables us not only to grasp the contours of this rather unknown state of mind (Homeric), but also to become aware of our deeply ingrained mindset due to historical developments and mental transformations in Western history or literacy (Platonic), it can be critically observed that that the dichotomy is rather absolute in Havelock's reconstruction. In no way do we find a positive or even neutral evaluation of preliteracy or oral culture. In contrast, the present study would argue that the phenomena of preliteracy/non-literacy as well as literacy should and must be valued on their own merits.

---

58. Havelock, *Preface*, 208.

59. In this way, we observe that the ancient subject-object problem comes to the fore. This problem of thought becomes related to the phenomenon of text. In section E below, this relation is addressed by Walter Ong.

In addition, Havelock does not deal with the question of how a present-day reader with their specific mindset should relate to transmitted documents which originate from communicative contexts determined by the Homeric or—in case of the Letter to the Galatians—a predominantly oral mindset. So, next to juxtaposing these mindsets as Havelock does, we have to ask how we can relate them to each other. To find answers we will now turn to the work of Walter Ong.

WALTER ONG: COMING TO GRIPS WITH DIFFERENT MINDSETS

A strong and influential advocate for the study of orality and literacy has been Walter Jackson Ong (1912–2003). Appointed professor of English and Psychiatry at Saint Louis University, he was also an ordained Jesuit Priest. In a major way, he contributed to the establishment of orality and literacy studies and their interface. He published a considerable number of articles and monographs across various disciplines.

In what follows, we will concentrate on two monographs, *The Presence of the Word: Some Prolegomena for Cultural and Religious History*[60] and *Orality and Literacy: The Technologizing of the Word*.[61] Both books read like anthologies of the main aspects of his work and are thus a useful avenue for exploring the significant pillars of Ong's thought.

Oral Residue: "Text" in Need of Historicization

We can summarize the contribution of Ong regarding orality and literacy in a rather simple axiom. As he writes in the introduction to *Orality and Literacy*,

> The subject of this book is the differences between orality and literacy. Or, rather, since readers of this or any book by definition are acquainted with literate culture from the inside, the subject is, first, thought and its verbal expression in oral culture, which is strange and at times bizarre to us, and, second, literate thought and expression in terms of their emergence from and relation to orality.[62]

---

60. Ong, *Presence*.
61. Ong, *Orality*.
62. Ong, *Orality*, 1.

Central to his scholarly efforts has been the exploration of this interrelatedness of "thought," on the one hand, and "verbal expression" on the other. Not without reason, does he draw on Eric Havelock the most. Although the relation between verbal expression and thought patterns may seem simple and clear at first sight, he issues a warning in which one can hear an echo of Albert Lord:

> We—readers of books such as this—are so literate that it is very difficult for us to conceive of an oral universe of communication or thought except as a variant of a literate universe. This book will attempt to overcome our biases in some degree and to open new ways to understanding.[63]

At the beginning of *Orality and Literacy*, Ong describes the interface of oralities and literacies in three categories. He introduces *primary* and *secondary orality*, on the one hand, and *oral residue* on the other. Primary orality refers to cultures that are not influenced in any way by the technology of writing and reading—for example, the fieldwork of Parry and Lord on preliterate bards. As examples of secondary orality, he describes the transformed role of the spoken word in the course of his own life, that is, the development of technology such as radio, telephone, television, and also the beginnings of computer technology. Although the world of primary orality seems to be far away from the present-day reader, Ong insists on the continued presence of this mindset: "Still, to varying degrees many cultures and subcultures, even in a high-technology ambience, preserve much of the mindset of primary orality."[64] We can recall earlier observations that when we are exposed to some sort of performance ourselves in real time (see Introduction). So, third, oral residue refers to reminiscences of speaking in all kinds of writing, such as repetitions, abundance of epithets, long sentences, and so forth. Oral residue connects the mechanisms in real-time speaking to the constitution of "text."

We turn to one of Ong's areas of influential research, Tudor prose. In this transmitted prose, oral residue as documented in writing reflects a transitory stage in the history and development of "text." Originating in the sixteenth and seventeenth centuries, this prose can be designated as an interface of the still aurally oriented mind and the further developing media of writing.[65] Texts contain parts, phrases, and fragments that, al-

---

63. Ong, *Orality*, 2.

64. Ong, *Orality*, 11. Remarks like these seem to weaken the accusation of Ong as advocate of a Great Divide thesis.

65. See Ong, *Rhetoric*, 47: "The new typographic media offered previously unheard-of opportunities to the impulse of the orally oriented performer to have as much

though practically appealing to the eye of the reader on the level of text, were composed for the ear. Based on the emerging *communis opinio* on the original communicative context of the biblical documents, we could argue that the whole corpus Paulinum is also to be understood as oral residue: all parts, phrases, terms, and themes were originally intended to function in this distinctive predominantly oral register.

When the identification of oral residue is valid, an uncritical and self-evident approach to ancient texts as "text" (without any explication on the level of text) becomes problematic. It entails the impetus to systematically "historicize text." For the present study, the consequence is that the letters of Paul cannot be equated anymore with "text" as a matter of course.

Ancient Rhetoric as Speech Art

Ong illustrates this necessity of historicizing text in yet another way. The discipline of rhetoric sheds an important light on the history of Western literacy. In *Orality and Literacy*, he writes that rhetoric is "the most comprehensive academic subject in all western culture for two thousand years."[66] In the Roman Empire, education for the privileged cumulated in the teaching offered by a *rhetor*. This training was directed towards influencing the public by means of the spoken word.[67] So education was fundamentally rhetorical.

In its Greek setting, ἡ ῥητορική (sc. τέχνη) meant "speech art." There is an interesting twist here in historical retrospect. The oral practice of rhetoric has been accompanied over the centuries by a reflective science on it. Testimonies to this science have been documented *in writing*. It is because of these transmitted documents (texts) that modern humanity knows about it. In the beginning though, writing as "the inscription of living speech" (Ricoeur) did not impair but enhanced rhetoric as speech art. "[R]hetoric, basically meant public speaking or oratory, which for centuries even in literate and typographic cultures remained unreflexively pretty much the paradigm of all discourse, including that of writing."[68] By the sixteenth century, the balance shifted to a context of writing. In this development, the transmitted documents started to be used as "text" to compose "text":

---

as possible on hand so that he would be prepared to extemporize in absolutely any eventuality."

66. Ong, *Orality*, 9.
67. See Corbeill, "Rhetorical Education ."
68. Ong, *Orality*, 9.

With their attention directed to texts, scholars often went to assume, often without reflection, that oral verbalization was essentially the same as the written verbalization they normally dealt with, and that oral art forms were to all intents and purposes simply texts, except for the fact that they were not written down.[69]

The role of rhetoric itself transformed then from the oral to the typographic and predominantly literate mindset:

> From classical antiquity the verbal skills learned in rhetoric were put to use not only in oratory but also in writing. By the sixteenth century, rhetoric textbooks were commonly omitting from the traditional five parts of rhetoric (invention, arrangement, style, memory and delivery) the fourth part, memory, which was not applicable to writing. They were also minimizing the last part, delivery . . . the 'art' simply followed the drift of consciousness away from an oral to a writing economy. The drift was completed before it was noticed that anything was happening.[70]

Ong states that—in line with rhetoric—the spoken word remained dominant over the written word up to the eighteenth century.[71] This exploration on the transformative history of rhetoric sheds light on the third governing question, that is, how our deeply ingrained processing of text influences our understanding of the rather unknown functioning of oral performance. A question which becomes more pressing when we contrast this original situation to the majorly textual practice of doing theology in the history of Western Christianity.

"Meaning" and the Text Area

For that reason, we will turn now to some considerations of Ong on the notion of "meaning." In *The Presence of the Word*, he states, "In literate

---

69. Ong, *Orality*, 10. An illustration of this critique, but in the reverse direction, can be found in the naming of the academic heritage of Milman Parry and Albert Lord: *The Milman Parry Collection of Oral Literature* (https://library.harvard.edu/collections/milman-parry-collection-oral-literature). On the one hand, the world of "oral" verbal art is referred to. On the other, the collection is framed as "literature." Although the *contradictio in terminis* is acknowledged today, the naming of this archive demonstrates how the scholarly community has been captive to the inherent predominantly literate mindset and how thought determines verbal expression.

70. Ong, *Orality*, 114.

71. Ong, *Orality*, 113.

cultures, the illusion is widespread that if one has the exact words someone has uttered, one has by that very fact his exact meaning."[72] "Meaning" is framed and experienced as unmediated; a direct relationship between the "words" and their meaning is presupposed.[73] In a similar vein, he addresses the commonplace of *literal meaning*:

> As philosophers and lexicographers well know, it is virtually impossible to assign to literal meaning a significance any more definite than the first or most obvious meaning of a passage as apprehended by one familiar with the language and context.

Literal meaning implies a clearness and self-evidence that cannot be superseded. Literally seeing the *litterae* equals grasping the meaning; the formulation pushes the claim beyond critical awareness.[74] The visual experience of print culture deepens our grasp of this commonplace:

> The sense of order and control which the alphabet thus imposes is overwhelming. Arrangement in space seemingly provides maximal symbols of order and control, probably because the concepts of order and control are themselves kinesthetically and visually grounded, formed chiefly out of sensory experience involved with space. When the alphabet commits the verbal and

---

72. Ong, *Presence*, 32. From another angle, we can turn here once more to Ricoeur, "What Is a Text?" After stating that "writing is fixed speech" and also that "the psychological and sociological priority of speech over writing is not in question," he argues for a kind of reversal. Regarding "writing," he comments that speech always precedes this activity. Hence, regarding "text," he formulates "that a text is really a text only when it is not restricted to transcribing an anterior speech, when instead it inscribes directly in written letters what the discourse means" (146). In the next paragraph, he elaborates on "this idea of a direct relation between the meaning of the statement and writing." In comparison to the self-evident referentiality of living speech in its "circumstantial milieu," "the interlocutors are not only presented to one another, but also to the situation, the surroundings and the circumstantial milieu of discourse" (148)—he argues that, regarding text, "the movement of reference towards the act of showing is intercepted." For this reason, he introduces the posture of interpretation. "The suspense which defers the reference merely leaves the text, as it were, 'in the air', outside or without a world." (149) Based on this reasoning, he posits his "quasi-world of texts" or "literature." The meaning in text(s) has to be construed in relation to text(s). Since Ricoeur rejects "the ideology of absolute text," he remains convinced—despite his apparently direct relation between inscription and meaning—that text has reference that has to be fulfilled in the activity of reading as interpretation ("What Is a Text?," 148).

73. Kelber argues, in this respect, that "our humanistic legacy has shown a preference for unmediated notions of meaning, sense, idea, proclamation, and even information, it is ill-disposed to concede any cultural force to the increasingly material means of mediation" ("Modality," 195).

74. In his words: "This term frequently implies that meaning which is literal, or according to the letter, is necessarily trim and easily manageable" (*Presence*, 32).

> conceptual worlds, themselves already ordered superbly in their own right, to the quiescent and obedient order of space, it imputes to language and to thought an additional consistency of which preliterate persons have no inkling.[75]

We get here a clue of how the invisible whole of our thought in a predominantly literate state of mind becomes visible—that is, "the alphabet commits the verbal and conceptual worlds, themselves already ordered superbly in their own right." The argument is that the visual experience of the "alphabet" or the "word" in print or pixels is reciprocal to how our thought is structured. In the present study, we relate this visibility to "the level of text." According to Ong, this disposition leads inevitably to degradation of other forms of verbal expression and knowledge.

> An alphabetic culture, which puts a premium on visualist qualities such as sharp outline and clear-cut sequences, is likely to regard the literal meaning, in the sense of plain or definite meaning, as something altogether desirable, and to regard other remote, perhaps more profoundly symbolic meanings with disfavour.[76]

The complexity and flux of the historical lifeworld, which we sensorially experience, is juxtaposed with the clarity, uniformity, and fixedness of the world of abstracted thought, which we control by our cognitive capacities. It is important to note that Ong equates a specific structure in visual experience with "meaning." In the latter, we recognize a resemblance to Plato's ideal world or Theory of Forms (see the discussion of Eric Havelock in Section D.).[77]

---

75. Ong, *Presence*, 46.
76. Ong, *Presence*, 47.
77. Given the field of the present study, a caveat needs to be given here. Biblical scholarship stems from the oldest of academic disciplines, theology. Although still current and familiar, this categorization tends to present more oneness and harmony than is the case. The designation "theology" (singular) is in itself already in need of critical and historical differentiation. Throughout the ages and regions of the world, several theologies have emerged and persisted. Moreover, nowadays, in the West, one has to take into account as well (diversity in) Jewish, Christian, and Islamic theologies amongst others. Already this brief differentiation illustrates an inherent tendency in this academic discipline—towards a single and harmonious world of abstracted thought. In this way, another example is found of Ong's warning against predominantly literate biases.

Oral Context: Simplicity and Accessibility

To deepen this line of thinking, we turn to Ong's discussion of the "psychodynamics of orality" in *Orality and Literacy*.[78] Here the oral mindset is contrasted with the literate one. Oral communication is framed by the event of live performances. What is crucial here is that this setting is structured by the approval or disapproval of the actual audiences: they need to be captured, touched in their hearts, and more so come under the influence of the performer. The audience should be able to follow the narration easily; the words of the orator should directly and concretely be attuned to the rhetorical situation or collective memory of his audience.

A related psychodynamic is *homeostasis*, that is, the dynamic in oral societies that only those memories and words are conserved that have immediate and self-evident relevance for that situation.[79] Already in an early stage of the debate, valid critique was made as to the absolute character of Ong's presentation of this psychodynamic. Some features of homeostasis, however, can help us to understand how human beings understand in primary, predominantly oral cultures and even ourselves when we are exposed, for example, to a captivating political speech or a sweeping sermon in a church. Print cultures have invented dictionaries with the various meanings attached to certain words and the history of its use. In oral cultures, the framing of words is directly linked to the collective memory of the actual audience. The room for semantic discrepancies is much smaller than in the writing-reading relation. The concrete human lifeworld of performer and audience controls to a high degree the single and univocal understanding. So, in the structuring of the spoken word, simplicity and accessibility is imperative.

Memorizing over against Analyzing

In a literate mindset, the relation of an author to the reader of his text is severed and abstracted. The immediacy and self-evidence of the participatory realm of history is transferred to the parameters of the abstracted communicative process inherent in text:

---

78. This discussion is related to the following psychodynamics as coined by Ong: i. Additive rather than subordinative, ii. Aggregative rather than analytic, iii. Redundant or 'copious,' and iv. Conservative or traditionalist (*Orality*, 37–42).

79. Ong phrases this psychodynamic, number viii., as Homeostatic (*Orality*, 46–49).

> Written discourse develops more elaborate and fixed grammars than oral discourse does because to provide meaning it is more dependent simply upon linguistic structure, since it lacks the normal full existential contexts which surround oral discourse and help determine meaning in oral discourse somewhat independently of grammar.[80]

In their development, written words have grown more and more complex. Due to the separation from the "normal full existential contexts," one can argue that through autonomous text a new context emerged. This idiosyncratic context, based on "more elaborate and fixed grammar" and "linguistic structure," severs the ties of time and place. These shared (though to a high degree abstracted) structures are needed to mediate the implied meaning of text. Thus, recalling Ong's axiom of the interrelatedness of verbal expression and thought structures, we witness once more in this emerging context of autonomous text the implied mental transformation towards high literacy.

In this respect, Ong also highlights another consequence. Once the written word is stored in the media of autonomous text and at the disposal of a society, the energy needed to uphold the collective memory can be used for other purposes. In this respect, the mechanism of *looking up* (e.g. in a dictionary, encyclopaedia, or on the internet) is typical:

> Fully literate persons can only with great difficulty imagine what a primary oral culture is like, that is, a culture with no knowledge whatsoever of writing or even of the possibility of writing. Try to imagine a culture where no one has ever 'looked up' anything. In a primary oral culture, the expression 'to look up something' is an empty phrase: it would have no conceivable meaning. Without writing, words as such have no visual presence, even when the objects they represent are visual. They are sounds. You might 'call' them back—'recall' them. But there is nowhere to 'look' for them. They have no focus and no trace (a visual metaphor, showing dependency on writing), not even a trajectory. They are occurrences, events.[81]

An important distinction between predominantly literate and oral cultures becomes clear: "Oral expression thus carries a load of epithets and other formulary baggage which high literacy rejects as cumbersome and tiresomely redundant because of its aggregative weight."[82] Since memory is of no concern anymore, a universe of text-to-look-up comes into existence.

---

80. Ong, *Orality*, 38.
81. Ong, *Orality*, 31.
82. Ong, *Orality*, 38.

> Thought requires some sort of continuity. Writing establishes in the text a 'line' of continuity outside the mind. If distraction confuses or obliterates from the mind the context out of which emerges the material I am now reading, the context can be retrieved by glancing back over the text selectively . . . In oral discourse, the situation is different. There is nothing to loop back into outside the mind, for the oral utterance has vanished as soon it is uttered . . . Redundancy, repetition of the just-said, keeps both speaker and hearer surely on the track.[83]

In line with this contrast, Ong concludes that linearity is not natural to thought and speech; they are artificial creations structured by the technology of writing.[84] Since thought structures and representations are externalized, stored, and available, one can go over them critically to dissect, reject, adjust, elaborate, and deepen them. One of the most prominent and valuable purposes of literate cultures is—instead of memorizing—analyzing.

Ong warns, however, that we should not assume that oral cultures lack originality:

> Narrative originality lodges not in making up new stories but in managing a particular interaction with this audience at this time—at every telling the story has to be introduced uniquely into a unique situation, for in oral cultures an audience must be brought to respond, often vigorously.[85]

Anticipating the next Chapters, regarding the originally intended effect of Paul's letters, we presuppose that the apostle is involved in aggregative communication as well. As a consequence, we will propose that the terms, themes, reasonings, metaphors—which are recorded in the letter and have been copied, transmitted, and, finally, transformed into autonomous text to us—should have been, as a rule, familiar and known to his intended hearers. This means that, in his envisioned oral performance, new themes and ways of reasoning would have been an exception. Put differently, new themes and reasonings must have been introduced explicitly. As a result, we should not ask "what" does the apostle say (to us?), but, in line with the previous quotation, the crucial question is, How does he introduce the already and mainly familiar themes and reasonings in the actual situation of his intended addressees? From this perspective, we can identify in the first example of Chapter 4 several terms and themes of Paul's opponents: "law,"

---

83. Ong, *Orality*, 39–40.
84. Ong, *Orality*, 40.
85. Ong, *Orality*, 41, 42.

"rectification," "sin," "Gentiles," and "faith." In the second example of Gal 2.19–20, the passage will be related to "baptism," as Gal 3.27 makes clear that his hearers must have been familiar with this ritual in the moment of delivery. The question, therefore, concerns how Paul attempts to structure their thoughts in this part of the oral delivery of the letter on this subject.

The Golden Rule of Walter Ong

This is one of the main critiques of Ong concerning the predominantly literate state of mind:

> Deeply typographic folk forget to think of words as primarily oral, as events, and hence as necessarily powered: for them, words tend rather to be assimilated to things, 'out there' on a flat surface.[86]

In its development throughout time, text has become isolated more and more from the diffuse and complex historical lifeworld of which the actual reader is inextricably part. Text can be grasped as "object." Once we are exposed to it, we enter the "world of objects" (see also Introduction, Section D.1. Corpus Paulinum: Some text from the start). This line of reasoning evokes the fundamental question as to the nature of this "object": Does t-e-x-t/"text" refer to a physical artefact at hand or is it a mental concept on the level of text? In this question, one recognizes the tension between concrete versus abstract, inner- versus extra-historical, becoming versus being, formal versus operational, and (inter)subjective versus objective.

To answer the question, we turn once more to Ong. In *Orality and Literacy*, he comments on the tension between concrete and abstract thought with the help of the example of "tree":

> All conceptual thinking is to a degree abstract. So 'concrete' a term as 'tree' does not refer simply to a singular 'concrete' tree but is an abstraction, drawn out of, away from, individual, sensible actuality; it refers to a concept which is neither this tree nor that tree but can apply to any tree. Each individual object that we style a tree is truly 'concrete', simply itself, not 'abstract' at all, but the term we apply to the individual object is in itself abstract. Nevertheless, if all conceptual thinking is thus to some degree abstract, some uses of concepts are more abstract than others. Oral cultures tend to use concepts in situational, operational

---

86. Ong, *Orality*, 32, 33.

frames of reference that are minimally abstract in the sense that they remain close to the living human lifeworld.[87]

For our purpose, this line of thinking is crucial. It contains two key perspectives. First, when we replace "tree" by "text," the problem of concrete and abstract or physical artefact and concept becomes clearer. *In concreto*, we can posit that text exists in the realm of history there-and-then as handwritten scrolls, codices, constituted by surfaces made out of thinly sliced wood, papyrus or parchment, or in the one here-and-now as printed books, journals, and pixels on screens. *In abstracto*, all these different kinds of concrete appearances can be referred to as "text"—as we indicated in the Introduction.

Since the masses were reached several centuries ago by the technology of reading, due to the commercialization of book print, t-e-x-t has become an overly familiar designator. As a consequence of large-scale and programmatic training in literacy in Western culture, text has been internalized beyond critical awareness (see Introduction). This process relates to the operational as well as formal dimension. We can argue that the operational and formal realm fuse in "text" *in optima forma*. "Text" functions on the level of text and is at the same time available as physical object (text) beyond or facilitating that specific level. This means that for us "text" is part and parcel of extra-historical thought.

A second observation is based on the conclusion that "all conceptual thinking is to a degree abstract." We turn here to *Orality and Literacy* as well. In his listing of oral psychodynamics,[88] Ong comments that the method of abstraction separates man as the knower from the known. In this process of analysing reality (*in abstracto*), one is heavily dependent on the "elaborate analytic categories that depend on writing to structure knowledge at a distance from lived experience."[89] Since primary oral culture cannot enter this alienating state of mind, all their thought and speech will be embedded in their lifeworld or actual situation: "Oral cultures tend to use concepts in situational, operational frames of reference that are minimally abstract in the sense that they remain close to the living human lifeworld."[90] *In conclusion, oral verbal expression—given the implied thought structures—limits the level of abstraction on the side of the participants.* When we apply this heuristically to the original functioning of Paul's letters, we as present-day readers should try to approach as closely as possible the sensorially experienced

87. Ong, *Orality*, 49.

88. In this section, his line of reasoning is related to numbers v. Close to the human lifeworld (42–43), and ix. Situational rather than abstract, (*Orality*, 49–57).

89. Ong, *Orality*, 42.

90. Ong, *Orality*, 49.

concrete lifeworld of the composer behind the ancient documents at hand. Likewise, in the opposite manner, we should acknowledge that the complex, elaborate, and extra-historical thinking on higher levels of abstraction that we can encounter in commentaries, articles, and monographs, needs to be made subject to critique. In some way—even dampened—our imagination should come to life and help us to scrutinize given prepositions and to textualize as adequately as possible the realm of history involved. In the first example in Chapter 4, this will become clear from the work of Moisés Mayordomo and Michael Bachmann on the syllogistic reasonings in Gal 3.10–12. Their proposals represent abstractions of a high level: they are complicated and fully dependent on the media of autonomous text. In this way, not only the second and third governing question come together, but Ong also provides a golden rule to counter the subliminal influences of our default mindset vis-à-vis text on the understanding of these ancient documents: *we can scrutinize the degree of concretization in our abstractions and representations of oral performances in which Paul's original addressees participated*; we have to bend our thoughts[91] as deeply as possible into the realm of the history involved in order to represent presence as adequately as possible.[92]

---

91. The phrase "to bend our thoughts into the realm of history" captures the sense of not just directing thinking towards, but entering into that realm intentionally.

92. Ong enables us to apply this even to "history" as a whole. This conceptualization in order to grasp past events demands a degree of abstraction unknown to predominantly oral-aural humanity. In that regard, we turn to *Presence* once more: "Perhaps one of the most striking and informative differences is that an oral-aural culture is necessarily a culture with a relationship to time different from ours. It has no records. It does have memory, but this is not by any means the same as records, for the written record is not a remembrance but an aid to recall. It does not belong to us as memory does. It is an external thing. In an oral-aural culture one can ask about something, but no one can look up anything. As a result, in an oral-aural culture there is no history in our modern sense of the term. The past is indeed present, as to a degree the past always is, but it is present in the speech and social institutions of people, not in the more abstract forms in which modern history deals" (*Presence*, 23). In no instance, should our approach to history be, therefore, pejoratively discarded. One has to be aware, however, that this relation to past events *as representation*, such as "D-day," "Napoleon's defeat at Waterloo," the implied "performances of Homeric epics," or the "letters of Paul," is typical of the present-day reader. One searches to find entrance to objectified events. In this way, "history" is external. The past exists separately from the present. The difference is that the transmission of the letter to the Galatians links us to that past, but the transformation into text distances us in terms of media and mindset from this same past. In Chapter 3, we will present the approach of *detextification* to overcome this tension. We cognitively know about but do not participate in an immediate and sensorial way in that specific historical period or event under scrutiny. The better the reconstruction, the more specific the event becomes to the researcher. The deeper the historicization the more our imagination comes to life—for example, the enormous

CONCLUSIONS

In their study of traditional oral epic, Milman Parry and Albert Lord broke new ground in academia. They forged a way into the preliterate state of mind. In the exploration of this newly broken ground, what emerged very clearly and strongly from the material is an explicit warning from Lord, and echoed later by Ong, to present-day readers in a predominantly literate state of mind: we are subliminally inclined to understand the unknown in line with the known, that is, to funnel the dynamics of "orality" into the one of "literacy." Parry's fieldwork proved particularly illustrative of this with regard to the apparently self-evident presupposition that oral performances were verbatim reproductions based on learning by heart—resembling the fixedness and order of wording in text. His overturning of that assumption leads to what this study contends is the crucial transition: Parry moved beyond the level of text into the actual presence of performers and their audiences *in actu*—asking the question, What is happening when this performer sings his tales? This is significant for the direction of the discussion in this research where the aim is to describe the original functioning of Paul's letters along the same lines. Moreover, in line with the agenda of the present study, the same, consistent historical perspective will be taken on the communicative process in which we ourselves are caught up right now: What is happening when we read autonomous text in silence and solitude?

The individual studies discussed in the Chapter each contribute particular insights that inform the contours of the research. In addition to the formative question noted above, Parry highlighted the importance of paying attention to the body. Based on his research into the *formula* and *epithet*, he was able to conclude that "words" there-and-then were not related to the kind of "meaning" with which we are familiar. The use of words was dependent on meter (rhythm). Abstracted thought reaches for cognition, whereas meter takes over the body. Once the performer has "captured" the

---

popularity of re-enactment of all kinds of historical periods. In oral cultures, the past is part and parcel of the present. Rather than existing as two differentiated realms—as we characterize them here—the past constitutes the present to them. Both are inextricably related and therefore one. We might think here of the Haggada at the Jewish Seder in which the exodus out of Egypt is consistently related to those celebrating at that moment (for example, Haggadah, Maggied 5.c.). The same pertains to the Christian ritual of the Eucharist or the Lord's Supper. A similar perspective arises out of studies in social memory. In remembrance, the past is always appropriated and reappropriated to the needs of the ever-changing present (see Kirk, "Social and Cultural Memory"). The familiar conceptualization of history is first and foremost a product of the abstraction typical of Western culture. This line of thinking affirms the earlier posed problem of the media muddle: the present-day reader is explicitly not part of those historical situations that constituted the intended functioning of Paul's Letter to the Galatians.

body, he can gain influence over the hearts of his audience. The body will be a focal point in our construction of the realm of history in which oral performance takes place.

Notable in the work of Lord, is his repeated emphasis on the decisive role of sound groups for preliterate bards. Contrary to the fixedness and free-standing nature of "words" with which we are familiar—on the level of text—he explains that sound is evanescent, bound to a specific time and place, and immediately directed towards addressees who are bodily present. In this state of mind, each performance is constituted anew and, according to the preliterate bards themselves, the "word" (as fixed basic unit to us) could change between being a single term up to a whole line of verse. Even we ourselves, despite our highly developed literate mindset, do not pause in living speech between every single word. So, in the preliterate worldview, but also in our own concrete lifeworld, the fixed visual basic unit ("word") is difficult to identify. From this, we can draw three conclusions. First, the present-day reader—especially when processing text in silence and solitude—has constant recourse to the objective dimension of the w-o-r-d. This is not only apparent in the media of text but also in the accompanying mindset. To quote Ricoeur again, "words cease to efface themselves in front of things; written words become words for themselves."[93] Second, this kind of knowledge was not present in primary oral humanity, nor was it required or at issue in the moment of exposure by an orator *in actu*. Third, we could see here in an ultimate way the affirmation that in the participatory realm of history there is only flux, change, and diversity (see, in the Introduction, Caution to the reader #1).

In terms of offering a way of understanding the structuring of thought with relation to ancient documents, John Miles Foley is of utmost importance. Systematically, he differentiates on the level of thought patterns. In his Theory of Metonymical or Traditional Referentiality, he explicates the role of the *structural element*. He argues that in a metonymic way the *partes* are visible and recorded in these ancient documents—on the level of text, so to speak—and the implied whole or *totum* consists of tradition or collective memory. As a major step forwards, this thought structure refines the first governing question: as present-day readers of ancient documents, we can grasp the distinctive way in which participation in oral performance structures thought by relating the visible parts (documented wording) to the collective memory of the originally intended addressees. In the actual performance, it is they who participate in the construal of that event—not

---

93. Ricoeur, "What Is a Text?," 149.

we who are reading these documents as "text" centuries later. The performer anticipates this matrix in which his words will be framed.

From another angle, Foley also helps us to bend our thoughts into the realm of the history involved. Regarding ancient documents, we should not any longer ask the question *What* does it mean? on the level of text and to us, but *How* does it function for them? In the first question, we put our bodies and a/our specific kind of participation—processing by reading in silence and solitude—in the place of theirs. From this perspective, repercussions of the earlier mentioned media muddle become intelligible: vis-à-vis text, the present-day reader comes to some sort of understanding; we have to come to understand, however, how the original addressees were intended to understand while being exposed to the emissary in performance.

This outlook coincides with the discussion of mindsets in Eric Havelock's *Preface to Plato*. By comparing the Homeric with the Platonic state of mind, he creates an insightful distinction. According to Plato, performances are like psychic poison. Through meter, imagination, and mimesis the participants—who are engaged bodily—are brought under a spell, as it were. The rhetorician or poet is not so much interested in the truth but in gaining influence over his audience. Thus, Havelock's discussion provides a firm basis for the relational or bodily parameters of the predominantly oral mindset (inner-historical). By contrast, the Platonic state of mind represents absolute truth, as expressed by the Theory of Forms. Contrary to the flux and complexity of the realm of history, Plato advocated that reality should be grasped as "'itself per se,' [that] which is 'one,' and [that] which is 'unseen.'"[94] We witnessed here some sort of birth of the method of abstraction. This kind of knowledge tends to move away from the specificities of the participatory realm of history in which the subject *in actu* exists. In this structuring of thought, in which the contours of the predominantly literate state of mind were recognized, the second governing question on the effect of eye-to-text communication on the academically trained reader is answered.

Notwithstanding the heuristic value of the dichotomy between "orality" and "literacy," Walter Ong makes clear that the historical interface is more complicated than that. He demonstrates that "text" can be living speech in disguise. Although the *Iliad* and the *Odyssey*, Tudor Prose, and the corpus Paulinum appear to us as "text," we must do justice to a possibly different original functioning than autonomous texts (*oral residue*). However, Ong points out, text is more usually perceived as a monolithic or extra-historical entity per se, involving the same processing everywhere, every time, and for everyone. So, he calls for a systematic approach to the historicization

---

94. Havelock, *Preface*, 256.

of "text" as such, or a differentiation of functionings. This is especially relevant in terms of the third governing question regarding how the prevailing mindset in scholarship affects our reading of ancient documents.

Ong is equally important on the other side of the dichotomy with regard to literacy. He answers the question: What is happening when we read autonomous text in silence and solitude? In short, autonomous text is a form of abstraction in itself; the physical appearance of text (*litterae*, w-o-r-d-s, order, sequence, text area) represents the unchanging and invisible forms of "being" and (abstracted) thought to us. Thus he succeeds in contextualizing autonomous text. Ong provides a simple golden rule to counter the impairment of our state of mind vis-à-vis text. Namely, to acknowledge that there are different degrees of abstraction. We have to concretize our abstractions, representations, or propositions on the level of text as adequately as possible. It is imperative to bend our thoughts into the specific realm of history. Our imagination should be brought to life to guide and critically scrutinize our explorations. Since the question What does it mean? is restricted to text, the other question How does it mean? forces us to deepen our representation of actual communicative processes (oral performance/text)—to push it beyond the level of text. In the following Chapter concerning the history of Pauline research, we will not only discuss what is said about Paul and the oral performance/public reading of his letters there-and-then, but we will also enquire into the role of "text" (at and beyond the level of text) in current biblical scholarship.

2

Pauline Scholarship and Oral Performance, but What about "Text"?

IN THIS HISTORY OF research, publications are discussed that approach the corpus Paulinum from the perspective of orality studies, with the intention of addressing the first governing question. The hypothesis is that the mental transformations of the Western mind—because of developments in the technology of reading and writing—lay beyond the critical awareness of biblical scholarship. For that reason, these studies will be scrutinized on the present-day processing of the letters as "text" as well. The questions that lie at the heart of this scrutiny address issues of How do these studies relate the different media cultures of oral performance there-and-then-to-them and text here-and-now-to-us to each other? What can be learned from the explicit and implicit ways in which they are related to each other?

This Chapter discusses a representative selection of publications. The criterion of selection is related to the field of Pauline scholarship, and in particular, those that deal with the Letter to the Galatians. In addition, some relevant studies that encompass the New Testament as a whole will be considered. The ordering is according to date of publication. Three sections can be distinguished. The first six scholars deal with Paul and oral dynamics in a more general way. The recent movement of Biblical Performance Criticism is then discussed. In the process of this movement gaining influence, Larry Hurtado published an article to correct some of its underlying premises, which prompted a response from Kelly Iverson and another from Hurtado himself. The perspectives of these various studies will lead to some important conclusions on the interaction of the two media cultures at issue.

WERNER KELBER: *THE ORAL AND THE WRITTEN GOSPEL*

In 1983, Werner Kelber published his seminal study *The Oral and the Written Gospel: The Hermeneutics of Speaking and Writing in the Synoptic Tradition, Mark, Paul, and Q*.[1] In the preface to the edition of 1997, he states, "I have written this book out of a concern for what seemed to me a disproportionately print-oriented hermeneutics in our study of the Bible." He disqualifies the search for the original form as a governing bias, rejects the paradigm of linearity and criticizes the form-critical presupposition that the written gospel is self-evidently in continuity with oral traditions.[2] The subliminal inclination of New Testament studies is "to treat words primarily as records in need of interpretation, neglecting all too often a rather different hermeneutics, deeply rooted in biblical language that proclaims words as an act inviting participation." He aims "to broaden biblical hermeneutics by developing a sympathetic understanding of both the oral and the written word, and by studying ways in which one acts upon the other."[3]

The main part of the book is devoted to the gospel of Mark.[4] Since this treatment provides the blueprint of Kelber's oral hermeneutics, we will first discuss the chapters on Mark's oral legacy[5] and textuality.[6] He claims that "the very genre of the written gospel may be linked with the intent to provide a radical alternative to a preceding tradition."[7] Thus, the explicitly written gospel indicates a radical incision to all previous oral stages. Based on Havelock's treatise of Plato's *Republic* (Chapter 1), Kelber explains Mark's written gospel as an inherent critique on the system of oral transmission. Similar to the poets in Plato's day, the disciples are the oral representatives of Jesus. This frame sheds light on a major theme in Mark's Gospel: Jesus constantly has to confront the disciples over their lack of understanding as to who he is and what his mission is. "This leads us to suggest that the dysfunctional role of the disciples narrates the breakdown of the mimetic

1. Kelber, *Oral and the Written Gospel*.
2. Kelber, *Oral and the Written Gospel*, xv.
3. Kelber, *Oral and the Written Gospel*, xvi.
4. Kelber, *Oral and the Written Gospel*, 44–139.
5. Kelber, *Oral and the Written Gospel*, 44–89.
6. Kelber, *Oral and the Written Gospel*, 90–139.
7. Kelber, *Oral and the Written Gospel*, xvii.

process and casts a vote of censure against the guarantors of tradition." According to Mark, the reason for this defect is "that oral transmission did not work because it could not work."[8] To do justice to "the theological complexities that characterize the fullness of Jesus," a fundamentally different mindset is needed. Only literacy can provide this. In a pejorative way, orality is juxtaposed with and judged as inferior to literacy. One can recognize here the critique coined as the Great Divide.[9]

Once he has formulated this fundamental opposition between orality and textuality, Kelber elaborates the consequences. His line of thought is that Mark composed the gospel in "writing" and that the addressees participated by "reading." He then adds the following parenthetical remark: "even if the gospel was meant to be recited or read aloud."[10] First, "reading" itself, or how Kelber is using the term, is not explicated. Second, no explanation is found as to how this "reading" differs from his assertion that "the gospel was meant to be read aloud." This remark remains a loose end. The conclusion seems to be that this radically new media relation to the gospel of Mark (reading) applies to all subsequent "readers"—including the contemporary, print- or screen-oriented biblical scholar.[11] Kelber then turns to Paul and starts with the following statement on the nature of the letter:

> A writer of letters has chosen a form that favours extension of one's personal authority into written verbalization. As far as his

---

8. Kelber, *Oral and the Written Gospel*, 97.

9. In his new introduction to the reprint in 1997, Kelber defends himself against these charges: "We must, thirdly, avoid any implications of what has come to be referred to as the Great Divide . . . Repeatedly, my critics have pointed out that in late antiquity 'oral operations (presentation and hearing) and literary operations (reading and writing) were . . . inescapably interlocked' (J. Dewey, 1994: 45). I do not myself use the term the Great Divide nor was it part of our vocabulary in the late seventies and early eighties when the book was written. Indeed, the attentive reader will observe that my understanding of tradition and gospel is more nuanced than the label of *the Great Divide* gives it credit for . . . I am, moreover, persuaded that the strong thesis of *The Oral and the Written Gospel* was, and to some extent still is, necessary to break theoretical ground and to challenge the chirographic-typographic hegemony that rules biblical scholarship and many of the human sciences" (*Oral and the Written Gospel*, xxi–xxii).

10. Kelber, *Oral and the Written Gospel*, 115.

11. See Achtemeier, "*OMNE VERBUM*," 5, note 7: "[This observation] would fall into the category of premature conclusions." In a similar vein, A. Dewey comments that "while Kelber made an important connection between writtenness and Law and noted that this connection does not refer to some legalistic character of the Law but to the sense of its written totality and complexity, he failed, in my opinion, to bring in the fundamental issue of the power conveyed through the written tradition . . . Again, the question is not simply one of orality versus writtenness but of how power was to be conveyed and augmented" ("Re-Hearing," 112).

> authorial identity is concerned, Mark has retreated behind his text. Paul, by contrast, plays up his first person singular authority in the manner of oral speech. The letter form allows him to keep in as close touch with the recipients of his message as is possible for a writer, and to address them almost as if he were present in person.[12]

Paul's letters function as a second-best form of mediating personal authority—"as if he were present in person." With a reference to Robert Funk, Kelber suggests that Paul even wrote reluctantly and regarded the "oral word more fully effective than letters."[13] This line of thought also proves to be a loose end, with no elaboration on the consequences of this alleged inferior quality of the letter form is found in evidence.

Several remarks follow that illustrate Kelber's oral hermeneutics. Gospel is the master metaphor of the apostle: "Paul links the word primarily not with content, but with the effect it has on hearers."[14] Since God is essentially invisible, Paul's mission is directed towards interiorization: "The heart is the central organ of reception that facilitates communication with Spirit and gospel."[15] Internalization means participation: "the epistemological principle of orality [is] that to know actuality is to participate in it."[16] Therefore, knowing means participating and participating means knowing. With this epistemological principle "nothing less than a fundamental creed of the apostle's oral hermeneutics" is given.[17] In this way, no separation is at stake between knower and known. Presence diminishes or excludes representation.

This perspective on oral supremacy is expounded in his theory of *oral synthesis*. Paul's message as spoken word "implicates speakers and hearers alike."[18] Oral synthesis is formed by the interrelatedness of message, speaker, and hearers: "Oral synthesis creates a tense world of personal loyalties and betrayals. Not only is the message inseparable from the speaker, but the speaker is as important to the recipients as his message." The subject of *mimesis* comes to the fore. Contrary to the origins of Mark's gospel, Kelber suggests that imitation is an integral part of Paul's oral hermeneutics:

---

12. Kelber, *Oral and the Written Gospel*, 140.

13. Funk, "The Apostolic Parousia," 259, note 1. Kelber, *Oral and the Written Gospel*, 141.

14. Kelber, *Oral and the Written Gospel*, 145.

15. Kelber, *Oral and the Written Gospel*, 146.

16. Kelber, *Oral and the Written Gospel*, 150.

17. Kelber, *Oral and the Written Gospel*, 145.

18. Kelber, *Oral and the Written Gospel*, 147.

"Because in oral hermeneutics words have no existence apart from persons, participation in the message is inseparable from imitation of the speaker."[19]

After this general overview, Kelber turns to 1 Thessalonians. At this point, Kelber seems to turn this view on its head to bring oral supremacy into question. The very way in which the apostle had originally conveyed the gospel to the Thessalonians, that is, the oral word/gospel, constituted the reason for the problematic enthusiasm. This negative effect of oral performance asked for correction by the counterpart, that is, the written word: "Distanced from the community by space and time, the apostle has to seize upon the written media that, despite the letter's close affinity to speech, locates him vis-à-vis the oral gospel."[20]

To drive this point home, Kelber turns to 1 Corinthians. The problem at hand is recapitulated as follows: "His [Paul's] polemic is distinctly directed against the oral powers of wisdom." The apostle counters the power of wisdom with the power of the cross: "There is a subtle but inescapable linguistic logic that casts the cross in a position of judging the oral powers of Corinthian wisdom."[21] Kelber concludes,

> When faced with the extreme consequences of oral wisdom, Paul, preacher of the oral gospel, is here compelled to reconsider his hermeneutical priorities and to invoke the norm of Scripture. "Do not go beyond what is written" is a wholly exceptional statement in Pauline theology, and in making it the apostle has at this point sanctioned the written media as a basis of the new wisdom.

Despite his original oral hermeneutics, the Paul of 1 Corinthians "is a subtle but consistent promoter of the values of literacy."[22] We can draw the following conclusions. The whole of his argumentation starts by stating that in essence the gospel is spoken; it needs to be heard so that participation and imitation can take place (oral synthesis). As readers of his book, our imagination comes to life. Kelber does not systematically relate, however, the "oral word" or "oral gospel," as delivered by Paul himself, to the—apparently inferior—oral delivery of the letters by the emissary. A number of questions thus arises: How is the effect of a sent emissary inferior to Paul travelling there and addressing the congregation himself? What role does the process of composition, the letter as physical artefact, and/or the event of delivery play in Paul achieving his goals? Concretization is also missing in his subsequent leap to the "letter" as "written medium" in the Thessalonian

---

19. Kelber, *Oral and the Written Gospel*, 151.
20. Kelber, *Oral and the Written Gospel*, 172.
21. Kelber, *Oral and the Written Gospel*, 174.
22. Kelber, *Oral and the Written Gospel*, 177.

and Corinthian correspondence. Kelber does not explicate the operational process in the realm of history there-and-then, again leaving a number of points to be addressed. One might raise the questions: Does "reading the written medium" mean that the addressees read in silence and solitude—as the modern reader is used to do? What then was the role of the emissary? Was the letter present in that situation as one physical artefact (autograph) or did Paul send several apographs? Neither does Kelber enter into any discussion as to how all these moments of individual reading might have taken place or looked like in the life of the congregation, in what way the recipients might come to a communal understanding or discussion of the content, or of who would have been in charge of that process and on what grounds did this person/these persons have the authority to act in this way. Conversely, when we imagine that this "written medium" (single artefact) was negotiated to the addressees in some sort of a public reading, then the question that arises is, How could the addressees, as they are exposed to the emissary and his reading aloud, be able to grasp and experience this radically opposed functioning of "writing"? But we can go even further: If the goals, which Paul wanted to achieve with the "letter," are dependent on the "written" form, what would be the consequence for the credibility of his prior gospel preaching mediated as "oral word"? Kelber's reasoning on "written medium" and "reader" remains abstract and ambivalent.

Here we might consider the intended audience of Mark's gospel which Kelber designates as the "readers." Since Kelber does not pay particular attention to this notion, the "reader" there-and-then can only be framed by the one he is familiar with, that is, he himself in actual practice. A huge gap in time is the result. A gradual development of the technology involved and possible mental transformative repercussions over time become blind spots. In the words of Casey Davis, "a scholar such as Werner Kelber, who argues that the New Testament writers were seeking to pull their readers into an abstract literate mentality and away from the concrete oral mindset, is condensing centuries of development into decades."[23] This critique pertains to the whole conceptual matrix of "reader," "hearer," "writer," and, in particular, "letter," and "text." This monolithic and extra-historical usage structures thoughts away from the concreteness of the realm of history. In view of the third governing question, this is a clear example of the tendency characteristic of the predominantly literate state of mind.

Therefore, we must ask whether the oral hermeneutics of Kelber is the inevitable result of this mindset. In this structuring of thought, "text" is free-floating. The phenomenon itself is left out of consideration; how

---

23. Davis, *Oral Biblical Criticism*, 28.

the present-day reader relates to it is not reflected upon. In a similar vein, "hermeneutics" is neither located in a specific realm of history (there-and-then-by-them or here-and-now-by-us), nor are the specific subjects *in actu* (the original addressees or the contemporary reader of his book) sufficiently identified. From the start, his hermeneutics is determined and constrained by the communicative situation of the contemporary biblical scholar, that is more precise, his particular technical relation to the available versions here-and-now of the New Testament documents as "texts." Nonetheless, despite this weakness, we will use his model of oral synthesis. Regarding the first governing question, the emphasis in his thesis on the participation of the intended addressees will be one of the focal points in defining body-to-body communication (Chapter 3).

PAUL ACHTEMEIER: *"OMNE VERBUM SONAT"*

In 1989, Paul Achtemeier, president of the Society of Biblical Literature for that year, delivered his presidential address, entitled *"OMNE VERBUM SONAT:* The New Testament and the Oral Environment of Late Western Antiquity."[24] In this lecture, he commences by hailing a salutary development in biblical research: "the recovery of the awareness that its documents were produced within the environment of late Western antiquity and that, therefore, knowledge of that [oral] environment will aid in their understanding."[25]

Achtemeier draws attention to the neglected aspect of the immediate cultural environment: "That aspect centers on the fact that we have in the culture of late Western antiquity a culture of high residual orality which nevertheless communicated significantly through literary creations." In this opening statement, "high residual orality" is related to "literary creations." The first phenomenon stems from Walter Ong (see Chapter 1), the second, however, is not explicated or defined. Since these "literary creations," "writings," "the written word," or "manuscripts" are distinguished from oral performances, public readings, or emissaries, Achtemeier seems to frame them as things or objects (being).

This tendency is also clear in the category of "residual orality," which subjects the spoken word to the written word. We recognize this hierarchy also in Achtemeier's focus on the "oral overlay": these are "indications in written documents that would make their oral performance understandable even in the absence of any formal rhetorical training on the part of

---

24. Achtemeier, *"OMNE VERBUM."*
25. Achtemeier, *"OMNE VERBUM,"* 3.

the writer or the listener." In this way, he addresses the question proposed in the introduction to this Chapter as to how these studies relate the different media cultures involved to each other. From the start of his article, the influences of the oral culture there-and-then seem to be dominated by the physical artefacts. And since no distinction is made between the approach of "these literary creations" there-and-then and here-and-now, we seem to have them at our disposal as the New Testament "texts" in real time.

What follows is an exploration of the outline of Achtemeier's argumentation. His contribution is to address the oral overlay in the writings of the New Testament by reviewing how written documents were created and read. Here Achtemeier makes the significant remark, "Of primary importance to this discussion is the realization that ancient culture remained committed to the spoken word."[26] He refers to the preference of Seneca and Papias for oral accounts over written records, and points to "the sheer physical nature of the written page in classical antiquity" which "militated against its ease of reading and in that way also contributed to the culture's reliance on the oral mode in communication."[27] These aspects illustrate a cultural bias in favour of the spoken word. Nonetheless, writing was known in a variety of purposes and types, and paper was readily available: "the wide distribution of copies of the writings of the NT gives evidence of the extent to which literature could circulate even among the less prominent members of the Hellenistic culture."[28] Achtemeier also deals with the rules of dictation. He concludes that the documents that were produced and read "were predominantly, indeed exclusively" oral.[29]

After this excursion into reading and writing in antiquity, Achtemeier launches his main point: "the oral environment was so pervasive that no writing occurred that was not vocalized."[30] Once more, this illustrates his

---

26. Achtemeier, "*OMNE VERBUM*," 9.

27. Achtemeier, "*OMNE VERBUM*," 10. As an illustration, Achtemeier describes the physical appearance of the text: "The written page consisted entirely of lines each containing a similar number of letters, lines that ended and began irrespective of the words themselves. Documents were written without punctuation, without indications of sentence or paragraph structure, indeed without separation of the letters into individual words" (*OMNE VERBUM*, 10).

28. Achtemeier, "*OMNE VERBUM*," 11.

29. Achtemeier, "*OMNE VERBUM*," 12.

30. Achtemeier, "*OMNE VERBUM*," 15. Many examples are mentioned, such as Zechariah in the gospel of Luke, a tombstone epigraph assuming that the deceased is speaking what is read (15, 16), Herodotus reporting that Croesus "hears" the written oracles from Delphi. In line with these examples, he extends this practice of vocalization to public presentations of literature in general. As final step, he subsequently frames "early Christian gatherings" likewise (16). To drive his point home, he concludes, "Most

emphasis on the oral inclination in late Western antiquity. For him, the research by Joseph Balogh had been decisive in shaping his view on this issue. In the beginning of the twentieth century, the question of whether antiquity was familiar with silent reading dominated the study of ancient literacy. In his article "Toward a Sociology of Reading in Classical Antiquity,"[31] William Johnson observes that some decades before Achtemeier's presidential address scholars had already disqualified the apparently revolutionary outcome of Balogh's research.[32] As a result, the *communis opinio* was that, next to the overly familiar practice of reading aloud in a predominantly oral culture, there is evidence of the practice of reading in silence and solitude in antiquity as well.[33] (See the Excursus on silent reading in antiquity below.)

Returning to his quintessential thesis, Achtemeier turns once more to the sheer physical nature of the written page. The ancient reader had a difficult task:

> The visual format of the ancient manuscript—words run together, and in addition often abbreviated, no punctuation to indicate sentences or paragraphs—conveyed virtually no information about the organization and development of the content it intended to convey.[34]

His argument seems to hone in on the absence of visual indications in the organization of the signs inscribed on the flat surface of the transmitted ancient documents. Implicitly, this absence is perceived as a problem, and is to scrutinizing this that we turn now.

In his formulation, first, "the visual format" is bound to the "ancient manuscripts." When we recall John Foley's question ("How does it mean?"), it becomes clear that a specific media is given (text/text area) and an isolated sense is in operation (vision/eye). Therefore we must ask, the rather rhetorical question, whether this "visual format" or the absence of visual

---

interesting from our perspective, and perhaps least generally understood is the fact that even solitary readers, reading only to themselves, read aloud . . . Reading was, therefore, oral performance *whenever* it occurred and in whatever circumstances. Late antiquity knew nothing of the 'silent, solitary reader'" (*OMNE VERBUM*, 16–17).

31. Johnson, "Toward a Sociology," 595.

32. As an unfortunate example of not being informed properly, Johnson explicitly refers to Achtemeier: "A startling example is the naive summary of the debate, which serves then as the basis for a study of New Testament texts, in Achtemeier 1990" ("Toward a Sociology," 597, note 11).

33. Johnson, "Toward a Sociology," 596. In his article "More Silent Reading," biblical scholar Frank Gilliard provides several examples that undermine Achtemeier's bold statement.

34. Achtemeier, "*OMNE VERBUM*," 16.

indications was problematic there-and-then-to-them (emissaries, professional scribes, public readers) or is it problematic here-and-now-to-us (contemporary reader, biblical scholar)? No explanation or explication is given. For the present-day readers vis-à-vis these ancient manuscripts (with their *scriptio continua*, abbreviations, no punctuation, and so forth) as text, this specific and atypical "visual format" is usurped by that level of text itself. The emphasis in the present study on the participation of the originally intended audiences in the oral performances of the letter makes clear that the role of this visual perspective is not directly relevant for them. Thus, Achtemeier's discussion lacks the question of to whom this visual format is important or apparently problematic.

Second, the visual dimension of the intended communicative process is related to the problem of "the content it intended to convey." Note that "it" refers to the physical object of the "manuscript." It is not the audience in reciprocity to the emissary that comes to a certain understanding, but it is the manuscripts which can freely float throughout time and place (objects) that are considered to convey "content." A priori the approach of the manuscripts there-and-then and the intended understanding is funnelled into our known and communal practice of reading them here-and-now in silence and solitude (text).

Given the problematic situation of the visual format and the conveyance of content, Achtemeier offers two possibilities. First, he makes the following comment,

> One way, of course, is to have someone deliver the writing who knows what it contains, and what the author intended with it, and have that person give such information. That in fact was frequently done with letters, itself an indication of the problem ancient writers faced in conveying their thoughts in understandable form. Yet such an expedient had limited utility at best, and in fact served virtually as a substitute for conveying information via the written word.[35]

Achtemeier proposes the emissary not as a solution to the problem of the visual format but as "a substitute for conveying information via the written word." He juxtaposes the process in which the emissary is crucial for activating the letter, with a distinctive communicative process based on "writing" or "the written word." An either-or structuring of thought is the danger here. In this way, we notice once more the inner tension in his argumentation as a whole.

---

35. Achtemeier, "*OMNE VERBUM*," 17.

We can make another observation on the presuppositional level. Achtemeier sees the role of the emissary as "an indication of the problem ancient writers faced in conveying their thoughts in understandable form." In this remark, we recognize the poles that cause the inner tension in his argumentation. Apparently, ancient writers faced a "problem." Now the question comes to the fore as to how does Achtemeier know (or, how can he demonstrate) that ancient writers faced (this as) a problem.[36] Clearly, in biblical scholarship, or even as early as 2 Peter 3.15–16, one experiences difficulties in understanding documented words that are severed from their original realm of history and that have to speak, therefore, more or less for themselves. The crucial and presuppositional question is whether Paul, his emissaries, and/or originally intended audiences experienced this as a "problem" in the one, envisioned, unrepeatable, and trenchant moment of oral delivery. One can only experience the problem as stipulated above when a writer is aware of an alternative, namely, conveying one's thoughts in understandable form via "the written word." We should add once more that in Achtemeier's reasoning these writings are seen as functioning independently from an emissary. In a Procrustean way, he seems to force *textum* into text. Put simply, either Paul is an inferior "ancient writer" or this was the normal and, therefore, non-problematic "visual format" at the time. The present study explores this latter line of thought.

Alongside the solution of an emissary, Achtemeier continues by providing an "alternative to visual structuring of a manuscript to indicate organization of meaning." He states,

> In short, organization of written materials will depend on sound rather than sight for its effectiveness . . . What we want to look for, are verbal clues that, by being heard (not seen!), would have aided the listener in understanding the organization of the kind of complex writings that are found in the NT, clues that helped the hearer determine when one unit of thought had ended and another begun.[37]

So the focus seems to shift here from the reader being exposed to the visual format as such to the aural participation by the hearer in the moment of

---

36. In this respect, we can turn once more to the article by Evans, "Creating a New 'Great Divide.'" In his argumentation, he addresses issues relating to "the complexity of both orality and literacy in reconstructing the function of scribes and their texts in ancient Israelite circles" (753). As an Old Testament scholar with a particular interest in matters of scribality, he rejects the position that text could not be read at first sight: "The fact that we moderns might have difficulty in reading these ancient scrolls does not mean that ancient users did so" ("Creating a New 'Great Divide,'" 753).

37. Achtemeier, "*OMNE VERBUM*," 19–20.

delivery. He presents three main structuring elements, that is, repetition,[38] parallelism,[39] and *inclusio*.[40] These clues were earlier designated by him as "residual orality" and "oral overlay in written media." On this basis, Achtemeier makes the following conclusion:

> Such, I would urge, are a few examples of the ways aural clues were built into the prose of the letters addressed to groups of Christians, clues that would aid the listener in following the course of some long and complex arguments contained in those letters, but which would also aid the reader in giving a coherent and meaningful presentation of the content.[41]

In line with the focus of the present study, we must ask: How does Achtemeier know that these "arguments" would be experienced by the intended addressees as "long" and—more importantly—"complex"? What makes an "argument" complex to everyone, everywhere at every time? Or is this perhaps his own experience as a twentieth-century reader approaching the letter as "text"? Furthermore, it remains vague as to what the differences are between an instructed public reader (emissary) and an uninstructed one, and how we should imagine the latter against the background of the oral environment of the New Testament. We can further observe that these clues help to organize the verbiage, but do not interfere with the structure of the (complex?) argument. These identified structuring features ("clues") solely function on the level of text. Once more, this perspective seems to be based on his own (uncritical) visual exposure to the available version (text).

Let us evaluate now Achtemeier's case for doing justice to the oral environment of late Western antiquity. Historically speaking, he rightly stresses the distinctiveness of the original context of the New Testament documents there-and-then-to-them. Also, his excursus on the role of the emissary is thoughtful and provides helpful material. Crucial is his uncritical turn from describing the specific process of delivering the letter by an instructed emissary there-and-then to the given product which seems to be also available here-and-now-to-us; on this basis, he formulates this problem of "visual

---

38. As an example of repetition, he elaborates on anaphora, that is, the repetition of a word or phrase at the beginning of successive clauses. For example, in 1 Corinthians, seven times reference is made by the phrase περὶ δὲ to topics dealt with in different settings (*OMNE VERBUM*, 23).

39. We can elaborate on one: In 1 Cor 1.27–28, the formula τοῦ κόσμου ἐξελέξατο ὁ θεὸς ἵνα is repeated three times. The third repetition, however, adds a second noun after τοῦ κόσμου and omits the ἵνα. In this way, the hearers are made aware that this unit has come to an end (*OMNE VERBUM*, 24).

40. For example, Rom 1.29–31; 12.9–13.

41. Achtemeier, "*OMNE VERBUM*," 25.

format." From the start of his article, however, we saw several indications that "text" ("manuscript," "writing," or "written word") as thing/object dominates the "oral context." These considerations may explain why the results of his call to do justice to this oral environment appear to be rather weak. He does not problematize the nature of the complex argumentation or penetrate the different ways in which thought can be structured (mindsets). This is due to the free-standing status in his argumentation of "literary creations," "writing," "the written word" and/or "text"—but also "argument." We deal with an a priori severing (abstraction) of the material[s] from a specific time and place (late Western antiquity) and functioning (emissary, oral performance, public reading). These oral clues do not affect our imagination; they do not bring to life the intended oral performance as an event. So, despite his good intentions, Achtemeier seems to leave us in the media muddle.

EXCURSUS: SILENT READING IN ANTIQUITY?

Achtemeier's *omne verbum sonat* urges us to ask whether there was a practice of silent reading in antiquity and, if so, what the nature of that type of reading was. Since the relation between silent reading there-and-then-by-them and here-and-now-by-us is pivotal, how well-known or unknown would this alleged ancient practice of silent reading be to academically trained readers?

To take a stance in this matter, we will turn to William Johnson's article on a sociology of reading in classical antiquity.[42] He traces the roots of this debate to Eduard Norden's *Die antike Kunstprosa*[43] and Josef Balogh's "*Voces Paginarum*: Beiträge zur Geschichte des Lauten Lesens und Schreibens."[44] They have set the stage for the assumption that (almost) all reading in antiquity must have been aloud. Particularly the practice of *scriptio continua* even led to the suggestion that silent reading was neurophysiologically not even possible.[45] This idea is still widespread. In 1968, Bernard Knox published an article on "Silent Reading in Antiquity."[46] Contrary to Balogh, he demonstrates that ancient letters and documentary texts could be read in silence.[47] Along the same lines, Andrei Gravilov published an article in

---

42. Johnson, "Toward a Sociology."
43. Norden, *Kunstprosa*.
44. Balogh, "*Voces Paginarum*."
45. Johnson, "Toward a Sociology," 595, 598.
46. Knox, "Silent Reading."
47. Johnson, "Toward a Sociology," 596.

1997 entitled "Reading Techniques in Classical Antiquity."[48] Referring to the field of cognitive psychology, he demonstrates that neurophysiologically speaking Greeks and Romans must have been able to read silently.[49] Despite cultural diversity, he suggests that we have to reckon with an underlying unity in silent reading in antiquity and modern times.[50]

Who is right in this debate? This is the moment where Johnson takes over. The question whether reading was aloud or silent is dismissed by him. It implies a too simplistic approach to historical reality: "We must proceed from a clear and deep perception that what we seek to analyze is an immensely complex, interlocking system."[51] Since there is clear evidence of silent reading *and* public reading and reading aloud, he reframes the question by asking what "reading" is and "how the ancient reading culture (as I [WJ] will call it) does in fact differ from the reading-from-a-printed-book model familiar to us today."[52] Johnson takes a sociological turn on reading: "Critical is the observation that reading is not simply the cognitive process by the individual of the 'technology' of writing, but rather the negotiated construction of meaning within a particular socio-cultural context."[53] According to him, reading comprises the following facets: *reading*—the experience of the action; *reading events*—the contextualization of a particular "reading;" and *reading culture*—the cultural construct that underpins the behaviours of groups and individuals involved in this particular "reading event." Johnson advances the following propositions:

> (1) The reading of different types of texts makes for different types of reading events ... (2) The reading of a given text in different contexts results in different reading events ... (3) ... the reader's conception of ... to what reading community s/he thinks to belong, is an important ... part of the reading event ... (4) The reading community normally has not only a strictly social component ... but also a cultural component, in that the rules of engagement are in part directed by inherited traditions ... (5) Reading which is perceived to have a cultural dimension ... is intimately linked to the self-identity of the reader.[54]

---

48. Gravilov, "Reading Techniques."
49. Johnson, "Toward a Sociology," 596.
50. Johnson, "Toward a Sociology," 599.
51. Johnson, "Toward a Sociology," 604.
52. Johnson, "Toward a Sociology," 600.
53. Johnson, "Toward a Sociology," 603.
54. Johnson, "Toward a Sociology," 602–3.

By contextualizing "reading" as specific "reading events" within a certain "reading culture," he points the way towards a differentiated and socio-culturally grounded conceptualization of ancient reading practices (plural). In this way, Johnson attempts to do justice to the "immensely complex, interlocking system" or "highly complex socio-cultural system."[55] In other words, he applies the golden rule of Walter Ong that the level of concretization in abstraction is crucial.

The second part of Johnson's article is dedicated to exemplifying this approach. Based on fragments from Lucian's diatribe on *The Ignorant Book Collector* (*Adv. Indoct.*) and Pliny the Elder (*Natural History*), he focuses on reading events related to prose literary texts in the first and second century BC of the Roman era.[56] In these particular socio-cultural instances, reading is situated in elitist circles in which the book rolls "were not . . . conceptualized as static repositories of information (or of pleasure), but rather vehicles for performative reading in high social contexts."[57] This social context of reading must have functioned as a springboard to intellectual discussion by members of the group.[58] Notwithstanding the notion "that at times the ancients read silently and in solitude," he emphasizes the force of tradition within the reading culture of using an out-loud reader. Referring to Raymond Starr,[59] Johnson suggests that the use of lectors has been adequately demonstrated and is so widely assumed that it is only rarely mentioned explicitly.[60] In conclusion, he posits reading aloud to a (elitist) group as the dominant practice.[61]

The treatment of the visual appearance of the book roll—clarity of letters, *scriptio continua*, the width of columns and intercolumn, the aesthetic dimension in the interplay of these features—already pointed in this direction. "The strict . . . attention to continuous flow in the design of the ancient book interlocks with the idea that it was the *reader's* job to bring the text alive, to insert the prosodic features and illocutionary force lacking in the

---

55. Johnson, "Toward a Sociology," 603.
56. Johnson, "Toward a Sociology," 605, 613–24.
57. Johnson, "Toward a Sociology," 616.
58. Johnson, "Toward a Sociology," 617.
59. Starr, "*Lectores*."
60. Johnson, "Toward a Sociology," 619, note 36.
61. It is important to note here a difference with the communities that Paul addressed in his letters. See, Johnson, "Paul's Letters," 26: "The claims of the discussion of ancient letters arise out of literate cultures; both writers and recipients were literate, elite classes of people . . . In contrast, the make-up of the communities to whom Paul wrote were primarily poor, working classes."

writing system."[62] He draws the parallel to a present-day reader relating to a play through text:

> Just as we, when we read a play, are conditioned to imagine the possibilities of the actor's intervention, so ancient readers (and indeed ancient authors) were, I suppose, conditioned to regard the text not as a voiceless and straightforward representation of the author's intent, but as a script to be represented in performance (whether actualized or not).[63]

This echoes what was said about *textum* in the Introduction to this thesis. Ricoeur's stipulation of writing as the inscription of living speech also comes to mind, since this takes place between actual human beings in a concrete situation in distinction from autonomous text.[64] In conclusion, not only do we have to move away from a monolithic and extra-historical framing of "reading," we can also infer from Johnson's study that the practice of reading aloud was predominant. Therefore "reading" is to a certain extent known to the present-day reader—as "the experience of the action," but he also has to take account of the unknown—as differing "reading events" and "reading cultures" in which the hearing of the word was central.

In the documents of the New Testament, we can find many examples of "reading" as well. Obviously, we think of Jesus reading out loud in the synagogue in Nazareth[65] or the Ethiopian eunuch reading aloud to himself

---

62. Johnson, "Toward a Sociology," 612–15.
63. Johnson, "Toward a Sociology," 620.
64. Ricoeur, "What Is a Text?," 146.
65. In his gospel, Luke depicts Jesus as reading in the synagogue (4.16–21): "When he came to Nazareth, where he had been brought up, he went to the synagogue on the sabbath day, as was his custom. He stood up to read (ἀνέστη ἀναγνῶναι), and the scroll (βιβλίον) of the prophet Isaiah was given to him. He unrolled the scroll and found the place where it was written (γεγραμμένον): 'The Spirit of the Lord is upon me' . . . And he rolled up the scroll, gave it back to the attendant, and sat down. The eyes of all in the synagogue were fixed on him. Then he began to say to them, 'Today this scripture (ἡ γραφή) has been fulfilled in your hearing (ἐν τοῖς ὠσὶν ὑμῶν).'" As part of the synagogue liturgy, the Jewish holy scriptures were read aloud to be applied to the concrete situation of the attendees and subsequently discussed. Elucidating is the combination of the active voice in "to read" (ἀναγνῶναι) and the completion of this reading of that which is written (ἡ γραφή) "in your hearing" (ἐν τοῖς ὠσὶν ὑμῶν). Here the holy scriptures are read to be fulfilled in literal and figurative hearing. Together with the synagogue as the typical Jewish place of gathering this practice reaches far back in time. Every synagogue had a genizah, that is, a room or closet in which several rolls were kept for the gathering on the Sabbath. In line with this purpose, there is also a *communis opinio* on a practice of individual reading or studying of these rolls. In the Roman era, the Jews already exhibited a vast array of exegetical methods. In this tradition of studying the holy scriptures, we can observe the objectifying effect when spoken words are written

on his chariot.⁶⁶ In line with Johnson, these two instances imply different reading events.

In the letters and the corpus Paulinum in particular, several relevant passages can be found. In 1 Thess 5.27, it says, "I solemnly command you by the Lord that this letter (τὴν ἐπιστολὴν) be read (ἀναγνωσθῆναι) to all of them [brothers]." In the letter to the Colossians (4.16), a more extensive instruction is found: "And when this letter has been read among you (ἀναγνωσθῇ παρ' ὑμῖν ἐπιστολή), have it read (ἀναγνωσθῇ) also in the church of the Laodiceans; and see that you read (ἀναγνῶτε) also the letter from Laodicea." The composer of this letter urges recipients to exchange the letters involved. Both the passive and the active voice are employed. The former implies that someone else is reading and the addressees will participate by hearing the reading aloud. Since the active voice is used in one and the same command—"that you, in turn, read the letter from Laodicea"—it points at the same functioning of this letter.

The second letter of Peter also contains an interesting remark (2 Peter 3.15–16):

---

down. As such the word as record becomes severed from the immediate and concrete contexts that enable and constitute the spoken word as evanescent sound (for example, Ricoeur's circumstantial milieu). Contrary to the spoken word, the documented word is without natural and immediate (inner-historical) context. Whenever read or referred to, these documented soundbites ask for recontextualization. Illustrative in this respect is the well-known introductory formula "for it is written." We encounter these in the letters of Paul as well as the gospels. *In nuce,* this standard phrase implies an explication and recontextualization of documented words that receive their value in relation to the actual situation in which they are activated and, therefore, in need of handling and application. In this way, one can recognize some of the typical communicative dynamics involved in the familiar media of autonomous text. The origin of these words, however, is out of reach. In their documented and transmitted status, they keep value within certain communities and are, as a result, in need of interpretation. We have to be aware that this practice in Jewish culture took place through vocalization. Although written down and affirming this particular status (cf., "for it is written," or "Scripture says"), in the communicative event itself these words become vocalized.

66. We find this scene in Acts, the story of Philip and the Ethiopian official (Acts 8.26–40): "Then an angel of the Lord said to Philip, 'Get up and go towards the south to the road that goes down from Jerusalem to Gaza.' (This is a wilderness road.) So he got up and went. Now there was an Ethiopian eunuch, a court official of the Candace, queen of the Ethiopians, in charge of her entire treasury. He had come to Jerusalem to worship and was returning home; seated in his chariot, he was reading (ἀνεγίνωσκεν) the prophet Isaiah. Then the Spirit said to Philip, 'Go over to this chariot and join it.' So Philip ran up to it and *heard* (ἤκουσεν) him *reading* (ἀναγινώσκοντος) the prophet Isaiah. He asked, 'Do you understand (γινώσκεις) what you are reading (ἀναγινώσκεις)?'" (emphasis mine). As in his gospel, Luke uses here once more the active voice of ἀναγινώσκειν (to read). The eunuch is reading for himself. Contrary to our habit, however, he is doing so aloud.

> ... and regard the patience of our Lord as salvation. So also our beloved brother Paul wrote (ἔγραψεν) to you according to the wisdom given him, speaking (λαλῶν [sic]) of this as he does in all his letters (πάσαις ἐπιστολαῖς). There are some things in them hard to understand, which the ignorant and unstable twist to their own destruction, as they do the other scriptures (λοιπὰς γραφάς).

The alleged authorships of Colossians (Paul) and 2 Peter (Peter) are disputed. On all accounts, however, we get a glimpse of how letters in the early Jesus movement and the Pauline communities could have functioned. After the intended and one-time-and-place deliveries of Paul's letters, these passages seem to point to a practice of (re-)reading (aloud) and studying them as physical artefacts as a community. Originally, the instructed emissary embodied the letter. In subsequent stages, the emissary is absent and the letter as physical artefact must have become more important as a starting point of the public reading and studying in the community.[67] There must have been exchange and a kind of distribution of the related physical artefacts. In this way, we witness in a sense the earliest beginnings of the *textification* of the letters.[68] Nonetheless, since there are no clear indications of reading in silence and solitude as practised in contemporary academia, an explicit differentiation between these kinds of "reading," as found in the previous examples, and the one with which we are familiar remains imperative.

---

67. It seems that letters deemed pseudepigraphical, such as Colossians and 2 Peter, must have been brought into circulation as manuscripts that suggested they started their life cycle as sent from an/one author in a single originating oral performance—something that, however, never actually took place. Nonetheless, once being written, copied, and distributed (funnelled?) in these communities, they could have functioned well in this procedure of public rereading and studying.

68. Brian Wright introduces the practice of "communal reading" as a control of literary tradition or a guarantor of the stability of documented wordings in key documents within the early Jesus movement. The fact that the practice of repetitious communal reading of specific documents took place in communities made these audiences sensitive to the specificity of words used in the public reading. Notwithstanding a focus on the gospels, he also deals with the Pauline corpus (*Communal Reading*, 153–83). The Foreword of this book is written by Larry Hurtado. For oral performance and/or public reading of the biblical documents and the approach of performance criticism, Wright refers to and agrees with the former's article "Oral Fixation" (see below). Since Hurtado does not engage this specific perspective on the documents, in the study we value Wright's discussion of communal reading in line with the comment above on the beginnings of the textification of the letters of Paul in the history of the church.

PIETER BOTHA: "LETTER WRITING AND ORAL COMMUNICATION IN ANTIQUITY"

In his article "Letter Writing and Oral Communication in Antiquity: Suggested Implications for the Interpretation of Paul's Letter to the Galatians,"[69] Pieter Botha aims at "locating Pauline letter writing within the context of ancient communication to make the constraints of an orally based culture relevant to the understanding of his letters." Despite Adolf Deissmann's distinction between "epistle" and "letter"[70]—which led to the valid and fundamental recognition of the situational character of Paul's letters—and the relevance of Greco-Roman rhetoric and epistolography, Botha claims that "the context of ancient communication still remains peripheral to these [Pauline] studies."[71] He observes a tendency "to study historical facets in isolation."[72] So how does he approach the subject himself?

Botha's first step is to clear "our minds of tacit assumptions," echoing the warnings of Albert Lord and Walter Ong (see Chapter 1), urging that "we must replace our misleading, modern literate view of ancient writing activities with a more responsible view that takes into account their historical, religious, intellectual, and psychological situation."[73] With respect to the first governing question regarding the effect of body-to-body communication, we see Botha identifying a clear and radical distinction between the two media cultures involved. He argues that the selection of modern scholarship in terms of witnesses from the past is governed by the availability of their writings. In this way, "we are misled by our prejudice towards the (*infinitesimal*) elite section of antiquity." Thus the witnesses chosen are, because of their relatively high literacy there-and-then, not representative of the culture in general.[74]

The second step is the discussion of ancient communication itself. Botha makes the preliminary remark that "by not critically defining our concepts we can easily fall into the trap of facile oversimplification."[75] This insight touches on the golden rule of Ong (Chapter 1). He suggests, also

69. Botha, "Letter writing".
70. Deissmann, *Bibelstudien*, 148–49 and 230–45.
71. Botha, "Letter writing," 17.
72. Botha, "Letter writing," 17–18.
73. Botha, "Letter writing," 18.
74. Thus he argues that we should also differentiate within the proposed predominantly oral state of mind in the first-century Mediterranean world; the elite could have been informed by practices and degrees of literacy not available to a majority of the population.
75. Botha, "Letter writing," 19.

citing the words of Ramsay MacMullen, that the primary difference with modern literacy is that "we are dealing with a different culture, a world that must be dealt with in its own right . . . [where] 'the explicit record at important points fits badly with what are, to ourselves, entirely natural expectations.'"[76] The present-day reader must become aware of their subliminal inclinations and distrust them, and the self-evident or given way of the original addressees to participate in oral performance must be subject to critical examination.

The next sections are more focused. In dealing with scribes and scribal culture, Botha states that, despite an oral world, people were familiar with writing. They used it, however, through the skills of others: "Writing was product and a commodity to be sold, not an intellectual process." Once more we recognize Ricoeur's distinction between "writing"—as the inscription of living speech—and text (Introduction). In light of this practice, Botha draws the important conclusion that the letters of Paul "are texts that originated as and were designed for oral presentations."[77]

After discussing co-authorship and the role of an amanuensis, Botha turns to the delivery. Although the imperial government maintained a postal service, private letters had to be sent by private means. Wealthy people had their letter carriers (*tabularii*). The role of a *tabularius* was decisive in this communicative process. The journey was full of dangers (shipwreck, robbery, illness). In winter, letter carrying was not even possible. There are also accounts of the forgery and disclosure of contents. To deal with all these problems, one selected emissaries based on their trustworthiness. They were not only instructed on the contents of the letter and given supplementary reports on matters that were not set down in writing, but "[t]he letter writer was careful to entrust the real message of the letter to the carrier, not merely the text of the letter itself."[78] The choice of the letter carrier was, therefore, more crucial than the "text" (note the use of the term by Botha) of the letter: "they receive authority to convey the letters to expand upon them, and to continue Paul's work."[79] The intentions of Paul had to be fulfilled by the letter carrier in the event of its delivery. In this respect, Botha critically reflects on the common conceptualization:

> All commentators refer to the 'readers' of Paul's letter, identifying the Galatian Christians, the recipients of the letter. How should this be pictured historically? Not as a little book passing

---

76. See, for his quote, MacMullen, *Christianizing*, 42.
77. Botha, "Letter writing," 21.
78. Botha cites here Doty, *Letters*, 268.
79. Botha, "Letter writing," 24. See Doty, *Letters*, 37.

from member to member! Even reference to "reading in the assembly" or "in worship" is not spelt out . . . There is abundant evidence that reading in antiquity was related to performance. Reading in antiquity, especially when it was not private reading, was similar to recitals or to oral delivery.

"Performance" is characterized by Botha as of the utmost importance in an oral environment, namely as "bodily incarnation of the word."[80]

We can start the evaluation of this article with the following observation: regarding media and mindset, Botha presents a well-thought through call for the need to pay attention to the modern, literate, and uncritical framing of ancient writing activities. The present-day reader brings their own "natural" expectations to the printed versions of the letter here-and-now that must be criticized. The communication at issue should not be conceptualized as a message "from one mind to another." He stresses the necessity to explicate the historical nature of the delivery and the specific persons and mindset there-and-then.[81]

For an adequate understanding by the present-day biblical scholar, another related observation is important: Botha downplays the role of the transmitted letter as "text." Based on his reconstructions of orality, scribes/scribal culture, co-authorship, amanuenses, deliveries, and oral performances, he suggests that the really intended "message" was not necessarily contained by the wording of the document but entrusted to and embodied by the letter carrier in the moment of delivery. Put simply, we have to focus on and imagine the emissary *in actu*. This is an important insight: the actual performance of the letter must be made concrete and specific. Nonetheless, we also note that the real "message"/"the work of Paul," on the one hand, and the "text" of the "letter," on the other, become severed from each other. This leads to a crucial point in his argument: the documented wording in the letter could be different from what the emissary would say in the

---

80. Botha, "Letter writing," 25. Given Achtemeier's oversimplification *omne verbum sonat*, Botha distinguishes between private and public reading. The latter has to be framed as oral delivery, that is, an orator performing in reciprocity with his specific audience. From this perspective, he criticizes how modern scholars think of rhetoric. The oral aspect of ancient rhetoric has been neglected. Summarizing the rhetorical principles of Hellenistic culture, he writes, "their rhetorical principles aimed specifically . . . at oral performance, and, consequently, also at creating successful communication through bodily presence." Referring to Quintilian, he elaborates on the detailed instructions in this respect. "The orator studies to deliver an effective performance: to stimulate the audience by the animation of his presentation, and to kindle the imagination, not through ambitious imagery, but by bringing the audience into actual touch with the things themselves" ("Letter writing," 26).

81. Botha, "Letter writing," 23.

oral performance. As a consequence, the role of the documented wording (sound groups) in the letter becomes critical. Through this argumentation, Botha forces us to choose between two perspectives: Do we want to grasp the delivery of the letter as envisioned by Paul in the moment of composition (*a priori/in spe*), or as the implied historical event of delivery by the emissary (*in actu/in re*)—who could expand on, deviate from, or possibly even contradict the documented wording? In the present study, we focus on Paul and his co-workers as composing *in actu* and on the intended goals for the anticipated event of delivery. This perspective can be taken independently from what might have happened in the assumed real delivery as such. The central question, therefore, is, What kind of understanding did Paul anticipate in the process of composition on the side of his hearers during the intended delivery?

LOUIS MARTYN: "EVENTS IN GALATIA"

In his "Events in Galatia: Modified Covenantal Nomism versus God's Invasion of the Cosmos in the Singular Gospel: A Response to J. D. G. Dunn and B. R. Gaventa,"[82] Louis Martyn responds to papers of other participants of the SBL seminar on Pauline Theology. The discussion focusses on the definition of the "theology" of Galatians. In his contribution, James Dunn defines it as "a responsive argument crafted in the light of previous developments."[83] Martyn comments that "while helpful, [this] does not reach all the way." He is convinced that Paul initiated the letter as a communicative act

> in the confidence that God intended to cause a certain event to occur in the Galatian congregations when Paul's messenger read the letter aloud to them . . . [T]he theology of Galatians is focused on that *aural event, as it was intended and actively anticipated by Paul* (emphasis original).[84]

Contrary to Dunn's "responsive argument," theology is related here to a specific "event" and also to the oral-aural media which apparently constitutes it. So an important layer is explicated here in the communicative process. Not only do biblical scholars have to hear the letter with the ears of the Galatians, but they also have to look over the shoulder of the composer to enter into his active anticipation of this aural event.

---

82. Martyn, "Events in Galatia."
83. Dunn, "Theology of Galatians."
84. Martyn, "Events in Galatia," 161.

As an inevitable next step, this textualization of the realm of history there-and-then-to-them urges Martyn to unfold this envisioned event. There is a focal point in his imaginative explorations: the presence of other teachers in the Galatian communities. Thus, he gives answers to questions in line with What is happening to them there-and-then?

> Paul knows that the Galatians will hear his letter with the Teachers' words still ringing in their ears, indeed with the Teachers themselves sitting in their midst, doubtless more than ready to assist them in interpreting the missive. . . . knowing their major motifs, even some of their favourite locutions and scripture texts, Paul can anticipate how the Galatians will hear his words when he borrows elements of the Teachers' vocabulary and when he gives his own exegesis of their texts.[85]

The role of these other teachers leads Martyn to distinguish three possible rhetorical strategies of Paul; and these offer possible ways of bending our thoughts into the realm of history there-and-then. First, the apostle could have accepted the questions and basic frame of reference of his opponents. He would argue then to defeat them on their own ground. Second, he could have taken a radically different starting point to arrive at a conclusion having neither a linguistic nor conceptual connection with the performances of these teachers. He chooses, however, a third option:

> [H]e could begin his argument at a different point . . . make contact with the Teachers' message . . . to modulate the terms of that message onto a radically new level of discourse consonant with his different point of departure . . . to arrive at a conclusion that ultimately silences the Teachers' themes not by contradicting them, properly speaking, but rather by being composed, as it were, on a radically different musical scale.[86]

Martyn argues that Paul in composing the letter is *doing* theology and anticipating a theological *event*.[87] Contrary to Dunn's "responsive argument," which tends to be an outlined and cognitive object of thought (product), he speaks of an "invasion" and an argumentation in progress (process). He broadens and transforms the frame of "theology."[88] So the second govern-

---

85. Martyn, "Events in Galatia," 161–62.
86. Martyn, "Events in Galatia," 162.
87. Martyn, "Events in Galatia," 161.
88. In Chapter 3, I argue for the preference of the notion of "rhetoric" over the one of "theology." Next to an inherent extra-historical tendency in the production and nature of theology—how thoughts are structured—I argue that "rhetoric" is more in line with the dynamics of the realm of history there-and-then-to-them.

ing sub-question in this Chapter comes to mind, namely, What can we learn from the ways in which the two media involved are related to each other?

In the second part of the article, Martyn deals with several passages from the letter to the Galatians itself. He presents his understanding of Paul's theology *in casu* through major portions of the letter (1.1—2.21; 3.6—4.7; 4.21—5.1; and 5.16—6.18). Since the apostle does not commence his anticipated performance with issues important for his opponents, "he makes them wait" on the subject of the "law."[89] Only one thing counts: in Christ's death and resurrection, the new age has been inaugurated. In line with his article "Apocalyptic Antinomies in Paul's Letter to the Galatians,"[90] Martyn juxtaposes the law with the gospel.[91] Regarding the inauguration of the new age, "Paul sees an antinomy between law observance and the faithful death of Christ."[92] As a comment on this reasoning, he adds, "The Galatians will have sensed his doing that; he will have anticipated their doing so; he will have intended them to do so."[93] Here we see an example of what he earlier demanded of his fellow Pauline scholars, namely the active anticipation of the aural event there-and-then-to-them in his own grasp of the letter here-and-now-by-us. He therefore rejects Dunn's idea of Paul modifying a form of covenantal nomism: "What Dunn says, about covenantal nomism seems fundamentally appropriate to the position of *the Teachers*."[94] Over against human movement into the covenant, Martyn places God's movement into the cosmos.

Next, Martyn deals with the major themes of Paul's opponents, for example, the "blessedness of Abraham's children." Over against the incorporation into Abraham, Paul points to the incorporation into Christ with "its necessary corollary the obliteration of the distinctions between Jews and Gentiles (3.26–28)." Paul is "unwilling (unable) to accept the Teachers' frame of reference in the writing of his letter."[95]

Then he turns to the notions of "promise" and "covenant." The event of the crucifixion has explicated an internal antinomy in the law. The cross symbolizes the collision between the law and God's Christ. Paul does not reject, however, the promise that is closely related to the law. So, in his depiction of the origin of the law, God is absent: "In Paul's picture—contrary

---

89. Martyn, "Events in Galatia," 164.
90. Martyn, "Apocalyptic Antinomies."
91. Martyn, "Events in Galatia," 167.
92. Martyn, "Events in Galatia," 165.
93. Martyn, "Events in Galatia," 166.
94. Martyn, "Events in Galatia," 164; see also 167.
95. Martyn, "Events in Galatia," 168.

to that of the Teachers—the covenant is tied *exclusively* to the Abrahamic promise, and it is emphatically *divorced* from the Law."[96] This radical divorce between law and promise is undergirded by the reference of the apostle, not to the seeds (plural) of Abraham (the Jews as a distinctive group as these teachers had done), but to his seed (singular) (Christ). Singularity as a line of thought now comes to the fore.[97] "Thus the covenantal promise uttered by God to Abraham . . . remained in a sort docetic state until the advent of the singular seed, Christ."[98] Before Christ, there was neither a covenant nor a linear history of a people of God: "For Christ was born not into the context of 'Israel's history' but rather 'under the dominance of the Law' and thus . . . into a context marked by a sort of covenantal docetism and by universal enslavement."[99] Based on the singularity of Christ, the end of *Heilsgeschichte* in the traditional understanding is marked. Gal. 4.21–25.1 undergirds this radical line of thought in terms of an invasion into the cosmos. Paul introduces here another covenant. Over against the Sinai/law covenant of Hagar which enslaves, he places the promise of Sarah which liberates. This sheds a subversive light on the effort of these teachers to bring Gentiles into the Sinai covenant.[100] We observe here that Martyn goes back and forth between the theology (frames of reference) of the teachers, Paul's rhetoric and the anticipated aural event that "explodes that frame of reference."[101]

When we relate this train of thought to the aspect of possible distinctive mindsets, Martyn offers several valuable insights. His main critique of Dunn's approach, that is, the theology (singular) of Galatians as a responsive argument (singular), is that it runs the risk of uncritically equating the frames of reference of the teachers with those of Paul. Over against this

96. Martyn, "Events in Galatia," 171.

97. In this respect, he explicitly agrees with one of the major emphases in the third essay by Gaventa, "Singularity."

98. Martyn, "Events in Galatia," 172.

99. Martyn, "Events in Galatia," 174.

100. Martyn, "Events in Galatia," 176.

101. Martyn, "Events in Galatia," 171. Although the thrust is clearly in line with the study of oral tradition and results of the debate on orality and literacy—compare the central notion of "aural event"—one does not find any explicit reference in that direction. Martyn exhibits a rather intuitive understanding thereof. One could argue that this intuitive understanding is due to his thorough and extensive study of apocalypticism regarding Paul. This phenomenon implies an independent view of history as totality. Since this encompassing frame of reference is alien to modern humanity and in need of pondering and reconstruction (textualization), implicitly one has to move away from one's own frame of reference (totality) which is overly familiar and internalized beyond critical awareness. In this way, one cannot escape also touching on the dimensions of communicative contexts (autonomous text in distinction from the one of the intended addressees participating in oral performance).

one-dimensional approach, Martyn explicates a plurality of dimensions or perspectives concerning the realm of history. He highlights aspects such as the reading of the letter aloud by an emissary amid the gathered Galatians (event), the teaching of these other teachers still ringing in their ears at the moment of delivery (theology), and the possible presence and willingness (or not) of the opponents to help the Galatians understand Paul's message (anticipation of participation).[102]

The fulcrum of this SBL seminar was the question: What is the theology of Galatians? When Martyn systematically elaborates on the anticipated aural event and in particular in reaction to the presence and performances of these other teachers, his understanding is in line with the collective memory of the intended addressees of Paul. His conceptualization is structured more in line with the concrete lifeworld of the original addressees than the more abstract "responsive argument" proposed by Dunn.

Martyn breaks here the spell of the implicit equation. *In particular, the present study is indebted to the idea that Paul in the process of composition is anticipating the delivery of the letter as a decisive event there-and-then-to-them.* Martyn does not locate his understanding of the letter in his encounter here-and-now with the letter as autonomous text, but in the reconstruction of two conflicting theologies that have to be located in the realm of history there-and-then taking shape in the carefully prepared and intended "aural event."

Therefore, regarding the leading sub-questions central to this Chapter on the effect of body-to-body communication on the actual hearers and also on how the studies discussed relate the different media cultures there-and-then and here-and-now to each other, we can now see that the introduction of the perspective on the letter as aural event provides many possibilities to explore and textualize the realm of history and/or the functioning of the letter there-and-then-to-them. In this framing of the letter as "aural event," Martyn disconnects the "gospel" or the "theology" of Paul from "text." The biblical scholar cannot relate himself immediately to the former as text here-and-now, for example in the text of the letter or academic publications; contrarily, he has to imagine, beyond that level, how the apostle envisions the oral performance of his emissary to counter—in that "aural event"—the

---

102. One could object here that there is no proof that these other teachers would still be there at the moment of delivery. That is a valid objection. Conversely, there is also no proof of the opposite, that they were not there anymore at the moment of performance. In the process of historical reconstruction, one has to take decisions on the one hand, yet one also has to check such assumptions in the course and process of coming to understand on the other. For that reason, we will apply in one of the test cases in Chapter 4 the criteria for mirror-reading Paul's letters as proposed by John Barclay in his article "Mirror-Reading."

influence of these other teachers. In this way, our understanding of the letter becomes detextified.

JOANNA DEWEY: "TEXTUALITY IN AN ORAL CULTURE: PAULINE TRADITIONS"

In what follows, two contributions to the SBL seminar in 1994 on the subject of "Textuality and Orality in the New Testament Literature" are discussed. In her contribution "Textuality in an Oral Culture: A Survey of Pauline Traditions," Joanna Dewey commences with the present situation in the study of early Christianity.[103] We hear an echo of the warnings uttered by Albert Lord and Walter Ong when she states that scholars have assumed on the whole "that the first-century media world functioned much as our modern print media world."[104] She then claims that "Christianity began as an oral phenomenon in a predominantly oral culture within which the dominant elite were literate and made extensive use of writing to maintain hegemony and control."[105]

From this sociological perspective on orality and textuality, Dewey surveys the Pauline traditions.[106] First, she starts with analysing the modern process of reading and writing.[107] She then turns to Pieter Botha and the ancient media world, citing his words that "Graeco-Roman literacy—the little that existed—remained a kind of imitation talking."[108] She concludes that reading in silence and solitude did not yet exist.

Regarding rates of literacy, she details how literacy was used for the arts, in trade, religion, to post laws inscribed in public places, and to rule the vast empire. In view of this, she notes that "it is virtually impossible for modern academics to realize how unimportant writing and reading were for the conduct of daily life." From a sociological perspective, she continues,

> On the other hand, writing was essential for the creation and maintenance of the Roman Empire (. . .) In a world in which most were non-literate, writing was both an instrument of power and a symbol of power. So although few could read or write,

---

103. J. Dewey, "Textuality."
104. J. Dewey, "Textuality," 37.
105. J. Dewey, "Textuality," 38.
106. J. Dewey, "Textuality," 39.
107. Regarding her hypothesis, she comments, "But to define it that way is to define it from the perspective of the elite, those few who could read and write" ("Textuality," 39).
108. Taken from Botha, "Letter writing," 206.

reading and writing were fundamental in structuring relations in the ancient world.[109]

So, as a symbol and an instrument of power, reading and writing in general structured relations in the realm of history there-and-then.

In the second part, Dewey turns her attention to the Pauline tradition. She asks the question of the degree and sort of literacy within the communities of Paul. According to Wayne Meeks,[110] they contained "a cross-section of the social scale, excluding at the top the ruling elite, and at the bottom, the most destitute."[111] This demonstrates the exclusion of the only social group for whom fluent literacy was normal, namely, the elite. The people who carried Paul's letters may have possessed some degree of literacy, "for that would assist them in using the letter as the basis for their recitation to the congregation."[112] In general, however, "the overall literacy of Pauline congregations would remain low."[113]

After these historical excavations, Dewey turns to her research question. Opposing the overestimated role of "literacy" and "textuality" in contemporary biblical scholarship, she examines the consequences of this sketch for our understanding of the formation of early Christianity. She turns to the role of Scripture in the Pauline congregations. Since reading and interpreting Scripture are nowhere mentioned in the Pauline material, she is convinced that this did not play a role in worship.[114] In the instances where Paul argues with Scripture, he did so solely because he was forced to by opponents. Subsequently, she contrasts the apostle with the practice of Oral Torah by the Pharisees: "it was quite precisely interpretation of a written (and probably memorized) text." To the apostle, the text "does not

---

109. J. Dewey, "Textuality," 44.

110. Meeks, *First Urban Christians*.

111. J. Dewey, "Textuality," 48.

112. J. Dewey, "Textuality," 50. In view of Doty, the picture becomes even more vivid: "I wonder if the Pauline letters may not be seen as the essential part of the messages Paul had to convey, pressed into brief compass as a basis for elaboration by the carriers. The subsequent reading of the letters in the primitive Christian communities would then have been the occasions for full exposition and expansion of the sketch of material in the letters." ("Textuality," 51) While not as radical and subversive as Botha's interpretation (see section C above), the letter is described here as the sketch in need of exposition and even expansion by the instructed letter carrier.

113. J. Dewey, "Textuality," 50. In line with Meeks, she designates the typical member as the free artisan or small trader. They could run their small businesses without being literate (see "Textuality," 48). Dewey also notes that some members were clearly wealthy. Though it is not clear that they were literate, nor that they needed to be; they could have employed slaves or freed people.

114. J. Dewey, "Textuality," 51.

appear to be the foundation for his understanding or the constant reference point."[115] Not text but Christ was central. She comes to the conclusion that "the only reading done during worship in Paul's churches was the reading—or rather performance—of Paul's letters."[116] Christians were not yet "people of the book . . . Authority was not yet vested in manuscripts." So, in the realm of history there-and-then, the produced artefacts (written documents) were of little importance.

Regarding the sub-question of the present Chapter on how the studies discussed relate oral performances to "text" and the functioning of the letters there-and-then-to-them and here-and-now-to-us, we note that the two media involved come to the fore. First, "orality" and "textuality" become absolute opposites. We can also observe, however, that these two explicated and juxtaposed media are concretized to a rather high degree, inasmuch as Dewey locates and describes them both in the realm of history there-and-then. Second, reflection on the situation of the present-day reader vis-à-vis the letter here-and-now ("text") is missing. There seems to be a huge leap involved here: the artefacts there-and-then-to-them float freely into those here-and-now-to-us, an implicit equation based on being "text."

Dewey brings both media together in the following way: "The seeds of manuscript-based Christianity are found in Paul: they are not, however, dominant in Paul. Orality remained the dominant media for Christianity for some time to come."[117] An earlier statement affirms this division in periods within Christianity: "While texts were produced that later became very important within Christianity *as texts*, these texts began as aids to orality, and seemingly had little importance in themselves" (emphasis original).[118] In short, although Paul had produced these documents, it was only later on that they became authoritative and autonomous texts.

This line of reasoning leads to a dichotomy, as can be seen in Dewey's statement that "[t]he oral memory of Paul seems to be more central to Christian debate and life than what he or his successors wrote."[119] She continues by arguing that Paul does not appear as a letter writer in the Acts of the Apostles or the Pastorals and that his successors did not quote or paraphrase him: "In all these writings we see not the textual Paul of the letters but the oral Paul of Christian memory." In her argumentation, we observe, therefore, another juxtaposition, that is, an "oral Paul of memory"

---

115. J. Dewey, "Textuality," 53.
116. J. Dewey, "Textuality," 52.
117. J. Dewey, "Textuality," 54.
118. J. Dewey, "Textuality," 51.
119. J. Dewey, "Textuality," 54.

over against a "textual Paul of the letters." Her argumentation seems to be contradictory here. In the opening of her article, she speaks about literacy as "imitation talking." In this later section on Paul, text has become a media in itself, functioning separately from or even opposed to the spoken word (talking): *textum*—after being introduced as such—has hardened into autonomous text. Dewey proposes an explanation of this alleged discrepancy between a textual and oral Paul with the following distinction: "I want to suggest that a major reason the letters were ignored was that Christianity still relied on oral memory and oral authority."[120] When we rethink this statement that "the letters were ignored," then the rhetorical question comes to the fore why Paul would have composed and sent them in the first place. Something important seems to get lost here.

The main thrust of her argument at this point seems to be that the Paul of the letters-framed-as-text first comes to the fore in the later history of Christianity when the literate Christian leaders turned away from oral memory and oral authority to manuscripts; then does "the Paul of the letters begin to creep into Christian discourse."[121]

In the third part, Dewey discusses several consequences of neglecting the distinction between the two stages. She explicitly introduces here the relation between "letter" and "text." Here she says once more that first the letter equals the spoken word and later on the written one. In reconstructions of Christian history, "we have tended to conflate these two stages, assuming that reliance on the text was present from the moment of the text's initial composition."[122] This is not the case. In the initial stage in early Christian history, "lack of literacy did not exclude one from leadership."[123] Later on, this oral leadership had to make place for the hierarchical, male, and educated form of leadership: "reliance on manuscript media drastically restricts access to leadership positions."[124] The literate elite gained control from then

---

120. J. Dewey, "Textuality," 55. In the following quotation from her article, we recognize the alleged problem of the "visual format" as identified by Achtemeier: "Since the rhetoric of the letters, unlike narrative, is not easily remembered, the letters never became as well known among Christians" ("Textuality," 55).

121. J. Dewey, "Textuality," 56.

122. J. Dewey, "Textuality," 58. The importance of Scripture as text in Judaism prompts her to posit the following: "It is perhaps reasonable to suggest, then, that where the influence of synagogues and Jewish teachers (either by Jews or by Christian Jews) on Christianity was greater, . . . the emphasis on reading and interpreting texts, would also be greater" (58). The later interaction with rabbinic Judaism might have pushed early Christian groups towards greater reliance on manuscripts as a distinct media ("Textuality," 58).

123. J. Dewey, "Textuality," 59.

124. J. Dewey, "Textuality," 57.

on. This is the point Dewey wants to make, that the still current perspective on Paul is uncritically determined by the literate elite. Already at an early stage, they took over control and up to the present day dominate the perception of this apostle. Therefore, her appeal is that the formative influence of orality on the beginnings of Christianity—which is neglected hitherto—leads to a fundamental revision of the history of early Christianity.

In any evaluation of Dewey's article, it is important to note that she brings to our attention the need to do justice to the distinctive predominantly oral context of early Christianity, in particular, regarding Paul and his letters. In doing so she brings helpful insight into the fact that "text" (in her terminology) functioned originally as "aid to orality" and not yet as an autonomous media. In and between both lines of thought, there is a tension: text-as-aid-to-orality stands over against text-as-having-importance-in-itself. It is important to observe that because of this approach the relation between "text" and "context" starts to shift. Dewey directs her thoughts on "text" into two different "contexts"—the realm of history there-and-then and subsequently the later stage, in which it starts to function in itself. This is rather revolutionary: she changes, in this way, the hierarchy in the text-context scheme. This intimates the proposed intellectual movement of textualizing history (Chapter 3).[125]

Similarly, however helpful the notion of text as an aid to orality is, there is need for this to be further concretized: How did "text" function in the realm of history there-and-then-to-them? What happened with this aid to orality, how was it physically or bodily mediated to the intended addressees? In her article, this context of text there-and-then-to-them remains abstract; deepening is much desired.

However, there is also a problematic dichotomy and an implicit equation that tends to weaken her argument. In wanting to bring focus to the oral context, we can trace the following dichotomy: she juxtaposes the original "Paul of oral memory" with the subsequent "Paul of the letters." The former prompts the question of his relation to and/or the function of his letters (artefacts). Since, however, this is not a theme for her, the explicit differentiation could lead to the impression that the Paul of oral memory—which should be considered as the true and original perspective on him—did not

---

125. J. Dewey refers several times to the writings of Paul as "manuscript." Given adequate conceptualization—or in the terminology of the present study textualizing history—this use seems to be more in line with the realm of history *illic et tunc*. To a certain degree, the letter as "manuscript" creates a distance between ourselves as present-day readers and the overly familiar phenomenon of "text." "Manuscript" appeals more to our imagination than "text" (text area). In this way, the functioning can be described more easily.

compose and sent letters. In the dichotomously structured phrase the "Paul of the letters," the latter are in danger of becoming limited in their operational functioning to the one familiar media of autonomous "text." So, this explicit differentiation frames the "letters" as "text" and seems to juxtapose them with the alleged historically valid depiction of an oral Paul, who, as a consequence, has nothing to do with the letters.

Another implicit equation can be discerned. On the formal level or the level of text, "text" is implicitly equated in a confusing or even—in terms of functioning—contradictory way: it covers the range of *textum* to autonomous text (see Introduction to the present study). Despite Dewey's considerations on the original functioning on the level of her own text, the "letter" is still and at the same time synonymous with "text." Therefore, in her reasoning, "text" has a docetic nature. It represents "orality/aurality" and at the same time it functions to us within a framework of "literacy/textuality." The problem is that the latter media and its attendant literate mindset dominate the actual operational matrix in which the biblical scholar processes these documents. For this reason, the present study proposes a textualization of the realm of history there-and-then-to-them which is void of the notion "text" or the phenomenon text-as-known-to-us (see the proposals of the Introduction).

ARTHUR DEWEY: "A RE-HEARING OF ROMANS 10.1–15"

As a second contribution to the SBL seminar referred to, we turn to Arthur Dewey's "A Re-Hearing of Romans 10.1–15."[126] He starts with lauding the pioneering work of Werner Kelber on Paul in *The Oral and the Written Gospel*. Alongside respect for the ground-breaking detection of the oral dimension however, Dewey also criticizes his use of the oral/written distinction "to understand Paul's acoustic field in absolute opposition to the regimentation of the 'letter.'" Bringing both media together, Dewey interprets them as ways of reaching for power: "Paul was playing creatively to utopian desires of his audience and of the first-century in general;"[127] both media are "different avenues of conveying power and breaking through the boundaries of space and time."[128]

Dewey then positions himself in relation to Kelber. Drawing upon the work of Ong, he expounds his own notion of *acoustic space*. In this definition,

---

126. A. Dewey, "Re-Hearing."
127. A. Dewey, "Re-Hearing," 110.
128. A. Dewey, "Re-Hearing," 111.

space as well as time are redefined as "a vast interior in the centre of which listeners find themselves together with their interlocutors."[129] In other words, central to the originally intended delivery of Romans is its effect upon the hearers. Subsequently, Dewey focuses (with Kelber) on the social effect of an oral performance. Spoken words create an audience, as it were. The rhetorical situation of this audience is often tense because of loyalties, interests, betrayals, and such like: "Thus the appearance of opposing parties (as happens quite often in Paul's letters) would have a divisive effect since there is a competition for acoustic space."[130] The oral performance of the letter aims at regaining the loyalty of the audience. As a key concept in acoustic space, he utilizes the relational dynamic of participation: "the intent of Paul's message is to create an ethos of participation." So, by their participation, the apostle can regain influence over the audience. Dewey juxtaposes this acoustic space with the absolute dichotomy of Kelber, making the point that "[a]gain, the question is not simply one of orality versus writtenness but of how power was to be conveyed and augmented."[131] He suggests that Paul's oral stance "could signal an alternative or even utopian stance."

In the next section, Dewey turns to the passage under scrutiny, Romans 10.1–15. Kelber called this passage the *locus classicus* of the oral hermeneutics of sound.[132] In this part of Romans, Moses and Isaiah are introduced more than once and several passages from the Jewish holy scripture are referred to. Dewey takes the following perspective on the material: "Not only do we have the creation of an acoustic space, but we may discern ways in which Paul is trying to negotiate social relationships, where the question of power comes into play."[133] This emphasis on relationships is based on Paul's frequent use of δικαιοσύνη (righteousness). The right relationship—termed by Dewey as "patronage"—guarantees fundamental stability in an unstable and harsh societal context.

In this passage, there is a tension between "Moses *writes* about the relationship from tradition" (Rom 10.5) and "the relationship of trust *says*" (10.6; emphasis mine).[134] He solves it by a personification of δικαιοσύνη. In this way, the proper relationship becomes imaginable in an ideal person.

129. A. Dewey, "Re-Hearing," 110.
130. A. Dewey, "Re-Hearing," 111.
131. A. Dewey, "Re-Hearing," 112.
132. A. Dewey, "Re-Hearing," 113.
133. A. Dewey, "Re-Hearing," 114.

134. "Moses writes concerning the righteousness that comes from the law, that 'the person who does these things will live by them.' 6 But the righteousness that comes from faith says, 'Do not say in your heart, 'Who will ascend into heaven?' (that is, to bring Christ down)" (Rom 10.5–6).

Δικαιοσύνη not only voices but also transforms the written tradition. This rhetorical use of the words of Deut 30.12–14 by Paul in this passage "would not only be appealing to their own experience but would be demonstrating inductively that Dikaiosune [δικαιοσύνη] herself is speaking from the midst of their own situation, that is, from their experience of a trusting relationship with God."[135] In this (re-)hearing, the audience could discover that they are part of what is already going on and that this is the genuine relationship of δικαιοσύνη, that is, the patronage of the Lord. Regarding the citation of Isa 28.16 (10.11), Dewey elaborates on the utopian vision taken up by Paul. The apostle supplements the original wording with "everyone." Everyone can "petition the Universal Patron, who gives generously and freely upon the establishment of this relationship." This utopian dream would reverberate in the experience of the Roman communities.

To compare Paul's use of Deut 30.11–14, Dewey surveys three passages from Philo (*De Virt.* 175–82, *Quod Prob.* 62–73 and *De spec. leg.* 4.160–69). He concludes that Philo uses the same paraphrase of Deut 30 (the imagery of a patron/client relationship) to make it accessible to his audience consisting of prospective proselytes. The proselyte did not only develop their potentialities as a human being by becoming a true citizen, but they were also engaged in the construction of the finest commonwealth. In this respect, Philo sees the technique of writing as counterpart of progression towards this utopian society:

> As one enters fully into this tradition, writing out the words, a different self emerges, which is free from the constraints of a senate-bound present. The dialectic within, the internal argument, allows the space for a reasoning ego to appear.[136]

Dewey then recapitulates both approaches to Deut 30. For Philo, the tradition comes to realisation when the individual utilizes the new chirographic technology and individuates to a self that is separated from the masses. Paul represents a counter-cultural position, because he wants to subvert the existing dynamics of patronage and kinship and establish a new community through the relationship to Christ as Universal Patron.

In conclusion, Dewey explores the oral dimension in one of Paul's letters. For the present study, it is particularly crucial that he states the goal of the letter to be the creation of an ethos of participation. Surpassing and transforming Kelber's orality-literacy dichotomy, he succeeds in presenting an apt description of how the intended audience could have heard the

---

135. A. Dewey, "Re-Hearing," 117.
136. A. Dewey, "Re-Hearing," 124–25.

oral performance of Romans 10. The paradigm of patronage structures the rehearing. The relationship is bound to the realm of history there-and-then-to-them; it is constitutive of the collective memory of the original audience. We note that by introducing this thought structure it is impossible for us, as present-day readers, to uncritically fill in an alternative structure from our own concrete lifeworld. In this way, Dewey directs our thoughts explicitly into this distinctive realm of history.

On a critical note, it is not clear how Paul would have anticipated these intended hearers to participate in this central metaphor (δικαιοσύνη). The answer seems to be dependent on the specific framing of a single term. So Paul must have been convinced that the intended addressees were able to fill in the paradigm of universal patronage at the first hearing of this singular term, without introduction or any form of explication. Thus, we are dealing with minimal anticipation (one common term) and maximal participation (the entire paradigm as such). Nonetheless—as we observed earlier in Louis Martyn's article—the historical dimension of the oral performance itself is integrated to an important extent in his understanding of this specific passage.[137]

CASEY DAVIS: *ORAL BIBLICAL CRITICISM*

In 1999, Casey Wayne Davis defended his doctoral thesis *Oral Biblical Criticism: The Influence of the Principles of Orality on the Literary Structure of Paul's Epistle to the Philippians*.[138] He wrote this study under the supervision of Paul Achtemeier. In this monograph, he seeks to present the rationale behind his method of Oral Biblical Criticism and applies it to the epistle of Paul to the Philippians. Davis states, "In particular, I seek to demonstrate the

---

137. Regarding the application of Deut 30, another structuring of thought is recognizable. The frame which Dewey applies is *the original context* of Deut 30: "In its original context Deut 30.12–14 speaks of a remarkable transcending of limitations so that the covenant of God can be kept" ("Re-Hearing," 116). In the present study, we feel urged to scrutinize such terms/phraseology as the "original context" of Deut 30. Despite his careful consideration of acoustic space concerning the intended Roman audiences of Paul's letter, at the same time on another level, he seems to relate to Deut 30 as text in a textual context (the ever-expanding universe of text)—as if Paul would relate to the "text" of Deut 30 in the same media and mindset as Dewey himself is used to doing. In this line of thinking, the realm of history in which these words from Deut 30 would have functioned *for Paul* or *from Paul's perspective on the intended hearers of the Letters to the Romans* (anticipated participation) is not addressed. The communicative context of autonomous text, in which Dewey participates, seems to usurp here the other historical communicative context there-and-then-to-them.

138. Davis, *Oral Biblical Criticism*.

extent to which these principles [of orality] affected the form, style, diction, scope, and interrelationships of the literary (or oral) units in this letter."[139]

Two preliminary observations are in order. First, the adjective between brackets, "oral," seems to suggest that to Davis the letter is first and foremost a construal of "literary units." Second, and despite this implicit hierarchy, he seems to treat the term "literary" as somehow synonymous with "oral."[140] Third, we recognize the agenda to look for "principles of orality" in this kind of literature as advocated by Achtemeier in his presidential address (see, in this Chapter, Section B. Paul Achtemeier: *OMNE VERBUM SONAT*). We see this affirmed in the first chapter where he elaborates on the principles of orality in the method of Oral Biblical Criticism:

> While each of the above characteristics is useful in describing oral compositions, it is dangerous to use anyone or two of them as criteria for judging the influence of orality on a given work. Any characteristic of orality, including formulaic style, can be found to some degree in even the most modern literature.[141]

The first governing question—How are the different media related to each other in the argumentations—comes to the fore here. When pinpointing the phrase "for judging the influence of orality on a given work," we might ask, Who is judging here? Inevitably, the answer seems to be ourselves as present-day readers of his text. Indiscriminately, we jump from the letter in the realm of history there-and-then-to-them to the one here-and-now-for-us. So, in speaking of "the influence of orality" on "a given work," the media muddle seems to be ingrained in this structuring of thought from the start.

Davis commences with a sketch of the extent of literacy in the New Testament world.[142] The quantitative influence of literacy in ancient times was limited; the qualitative influence of literacy would have been negligible

---

139. Davis, *Oral Biblical Criticism*, 11.

140. It would also be possible, though less plausible, that Davis is referring solely to "literary units." We follow the explication as given in the main text.

141. Davis, *Oral Biblical Criticism*, 20. For chapter 1 on the principles of orality, see *Oral Biblical Criticism*, 11–63.

142. Davis, *Oral Biblical Criticism*, 23–26. He summarizes the situation as follows: "(1) Practical writing materials were expensive and hard to come by. (2) Availability of eyeglasses was extremely limited. (3) There were virtually no open school systems and the private schools could only be afforded by the rich. (4) The society was still primarily rural. (5) Finally, literacy was simply not necessary, even for cultural success. The society as a whole was still basically oral, and its traditional education provided the essentials for social life. Literary materials were also readily available to the illiterate through performances, speeches and recitations in the market place, the theatre and in various governmental and religious settings" (*Oral Biblical Criticism*, 24).

as well.[143] Since there was no real widespread growth of literacy, the mental transformation implied was not yet at issue. He argues that, as a rule, we are dealing with performance in line with oral composition.

Then Davis turns to his methodology.[144] Source and form criticism isolate sources and units to determine their history. Contrarily, Oral Biblical Criticism focuses on the final form of the text—which is emphasized in its canonical form (later more on this). Subsequently, an anthology of methods is presented. We will pay attention to his discussion of all these different methods on a meta-level. It will help us to evaluate his approach. He starts with the rhetorical critical approach by George Kennedy in his *New Testament Interpretation through Rhetorical Criticism*.[145] Kennedy argues that the modern critic should analyze the biblical text in six steps. He should start with determining rhetorical units: first, one should determine the smaller units and then the larger ones in which they are embedded. This step thus concentrates on the biblical text as such. The second step is to define the rhetorical situation.[146] Exigency is pivotal in this respect, which Davis defines as "a situation in which a person is called upon to make some response which will affect that situation."[147] This step goes beyond the level of the biblical text itself and reaches into the context or realm of history there-and-then; our imagination comes somehow alive. As steps three and four, the critic should establish the occasion that caused the speech (*stasis*) and the species of rhetoric involved (judicial, deliberative, or epideictic). The fifth and sixth steps are to examine the persuasive effects of the ordering of the elements that constitute the argument (assumptions, topics, enthymemes, devices of style). These steps are made in order to examine the efficaciousness of the entire unit "in meeting the exigencies and its implications for the author and audience." In Davis's description, Kennedy forces the present-day reader to reconstruct the realm of history there-and-then-to-them, that is, the historical horizon of the causative event as well as the effects on the audience.[148]

In light of discourse analysis, Davis suggests that the modern critic should prefer synchronic to diachronic study. The critic should relate the

143. For a recent overview, see Wright, "Ancient Literacy."
144. Davis, *Oral Biblical Criticism*, 29–61.
145. Kennedy, *New Testament Interpretation*.
146. In his words, Davis: "Critics should analyze the 'categories' of persons, events, objects and relationships involved, time and place (. . .) Note should also be taken of the overriding 'rhetorical problem' with which the speaker is often faced. It is usually evident at the beginning of the discourse" (*Oral Biblical Criticism*, 44–45).
147. Kennedy quotes Bitzer, "Rhetorical Situation."
148. Davis, *Oral Biblical Criticism*, 45.

basic meaning of words in texts not to the dictionary definition but to the particular context in which the word occurs. Based on Ferdinand de Saussure's structuralism, the linguist can only study *langue* based on *parole*.[149] So, once more, context is crucial.[150]

With regard to this, Davis turns to the method of George Guthrie presented in his article "Cohesion, Shifts, and Stitches in Philippians."[151] The first step is to analyze the discourse grammatically.[152] The second step then is based on Chomsky's Transformational Grammar. It involves the dissection of a passage to its "kernels" which are the most significant units of the total discourse.[153] Guthrie's third step is to identify unit boundaries.[154] The fourth step is to analyze the relationship between these units.[155] The final step is to analyze the progression from unit to unit. In his evaluation of Guthrie, Davis objects that this method is directed and limited to the text as such: "The results of primarily sub-conscious oral habits are seen primarily as intentional literary devices. The difference is subtle but can be significant."[156] There is apparently a difference between "oral habits" and "literary devices." In contrast to Kennedy and discourse analysis, all steps of Guthrie remain on the level of (or limited to) the text. The rhetorical situation or historical context does not seem to be constitutive of this approach.

After this caveat, Davis introduces the following imperative: "Interpreters must seek to determine the influences of orality and literacy on the author, the readers, and the general society in which a document was composed." In this quote—despite the location of "author" and "readers" in the realm of history there-and-then ("the general society in which it was composed")—once more the "document" seems to float freely from the original situation to the present-day one and back: we relate to it, without any further consideration. When we follow his argument further, Davis suddenly

---

149. Davis, *Oral Biblical Criticism*, 49–52.

150. The communicative value of a given text becomes prominent for Davis in terms of its *cohesion* in syntax; *coherence* of used concepts; *intentionality* of the speaker, that is, the author intends to communicate coherently and cohesively; *acceptability* of the audience, that is, the willingness of the addressees to participate in accomplishing the intentions of the author; *informativity*, that is, the reaction of the audience in being captivated or bored by it; *situationality*, that is, relevance of the text given the situation that produced it; and *intertextuality*, that is, the relation of the given text to other texts (*Oral Biblical Criticism*, 54–55).

151. Guthrie, "Cohesion."

152. Davis, *Oral Biblical Criticism*, 56.

153. Davis, *Oral Biblical Criticism*, 56.

154. Davis, *Oral Biblical Criticism*, 57–59.

155. Davis, *Oral Biblical Criticism*, 59.

156. Davis, *Oral Biblical Criticism*, 60.

speaks of "principles" instead of "influences": "those principles may then be used to more accurately interpret the structure and meaning of a document composed in that setting."[157] These "influences" are explicitly located in the realm of history there-and-then. Implicitly, however, these "principles" are related to the documents with which the biblical scholar works here-and-now. So, a sudden and implicit shift takes place from describing influences in the historical process as such (composition) to identifying these principles in the fixed and given product here-and-now (reading). In this substitution, we witness a turn from describing the process of production to the product as such, which seems to be free-floating and, therefore, equal to the one here-and-now-to-us ("text").

Finally, Davis turns to his own method. The rich anthology of insights and critical methods of chapter 1 is now streamlined into a method consisting of three steps. The first step is to analyze the author's rhetorical style (A).[158] The subsequent step is to identify and analyze units (B).[159] The final step is to analyze the method of progression from unit to unit (C).[160] In these three steps, a variety of oral characteristics are paid attention to. We can distinguish micro- (repetition in sound and rhetorical figures of speech [antithesis, vagueness and so forth]), meso- (literary or oral units) and macro-characteristics (the progression from unit to unit).

Davis posits that all these steps have to be made regarding the letters as "canonical text." In the adjective "canonical," the text becomes determined

---

157. Davis, *Oral Biblical Criticism*, 61.

158. In this step, the development of *ethos* and *pathos* is important. This is connected to heightened awareness of the speaker/audience relationship (A.1.). This comes to the fore in the use of dialogue and the diffusion of objections, the creation of adversaries, the presentation of examples, praise and blame, and stress on the relationship rather than philosophical position of right versus wrong (A.1.a.). Another element in this first step is the treatment of topics which apply to the present situation rather than to the theoretical (A.1.b.). In addition, various rhetorical figures of speech—such as antithesis, synonymy, vagueness and metaphor—should be paid due respect in this first step (A.2.). Also, an awareness of repetition in sound or of grammatical construction, words and topics is required (A.3.). Finally, this step includes attention to rare words chosen because of aural and rhetorical considerations, oral formulas and themes (A.4.–6.). Thus, it is on the basis of features in the text that he wants to define the "author's rhetorical style." Notwithstanding partial overlap, this does not cohere with reconstructing the realm of history there-and-then.

159. For example, concentric and parallel structure (B.1.), introductory and concluding formulas (B.2.), changes in genre (B.3.), logical relationships (B.4.), grammatical inconsistencies (B.5.), sound, word, and topic grouping (B.6.), temporal and spatial frames (B.7.), and climaxes (B.8.).

160. This step is structured by asking for logical relationships (C.1.); changes in location, time, characters, or referents (C.2.); transitional techniques (C.3.) and development of previously stated themes (C.4.).

by the process in the early church, centuries later, in which a distinction was made between authoritative and non-authoritative documents. An uncritical leap in time shifts the perspective from the oral dimension to an affirmation of the text-ness of the letters or constitution of them as text. Put differently, a confessional category (canonical in combination with text) supersedes and governs a historical one (oral).

In assessing/evaluating Davis's methodology from a meta-perspective, the first comment would be that in order to establish Oral Biblical Criticism as a critical method, Davis deals with such an abundance of theories that it is sometimes difficult to comprehend how they matter or relate to each other. We observe, however, that, in the first chapter, he openly declares his indebtedness to the rhetorical-critical method of Kennedy, whose approach is directed towards a reconstruction of the rhetorical situation. In Kennedy's method, a tension is apparent between the interpretation of a text on the one hand, and historical reconstruction on the other. When we take this into account, it is all the more surprising that in his step-by-step method Davis then goes on to actually employ, the rhetorical situation is completely lacking. In the end, all three steps are confined to present-day readers vis-à-vis text.

When Davis applies his method to Philippians, one encounters a wide-ranging and meticulous analysis of this letter *as text*. In this gathering of data, the analysis of the realm of history there-and-then is absent, in particular, with regard to how the original addressees related to and participated in the delivery of the letter. The audience of the letter is not "concretized." Apart from a minimum of explicit references, the addressees also remain anonymous and highly abstracted.[161] This pertains to the rhetorical situation as well: it is virtually absent and does not gain depth.[162] Regarding the category of Paul's enemies, Davis comments in a footnote,

---

161. For examples of highly abstracted formulations: "Because of the high degree of interplay between a storyteller or teacher and the audience in an oral culture" (*Oral Biblical Criticism*, 64); "Such data is recognized through the ear. It is influenced by the special relationship between the speaker and the hearer in an oral setting" (*Oral Biblical Criticism*, 96); 100; 102: "An audience listening to an oral recitation or the reading of a composition in an oral setting would be particularly aware of these formulas" (*Oral Biblical Criticism*, 100, 102); other examples can be found on 103, 105, 106, 107, 108, 120, 125, 146, 159, 160.

162. A view of the rhetorical situation can only be found regarding Phil 2.13, where Davis suggests that particular references in the verse "may give a hint of disunity in the church" (*Oral Biblical Criticism*, 157). See also: "It has been stated in many sermons and books that the theme of Philippians is joy in the Christian life. There *is* a tremendous emphasis on joy in the letter. However, this joy is linked to the topic of unity. Paul needs to address some problems in the church resulting from disunity, specifically the difficulty between Euodia and Syntyche" (*Oral Biblical Criticism*, 158–59).

> There has been a great deal of debate concerning the identity of the adversaries whom Paul has in mind. *It is my contention that their identity is of little concern to Paul in this letter* (...) Whether the opponents are within or outside of the church in 1.28, Jews or Judaizers in 3.2, or Judaizers or libertarians in 3.18–19, is neither discernible from the letter nor important to his discussion (emphasis mine)[163]

We seem to witness here an explicit denial of the importance of the role of adversaries in understanding the letter. Once more, this is remarkable in light of the historical-critical agenda and Kennedy's method. Davis's method is directed towards the understanding of the letter-equated-with-("canonical")-text by the present-day reader in his unquestioned predominantly literate state of mind. As a result, his presentation of the structure of Philippians remains highly abstract and text-bound. His reading of the letter does not activate our imagination; the question, What is happening? does not immediately come to mind.

In line with this critique, we must add another concern. In the opening sections of the first part of his book, the phenomenon of oral composition and oral performance was often encountered. When critically scrutinizing the steps of his method, however, we must conclude that they are not well-integrated. This is also apparent in his emphasis on the "text" being "canonical." What is the reason for this contradictory outcome? A clue may be found in Davis's own words about those who actually did the writing of the New Testament literature/documents:

> The literature of the New Testament was composed predominantly by writers who had learned to write for practical reasons and had little, if any, training in aesthetics. They viewed literature as a practical means of communicating with others when they were absent but saw it as inferior to the spoken word. They expected their compositions to be read aloud to a gathered community, who would, in turn, use that material to establish dialogue among themselves and, especially in the case of a letter, with the reader, who was often the writer's official representative.[164]

Although "literature" was seen "as inferior to the spoken word," this is not reflected in his approach. First, when we critically scrutinize concepts, such as "literature," "writers," "to write," and the letter as "material," we see once more that the matrix of text-as-known-to-us structures his reasoning.

163. Davis, *Oral Biblical Criticism*, note 93, 125–26.
164. Davis, *Oral Biblical Criticism*, 612.

Moreover, he implicitly equates the "letters" with "literature." In no way does he elaborate on what he means by, what is for us, such an overly familiar notion. When we use "literature" in an uncritical way, it will function in our predominantly literate state of mind as extra-historical thought, that is, everywhere, every time, and for everyone the same. He also does not consistently differentiate between the spoken or heard and the written word or "text." He argues that, as we saw earlier, next to "literary" units, the "principles" of orality are related to "oral" units as well. It is meaningless, however, to argue that "principles of orality" influence "oral" units. Such principles do not affect but constitute oral units; they influence literary units (consider Ong's oral residue). These inner tensions provide answers to the second question which governs this Chapter—What can we learn from how the different media are related to each other? It illustrates once more that the use of certain concepts on the level of text ("oral," "oral composition," or "oral performance") and propositions about the context ("the written material is inferior to the spoken word") do not automatically direct or correct how the thoughts of the actual reader are structured on that same level. As stated in the Introduction, addressing adequately the role of the media of oral performance will infringe on the communicative process as constituted by the other media (text). In Davis's study, we observe how text on oral performance can veil oral performance.

DAVID RHOADS: BIBLICAL PERFORMANCE CRITICISM

In 2006, David Rhoads published his two-fold article "Performance Criticism: An Emerging Methodology in Second Testament Studies (Part I and II)."[165] These articles now function as a general introduction to Biblical Performance Criticism as found on the website under the same name.[166] The insight that drives Rhoads is the following: "Performances were a central and an integral part of the early Christian experience of the compositions that have now come down to us in written form in the Second Testament." In this phrase, a layered distinction between media cultures comes to the fore: The "composition" was experienced then as "performance" and has come down to us in "written" form. He defines performance "in the broadest sense as any oral telling/retelling of a brief or lengthy tradition . . . in a formal or informal context . . . by trained or untrained performers." This

---

165. Rhoads, "Performance Criticism (Part I and II)."

166. See https://biblicalperformancecriticism.org/index.php. Note also the program unit in the annual meetings of the Society of Biblical Literature, "Performance Criticism of Biblical and Other Ancient Texts."

broad definition sheds light on the documents of the New Testament: "they [traditions] were either written 'transcriptions' of oral narratives that had been composed in performance or they were composed orally by dictation and written for use in oral performance."[167] One way or the other, the "compositions" were in fact "oral presentations." This contextualization of the New Testament writings leads him to refer to them as "performance literature." Note his use, without further explanation, of the term "literature."

Once having defined New Testament documents as "performance literature," he asks "why Second Testament scholars do not function more like musicologists or dramatists." He criticizes the praxis of biblical scholars who interpret documents "without ever experiencing performances of them." Therefore, "performance should be an important site for the interpretation of the biblical writings."[168] It is important to note that he explicates the goal of his method as "interpretation."

The focus of Rhoads's method is two-fold. On the one hand, he presents performance there-and-then-to-them as an "object of study." On the other, he introduces the practice of real-time performing here-and-now so that we can grasp the meaning and rhetoric of these ancient writings.[169] In his reasoning hitherto, the status and function of "text" as well as "interpretation" remain in need of further explication. Regarding "meaning," we will see that he proposes a different understanding.

After the opening statements, he briefly discusses how the precise mode of oral tradition has been neglected in form-, genre-, and narrative-criticism, in reader-response and rhetorical criticism, and similarly in orality and gender studies. He then explains why performance is a blind spot. In the contemporary Western world, one is only acquainted with private and silent reading of texts; in the scholarly community "we have not even thought about experiencing whole texts in a theatre setting."[170] Therefore, reflection on the "holistic, communal experiences of oral performance in the early church" is imperative. He advocates "doing a performance ourselves as an act of interpretation."[171]

167. Rhoads, "Performance Criticism (Part I)," 118.

168. Rhoads, "Performance Criticism (Part I)," 119.

169. The repertoire of Rhoads himself includes all kinds of genres within the New Testament writings, such as the Gospel of Mark, the Sermon on the Mount, and Paul's Letter to the Galatians. For a performance of the Letter to Philemon, see YouTube, https://www.youtube.com/watch?v=48YWFNWvzKo.

170. Rhoads, "Performance Criticism (Part I)," adds the remark that "public reading that has fragmented the text into lectionary lessons in the context of parish worship and teaching" ("Performance Criticism [Part I]," 120).

171. Rhoads, "Performance Criticism (Part I)," 120.

After the presentation of this two-fold approach, Rhoads sketches the first-century Mediterranean world. No more than five to eight percent of the people were able to read. Even fewer were able to write, let alone both. Their world was constituted by the media of sound. Sound implies event. Everything that is learned or passed on takes place in conversation in a specific historical situation. Real time conversation is based on relationships: "Because speech is relational, the interaction is empathetic and participatory." Over against our contemporary Western introspective and private values, the focus of people in oral cultures is outward and governed by the community. In oral cultures, knowledge is limited to and constituted by "what is shared and remembered by the community through social interaction." One deals with a world "very different from our print/electronic culture."[172] There were manuscripts (for example, Scripture), professional scribes, limited educational practices, and writing as a means for authorities to govern and control. He rejects, however, designations such as "manuscript culture," "scribal culture," and "rhetorical culture,"[173] because they are not representative of life then and there. The vast majority of peasants did not have direct contact with manuscripts. If that were so, "the presence of a scroll, such as a scripture text, could serve as a symbol to enhance oral authority."[174] Rhoads minimizes the role or presence of "text"—as we are used to—up to the point of negation. He concludes: "Studying the Second Testament writings as performance literature will involve a radical shift from our exclusive focus on them as 'writings.'"

In a following section, Rhoads pays attention to the act of performance in oral cultures. He states that, as a rule, public performers then were not dependent on manuscripts in the act of performing. To frame and envision how performers in antiquity prepared for performing, he draws a parallel to contemporary stand-up comedians, who prepare for lengthy televised monologues. In advance, they practice their material before many diverse audiences in different settings. Similarly, ancient performers composed and recomposed their material.

Subsequently, Rhoads deals with the situation in which performers did use manuscripts.[175] Despite some evidence for rote memorization, he questions the legitimacy of the comparison with modern actors learning a theatre script by heart. The question of freedom in improvisation

---

172. Rhoads, "Performance Criticism (Part I)," 121.

173. It does not become sufficiently clear what he means by "rhetoric" in this respect.

174. Rhoads, "Performance Criticism (Part I)," 122.

175. Rhoads, "Performance Criticism (Part I)," 123.

concerning manuscripts can be understood as the dichotomy of "fixedness" and "fluidity." In his depiction of first-century oral cultures of the Mediterranean world, the latter supervenes the former: "So, the transmission and reception of the text did not go primarily from manuscript to manuscript but from audience reception to audience reception in memory."[176] Regarding the second sub-question of the present Chapter as to how the distinctive media are related to each other in these studies, and the third governing question in which we address the ramifications of the functioning of text here-and-now on our perception of the intended oral performances of the letters, we observe here that he distinguishes between "manuscript" and "audience reception," on the one hand, and "reception of the text" on the other. So he seems to grant "text" also an existence independent of or at least severed from "manuscript."

As a next step, Rhoads turns to the gospels and the corpus Paulinum. Referring to several publications, he states that "we know that the letters of Paul were composed orally by Paul and recorded by a scribe or amanuensis, perhaps in several sessions—a possibility that may explain the stops and starts of a letter such as Philippians." Regarding the emissary, he states: "It is likely that the emissary who delivered a Pauline letter was the one who performed it for the community," and that the oral delivery of the letter was "presumably performed by heart or performed as a 'reading' in a public setting before a house church or other gathering." Since the letters were also passed on to be presented to other assemblies, the performers may have adapted the letters/compositions to divergent audiences in different circumstances.[177] In this way, the emphasis on "fluidity" becomes all the more clear. The point Rhoads wants to make is that oral performances formed the "primary medium" through which the original and intended addressees received the compositions now comprising the New Testament.

Referring to Thomas Boomershine, Rhoads designates the present situation in biblical scholarship as "media anachronism."[178] We interpret the texts involved "in a written medium that is different from the oral medium in which they were first composed and performed." He continues: "Indeed,

---

176. Rhoads, "Performance Criticism (Part I)," 124. The fixedness, typical of default text, is alien to this world then. Based on this rule of fluidity, he is even able to subvert the traditional picture of the scribe. Differences in the written traditions of Judaism and early Christianity can be explained as a result of scribes "who did not copy slavishly but who functioned like performers—recomposing the tradition as they wrote" ("Performance Criticism [Part I]," 123/4).

177. Rhoads, "Performance Criticism (Part I)," 125.

178. Boomershine, "Peter's Denial" (see also the Introduction). Note that in the article itself Boomershine speaks of "media eisegesis" ("Peter's Denial," 48).

to study these texts now as oral compositions that were performed in an oral culture can potentially transform our experience of the writings of the Second Testament and our picture(s) of early Christianity." Regarding the third governing question, we rephrase that "our experience" of "the writings" can be "transformed" when we "study" the "texts" as "oral compositions" that "were performed." The use of the past tense is significant as it implies oral performances there-and-then-to-them. So within this reasoning, our study of the text here-and-now is based on the intended performance there-and-then. The object of study is "the whole complex dynamics of a performance in the ancient (and contemporary) world." In this definition of the object of study—that is introduced without warning and in parenthesis—performances here-and-now-by-us are surreptitiously introduced ("contemporary"). They are not only equated with those there-and-then, but also their nature or constitution is taken for granted. So, all the more, in Rhoads's Biblical Performance Criticism we have to inquire as to the relationship between the functioning of "text" here-and-now-to-us and the functioning of oral performance there-and-then-to-them, as well as his advocated performances here-and-now-to/by-us.

Along the same lines, Rhoads transforms the frame of "meaning." It is "not words on a page as understood by a reader," but it is found "in the whole event at the site of performance—sounds, sights, storytelling/speech, audience reaction, shared cultural beliefs and values, social location, and historical circumstances."[179] The question comes to the fore: What does that mean for "meaning"? It is important to observe that he locates it somehow in the sensorially experienced realm of history. In this formulation, once more, the specificity of the realm of history does not become clear (either there-and-then or here-and-now).

In this reframing, Rhoads deals with several key components of the performance event. One of them is the notion of "The Composition-as-Performance": One should not investigate the oral traces in the composition (for example, Achtemeier, Davis), but realize that the whole piece was performed. This is important, because the performances are constituted by the "power to transform." "Therefore, we have to seek to understand how every part and how the whole 'worked' as a composition-in-performance."[180] Now we can observe that two distinctive realms of history come together, namely, the imperative is related to our contemporary understanding, and the pronoun is significant here ("we have to seek to understand") and the past tense ("worked") is related to the audience of the performance there-and-then.

179. Rhoads, "Performance Criticism (Part I)," 126.
180. Rhoads, "Performance Criticism (Part I)," 127.

In a similar vein, Rhoads implicitly and surprisingly changes the perspective regarding "the Performer."[181] Sidestepping the historically implied emissary, all of a sudden *we* are the "performers": "By placing oneself in that position [performer], the contemporary exegete-performer enters the world of the story or letter through a fresh medium." No attention is paid to the emissary as crucial historical constituent of the oral performance there-and-then-to-them. How the contemporary exegete-performer relates here-and-now to the physical artefact (text) is also not an object of study. So, despite the mentioning of a "fresh medium" on the level of text and the call to perform here-and-now, Rhoads—with his academic training and being part of this sociocultural context of hight literacy—still relates to the "text"-by-reading as the uncritical starting point to which one continuously returns.

After dealing with the performer, Rhoads turns to "The Audience," which, he deems to be intrinsically linked to the performer. He remarks, "We cannot separate audience from performer."[182] The performance is an interactive event: "As such, compositions may have anticipated audience response and, in turn, audiences were quite capable of shaping a performance as it went along." So, he continues, we do not need to differentiate, because "performer" and "audience" come together in "the performance." When we distinguish performer and audience as distinctive subjects (plural) in the intended communicative process, an interesting shift takes place—on the level of his text—to the solely singular "the performance," which is an object, that is, his "object of study." In combination with the earlier observed ambiguity of past and present, "the performance" becomes somewhat abstracted and, therefore, free-floating—being everywhere, every time, and for everyone the same.

This tendency can also be seen in Rhoads's emphasis on the communal character of audiences. Over against our deeply ingrained habit of individual and silent reading, he pleads for communal experiences of these writings as performances. In this way, the dynamics of "group response" can be investigated.[183] In the flow of his reasoning, it becomes clear though that this observation is related to his advocated performing of these writings here-and-now. In his conclusion to part one of his methodology, he contends for the analysis of "all these elements of the performance event together."[184] As a critical observation, we note that it does not become clear whether the

---

181. Rhoads, "Performance Criticism (Part I)," 128.
182. Rhoads, "Performance Criticism (Part I)," 128–29.
183. Rhoads, "Performance Criticism (Part I)," 129.
184. Rhoads, "Performance Criticism (Part I)," 131.

performance event referred to lies in the past or in the present/future.[185] In his argumentation, this is a recurrent issue. From this perspective, though, he provides in the second part of his article an important key for our present approach and efforts to understand the text: "We often give interpretations of the text without ever asking: Could the lines be read in such a way that the hearer would understand the meaning you are giving to it?"[186] Performance here-and-now-by-us as such may provide a way to test the limits of viable interpretations.

We will turn now to a more detailed and critical evaluation of this methodology in the making. It is clear that Rhoads presents an unconventional agenda for biblical scholarship, calling for the performance of the New Testament documents here-and-now-by-us. In Rhoads's approach, two aspects require clarification. The nature of "performance" as well as "text" demands further scrutiny. As repeatedly mentioned, his emerging methodology is comprised of two endeavours. He continuously phrases his two-fold focus on the reconstruction of oral performance there-and-then-to-them and the contemporary praxis of performing here-and-now oneself as a new way for us to interpret the transmitted texts.

In the first movement (the historical reconstruction of the originally intended performance), the media of the spoken word dominates his view of them. At the same time, present-day readers—also when performing themselves—still relate to the writings as "text" in real time. Rhoads does not answer the underlying question of how these two activities in their distinctive realms of history relate to each other (third governing question). In the passage in which he compares the New Testament scholar with musicologists and dramatists, he concludes, "When viewed this way, we realize that performance should be an important site for the interpretation of the biblical writings. Performance is the place where interpretations are

---

185. Since Rhoads, "Performance Criticism (Part II)," is not relevant to the present study, we will deal briefly with it here. According to Rhoads, performance criticism is not just another discipline alongside others. As a result of the media shift, performance criticism informs other disciplines and can transform their strategies, methods, and results (165). After a short discussion of each discipline, he concludes that a new kind of commentary might emerge, that is, "to put flesh and blood on the skeletal remains of the text—by filling in and by filling out the many performance/orality dimensions of these Second Testament 'scripts'" (173). Crucial to this viewpoint is the practice of performing here-and-now. The act of performing is as "a methodological tool for interpretation." He comments, "We can never recover a first-century performance event, but we can experiment with twenty-first-century ones" ("Performance Criticism [Part II]," 173). For thirty years, Rhoads has been translating, memorizing, and performing New Testament writings. On this basis, he addresses several dynamics.

186. Rhoads, "Performance Criticism (Part I)," 179.

expressed, interpretations are tested, and interpretations are critiqued."[187] The praxis of performing biblical material here-and-now is consequently framed by him as "interpretation": his call to "perform" should help the biblical scholar to "interpret." Since the nature or subject of "interpretation" is not thematized and "text" forms the starting point, the implicit presupposition seems to be that "interpretation" forms a pair with "text" and that as present-day readers, we are the subjects *in actu*. In the end, our thoughts become structured once more in line with the free-floating question, What does it mean? In this respect, the call of Rhoads to locate "meaning" in the event of performance becomes even more urgent: What is the difference in the nature of meaning then?

Subsequently, in Rhoads's description of the historical realm there-and-then-for-them, the role of text is minimized or even obliterated:

> Again, written texts assisted in circulation. At the same time, because of the nature of performances, all these narratives, letters, and apocalypses may just as well have circulated orally, without the aid of a text, even after they were written down.[188]

We observe, first, that "text" in Rhoads's argumentation and praxis is an unquestioned given here-and-now-to-us. On that basis, he can perform. These performances constitute his additive or corrective way of interpretation. Second, he argues that at most, text "assisted" performance there-and-then-to-them. The question is, How does Rhoads solve this fundamental reversal, namely moving from the situation of denial of text as independent media there-and-then to the given functioning of it to us—even in his praxis of live performances? An answer is found in Rhoads's formulation of "performance literature." So here the second governing question comes to the fore at a deeper level—What can we learn from how the different media are related to each other?

Rhoads does not seem to be consistent or clear in this respect. The New Testament consists of "writings" or "texts"—apart from a single reference to "manuscripts."[189] More so, he describes them as "written texts."[190] So,

---

187. Rhoads, "Performance Criticism (Part I)," 119. As suggested in the abstract of the paper, where Rhoads sets out his intentions: "I seek to identify the various features of a performance event—performer, audience, material setting, social circumstances, and so on—as a basis to construct and analyse performance as the site of interpretation for Second Testament writings" (118).

188. Rhoads, "Performance Criticism (Part I)," 126.

189. Rhoads, "Performance Criticism (Part I)," 123.

190. Rhoads, "Performance Criticism (Part I)," 120, 124, 126. In terms of "writings," Rhoads comments, "Studying the *Second Testament writings* as performance literature will involve a radical shift from our exclusive focus on them as '*writings*'" (123,

while he seems to deny the existence of autonomous text there-and-then, he states at the same time that "text" equals "writings" which were present there-and-then. One could argue that in Rhoads's argumentation text has a docetic nature in the realm of history there-and-then-to-them (as noted with Joanna Dewey). On the one hand, "text" as mere assistant is usurped by oral performance. Put differently, although it is there it is not there. On the other hand, in his argumentation, and more importantly regarding his praxis of real-time performances, "text" is presupposed as an operational given; it is there, forming the starting point and thus a *conditio sine qua non*. In this way, a change in media—"orality" in distinction from "manuscripts" or "writings"—does not affect "text." The problem is that the mental transformations of the technology of reading and writing are not taken into account. "Text" will be the same every time, everywhere, and for everyone. This extra-historical status fits perfectly with our operational familiarity with text. In conclusion, regarding the second governing question, we see once more how complicated our relation to and subliminal dependence on "text" is—as indicated by the warnings in the Introduction to this thesis, and by Albert Lord and Walter Ong in Chapter 1.

In a similar vein, "composer" and "composition" are not differentiated sufficiently enough by Rhoads. "Composer" represents the historical person with his intentions, mindset/way of thinking, specific relation with the original audiences, and specific historical context. The composer composes. There is an emphasis on the communicative process (becoming). Contrarily, in his reasoning, "composition" tends to emphasize the outcome or end-product (being). Once more two distinctive ways of structuring thought are fused here. One can recognize this tendency, in particular, in his section "Clarifying the Object of Study: The Performance Event." Here Rhoads describes the key components of the moment of performance in real time. A section on the a priori process of composing, however, is lacking. Relating to the event of performance as object means that this event becomes isolated from the decisive and prior process of composition.

On the level of Rhoads's text, the "performance" functions separately from two explicit and distinctive historical and communicative contexts (there-and-then in distinction from here-and-now); it becomes one,

---

emphasis mine); see also the paragraph entitled "*Second Testament Writings* in Relation to Performance" (124–26, emphasis mine). With regard to "text": "Our cultural experience of the *Second Testament texts* in contemporary Western world has been private and silent reading by individuals or public reading that has fragmented *the text* into lectionary lessons in the context parish worship and teaching. In scholarship, we have fixed our attention on *written texts* so exclusively that we have not even thought about experiencing whole *texts* in a theatre setting or about listening to the Greek Testament as a way to interpret" ("Performance Criticism [Part I]," 119, emphasis mine).

remains unchanged and can float freely throughout time and place. His own experiences in performing here-and-now provide the determining horizon against which he himself interprets the biblical texts as texts. In this way, the final functioning of the letters as text-here-and-now-to-us-being-vocalized-by-Rhoads usurps the originally intended one. Since Rhoads is performer and interpreter in one and the same person, Paul as anticipating composer, and the original addressees as participants in the moment of delivery become eclipsed. This specific structuring of thought on the level of text exemplifies a derailing dynamic. Here we touch on the contribution of the present study: by locating the anticipated performance there-and-then-to-them in the moment of composing by the apostle, a perspective in the realm of history there-and-then can emerge. Contrary to the free-floating "performance" of Rhoads, we can oversee and integrate different actors or subjects *in actu* in one intended and envisioned communicative process, namely, Paul as anticipating the participation of his intended audience in the envisioned moment of delivery regarding their rhetorical situation.

BERNHARD OESTREICH: *PERFORMANZKRITIK DER PAULUSBRIEFE*

In 2012, Bernhard Oestreich published his monograph *Performanzkritik der Paulusbriefe*.[191] In his introduction, he comments that he embarked on an exploration of a world "wo das in der Bibel Geschriebene nicht nur schriftlicher Text, sondern gemeinsam gelebtes Ereignis ist."[192] Two key notions are "schriftlicher Text" and "Ereignis." Before the presentation of his method, Oestreich discusses "das Wesen der Performanz."[193] This seems to mean "performance" in and of itself or performance as being the same to everyone, every time, and everywhere. The perspective of "das Wesen" (being) is, therefore, in tension with performance as "Ereignis" (becoming). This atomizing tendency is confirmed by the fact that in this introductory section the moment of composition is not explicated or incorporated in any way.

---

191. Oestreich, *Performanzkritik*.

192. Oestreich, *Performanzkritik*, viii. On the one hand, he comments that he participated and learned much from the SBL seminar on "Performance Criticism of Biblical and Other Ancient Texts." On the other, he does not explicitly frame his study as a contribution to Biblical Performance Criticism. In distinction to the broad agenda of Rhoads, his development of performance criticism concentrates on the corpus Paulinum. He delineates his proposal as being limited to the performance there-and-then as implied by the letters of Paul. More so, he contradicts the idea that this method also entails performances here-and-now-by-us (*Performanzkritik*, 62).

193. Oestreich, *Performanzkritik*, 45–59.

Regarding his method of performance criticism, Oestreich turns to John Austin's "Performativität."[194] This notion emphasizes the effect or outcome of speech-acts.[195] Contrary to abstracted (*außersprachliche*) meaning, performativity structures understanding in terms of the goal(s) that are striven for. Language framed as speech-act always involves the one who is speaking as well as the one who is addressed.

Oestreich then engages with the work of Richard Bauman in which the essence of performance is comprised of the following aspects: *Materialität* and *Körperlichkeit*, interaction with and also within the implied audience, social conventions, *Emergenz* and *Ephemerität* and *Rückverweis auf bereits Vorhandenes*.[196] Regarding "matter-ness" (*Materialität*) and "bodily-ness" (*Körperlichkeit*), Oestreich observes that the original audiences of Paul always consisted of a plurality of persons. One has to consider—next to the relation between speaker and audience—that audiences consist of factions and groups. In this way, he concretizes the rather abstract "audience" to a greater degree.[197]

The notions of emergence (*Emergenz*) and a very short life cycle (*Ephemerität*) require attention for the specificity and the changeability of actual performances. Here the perspective shifts from performance as object to performance as event. Based on the research by Bauman, he describes the consequences of the event feature of a performance:

> Auch die Aufführungen kultureller mündlicher Traditionen . . . oder traditioneller Theaterstücke, deren Text schriftlich vorliegt, werden unter Performanz-Gesichtspunkten nicht zuerst als Übermittlung eines permanenten Inhalts verstanden, sondern als unwiederholbare Präsentation der rhetorischen und darstellerischen Kompetenz der Akteure.[198]

In a performance, the emphasis is placed upon "Akteure," those who perform or read aloud.

In this unrepeatable and unique historical event, the audience participates in an essential way. Following Erika Fischer-Lichte, who addresses the emergence of performance through the *autopoietischen feedback-Schleife*, he writes, "Alles, was in der Performanz geschieht, sowohl auf der Seite der

---

194. Austin, *How to Do Things*.

195. Oestreich, *Performanzkritik*, 46.

196. Oestreich, *Performanzkritik*, 46–59. References are made to Bauman, *Verbal Art* and *Story*.

197. Note that this structuring of thought (abstraction), which he wants to counter, seems to be implied by the singularity and oneness of this overly familiar concept.

198. Oestreich, *Performanzkritik*, 55.

Darsteller als auch auf der Seite des Publikums, wirkt zurück auf der Seite der Darsteller als auch auf der Seite des Publikums, wirkt zurück auf die Performanz selbst."[199] In short, every actual and unique performance should be valued in relation to itself (*Selbstreferentialität*).

Two observations are in order. First, Oestreich builds on insights from performance studies. This discipline concentrates, however, on contemporary performances *in actu*; for example, one can go to a theatre and participate in a performance oneself in real time. When biblical scholars attempt to reconstruct past performances that took place approximately two thousand years ago, they touch on a boundary inherent in historical-critical research or performance criticism of the biblical texts. We must, therefore, distinguish between intended performances there-and-then-to-them, as envisioned by Paul, and actual performances taking place before our very own eyes.

Second, we have to note—in line with Bauman—that the source of "kultureller mündlicher Traditionen" and the writer of "traditioneller Theaterstücke" do not play a significant role for the object of study. The focus is, after all, on the "unwiederholbare Präsentation der rhetorischen und darstellerischen Kompetenz der Akteure." There is an emphasis on the actuality of the performance. As a result, the specifics of the prior process of composition by Paul—that is, with respect to his spiritual fatherhood, other teachers as opponents, and the danger of apostasy of the converts—tend to be marginalized. Not to mention the difference, in this respect, with composing and directing a theatre play in the twenty-first century.

Regarding materiality and corporeality, Oestreich recapitulates the difference between "text" and "performance" as follows:

> die Aufführung [ist] zuerst einmal ein Erlebnis, nicht gleich und allein ein intellektuelles Verstehen eines Textes oder Stückes ... es erschliesst zusätzliche Deutungsmöglichkeiten, die über das hinausgehen, was im aufgeführten Stück oder präsentierten Text steht.[200]

Oestreich provides a frame of understanding in which text is processed in the overly familiar way ("intellektuelles Verstehen"), but additional dimensions ("zusätzliche Deutungsmöglichkeiten") should be discerned in the "Aufführung" of the text. So "texts" can be read, but more so these texts should be performed. However, in both procedures, "text" is the unquestioned starting point.

---

199. Oestreich, *Performanzkritik*, 55.
200. Oestreich, *Performanzkritik*, 60.

Subsequently, Oestreich asks how these additional possibilities in understanding are related to "was der aufgeführte Text aussagt." His answer is that "Die im Text liegende Bedeutung" or "ein intellektuelles Verstehen eines Textes" can be compared to "eine Abstraktion":

> So wie ein abstrakter Begriff (etwa "Kreis") eine Fülle von konkreten Erscheinungen bezeichnet, aber als solche Abstraktion nicht existieren kann (den Kreis gibt es nicht, nur konkrete Ausführungen), so muss ein Text durch eine konkrete Person unter konkreten Bedingungen verkörpert werden, um in Erscheinung zu treten.[201]

So text relates to actual performance as abstraction relates to concretization.[202] More precisely, the text needs embodiment by a specific performer in a concrete situation to be able to appear ("in Erscheinung zu treten"). The latter phrase is synonymous with "the realm of history" as used in the present study. This train of thought implies a process. Initially, there is only text—that is, the letter as text (abstraction). Subsequently, it appears (concretization); the movement is from "abstraction/text" to "concretization/performance." For example, in the text, a circle exists as an abstraction. In the performance, however, it has to appear to the participants as that specific circle to which they necessarily will relate. This line of thought has an important consequence. When the letter is equated with text in this way, Paul as "author" would have framed the term ("circle") in a general and extra-historical way, independent or even unknowing of and not interested in the specific situation of the concrete addressees. To the contrary, the present study would argue that instead of a free-floating "circle," the apostle as composer anticipates from the start the specific circle vis-à-vis his intended addressees, which he wants to direct their attention to.

Since it is inherent in Oestreich's reasoning that the abstraction precedes and determines the concretization, one can ask—regarding the first question of this Chapter as to how the different media are related to each other—What are the consequences of this understanding and the primacy of

---

201. Oestreich, *Performanzkritik*, 60.

202. Consider, in this respect, Rodríguez, "Reading and Hearing." In his critique on the reasoning of Casey Davis, as found in his article "Hebrews," we see a similar situation: "Davis portrays the author of Hebrews as a cultural monstrosity who wishes to communicate complex (literate?) ideas but finds himself constrained by the inability of his audience to follow 'analytic,' 'objectively distanced' or 'abstract' discourse. Davis's author, among other things, seems to grasp the truth he conveys in ways unconstrained by cultural or historical forces, and the tasks before him as he writes is to express that truth in terms that are accessible within the cultural limitations affecting his hapless readers" ("Reading and Hearing," 153–54).

"text"? First, regarding his section on "das Wesen der Performanz," we signal that Oestreich does not address "das Wesen des Textes." So, on and beyond the level of text, "text" *is*—a conceptually unquestioned given. Alongside appearances (plural) in performances there-and-then—which are his object of study—the "text" (singular) was there-and-then and is here-and-now the same. In his argument therefore, text does not become concretized either to the original addressees, or to the present-day reader. Whether the letters or Oestreich's own publication, everything *is* "text." Text enables and facilitates abstraction, but it does not become abstracted—or, better, concretized—itself (see Chapter 3, Section A.1. Textualizing text *hic et nunc pro nobis*).

Second, Oestreich determines the role of text in performance criticism as follows: "Performanzkritik der neutestamentliche Texte geht davon aus, dass diese Texte auf das Ereignis ihrer Aufführung vor einem Publikum zielen und Zeugnisse solcher Ereignisse sind."[203] On the one hand, he argues that New Testament texts—in their genesis—point to a future performance. On the other, these same texts—as given products—are witnesses of these past events.[204] In this one notion of "text," two different communicative processes (*textum* and autonomously functioning text) become mixed. Also, the question as to who does relate to the letter receives two answers: "Ereignis ihrer Aufführung" for the originally intended audience and "Zeugnisse solcher Ereignisse" for the present-day reader. The autonomous way in which text functions—which is an operational given in the socio-cultural context of academia—dominates and determines the former: "Methodisch wird Performanzkritik vom Überlieferten Text ausgehen."[205] Since his proposal of performance criticism starts with the text (which makes Paul an author who abstracts), the role of the emissary, the original addressees, adversaries, and also the apostle—while composing/envisioning the oral delivery—are addressed as separate aspects and do not become interlocked in one overarching approach.[206]

---

203. Oestreich, *Performanzkritik*, 60.

204. A similar tension is involved when Oestreich argues that texts "auf das Ereignis ihrer Aufführung vor einem Publikum zielen" (*Performanzkritik*, 70).

205. Oestreich, *Performanzkritik*, 70.

206. This critique is affirmed in the double way in which Oestreich uses "interpretation" in his reasoning. On the one hand, the present-day reader interprets the letters as texts. On the other, the public reader who addresses the gathered audience interpreted the letter at that moment: "Was aufgeführt wird, ist also trotz vorbereitetem Text eine jeweils eigene und einmalige Komposition, eine verkörperte Interpretation des Textes" (*Performanzkritik*, 38, see also 126 and 136). So "performance" seems to be categorized here as "interpretation" as well. Since the notion is not elucidated and explained, and in his reasoning "text" is free-floating, the equation of what the highly trained reader is used to do ("interpretation") with how the emissary would have participated in the oral

LARRY HURTADO: "ORAL FIXATION AND NEW TESTAMENT STUDIES?

In 2014, Larry Hurtado published "Oral Fixation and New Testament Studies? 'Orality', 'Performance' and Reading Texts in Early Christianity."[207] The article is rather polemical; the aim is to counter the agenda of the emerging discipline of Biblical Performance Criticism. Two years later, a response by Kelly Iverson was published.[208] Hurtado responded to Iverson in the same issue.[209]

---

delivery ("interpretation") is difficult to avoid. As a result, the intellectual endeavour remains directed by the question, What does it mean?

207. Hurtado, "Oral Fixation."
208. Iverson, "Oral Corrective."
209. Hurtado, "Correcting Iverson's 'Correction.'" The first correction by Hurtado of Iverson's corrections is relevant to the present evaluation. The former writes: "Perhaps the fundamental problem is that Iverson mistakes my article as if it were some kind of broadside against the entire body of scholars and publications that refer to 'performance' of texts in early Christianity" (201). Hurtado's defense is the following—the emphasis is mine: "I hoped to have made it perfectly clear that I was addressing problems in the work of '*some* scholars' and '*some* of the crucial claims and inferences' (abstract), referring to '*some* advocates' (327, n. 34, 329), and '*some* studies taking a performance criticism approach'" (334)—as found in his "Correcting Iverson's 'Correction'" (201). He continues: "To reiterate this point for emphasis, I gave no indication that my article was some sort of comprehensive assessment of 'performance criticism,' and I made it rather clear, instead, that my purpose was to correct *certain* claims and assumptions made by *some* of those who identify themselves with this emphasis" (202, emphasis original). So, contrary to the complaint by Iverson of erecting "something of a straw man," Hurtado ends his first section with the exclamation: "So, I really must complain of being misrepresented myself!" ("Correcting Iverson's 'Correction,'" 201). Several reasons can be provided that suggest and also seem to affirm Iverson's impression that Hurtado wants to address or more so oppose the whole of this movement. First, regarding a paper of almost twenty pages in total, he can bring together only six rather common, dispersed, and in the original text not emphasized adjectives ("some" and "certain;" for four of them, see above). Second, when we consider the intentions of the paper as a whole, the overall impression is one of generality rather than specificity. The title, "Oral Fixation and New Testament Studies? 'Orality', 'Performance' and Reading Texts in Early Christianity" presents a horizon that is as broad as the mentioned notions of "Oral," "New Testament Studies," "Performance," "Reading Texts," and "Early Christianity." There is no hint as to a restriction to specific (some) scholars regarding their specific perspective on performance criticism. In terms of the abstract, the first sentence does indeed mention "some scholars" who "have asserted that in early Christian circles texts were 'performed,' not 'read' (and could not have been read), likening this action to descriptions of oratorical delivery of speeches (from memory) or theatrical performance" ("Oral Fixation," 321), but in light of the title linking "Oral Fixation" and "New Testament Studies," one is inclined to frame this identified group of scholars as those within the community of New Testament scholarship as a whole who engage matters of "orality" and "performance." In his response, Hurtado explains that this usage of "some" should

In the words of Hurtado, the movement of performance criticism consists of a small but increasing number of scholars who have postulated,

> that in early Christian circles texts were originally "performed," by which they appear to mean something more than skilful reading, something more akin to ancient oratorical delivery and/or theatrical performances, involving (it is proposed) recitation of the texts from memory (not reading from a manuscript), animated or theatrical use of voice and bodily gestures/actions, and even various lively responses from the "audiences."[210]

Before we turn to the main idea of his paper, attention has to be paid to the first footnote in which he opts for a "more precise sense of the term of 'performance.'"[211] His point of reference is based on studies by Whitney Shiner and William Shiell.

> Shiner proposes 'applause of different types, including waving hands, loud exclamations, and rhythmic clapping,' people leaping from their seats and thumping the floor with their feet, and being 'just as boisterous in condemning what they did not like' ... It is this more precise sense of the term of 'performance' that I engage here.[212]

In his polemic, "performance" entails a rather outspoken and narrow version of it. In this way, we touch on two main reasons why Hurtado's polemical paper causes confusion and prompts responses such as that by Kelly Iverson. Not only does he restrict his usage of "performance" to an outspoken theatrical version of it, which is not self-evidently implied by the current usage of this key notion, but he explicates this important presuppositional matter simply in a footnote.

---

be seen, however, as a restriction *within* those who represent performance criticism. This later remark is more or less necessary to read this sentence in this way. In the words of Iverson: "Though Hurtado, in places, seems to engage in a more qualified discussion with certain scholars, the title, abstract and introductory comments are articulated in a manner that depicts performance critics as a homogeneous group whose perspectives are represented in the following pages" ("Oral Corrective," 188). Since we do not find any hint of a limitation in the rest of the abstract, the following formulation would have been more appropriate: "These claims *as posited by some within the movement of performance criticism* ..." If he had done so, however, the question does arise as to what the value and impact of this free accessible article would have been.

210. Hurtado, "Oral Fixation," 321–22.

211. Hurtado, "Oral Fixation," 322.

212. Hurtado, "Oral Fixation," 322, note 1. For the points of reference, see Shiner, *Proclaiming the Gospel*; Shiell, *Reading Acts*.

In the same extended footnote, Hurtado also mentions the juxtaposed and broader definition of performance, "as to encompass practically any conveyance of Jesus tradition in any form." The latter—despite the unexplained limitation to the Jesus tradition—is the broad definition as encountered, for example, in the articles by David Rhoads and as applied in the present study. He does not argue why, in view of this, he chooses to confine his definition to the outspoken theatrical kind of performance. Later on, we will observe that he juxtaposes a position of reading (out loud) with this theatrical kind of performance; instead of a continuum, a clear and simple opposition between (reading) "text" and "performance" is the result.

We turn now to the start of his argumentation. The newly discovered oral dimension of the Bible has brought the origin of the gospel of Mark under debate. An increasing number of scholars claim that it was composed in the process of several oral performances delivered in various settings. Hurtado concludes, "So what we know as the Gospel of Mark is (in this proposal) perhaps only a transcript of a given performance, and/or a script to be memorised for subsequent performances."[213] Two observations can be made regarding his formulation. First, neither the media of "the Gospel of Mark" is defined—so uncritically we fill in "text"—nor is the relation between the subjects *in actu*—"we" here-and-now and those there-and-then dealing with "a transcript of a given performance, and/or a script to be memorised"—explicated. This is another example of the media muddle; from the start, both functionings, realms of history, and subjects *in actu* become muddled on the level of his own text. Second, he does not make any further exploration of the proposal that the product follows on from the production. He confines, then, (one-sidedly) his framing of performance in terms of the product preceding the production/performance. A subsequent confinement is his framing of performance solely to the latter, that is, the product precedes the production/performance. Regarding the first governing question on the effect of body-to-body communcation, we can observe that Hurtado equates ourselves with those who have to come to an understanding and, at the same time, he posits the Gospel of Mark as (free-floating?) text to be the starting point of his evaluation of performance criticism.

Another preliminary observation can be made regarding the representatives of this approach. Hurtado identifies two particular scholars: Pieter Botha and David Rhoads. He addresses the latter's call to actual performances of the New Testament writings by biblical scholars also in a footnote, commenting that this is "a matter I do not engage here."[214] Since

---

213. Hurtado, "Oral Fixation," 322.
214. Hurtado, "Oral Fixation," 322, note 3.

he sidesteps this central appeal of Rhoads, he does not engage the agenda of performance criticism as posited by these scholars themselves. This prompts the question: What is his own agenda?

Hurtado formulates the aim of his paper as follows:

> In this essay . . . I show that key assumptions of 'performance criticism' advocates comprise a number of oversimplifications (and so distortions) of relevant historical matters, and that, consequently, the inferences drawn about the composition and use of texts in early Christianity are the more dubious.

In stating that performance critics oversimplify and distort the realm of history there-and-then-to-them,[215] his own formulation gives rise to the observation that "texts" are constitutive of his grasp of early Christianity without further explanation. Subsequently, he affirms, referring to Werner Kelber, that the "appreciation of the spoken word" in the Roman era "may be taken now as widely accepted and not under dispute here."[216] He questions, however, "whether the prominence of this 'orality' should be taken as a basis for minimising the place of texts and the activities associated with them (writing, reading, copying etc.) in that same period."[217] Uncritically, "text" is once more located in the realm of history there-and-then-to-them. He adds that a kind of zero-sum game is at stake "in which emphasising the place of Roman-era 'orality' is at the expense of recognising the significant place of written texts and their various uses in that period."[218] This is the oversimplification that he wants to address, namely a mutually exclusive dichotomy between orality and "written texts" where, due to the dominance of orality, literacy could not inform the culture involved. Once more, we have to take recourse to a footnote to find an explanation for this allegation of oversimplification: "This may arise from their [advocates of performance

---

215. Botha (see, in this Chapter, Section C.)—mentioned by Hurtado as one of the exponents of Biblical Performance Criticism—commences with exactly the same warning against oversimplification regarding the study of literacy in Greco-Roman society: "Furthermore, by not critically defining our concepts we can easily fall into the trap of facile oversimplification" ("Letter writing," 19).

216. Hurtado, "Oral Fixation," 323. He describes this sense of appreciation extensively: "Roman-era people valued the sound of words/speech, relished and promoted effective speaking (rhetoric), enjoyed lively recitations of poetry and performance of theatrical works, read literary texts aloud and enjoyed having these texts read to them, or used dictation (variously) as part of the process of composition. All these things seem to be the case. In these phenomena and others, certainly, we can characterise the Roman period as one in which an 'orality' (in the sense of the use and enjoyment of the spoken word) was a prominent feature." ("Oral Fixation," 323)

217. Hurtado, "Oral Fixation," 323.

218. Hurtado, "Oral Fixation," 323-24.

criticism] construction of Roman 'orality' from anthropological studies and theories based on pre-literate societies, with insufficient attention given to relevant cultural specifics of the Roman era as illustrated in this essay."[219]

Let us now recapitulate and evaluate Hurtado's train of thought hitherto. Within performance criticism, the reconstruction of the dimension of orality in Roman culture is based on research into pre-literate cultures. In this way, there is a lack of sensibility towards relevant cultural specifics of the Roman era as such, for example, in terms of the role of literacy there-and-then-to-them. Pre-literacy and the "orality" of the Roman era cannot be related in such an oversimplified way. On the one hand, this acknowledgment of actual interfaces between orality/aurality and literacy, in that specific realm of history (Roman era), is valid. On the other, we have to ask critically: To what extent does the implied conclusion mean that "pre-literacy" cannot be related to or shed light on (Roman) "orality"? The related and more fundamental question is, How can we—as products of a highly literate socio-cultural context and actually working with (the biblical) text—explore and know this distinctive (and rather unknown) context of orality in any absolute way, whether that orality is preliterate or in the first-century Roman context where all kinds and degrees of literacies were present? In some way, one would now expect a proposal to distinguish first-century Roman oralities from ancient Greek ones, and to explore and describe the specificities of the oral dimension in the Roman era. This, however, is not the case. Despite the call for historical sensibility, Hurtado does not engage the question as to what this presence or even dominance of orality-aurality in the Roman era means for the constitution of literacy there-and-then. In his argumentation, "orality" becomes dichotomously structured to "pre-literacy"; they remain coarse, unrelated and, therefore, *freischwebende* categories. We will see that this is typical of his way of reasoning in general.

We can also evaluate this part of his reasoning from another angle. When Hurtado states that the appreciation of the spoken word in Roman era is a *communis opinio* in biblical scholarship and, therefore, not a matter of dispute for him, he seems to ignore the primary point of emphasis of performance criticism. To quote Iverson,

> Of primary concern is that for the overwhelming majority of people in the ancient world, texts were experienced in an oral context. That is, although manuscripts may or may not have been present and/or used at times of presentation, the audience encountered 'the text' through oral recitation.[220]

219. Hurtado, "Oral Fixation," 324, note 6.
220. Iverson, "Oral Corrective," 198.

Therefore, Hurtado not only does not dispute this *communis opinio*, but he also does not engage in the debate on the consequences. In his response, Iverson introduces the specific perspective of the subjects *in actu* of performance there-and-then (body to body) in distinction from our overly familiar one of eye to text area. Instead, Hurtado calls for consideration to be given to the alleged problem that performance critics want to minimize, "the place of texts and the activities associated with them (writing, reading, copying etc.)," based on "the prominence of this 'orality.'"[221] In line with his earlier observed location of "text" in the realm of history there-and-then, he posits here—without explication or explanation—the product as the starting point. So, in his thought structure, the free-standing product overrules or transcends the historical process. Iverson comments on this reasoning as follows: "To confuse silent reading with public recitation ignores a host of interpretive issues and reflects a misunderstanding of media types."[222] Hurtado seems to advance his own agenda from the start. Since he does not explicate or justify his own presuppositions, constructive discussion becomes difficult or even impossible.

Returning to the first main issue Hurtado raises as an oversimplification on the part of advocates for performance criticism, we now examine his own assessment of the claim of a first-century cultural bias in favour of the oral over the written. He counters this with the following assertion:

> As reflected in the many thousands of manuscripts that survive from the Roman period, the many literary works produced and circulated, the many inscriptions and the many kinds of 'documentary' texts (letters, contracts, business/commercial documents, *et al.*), writings were not mere appendages to the spoken word but were important in themselves as a major factor in many areas of life and among various levels and sectors of societies.[223]

We start our scrutiny of this line of thinking with the premise of quantity, as reflected in the repeated use of the word 'many' in the above quotation. The difficulty with such data is interpreting the value of any quantity mentioned and it does not become clear on what basis Hurtado claims that we are dealing with a large quantity. He assumes this to be self-evident. Given the timeframe and area of the Roman empire, one could ask why this number could not be a sign of the opposite, that is, a sign of sparsity. Similarly, Hurtado offers little comment on the nature or function of these writings and whether they should all be quantified as being important "in themselves," or

221. Hurtado, "Oral Fixation," 323.
222. Iverson, "Oral Corrective," 199.
223. Hurtado, "Oral Fixation," 324.

whether there are also genres and categories that can be valued in line with manifestations of the spoken word (*textum*/"inscription of living speech"; see Excursus: Silent reading in antiquity?). In a more philosophical way, we can question whether the statement on the importance of these writings in themselves grants them this *freischwebende* status that we are concerned to identify in the present study as typical of the mindset of the socio-cultural context of academia.[224]

A related difficulty that follows on from this lack of clarity in terms of quantifying texts, concerns the way such texts are then characterised. Since he has introduced the opposition of "orality" and "texts" and does not explain what he means by this phrase "(being) important in themselves," the necessary implication is that these physical artefacts functioned independent of the spoken word in an idiosyncratic or autonomous way. So the (unwarranted) claim of the large quantity of "writings" there-and-then-to-them has to ground their status (quality) as autonomous text. If this analysis is valid, we are dealing with a category mistake.

In an ensuing section, Hurtado refers to "exaggerated claims in some earlier and influential publications of classicists that subsequently have received justifiable correction." Referring to studies by Holt Parker[225] and Emmanuelle Valette-Cagnac,[226] he writes in a polemical but also nuanced way:

> So, to reiterate the point for emphasis, the Roman period is better characterised as a time of rich interplay of texts and readers (both private and to/before groups), writers and speakers,

---

224. In an extended footnote, we turn to Thomas, *Literacy and Orality*, to shed more light on the dimension and value of an argument on the basis of quantity: "The tendency to see a society (or individual) as either literate or oral is over-simple and misleading. The habits of relying on oral communication (or orality) and literacy are not mutually exclusive... the evidence for Greece shows *both* a sophisticated and extensive use of writing in some spheres *and* what is to us an amazing dominance of the spoken word" (4). "Given the complexity of literacy and paucity of detailed ancient evidence, all we can say with any plausibility is that probably more people could read than write; the ability to read or write very simple messages, often in capitals was probably not rare and in cities like Athens... most citizens had some basic ability and perhaps 'phonetic literacy' was pretty widespread; but the written texts of poetry and literary prose had a reading audience confined to the highly educated and wealthy elite, and their secretaries" (*Literacy and Orality*, 11). In this respect, we can also quote Foley on the diversity within the concept of "literacy": "brute measures like percentage literacy or the mere existence of some sort of writing must not lead us down the garden path of assimilating other cultures' literacies to our own" (*How to Read*, 69). Regarding the reasoning of Hurtado, much more precision is needed in definitions of "literacy" and "orality" and more argumentation is required regarding the quantity and quality, or types, of literacy.

225. Parker, "Books."

226. Valette-Cagnac, *La lecture*.

> and appreciation of both oral/aural and written expressions of thought and entertainment, and it is a fallacy to make the one subservient to the other in any generalising way.[227]

Here Hurtado advocates for a more balanced paradigm: over against a dominance either of the spoken/heard or the written word "in any generalising way" one has to evaluate every specific situation in its own right.[228] Following Valette-Cagnac, he emphasizes that exchange took place in both directions. So contrary to clear and simple oppositions, he calls, at the beginning of this section, to explore the continua between both media.

The subsequent examples, however, show only one of the two directions implied—that is, from the written to the spoken word. He introduces Quintilian and Pliny who state that composition-in-writing produces the better results in the actual delivery of oratory.[229] In short, the outcome of these examples is an extensive illustration of the dominance of the written over the spoken word. Once more, we see that the consistency of his argumentation is under strain.

To undergird the implied dominance of the written word, Hurtado immediately continues with the following affirmation: "*Indeed*, in many cases the written text was simply intended to be read in its own right and by individuals" (emphasis mine).[230] We recognize in the phrase "in its own right" a synonym of "being important in themselves." In conclusion, the section on the first oversimplification moves from an explicit plea for mutual exchange between the two media, via examples which consistently illustrate the dominance of one over the other, to an implicit conclusion ("[i]ndeed") on the priority and dominance of the written word (being important in itself) over the spoken one in the Roman era.

---

227. Hurtado, "Oral Fixation," 325.

228. Confusingly, this comment fits Iverson hand in glove! In this respect, we can ask to what extent or in what way can this reasoning be related to the previous point that all the writings that have survived from the Roman era are important in themselves. The latter structuring of thought would preclude mutual exchange a priori. So, what is the cogency of his article in this respect?

229. This train of thought is directly based on Parker, "Books," 215. See also Parker's comment: "It is not the case that the written text is considered a copy or record of the oral presentation. Pliny explicitly states [*Ep. 1.20.9*] that the opposite is true: the written text is the model and archetype for the speech as actually delivered" ("Books," 225-26). The question is, though, whether these writings were perceived as being "important in themselves" and, as a result, in opposition to "speech" by Pliny.

230. Hurtado, "Oral Fixation," 325. Consider examples of poetic texts—once more provided by Parker—that are clearly intended for the eye: acrostics, picture poems, poems in the shape of eggs or wings etc.

The second oversimplification Hurtado addresses is the claim by advocates of performance criticism "that Roman-era reading, even private reading, was almost always reading aloud." Hurtado in no way wants to deny the practice of reading aloud. Notably though, this qualification of his opponents ("almost always") is subsequently replaced with "often": "Certainly, texts were often read out (aloud)."[231] In particular, reading aloud was the case in elite circles, as well as sub-elite settings such as synagogues and early Christian gatherings.[232] However, Hurtado claims that the implication of this practice for advocates of performance criticism is "that texts were radically subordinate to 'orality.'" Despite the quotation marks, it is not clear what "orality" involves in this reasoning. "So it is simply misinformed to assert that texts were only (or even predominantly) read aloud in groups, and were, thus merely appendages to 'orality.'" Implied in the structure of this proposition, one media (orality) always subordinates and neglects the other (text).

We recapitulate the argument. First, the situation that texts were read out "almost always" is nuanced by Hurtado into "often." Then, as next step, "often" is, suddenly, turned into "only": performance critics claim that writings were only read aloud. This situation is then self-evidently and correctly rejected by Hurtado.

At the end of this section, Hurtado provides a conclusion that seems to be presupposed from the start: "Even texts that were written to be read out (for example, Paul's letters) were foremost *texts*, and what was delivered orally was the *text*" (emphasis original). We will scrutinize now the structuring of thought of this statement. This critical analysis will be in light of the dichotomy between the realm of history and that of extra-historical thought as set out in the Introduction to this thesis (Caution to the reader #2). Hurtado commences with "texts that were written to be read out (for example, Paul's letters)" (plural). So, on the level of text, he starts by framing these "texts" as the historical artefacts that enabled public reading. The

---

231. Here he refers to several important "but insufficiently noticed" studies: Knox, "Silent Reading";. Gavrilov, "Techniques of Reading"; Burnyeat, "Postscript"; Snyder, *Teachers and Texts*; Johnson, "Toward a Sociology"; Johnson, *Readers and Reading Culture*. Evidence can be found that it was usual practice to read letters silently. Regarding larger literary texts, plenty of evidence can be provided as well that these were read privately and silently. Valette-Cagnac has shown that the Latin verb *legere* appears to be used in contexts designating reading in silence and solitude. Gavrilov has demonstrated that Roman-era readers were well aware of the different features and also advantages of reading in public as well as in silence and solitude. As we argue in the present study, this evidence should not lead us to (uncritically) jump to the implicit equation with the socio-cultural context of present-day academia.

232. Hurtado, "Oral Fixation," 326.

past tense makes clear that we have to locate them in the realm of history there-and-then (autographs). Subsequently, he defines these autographs "foremost" as the single un-explicated term in italics "*texts*" (plural). The adverb (foremost) structures hierarchy. Notwithstanding the acknowledgment "being written to be read out," their categorization of "*texts*" is the most prominent in rank. However, notwithstanding the use of italics, the term itself is repeated ("texts" becomes "*texts*"). Accordingly, the definition hinges on the omission of the specification "that were written to be read out" and the adding of italics. In the next phrase, he repeats the purport of his argument: "and what was delivered orally was the *text*." Now plural ("*texts*") has become singular ("*text*") and the process or historical event ("was delivered orally") is distinguished from the "what" or the essence: that is the *text* itself. The use of italics and the articulate singular ("the *text*") structure our thoughts away from the specific realm of history towards the one of extra-historical thought. He argues that, despite an unfamiliar functioning there-and-then (public reading/oral performance), the *text* as such is the same everywhere, every time, and for everyone. Essence and historical manifestation or form and content are separated. In short, the *text* (articulated and singular) transcends the realm of history. Some reflections on this reasoning are offered. First, according to Hurtado, the provocative call of Rhoads to perform the New Testament here-and-now, along with the *communis opinio* on the appreciation of the spoken word in the Roman era, will not and cannot touch on the *text*-ness of these documents. Second, as in the articles by Joanna Dewey and David Rhoads, we witness once more some sort of conflict between the status and role of "text" on the level of text and in the realm of history (beyond that level). Dewey speaks of text as aid to orality in distinction from text as having importance in itself, whereas Hurtado denies the importance of the aid to orality so that text will always have importance in itself. Third, when he states *text* as singular, articulate, and in italics on the level of text (as part of the realm of extra-historical thought) and has denied the importance—on that same level of text—of the oral delivery or public reading thereof, the actual functioning of text will be determined beyond that level (in his own realm of history here-and-now)— that is, as processing by reading. Fourth, this reasoning seems to represent in an intentional way the movement of *textification*: despite acknowledging the historical functioning of the New Testament documents (oral performance/public reading), their nature, content or essence is declared to be extra-historical ("the *text*") and cannot, therefore, be subject to change (Introduction: Caution to the reader #4). Fifth, the structuring of this statement by Hurtado—that is, from the concrete or specific ("texts were written to be read out") to the abstract and general ("the *text*")—is precisely the opposite movement of detextification. Although logically flawed, this reasoning is rhetorically strong: somehow the deeply ingrained proposition in biblical scholarship—there is some "Greek text" from the start—has to be done justice (Introduction).

In the following section, Hurtado elaborates on what he regards as another oversimplification, namely that reading was a physically demanding activity.[233] In this section, the object of reading becomes historicized or concretized. He deals with features of the scroll book such as *scriptio continua*, how columns were formed, and the Roman-era educational process of learning to read. He continues,

> Moreover, just as those intending to read a text publicly today do, people in the ancient setting who read a text aloud for a group did not approach the task 'cold,' trying to read it without first acquainting themselves with the text so that it could be read smoothly, with appropriate pauses, emphases and intonation.[234]

According to advocates of performance criticism, the awkwardness of the scroll book should explain a general practice of the memorization of texts. Hurtado argues that this presupposition is not valid per se. The present-day reader should not impose his own reading habits or should not project his own acquaintance with the standard text area upon ancient readers.

This practice of reading urges him to comment on memorization. He does so in a footnote: "this preparation to read literary texts out to a group did not typically involve memorisation, but instead a familiarisation with the text so that it could be read out competently."[235] Although this remark is an addition to the main argument of the paper, it remains a loose end. It prompts the questions: How does "reading out competently" relate to "public reading" and/or "oral performance"? What are the possible differences between reading in silence and solitude and this kind of reading? How does composition regarding reading out differ from reading in silence and solitude? One of the consequences is that Hurtado does not elaborate on research on memorization and memory; for that reason, he cannot penetrate the dimension of mindsets and how thoughts are structured. He acknowledges fundamental differences between the format, that is, scroll book and printed leaf book (product). Nonetheless, the process of "reading" is one and the same. So, from correcting one oversimplification on the part of performance criticism, we end with one on his side: the "reading" and the

---

233. Hurtado, "Oral Fixation," 327.
234. Hurtado, "Oral Fixation," 330.
235. Hurtado, "Oral Fixation," 329, note 4.

process of coming to understand there-and-then-by-them is the same as ours; there is no differentiation between media and mindsets.

Subsequently, Hurtado proceeds to a third oversimplification, namely estimates of rates of literacy as a reason to minimize the role of literacy.[236] This point has been critically engaged by Iverson in his article.[237] Once again Hurtado's reasoning commences with a view close to the performance critics: "We may grant that it seems broadly correct that probably only a minority (perhaps a small minority) of the total population of the Empire were able to read easily and fluently, or at least able to read the more demanding literary texts with ease."[238] After acknowledging that only a (small) minority were literate,[239] Hurtado urges us, however, to avoid oversimplification of the historical situation. He points to several recent studies of education in the Roman imperial era[240] and, in particular, in the city of Pompeii.[241] He summarizes them as follows: "[T]he period actually seems to have been one of comparatively wider and greater literacy than any time before it, and probably greater than in the subsequent medieval period as well, even if the majority of the Roman-era population may have been functionally illiterate."[242] At the end of this section, he turns to Wayne Meeks and his description of the typical member of the Pauline communities, commenting that

> This seems to me a rough fit with the sort of individuals depicted in the Pompeii paintings, the sort of people who would have, or

236. Hurtado, "Oral Fixation," 330.

237. Iverson, "Oral Corrective," 189-92.

238. Hurtado, "Oral Fixation," 330.

239. This statement casts light on our previous questions on the value he assigns to the quantity ("many thousands" as indicating large) and why this could not be a sign of sparsity.

240. Morgan, *Literate Education*; Cribiori, *Gymnastics of the Mind*.

241. Franklin, "Literacy"; Milnor, "Literary Literacy"; Bowman and Thomas, "Vindolanda 1985"; Bowman, "New Texts." A subsequent argument of Hurtado in favor of a more widespread literacy is based on findings in Pompeii. First, an argument on quantity is again given, that is, the evidence of around 11,000 pieces of writing (331). Second, in terms of degree, widespread literacy is suggested by graffiti as found in Pompeii. These findings indicate that various sub-elites such as prostitutes, lower-class workmen and others were capable of reading and also some level of writing in Pompeii. He proceeds by highlighting the study of graffiti from Smyrna in ancient Greece by Bagnall, *Everyday Writing*. He concludes that, despite a minority that was able to read and write, the use of written language was not limited to a small high-status group. Writing was ubiquitous and several social strata were deploying writing in some fashion. Also, paintings as found in Pompeii support this view. "These paintings suggest that people of sub-elite levels prized abilities to read and write, including, so they claimed, the ability to read what looks like literary texts" ("Oral Fixation," 331).

242. Hurtado, "Oral Fixation," 331.

want to acquire, a reading ability to advance themselves. Such individuals (probably not as rare as some have assumed) who embraced Christian faith would also have been able to read out texts to the Christian gatherings of which they were a part.[243]

This line of thought contains some unexplained leaps. From the general view that a majority of the Roman-era population was functionally illiterate, via an implicit interpretation of findings, graffiti, and persons depicted in paintings found in Pompeii, and the depiction of urban Christians by Wayne Meeks, he deduces the literate emancipation of the first urban Christians. Finally, Hurtado draws the conclusion of "widespread literacy" in the Roman era.[244]

In his response, Iverson criticizes this unsubstantiated claim of "widespread literacy," observing that "[u]nfortunately, Hurtado does not define what he means by 'literacy.'"[245] Iverson turns to the definition of "literacy" by Michael Macdonald: a society is literate when reading and writing has become essential to its functioning, independent of the majority who possibly do not possess the skills to read and write in any advanced manner.[246] Iverson concludes, "In this respect, it is legitimate to describe Rome as a literate society, despite the fact that the majority of individuals would have been incapable of reading or writing texts similar to those found in the biblical literature."[247] In this manner, he makes clear that Hurtado does not provide accurate definitions of "literacy" and "widespread literacy." So, despite his initial confirmation of low literacy rates, Hurtado presents, in the end, a view of a widespread ability among early Christians to read written documents.

After these three oversimplifications, Hurtado proceeds by thematizing two more problems. The first he defines as "the confusion of the reading of texts to groups with the actions of orators and/or actors." He refers to visual evidence to confirm the clear difference between poets and "orators." Poets are visibly reading manuscripts out loud to small groups of people. In his depiction, the emphasis is on the activity of reading (which might be characterised as the familiar eye to text area experience). The orators are depicted, however, with closed rolls in one hand and gesturing with the other. The emphasis is on sensorial experiences which are more in line with the theatre (which might be characterised as body-to-body communication). The relation between poets and orators is not elaborated. The outcome of his

243. Meeks, *First Urban Christians*.
244. Hurtado, "Oral Fixation," 334.
245. Iverson, "Oral Corrective," 189.
246. Macdonald, "Literacy," 50.
247. Iverson, "Oral Corrective," 191.

reasoning is dichotomous: either one is a lector dependent on text/reading literature or poems aloud or one is an orator without text/speaking freely and gesticulating abundantly. We see this more clearly in his final response to Iverson:

> So ... I also hope now that scholarly discussion of 'orality' and 'textuality' in early Christianity can proceed on a more informed basis and with due recognition that we need to take full account of various activities without confusing them: strictly oral performances (for example, preaching), the 'performance' of written texts (reading aloud to groups), and the place of reading and study of texts as well.[248]

In this categorization of activities, the first is constituted by "performance" and does not touch on the nature of the New Testament as "text," the second and third are dependent on "text." Instead of tentatively exploring continua between "text" and "oral performance," Hurtado creates a clear-cut and simple dichotomy between them. It takes the shape of "text" versus "textless oral performance."

Iverson reacts to this mutually exclusive categorization: "Though this assertion seems straightforward, Hurtado provides no specific examples nor does he interact with the performance literature."[249] Iverson himself provides several examples of cross-fertilisation between different kinds of performances. First, he affirms the instances in which Quintilian (*Inst.* 11.3.182–84) and Cicero (*De Or.* 3.59.220) openly refute the influence of theatrical arts on oratory to provide also several examples to the contrary.[250] As a result, Iverson concludes as follows:

> To posit that early Christian communities in various regions were somehow insulated from the delivery and performative practices in the wider cultural area—either Greco-Roman or Jewish—or that they adopted a uniform model of scripture reading ignores the diverse performative winds blowing from various quarters within the Empire.[251]

So instead of affirming the simple and rigid dichotomy of Hurtado, Iverson calls us to take heed of diversity in performances.

---

248. Hurtado, "Correcting Iverson's," 206.

249. Iverson, "Oral Corrective," 193.

250. These examples include Demosthenes (Quintilian, *Inst.* 11.3.7), Cicero as described by others (Macr., *Sat.* 3.14.12; Plutarch, *Cic.* 5.3), Quintus Hortensius (*Val. Max.* 8.10.2), and Pliny the Younger (*Ep.* 9.34).

251. Iverson, "Oral Corrective," 197–98.

The other problem in the agenda of performance criticism, according to Hurtado, is the framing of "dictation": "Finally, we should note the confusion over the use of dictation, as if this amounted to *composition* of texts in 'performance'" (emphasis original). Disturbingly, the emphasis in this section is not on dictation but on composition. Contrary to the rejected assumption that dictation "amounted to *composition* of texts in 'performance,'" he frames this practice as "a step in *writing*" (emphasis mine). Subsequently, a detailed depiction of the process of "dictation"—what one would be inclined to frame as or at least relate to "composition"—follows:

> This involved speaking thoughts, which were taken down by a secretary, after which the author worked up a complete draft of the poem, speech, letter or treatise. This draft might be read out to a circle of acquaintance for comments (*recitatio*), after which a final draft would be made for delivery/performance (for example, an oration) and/or for circulation (for example, poetry, prose writings).

The process starts with the spoken word ("speaking thoughts"), but aims at ("by a secretary") and is perfected in the written word ("the author worked up a complete draft"). No real attention is paid to this apparent first phase. Questions arise as to why "the author" does not skip this technically non-logical and superfluous dictation phase—especially when thinking through the contemporary material aspect that rewriting would be factually writing oneself anew—and directly write and rewrite themselves, and whether there might be a difference between the mindset behind "speaking thought" and composing autonomous text. This neglect of the spoken word becomes clear once more in a subsequent conclusion: "But such a 'performance' of a speech or poem involved the oral presentation of *the previously written text*" (emphasis original).[252] In his italicized phrase, we recognize again a clear hierarchy or the given dominance of "text" (singular, articulate, italics).

In the next section, Hurtado turns to another feature characteristic of early Christian manuscripts, namely, *nomina sacra*. Because of the distinctive way in which they were written down, these words formed a visual expression of piety.[253] The phenomenon is already present in the earliest Christian manuscripts. "My point here is that, along with an appreciation for oral/aural phenomena, the *nomina sacra* show a surprising early physical and visual dimension to texts in manuscript form in early Christianity." Since they cannot be vocalized, *nomina sacra* emphasize the visual dimension for those who related to the manuscripts as artefacts themselves by

252. Hurtado, "Oral Fixation," 335.
253. Hurtado, "Oral Fixation," 337.

reading. Rightly, he draws attention to this phenomenon—which does not become visible in the standard versions with which the biblical scholar is acquainted. On this basis, however, he suggests that from the beginning the visual dimension of the written word was prevalent.[254]

A following argument is based on the presence of aids to reading in copied manuscripts. These aids originate from even earlier times. So specific attention to the act of reading is rooted deeply in the beginnings of Christianity. This format as predominant in Roman-era literature has led him in an earlier publication to argue "that the use of readers' aids in Christian biblical manuscripts was intended to enable a wider spectrum of people to read them, including readers of sub-elite social levels."[255] These aids would have facilitated and unintentionally promoted the spread of "reading." The implication is that "readers' aids" in ancient manuscripts enhanced "reading." The notion of "reading" is not explicated or explained here. Therefore operationally, it will be framed as the way of "reading" with which we are familiar here-and-now. As a result, our understanding of the text has to be identical with the one of the intended addressees.

We can conclude that the argument of Hurtado is distinctive from Werner Kelber, Paul Achtemeier, Joanna Dewey, Casey Davis, and David Rhoads. They made a turn from process to product. Hurtado projects the product ("the *text*") firmly and openly into the historical situation there-and-then-to-them.[256] For him, text is the unquestioned and ultimate starting-point of all research. In this respect, the close of his article is illustrative:

> As was the case for other Roman-era authors, NT writers often (typically?) composed their texts with a view to them being read aloud to groups and experienced aurally. But NT texts are the products of authors who wrote for readers and for those who would hear their texts read out.[257]

Throughout his article, Hurtado explicitly uses vocabulary from the literacy matrix, such as "text," "author," "reading," "reader, "writings," and "to write."

---

254. In the first and last quotation, "manuscript" is not equated with "text"—c.f., "manuscripts of Christian texts" and "texts in manuscript form in early Christianity." Hurtado creates a distinction between historical artefacts, i.e., manuscripts and *texts*. Text as *freischwebendes* or extra-historical thought is not as susceptible to historicization as manuscripts are. Later, we will pay explicit attention to this feature in his reasoning. On the *nomina sacra*, see further Hurtado, *Earliest Christian Artifacts*, 95–134.

255. Hurtado, "Manuscripts," 49–62; Hurtado, "Earliest Christian Manuscripts," 179–92.

256. Paraphrasing a famous biblical passage, one can say: "In the beginning was the text."

257. Hurtado, "Oral Fixation," 340.

These concepts do not in any way gain historical depth. In this final recapitulation, he defines—without argument—the creators of what is now perceived as the New Testament as "writers," frames the end of the process of composition as "text" and objectifies the New Testament documents as free-floating "products of authors who wrote." The outcome of his polemical treatise of performance criticism is fixed from the start. Unfortunately, remarks such as "with a view to them being read aloud to groups and experienced aurally" and "those who would hear their texts read out" remain empty epithets. They give the impression that he has listened to his opponents, but this fixed-ness of "text" from the start will not only preclude any fruition of insights from the debate within performance criticism but more so will prevent any change taking place in the conceptualizations and practice of biblical scholarship. We are confronted—more clearly than in the other studies discussed in this Chapter—with an encompassing circular system of thought: when we begin with "text" in our own participatory realm of history (physical artefact) and on our level of text (concept) and we do so without explication, we will not only conclude with this situation there-and-then but we will also stay, operationally speaking, in this situation here-and-now. One could argue that a central and unquestioned pillar of biblical scholarship seems to be at stake, that is, "text" and, as a result, the "biblical text." Despite acknowledging on the level of his text that these documents were "written to be read out," "orally delivered," and "composed their texts with a view to them being read aloud," he implicitly declares them to be *text*, that is, our perception of, engagement with, or understanding of them cannot be influenced by the originally intended media functioning.

GLENN HOLLAND: "DELIVERY! DELIVERY! DELIVERY!"

In 2016, Glenn Holland published, in the volume *Paul and Ancient Rhetoric: Theory and Practice in the Hellenistic Context*, his article "'Delivery, Delivery, Delivery': Accounting for Performance in the Rhetoric of Paul's Letters."[258] He commences by emphasizing that in either Greek or Roman rhetoric "delivery—the actual performance of the speech before an audience—was among the most important aspects of the art of persuasion."[259] He refers to the story about Demosthenes. When somebody asked him what is most important in rhetoric, he responded by exclaiming three times, "Delivery! Delivery! Delivery!" By examining writings of Aelius Theon, the author of

258. Holland, "Delivery."
259. Holland, "Delivery," 119.

Rhetorica ad Herennium, and, in particular, Quintilian, Holland sets out that the attention to tone, volume, strength of voice, gestures, and movements of the body makes clear that delivery is all about the impression the orator makes on the audience. Consequently, the physical appearance of the orator should be in accordance with his status and should make him worthy of the attention given to him in oratory.[260] The impression of authenticity, regarding age, profession, social status, and so forth, was imperative: "In fact, the way a speaker presented himself through both words and personal presence was believed to embody his moral worth as a person."[261] On the other side of the coin, is the audience and the occasion. Quoting Quintilian, Holland gives illustrations in which different styles of eloquence are required, for example in speaking before the senate or the public, before various types of judges, or soldiers and farmers (*Inst.* 11.1.45).

After having dealt with delivery from the perspective of the ancient sources, he turns to the delivery of Paul's letters. In an extended footnote, he defines "performance" as "a reader giving voice to what was conveyed by the marks that made up the text in order that its contents could be heard and understood by others." In that same footnote, he denies, with a reference to the article by Larry Hurtado (see before), more theatrical framings of the event and underscores that the task of the reader was not "to do anything other than convey a letter's sense and content to an audience."[262] Although preferring "performance" over "reading" or "reading aloud" because of the emphasis on the oral/aural nature of the communicative act, we observe a framing of the act of delivery that centres on the "sense" and "content of the letter." To this framing of the act of performance, he brings the earlier presented insights from ancient Greek and Roman sources. By reading the letter aloud, the reader spoke to the congregation "as Paul." Holland stresses the fact that the apostle was dependent for the effectiveness of the delivery on the one who was reading. As a result, "the persona of the reader would affect the way the letter was heard and understood by its audience, either for good or for bad."[263] On the basis of the strong conviction in ancient rhetoric that the delivery itself was decisive, he expresses an interesting question: "[I]f Paul's rhetoric was conveyed to an audience only through the vehicle of another person reading his letters aloud, how did Paul seek to ensure that it would have its desired effect upon the audience?" Thus, What were the possibilities open to the apostle in this respect?

260. Holland, "'Delivery,'" 120.
261. Holland, "'Delivery,'" 121.
262. Holland, "'Delivery,'" 123.
263. Holland, "'Delivery,'" 124.

This vista leads to the subject of Paul as "author." Since an author always writes with a specific purpose in mind, "he [Paul] had to deal with the nature of communication via letter read aloud by an intermediary who would help determine through performance how the contents of the letter—and Paul himself—would be (re)presented to its audience."[264] In this expressing the idea that Holland does not seem to see or envisage any active role for the emissary in terms of being instructed on the nature of how they might carry out the delivery or in what ways they might embody the apostle, but the weight seems to be placed firmly on Paul's writing capacities to see his intentions realised. Subsequently, Holland adds that the apostle would have composed with the performance in mind. What Holland does helpfully do in highlighting this, along with the observation that the composition of a letter in the first century CE was collaborative in the broadest sense, is to shift the notion of "author" for us. One should think not only of a "scribe" or "amenuensis" next to Paul as "author," but should also consider the influence of the community of addressees on the common language, assumptions, perspectives, desires, and vocabulary—"[t]his common understanding made the communication of ideas through a letter possible." Here more elaboration would be possible as to what kind of "author" and "writing" we are speaking about.

Then he hones in upon the "content" of the letter. First, he addresses the role of the letter carrier "who was in some cases presumably also the performer of the letter, [and] would often have received additional information from the writer and conveyed it to the audience to augment the letter."[265] A letter carrier could elucidate the content and, during the delivery itself, he could feel forced to react and anticipate certain reactions from his audience: "Audience members would inevitable determine the ultimate 'meaning' of what they experienced for themselves."[266] Here his argumentation takes an interesting turn, because the earlier mentioned notions of "sense," "content," and "communication of ideas" become more contextualized and/or—one could say—are losing their absolute glare. The importance of the role of the audiences leads to the argument that the texts were subject to emendations, expansions, and other forms of editorial variation by the Pauline communities themselves, because they preserved and circulated these documents. He sees this affirmed in the appearance of variant placement of parts and interpolations in Paul's letters (think of the constitution of the so-called second Letter to the Corinthians). As a consequence, the operating assumption in

---

264. Holland, "'Delivery,'" 125.
265. Holland, "'Delivery,'" 126.
266. Holland, "'Delivery,'" 127.

biblical scholarship "to understand the texts of Paul's letters as products of a long history of transmission" comes under strain. The texts of Paul's letters are only partially from his hand, because "[t]he letters are what a series of audiences have made of them." Instead of focusing on the autograph, textual criticism should do their reconstructive research against this background.[267]

His conclusion starts with the statement that our efforts to discover the intentions of Paul in his writing activities are under strain because of "the limitations of rhetoric and delivery." The texts at our disposal are transmitted versions of artefacts that emerged out of series of performances initiated by Paul and preserved by scribes, readers, and congregations. Subsequently, he states that "the most important determinant of the 'meaning' of those texts for their original audiences—their delivery in very specific circumstances by some person other than Paul—is lost to us and cannot be recreated." Contrary to a rather absolute or single meaning of the letter, he bends his thoughts into the moment(s) of delivery and how the letter would have meant in the experience of the intended addressees. However, he declares this moment to be lost for us. This thought prompts another one: "Even if those circumstances and that performance could be recreated, however, the result would only be another performance."[268] Should we be able to recreate the complexities of the historical situation, we would, he suggests, not so much re-enter that specific performance of the letter involved, but just be participants in "another performance." It would be one performance among many others, a performance with its own dynamic of appropriation because of that specific rhetorical situation.

Let us now evaluate Holland's analysis of the ancient evidence on the importance of delivery and thoughtful application thereof on the letters of Paul. Central to the ancient sources is that the event of delivery, and more precisely the quality thereof, is cardinal. Regarding the apostle and his letter writing activities, he first provides a definition of performance: instead of

267. In the following sections, Holland turns to passages in the Corinthian correspondence and the Letter to Philemon. He draws attention to aspects in the text that can be related to the dynamics of these letters being performed. For example, in 2 Cor 10.1-11, Paul is accused of being "weak" face to face but "strong" when he is away. Holland makes the case that this is not a comparison of arguments but one of physical appearance in delivery. When embodied by a skillful reader, the contents of his letter would be perceived as being much more powerful (129). Another example is based on 1 Cor 5.3-5 in which his bodily absence is overruled by his claimed spiritual presence. In the cursing of the adulterous man, it becomes especially clear that this is a strategy of the author of the letter to wield power in the actual delivery ("Delivery," 130-31). In this way, he provides some answers to the question which he earlier asked of/as to how Paul can anticipate in writing his letters his dependence on the sometimes poor quality of the performance of his letters by others than himself.

268. Holland, "'Delivery,'" 140.

acting out the letter, the emphasis is on the "conveyance" of "the content." For the effectiveness of this conveyance, Paul is dependent on those who read the letters aloud: Will their appearance and performance be perceived to be strong or weak? Holland asks the crucial question of what possibilities does Paul have in the process of writing to anticipate a possibly weak delivery. So, he depicts here a situation in which Paul is distanced from the actual delivery and becomes tightly related to the activity of writing the letter as physical artefact. As we observed, in a following comment, he speaks of the letter carrier who could also be the one who performed the letter and could have been instructed to augment the content to the actual audience in the event of delivery. Now a situation is described by Holland in which the emissary is closely related to the content of the letter in the moment of delivery; the emissary is not only reading it aloud but is also able to explain it. Paul as writer and the letter carrier as performer seem to be connected in the content of the letter, their activities, however, are seen as separated from each other. Questions come to the fore: What would happen when the letter carrier, who will deliver, is perceived as a co-worker of Paul and projected into the former depiction of the apostle caught up in the process of composing the letter? Did the letter carrier convey the content of the letter by reading aloud in order to explain and elaborate on the content or did they wholeheartedly embody the collectively prepared rhetoric for this particular congregation? In this respect, there seems to be a tension in Holland's argumentation: he commences by emphasizing that performance is only conveyance of the content and not forms of acting out; his reasoning also seems to be structured by addressing the search for the "intentions in writing" and "meaning" and "conveying" "the content" and "the communication of ideas." Although, his conclusion is that the "meaning" of "those texts for their original audiences is lost to us and cannot be recreated." In short, the purpose of Paul's writing is to convey content or meaning, but this is (unfortunately) lost to us. This raises the obvious question: Why should one (still) study these texts? There is also an interesting shift in a subsequent conclusion. Even if we could recreate the historical situation of one of the many oral performances following on from the original reading aloud of, for example, the letter to the Romans, then we would only have one more performance in the series that finally constituted the texts of the letter as we know it. Some questions and observations arise: First, why does Holland not pose the recreation of the historical circumstances of the originally intended first reading of the letter to the Romans? What value or independent position has the originally intended or primary performance as envisioned by Paul in the moment of composition—according to Holland? Second, in line with the approach of detextification, he seems to jump, in an indiscriminate and uncritical way, from the level of text to the concrete lifeworld. The first mentioned level or media is found not only in the composition of his own argumentation and the dissemination thereof as an article, but also in his reasoning that Paul wrote to communicate his ideas or convey content. The latter is indicated in the suggestion of the recreation of the historical situation in which one bodily or in real time can participate in the performance of this letter. What the present study seeks to do is locate this historically lost moment in the perspective of Paul in the very process of composition. In this way, it becomes an integral part of the way in which the apostle composed the letter, that is, Paul himself envisioned how the emissary would perform and what reaction that would evoke on the side of his audiences.

CONCLUSIONS

In this Chapter, we examined a selection of studies on Paul and the dynamics of orality. Besides the three governing questions from the Introduction, we did so according to two governing sub-questions: How do these studies relate the different matrix of a predominantly oral culture there-and-then (oral performance/public reading) to the overly familiar one in academia here-and-now (text)? What can be learned from this interplay?

More generally, we observed that most of the studies tend to be separate and explorative endeavours into this new field of research, that is, orality studies. Biblical Performance Criticism is beginning, however, to bring scholars together and to generate debate in biblical scholarship. As introduced by David Rhoads, this methodology implies that the biblical scholar too should not only read the biblical text in silence and solitude, but should experience themselves these documents as performances—similar to musicologists and dramatists. We noted also that Larry Hurtado felt urged to address what he deemed to be several oversimplifications apparent in this movement. Notwithstanding the corrective intent of his article, he underscores the *communis opinio* on the predominantly oral background of the New Testament. At the same time, he argues that "performance" should not jeopardize the position and status of the biblical text as "text." Thus, his polemical article suggests that the stakes are high.

Regarding the first governing subquestion in this Chapter, we observed that a majority of the studies elaborate in some way on the unfamiliar media culture there-and-then. In particular, two theories were valuable. First, Werner Kelber pioneered what he called *oral synthesis*. In this theory, he emphasizes a specific feature of the spoken word: it is an act of inviting the hearer to participate in this communication. Arthur Dewey echoes the theory of oral synthesis as he describes a power struggle between Paul and his opponents for *acoustic space* and argues that it is the former's intent to create an ethos of participation. So, in the present study, the dynamic of the *participation* of the intended addressees has to be decisive in the proposed grasp of the letter as oral performance there-and-then-to-them. Second, Louis Martyn enabled us to explore further the originally implied communicative process. Contrary to the letter as product, he frames his understanding in line with the intended *aural event*. Although no vocabulary from the field of orality studies was evident, he does perceive the letter from the perspective of Paul in the process of composition, who is envisioning the real-time delivery by his emissary to the specific audience. Thus Martyn highlights the aspect of *anticipation*. In line with this perspective, the other teachers in Galatia are integral to his reconstruction of the rhetorical situation. Instead of there being one or the "theology" of Galatians, Martyn argues that there must have been two "theologies" operative. Bringing both constituents together, we can conclude that *Paul anticipates a specific participation of his intended hearers in the aural event of delivery* (the first element in the first leading question).

Botha forced us to make a distinction between the originally intended oral performance of the letter(s) as envisioned by Paul (composition) and how the actual performance or public reading takes place ([f]actual delivery) and—once the letter started to circulate as an artefact—the reading, copying, and studying of it up until today (reception). In this way, "composition" does not become opposed to "reception," but the former includes the apostle's anticipated reception by the intended first addressees there-and-then in the aural event.

Regarding the second governing sub-question, we paid attention to the function of "text" in these studies. Joanna Dewey and David Rhoads use this concept rather indiscriminately in their reconstruction of the historical situation there-and-then. So, according to their texts, there was "text" there-and-then-to-them. Both argue, however, that the latter functioned differently from text here-and-now-to-us. Although affirming the operational distinction, we concluded that the nature of text in their argumentations is *docetic*: in view of the realm of history there-and-then, it is there (physical artefact) and not there (processing by reading in silence and solitude). Oestreich equates the letters-as-text with abstraction and the actual performance with concretization. The movement is from "text" to "oral performance." The problem is that he does not differentiate between the letter as "text" there-and-then-to-them (*textum*) and here-and-now-to-us (autonomous text). Since he relates "Paul" to "text" without further explanation, the apostle is for him "Autor"[269] of an abstracted or autonomous text. This would imply that he does not consider nor is interested in how the addressees would concretize the used concepts in their direct environment (think of the "circle" as example; see Section I.). From the perspective of the present study, we ask rhetorically whether the apostle would not have anticipated his audience's concretization. In Hurtado's article, we identified an underlying circularity in his reasoning as a whole: since "text" is a given from the start, it will constitute the conclusion. We concluded moreover that the article exhibited a systematic *textification* of the New Testament documents. These troublesome structurings of thought appear to be caused by the media muddle in biblical scholarship (Introduction).

What appears from the literature is the persistent difficulty inherent in dealing with "text" in terms of our own experience. On the level of text, one can explicate the original functioning of the letters—the gathered addressees exposed to and participating in the construal of the oral delivery by the emissary—while the functioning of these ancient documents in our own actual practice remains unchanged ("text"). The main cause of this effect is that the word "text" floats freely from the description of the realm of history there-and-then-to-them to the one here-and-now-to-us; it is constantly just there without explanation. In the Introduction, we framed this mechanism as the implicit equation of "letter" and "text." In light of this critical observation, we see first the warning of Albert Lord and Walter Ong affirmed on the difficulty of entering the rather unknown, predominantly oral universe of Paul (Chapter 1). Second, the systematic thematization of the role of "text" on the level of the text of these publications (this is the concern of the second sub-question) discloses the related kind of structuring thought on that level (Introduction).

In several instances, we witnessed this implicit equation of letter and text *in actu*. A notable illustration of this can be found in Kelber's exposition of Paul's letters. The preceding description of oral synthesis did not prevent him from equating his own way of understanding the letter as text with the understanding of the original audiences in the oral performance. In Achtemeier's article, we encountered a similar paradox in his dealing with the problem of the "visual format" of the letters. In the first part of his

269. This identification of Paul as "author" is congruent with the vocabulary used in handbooks on exegesis. When "text" is taken as a self-evident starting point, one necessarily has to speak of "author" as counterpart. For example, see Fee, *New Testament Exegesis*, 27: "Exegesis, therefore, answers the question, What did the biblical *author* mean? It has to do both with what he said (the content itself) and why he said it at any given point (the literary context). Furthermore, exegesis is primarily concerned with intentionality: What did the *author* intend his original readers to understand?" (*New Testament Exegesis*, 27; emphasis mine).

article, he historicizes extensively the way in which the letter should have functioned to the original addressees. In the second part, all of a sudden, a situation is implied in which the present-day reader themselves relate immediately to the letter in the way they are used to (text area). In this way—we concluded—this visual format becomes problematic to us—not to Paul or the emissary. From a formal treatment of the process of production there-and-then (becoming), Achtemeier turns out of the blue to the letter as product (being) in his own practice. In the study of Casey Davis, we also observed this turn. In the first part of his monograph, he emphasizes the importance of the rhetorical situation, that is, the question of to whom was the letter directed originally and what kind of situation had they been caught up in. When he finally presents his Oral Biblical Criticism, however, this whole process of production is missing. He is only concerned with identifying oral principles in the letter to the Philippians as product. Since media and mindset in the originally intended communicative process are not explicated, the givenness of text and his own highly literate state of mind determine the whole process of coming to an understanding. Once more, we witness that Davis is caught up in the actuality of the media muddle.

We conclude that the previous examples exhibit dynamics of *freischwebendes Denken*. Thought is structured away from the concrete realm of history there-and-then-to-them. We might point to Rhoads's reasoning on "performance," "composition," and "interpretation." He moves back and forth between the letter in the situation of the apostle and his own advocated practice of performing the biblical text here-and-now. Since the biblical documents as "text" form the starting point of his advocated vocalizations here-and-now, we demonstrated that in all instances his own text-based practice usurps the (possibly distinctive) processes of "performance," "composition," and "interpretation" there-and-then-to-them. We also observed this mechanism in Kelber's "oral hermeneutics." In the end, the present-day reader is still preoccupied vis-à-vis the text with the question: What does it mean?; rather than the original addressees, we ourselves, in our predominantly literate mindset, are the knowing subjects *in actu*. The communicative dynamic of anticipated participation is eclipsed. This critique does not imply that Rhoads's approach or Kelber's perspective are not enriching for our understanding of the New Testament documents, but the conviction is that differing ways of "performance," "composition," "interpretation," and "hermeneutics" deserve an explicit appraisal.

Based on these observations, we turn now to the third governing question as set out in the Introduction: Can we deepen our insight into the impact of literacy on our grasp of orality? The distinction between "production" and "product" reflects the distinction between "becoming" and "being."[270] Production describes the realm of history (inner-historical). Once the letter has reached the state of product, though it travels around unchangingly and independent of time and place—it reaches us in this state. In this way, we witness that, implicitly and unwittingly, a process of *textification* takes place. Despite explorations in the realm of history there-and-then, the documents receive on the level of text the status of "the *text*" and, as a result, their actual functioning here-and-now to the biblical scholar equates with the media of autonomous text. The dynamics of oral performance become veiled by the structuring of thought on the level of text.

There are two consequences involved. First, the only remaining dimension of the process of production that can be looked for in the product consists of an "oral overlay" (Achtemeier), "oral principles" (Davis), or "oral qualities" (Hurtado). Second, as long as the historical emergence of the letters is described, the reconstruction is directed by an unfamiliar *process*: the question of what is happening there-and-then-to-them. At the moment that the scholar themselves turn to the letter as physical artefact in front of them, the scholar relates in real time to the overly familiar *product*—What does it mean? None of the previous studies identifies or explicates this fundamental shift from describing a specific process to participating oneself in a different processing of the product. A link is missing. A leap is involved from the level of formalization to one's own actual realm of operation (Introduction). We conclude that a self-evident logic in this turn is lacking. Without any apparent specific or explicit logic in evidence, we seemingly just do it, jumping from the formal level to the operational realm. Are we confronted here with an anomaly or a cognitive dissonance in biblical scholarly practice? Is this in essence the veil of text?

---

270. This conclusion pertains also to the following studies that were researched for this Chapter, but not subsequently included: Harvey, *Listening to the Text*; Ito, "Written Torah."

3

Detextifying Paul's Letters

THE INITIAL AIM OF this Chapter is to develop further the leap encountered in the previous Chapter, from the description of the process of production there-and-then (oral performance) to the product as such and/or the latter as floating freely from there-and-then-to-them to here-and-now-to-us and back (text). This analysis is concerned to deepen our grasp of the impact of autonomous text on our typical way of understanding (third governing question). Parallel to this analysis, we can turn to how we might bring an alternative perspective, namely the approach of detextification itself. In order to make as thorough an exploration of this approach as possible, the Chapter then examines two necessary movements concerning the historicization of text, that is, textualizing history (Section A.) and historicizing text (Section B.).

To deepen our grasp of the impact of autonomous text on our typical way of understanding (third governing question), the work of John Miles Foley is highly relevant. In his online Pathways project, he draws attention to the force of ideologies, because "[t]hey short-circuit critical thinking by automatically defaulting to familiar, comfortable, pre-designated positions."[1] He states that "critical thought" is cut off by an uncritical and "familiar position." Once we are exposed in real time to the text area, this mechanism is at work:

---

1. Foley, "Ideology of the Text."

> ... how often do we stop to contemplate just what we're doing when we scan the lines and turn the pages of a book? Instead, we conventionally skip the preliminaries and get down to reading— all without giving much if any thought to precisely what we're doing. . . . In other words, reading habits trump comparative analysis of media. It's precisely because we don't pause over how texts work . . . that we're able to use them so well. Like any medium, the book and page require that we categorically ignore other realities in favour of the reality they construct and represent.[2]

Foley puts his finger on the deeply ingrained nature of our reading habits: in the participatory realm of history—in which we study the Bible in real time—one always starts with the "biblical text." This is the "familiar position." Once exposed to the text area in real time, the trained reader by habit will start (from then on) his critical processing of what it means. The functioning of text remains beyond critical awareness. So, this process in real time—that which is actually taking place beyond the level of text (right now by you regarding the current text!)—precedes formalization; we do it uncritically, it takes place in real time, it is a blind spot. One could wonder whether this situation is too obvious to be stated or, recalling the warnings by Albert Lord and Walter Ong, it is too complicated to be grasped without further systematic explication.

In the present study, we differentiate between the realm of history and the one of extra-historical thought (see Caution to the reader #1 in the Introduction). However, within the realm of history (singular) we distinguish between the realm of history here-and-now-to-us and the one there-and-then-to-them (plural). The daily practice of biblical scholarship is located in the former, whereas the original functioning of these documents belongs to the latter. As mentioned earlier, the situation in biblical scholarship is that, in a historical-critical approach, these texts prompt the search for their original historical context,[3] also—as the studies discussed in Chapter 2

---

2. Foley, "Ideology of the Text."

3. For example, see Trebilco, "Jewish Background," 359: "Any study of New Testament texts needs to be informed by an understanding of the Jewish world of the first century. Jesus and his disciples were a part of this world, many details of which feature in the texts, and the main agents of the spread of Christianity into the Gentile world were Jews who continued to see themselves as part of God's chosen people"; Gill, "The Roman Empire," 389: "Any reading of the New Testament background needs to take account of the local setting as well as the broader issues of empire"; Fee, *New Testament Exegesis,* 96: "The very nature of Scripture demands that the exegete have some skills in investigating the historical-cultural background of NT texts. The NT, after all, does not come in the form of timeless aphorisms; every text was written in a given first-century time/space framework. Indeed, the NT authors felt no need to explain what were for

demonstrate—for their original media functioning. The description of this unknown situation is categorized in the terminology as *context*. Regarding the Pauline letters, the realms of the intended oral performances are not (immediately) accessible to us through our senses. It is worth noting the contrast here with the fieldwork of Milman Parry (Chapter 1). When one is present oneself in a situation and able to critically describe the processes involved, the level of concretization and accessibility is rather high. When there is a huge gap in time, as is the case in view of the biblical documents, then the relation between presence and representation changes: these representations become more abstract and less attuned; consider, for example, the "Greek" and "Byzantine world" of which Ricoeur speaks (Introduction). The point to make is that since we, as biblical scholars, cannot be present ourselves in that realm of history there-and-then-to-them, "context" is always an abstracted form or representation of history. So, in this text-context scheme, there is a fundamental difference between "past," "representation," and "absence" (context) and "present," "physical object," and "presence" (text).

The crucial leap now is that these proposals of the "context" are available in scholarly publications ("text"). Next to these "texts" on the context, we also have—at the same time and in the same functioning—the biblical text as "text" at our disposal. So, in addition to the formal dichotomy of the text-context scheme, there is an operational similarity: "context" and "biblical text" both function to us as text. They are (uncritically) mediated on the same level of text. We can argue and state—on the level of text—that the letters were orally delivered, yet the consequences do not automatically reach beyond that level into our own daily media practice. That is to say, we are still dealing with the biblical text as text that has to be read by us. And precisely here is the turn from describing the process of production there-and-then-to-them on the level of text to participating oneself in the product here-and-now as level of text beyond that level: everything is representation. Hence we touch on one of the conclusions in Caution to the reader #1 (Introduction): in distinction to the traditional hermeneutical gap, this gap is between the uncritical operational level (presence/realm of history) and the critical realm of formalization (representation/level of text/realm of extra-historical thought). I would suggest that we touch here on the main cause of the earlier mentioned veil of text.

Besides considering the letters of Paul in terms of their original functioning there-and-then, we will approach the product in its operational matrix here-and-now as well, as part of the process of coming to understand by reading. Therefore *we propose that, contrary to the text-context scheme,*

---

them and their readers common cultural assumptions."

we are dealing solely with context.⁴ Put simply, "text" as "product" also has a context; it involves a "process" or "functioning" in our realm of history here-and-now as well (processing by reading).⁵

In the Introduction, we related our roles as readers and historians to each other. In this stance, we find a solution to both activities or roles: stating that there is solely context is similar to giving priority to the historian and the question: What is happening? For this reason, we continue by explicating two intellectual movements that enable us to detextify our understanding of the Letter to the Galatians. We will textualize the participatory realm of history here-and-now-to-us (the functioning of text) to make it subservient to our understanding of the one there-and-then-to-them (public reading or oral performance of the letter). This complex and layered stance towards the totality (*totum*) of history defines the first movement of *textualizing history* (Section A): we move from the realm of extra-historical thought into specific realms of history (A.2.), such as the realm of the Galatian converts being exposed to the emissary delivering Paul's letter, as well as the biblical scholar studying this letter in the available (scholarly) editions of the New Testament (A.1.). The second intellectual movement is related to the concrete object (*pars*) in the realm of history here-and-now-to-us, more precisely, the moment in which we turn to the letter as "text" and "our reading habits trump comparative analysis" (Foley). This movement is intended to counter the mechanism whereby the reader becomes the knowing subject *in actu* (Caution to the reader #3 and 4 in Introduction). In the present study, this second movement is called *historicizing text* (Section B). After expounding these two intellectual movements, the approach is presented

---

4. One could recognize here an aspect, which we discussed earlier, from the thinking of Jacques Derrida in his *Of Grammatology*. As indicated earlier, he argues that the typical tendency in metaphysics is to structure thought in a system of oppositions (9). In this instance, we discuss the text-context scheme as such an opposition. He proposes a new situation to think of speech in terms "of its subordination within a structure of which it will no longer be the archon." In this line of thought, he posits the *grammè* as "[a]n element, whether it is understood as media or as the irreducible atom, of the arche-synthesis, *of what one must forbid oneself to define within the system of oppositions of metaphysics*, of what consequently one should not even call experience in general, that is to say the origin of meaning in general" (*Of Grammatology*, 9, emphasis mine). So, according to Derrida, the origin of meaning is found beyond oppositional structuring. According to the approach of detextification, understanding the anticipated participation of Paul's letters is found beyond the opposition of text and context.

5. In Caution to the reader #4 (Introduction), we speak of *textification* when, intentionally or unintentionally, the New Testament documents are declared to be or exist as text as such. For that reason, we could designate the stance as described in the main text as *contextification*, that is, everything is context. This starting point or preposition enables the approach of detextification.

in an Infographic to visualize the realms of history, distinctive movements between them, and key terms in detextification (Section C).

TEXTUALIZING HISTORY

In this Section, the first intellectual movement of textualizing history will be explored more in-depth, beginning with an inquiry into the structure of this endeavour. On the one hand, the functioning of text here-and-now-to-us will be textualized (A.1.) and, on the other, oral performance or public reading there-and-then-to-them (A.2.). Later, it will become clear that this latter direction has to be pursued in two sequential phases. The logic of this repetitive procedure is related to the fact that this past realm of history has vanished. We need text and representation to approach the presupposed presence in that realm. As present-day readers, we first have to grasp the implied structure of this communicative process there-and-then-to-them in a more general way. Via this structure, we can represent presence, that is, the intended oral performance of specific passages from the Letter to the Galatians (Chapter 4).

The first phase is based on the reasoning of John Miles Foley as dealt with in Chapter 1. Instead of the common question What does it mean?, he argues that the acknowledgment of the presence of different media (plural) prompts the preliminary question How does it mean? Since in the present study, we problematize the tight relation between processing text and construing meaning by the reader ("What does it mean?"), we will use in Foley's question the verb "to function" instead of "to mean": How does it *function*? In this way, the intellectual movement of textualizing history gains more depth. In light of our stance towards the realm of history, and in terms of doing justice to it, this is a major step to make. So, by textualizing history and historicizing text, the subliminal media monopoly of (autonomously functioning) text in the socio-cultural context of academia can be hopefully overcome.

Already at this stage there is a need to step back. Several times we have used the notion of "media." On the level of text, this term is adequate and valid. However, the intellectual movement of textualizing history urges us to consistently contextualize or push concepts beyond the level of text. In this light, we can observe that the word "media" can remain to a greater degree *freischwebend* or extra-historical. Namely, there is a difference between the situation that we ourselves relate to the words "oral" and "performance" (referring to a specific media) on the level of text, and the situation to which we are ourselves exposed in terms of an actual performance of some sort—beyond the level of text. The latter experience involves all our senses in real time and takes place in a communicative situation, in which we do not relate to reality through text: we do not represent, we are present! This was expressed in the agenda of Biblical Performance Criticism (Chapter 2). The differences become even more fundamental when we realize that we ourselves relate on the level of text to the originally intended addressees who were, in their turn, familiar with this other specific media beyond that level. Thus the word "media" on the level of text and the real time experience of "media" beyond that level implies different subjects *in actu*: regarding "text," we deal with the "reader," regarding "oral performance" there-and-then with the "original addressees."[6] In the light of Foley's question, this example of textualizing "media" provides an important extension. When we locate "media" in whatever concrete and participatory realm of history, the question is extended: How does it function *to whom*?

As a following step, another presupposition has to be dealt with. We turn here to the acknowledgment that these subjects *in actu* there-and-then may know theoretically in a different way than the present-day reader. In the Introduction, we argued for a predominantly oral mindset. This illustrates the complexity of the intellectual endeavour to cross the gap in time, place, and subject *in actu* and textualize history there-and-then-to-them as adequately as possible (Introduction). As we observed in the studies by Casey Davis and Larry Hurtado amongst others (Chapter 2), the identification of "readers" there-and-then with those here-and-now led to an implicit equation of the originally intended understanding with our own understanding. In the formulation of the question, this results in another extension: How does it function to whom *in what mindset*?[7]

---

6. Now one could object that present-day readers as knowing subjects can give different interpretations. This is true. On the one hand, we see then an affirmation in the present study of the validity of textualizing history: diversity is integral to the realm of history and we need to inquire into the various distinctive interpretations given. On the other hand, since these interpretations tend to be conserved in writing, transmitted by, and available in academia in text, the readership is limited to those in the socio-cultural context of academia. The implied media entails one and the same mindset or communicative process—all these interpretations are structured by and presented at the level of text. Explicating "media" on the level of text is not the same as relating specific media to the actual participants in the implied communicative processes on their own terms—compare the original addressees of Paul in the moment of oral delivery, which is beyond the level of text, over against the present-day reading of these letters as text in silence and solitude. As a result, one has to ask more specifically: How does it function to whom?

7. Given this element, we can hear once more reminiscences of the earlier mentioned (Introduction) form-critical distinction between "epistle" and "letter" made by Deissmann: "Der Brief ist ein Stück Leben, die Epistel ist ein Erzeugnis literarischer

As observed earlier in the Theory of Metonymical or Traditional Referentiality (Chapter 1), however, the singer, as well as their audiences, are veiled in the mist of history. In this respect, "Homer" (singular)—or the original group of bards—can function as a clear example: we know so little about him (them), let alone the innumerable audiences we presuppose he (they) sang for. There is only limited ground to textualize them; both necessarily remain on a high level of abstraction. There is a difference regarding the corpus Paulinum.[8] Scholarship has devoted energy to dealing with the specificities of Paul's addressees who lived centuries later and also in different cultural contexts (Galatian, Roman converts and so on). Moreover, we can identify him as the composer. So, in situations where there is a greater degree of historical identifiability, another layer can be added to Foley's theory. We know the source behind this referentiality; it is this apostle who wants his audiences to understand in a specific way. We have to approach the intended addressees and their realm of history, therefore, from the perspective of the apostle. We can formulate the question now as follows: How does it function to whom in what mindset *from whose perspective*?

Based on this line of thinking, conclusions can be drawn regarding Paul's letters. First, we see how crucial it is not only to distinguish between the realm of extra-historical thought and the realm of history, but also to take the latter as the criterion or starting and end point (Introduction: Caution to the reader #1). Second, the extensions to the question which we have formulated hitherto, circle around the intended original addressees, that is, the specific knowing subject *in actu* (that you, as present-day reader, are not while reading the letters as text); with his body as the focal point, we can represent layers in the realm of history there-and-then-to-Paul-and-his-addressees. Through these elements, we as present-day readers can structure our understanding of how the letter originally was intended to function. Instead of a hermeneutical circle in the realm of extra-historical thought, we can follow a textualizing spiral into the realm of history involved.[9] We see that

---

Kunst" (*Licht vom Osten:*, 159). Since he framed the corpus Paulinum as letter instead of epistle, a radically different approach emerged. This distinction, however, is not a *communis opinio* anymore (see Bauer, *Paulus*, 1–8). An increasing number of contemporary Greek and Jewish letters have been studied. Contrary to Deissmann's suggestion, the results lead to the conclusion that Paul had a sophisticated *Bildung* and actually must have received some sort of epistolary training. In the present study, the value is emphasized of the fundamental differentiation between a generalized and abstracted readership (epistle) and the historically specific and originally intended addressees of these documents involved (letter).

8. For a description of differences between the letters of Paul and the genre of the gospels, see footnote 9.

9. The distinction between the realm of history and the realm of extra-historical

the more questions and dimensions addressed, the deeper one can enter the aural event there-and-then-to-them. This textualizing history will overcome to a certain extent the way in which the letters as text function to us.

Textualizing Text *Hic et Nunc pro Nobis*

We will attempt now to systematically contextualize the functioning of text here-and-now-to-us. According to the purport of the present study, we will concentrate on reading prosaic and academic texts. This section will be mainly built on the study of oral tradition, the subsequent debate on orality and literacy, and the article by Paul Ricoeur, "What Is a Text?" (see Introduction).[10]

How and to Whom: "Text" Has to Speak for Itself to the Reader

The impetus to contextualize text makes us start with an external perspective. Imagine a student in theology who is studying in the college library. He sits behind a desk with a laptop and an open book in front of him. His attention is directed towards the book. He is holding a mug of coffee in his left hand. More students are sitting (or slumping?) behind desks. This description of this imagined real-time situation can be spun out endlessly. When we try to imagine this situation, we have to disengage ourselves somehow from the words and sentences of this very text area—*hic et nunc pro tui et mei*. At the same time, we still engage this external perspective through the

---

thought, as proposed in Caution to the Reader #1 (Introduction), sheds an interesting light on the notion of "meaning." One can state that (the search for) meaning is omnipresent not only in academia but throughout our concrete lifeworld. In the Introduction, we set out the automatism embedded in text that evokes the question: "What does it mean?" Since the reader *in actu* as well as the text as actual object is necessarily singular, the outcome is also expected to be singular, that is, *the* meaning of the text. This reasoning is extra-historical in nature. In the realm of history, that is, in biblical scholarship as well as in the Christian church, a singular text can carry a plurality of meanings. More so, this plurality of meanings is openly admitted and debated. Regarding "meaning," one could argue, therefore, in line with the approach of detextification, that there is a short circuit at stake between an extra-historical presupposition (singular/being) and inner-historical experiences (plurality/becoming). We see the presupposition that meaning is singular and absolute confirmed in *Of Grammatology*. Contrary to a metaphysical system of oppositions, he posits the *grammè* as "the arche-synthesis, . . . *that is to say the origin of meaning in general*" (*Of Grammatology*, 9, emphasis mine). In this way, an apparently absolute nature is granted to "meaning" by Derrida.

10. In footnotes, we will also take into account the earlier mentioned study by Eco, *Role of the Reader*, 3–46.

previous lines in one and this same text area. An important difference is that in this external perspective our senses and imagination become (somewhat) activated automatically—we somehow see this student, hear a stifled cough, and a page being turned. Here the formal level and operational or participatory level intrude on each other and can interact; we can look over the gap between them.

Let us imagine the student again. Apparently, not much seems to happen. More so, in every library, one is cautioned and conditioned to be silent. Nothing should happen there. At least nothing that could distract or attract one's attention. From this particular silence, we can learn that someone who reads engages in a solitary activity. When reading—ideally speaking—one does not hear, see, smell, or sense anyone or anything else. This silence enables the particular activity of reading and makes clear that one is not (directly) dependent on others. We can conclude that the overly familiar kind of reading here-and-now is a solitary activity which takes place in silence. In the student who is reading, we find an obvious answer to the element of "to whom": *the actual reader*. We also find an indication or aspect of the element of "how," namely autonomously functioning text is meant and designed to be processed by reading *in silence and solitude*.[11]

When we return to the external perspective, however, we should not overlook another rather obvious constituent: we can imagine a "reader" only vis-à-vis a physical artefact of some sort. It is this thing that makes this activity possible or recognizable for us. In this way, we find another indication of how text "means" to us. The physical object—such as the book, pile of papers, or screen which is read—is necessary. So "text" cannot "mean" to us when it is not physically available in the participatory realm of history.

This observation can be deepened. The texts, with which we are familiar in academia, are composed and edited to be printed or disseminated and published. They are explicitly meant to be severed from the physical presence and guidance of the writer. In a similar way, the intended reader is abstracted from the writer in the very process of writing itself. Since writer and reader are distanced from each other in time and place, we find a reason why text has to function as a thing in the realm of history. It has to bridge the gap in time(s) and place(s) between writer and readers. As mentioned earlier, Paul Ricoeur distinguishes in his article "text" from "writing"— which he defines as "the inscription of living speech." According to him,

---

11. Self-evidently, there are situations in which biblical scholars, students and, in particular, believers read the biblical text aloud and together. The point to make is that the media of text in general is meant to be processed by the individual reader and designed so that it can be processed without the necessity of vocalization.

living speech is structured by dialogue. The act of reading is fundamentally different however:

> It does not suffice to say that reading is a dialogue with the author through his work, for the relation of the reader to the book is of a completely different nature. Dialogue is an exchange of questions and answers; there is no exchange of this sort between the writer and the reader. The writer does not respond to the reader.[12]

He elaborates on this relation between writer, reader, and book, when he describes the experience of a live encounter with the author as "a profound disruption of the peculiar relation that we have with the author in and through his work." He goes as far as claiming that a book becomes complete when the author is dead. "The author can no longer respond; it only remains to read his work."[13] The disseminated text is predestined to live a communicative life of its own. Therefore, we can formulate a partial or initial answer to the question: How does it function, to whom, in what mindset, and from whose perspective? In its own manner—distanced from living speech and dialogue—text has to speak for itself.[14]

---

12. Ricoeur, "What Is a Text?," 146.

13. Ricoeur, "What Is a Text?," 147.

14. Eco reports, regarding the tradition of structuralism and contemporary literary criticism, that "in a structuralistically oriented milieu, the idea of taking into account the role of the addressee looked like a disturbing intrusion, disquietingly jeopardizing the notion of a semiotic texture to be analysed in itself for the sake of itself" (3). We see here that he criticizes structuralism, because in this movement text is approached as an autonomous media which functions independent of writer or reader—cf., "a crystal" (4, 5). On the other hand, though, and contrary to the role of the reader, Eco mentions "the author" only a few times in his own semiotics. He argues that "to make his text communicative, the author has to assume that the ensemble of codes he relies upon is the same as that shared by the possible reader . . . supposedly able to deal interpretatively with the expressions in the same way as the author deals generatively with them" (7). Thus, the writer in his activity, that is, "the generative process," has to mirror somehow the reader, that is, "the interpretive cooperation." In general, he formulates his sentences in such a way that "the text" is the subject: "At the minimal level, every type of text explicitly selects a very general model of possible reader . . . But at the same time text *creates* the competence of its Model Reader" (7, emphasis original). We also find another perspective on how the author relates to the text. Contrary to other communicative processes (for example, closed texts) in which sender and addressee are grammatically manifested by the message—"*I* tell *you* that . . ."—he states that "as far as a text is focussed *qua* text, and especially in cases of texts conceived for a general audience (such as novels, political speeches, scientific instructions, and so on), the sender and the addressee are present in the text, not as mentioned poles of the utterance but as actantial roles of the sentence" (10). Based on Wittgenstein's *Philosophische Untersuchungen*, in which the latter speaks of "I," Eco concludes that "Wittgenstein is nothing else but a *philosophical*

In What State of Mind:
"Text" (Singular) and Texts in Real Time (Plural)

We can continue this exploratory textualization by rephrasing the question: How does text speak to the reader? In the above introduction to this Section (A. Textualizing History), we provided an exemplary textualization of "media." In a comparable way, we can look at the specific formulation of the question above. When we reason about "text" and the "reader," nobody will immediately utter complaints or objections; the usage of these nouns is common and valid. When we bend our thoughts into the realm of history and ask where this specific text or "the text" can be found, we can point to the printed letters and sentences of a text area in an opened book or as pixels on a screen in front of us. Pressing this question regarding the realm of history, there exists a problem when we argue that "text" functions as a singular. Because in the realm of history, we deal with "texts" (plural) which are printed in editions of hundreds or thousands of copies, or appear on different screens throughout the world. We touch here once more on the paradox between on the level of text and what exists beyond.

Concerning the "reader," we can offer a similar line of reasoning. We all know and somehow sense that the "reader" does not mean that there will and can only be one reader found in the world or course of history. We fill in that the singular reader on that level represents a plural or group beyond. The "reader" means everyone who can—technically speaking—read in a basic manner, notably so everywhere and every time. Furthermore, we intuitively make a distinction between a five-year-old child, who just starts to vocalize the letters of the alphabet in a children's book, and the trained academic reader. This rather trivial observation leads to an important conclusion on the functioning of text to us. On the one hand, *this specifying intellectual movement (distinguishing a five-year-old reader and an academic reader) is self-evident and part of academic training—it is critical thinking in practice.* On the other hand, *though, we could not effectively develop or even start an argument if we had to mention all the different types and levels of "readers" in all places in past and present*, when we want to argue on "reading." Vis-à-vis text, we are somehow caught up in this paradox.

We can observe this same movement when Paul Ricoeur argues that discourse is only fully meaningful in relation to the circumstantial milieu: "the return to reality is ultimately a return to this reality, which can

---

style, and his Model Reader is nothing else but his capability to cooperate to reactualize that philosophical style" (*Role of the Reader*, 11). So, according to Eco, text has to function as such and of itself.

be indicated 'around' the speakers, 'around' . . . the instance of discourse itself."[15] Thus, extra-historical or highly abstracted statements should be—in the end or as criteria—relatable to the realm of history. Therefore, on the level of text, we need to start with a presupposed basic or rough referential matrix—for example, "reader" and "text." Subsequently, we have to ask critically how far, or for how long, the implied level of abstraction is adequate and (still) in line with the realm of history; we apply the golden rule of Walter Ong (Chapter 1). In the present study, we argue that these concepts of text and reader do not suffice anymore; they hinder an adequate and accurate textualization of the original functioning of Paul's letters.

In this respect, our attention is drawn once more to the argument of Eric Havelock concerning Plato's *Republic* (Chapter 1). Regarding the Theory of Forms, we can recognize the fixed matrix of oneness, unchangingness, and being when we consider the "text" and the "reader" (singular). When we structure our thoughts in this way, we reach a high level of clarity and abstraction. When we intentionally bring our thoughts on the "text" and the "reader" into the realm of history, the inevitable plurality of handwritten, printed, or digitalized versions and distinctive forms of literacy activities represent the flux and complexity inherent in the category of becoming (realms of history). In retrospect, we recognize the ideal situation, which Plato strived for. His search for absolute truth resembles the way we, as present-day readers in academia, have been trained in essence to structure our thoughts on the level of text. We do so beyond critical awareness. In light of the Allegory of the Cave, we can say that the academically trained reader has become accustomed to looking in the clarity of sunlight—in the present study formulated as structuring thought on the level of text or in the realm of extra-historical thought. The emerging *communis opinio* and the related media muddle urges us, however, to take the hazy shadows into account because of the flickering flames of the fire in the cave. These flickering flames are the differences between a five-year-old child who just learns to identify letters written down and pronounce simple words in that way and the highly trained academician, who are both objectified as "reader" on the level of text.

Now the element of "in what state of mind" comes to the fore. Text can only mean to us in the mindset in which these singular and formal concepts do not cause cognitive problems. This mindset is governed by (levels of) abstraction. Even when we increase the focus and concretize—as we did in the previous paragraph, this level or realm is still "drawn away" [*abstrahere*] from the concrete lifeworld. Even when abstracted on the lowest

---

15. Ricoeur, "What Is a Text?," 148.

levels imaginable or made as concrete as possible, there is a fundamental transition at stake. Still we relate via the text area (level of text) and not immediately and uncritically through our senses to "reality" or the "world" around us.

From Whose Perspective: The Same for Writer and Reader

We now proceed to the element "from whose perspective." In textualizing text, the perspective is in line with the level of text. Because of training and habit, the reader should be able to take the same perspective or technical approach as the writer. Put shortly, the perspective on how (a) text means is bound to the particular state of mind which defines both writer and reader. As John Miles Foley states: "It's precisely because we don't pause over how texts work."[16]

We step back now to draw another conclusion. First, we observed the nature of the differences that come into play when thought is structured not on the level of text—that is with a free-standing and singular use of concepts such as "media," "text," "writer," and "reader"—but is structured along the parameters of the realm of history. Vis-à-vis text, the imaginary starts to play a role only when the thoughts of the reader are structured into the realm of history. This is the point to make: it is the writer who decides whether or to what extent the structuring of thought is intentionally directed towards the realm of history or remains *freischwebend*. Regarding the polemical article by Larry Hurtado, we saw that even his argumentation as a whole aims at stating the extra-historical nature of "the *text*" (see Chapter 2, Section J. Larry Hurtado: Oral Fixation and New Testament Studies?). In this respect, the perspective of the writer tends to determine that of the reader.[17] Earlier, we saw that Umberto Eco describes a similar process regarding certain poetic or narrating texts: open texts cannot be used as the reader suits, but the real-time process of interpretation is a structural element of the generative process. It is the writer who plays "upon the prerequisites of such a general process" to determine the perspective of the reader.[18]

---

16. Foley, "Ideology of the Text."

17. Of course, we should note here that historical-criticism entails the possibility to and many examples of scrutinizing the perspectives taken by writers. However, de-textification advocates this approach in a systematic manner: The perspective of every writer or every text should critically be related to the inner-historical realm.

18. Eco, *Role of the Reader*, 5.

The Inner-historical "Text" as Portal to Extra-historical Thought

We now pursue further the tension between "text" (formal, that is, as concept functioning on the level of text) and "texts" (operational, that is, functioning to us in the realm of history or our own praxis as things). What happens when text—on the level of text—is implicitly equated with the physical object of a book or pixels on a screen? The consequence is that this freestanding object in the extra-historical realm of thought functions, all at once and at the same time, as a sensorially available and inner-historical artefact; from the formal, it suddenly functions on the operational level to us. This is the mechanism behind the turn from describing the process of production to the product as such (see, Chapter 2, Section K. Conclusions). When this is indeed the case, we are dealing—in biblical scholarship as well—with a continuous and uncritical transition from "text" as singular formal concept to the numerous artefacts available. The former ("text") is part of the realm of extra-historical thought; to the latter (artefacts) we relate bodily in real time. This transition occurs all the time without explication or explanation. Since taking place beyond critical awareness, the structuring of thought on the level of text will dominate and suppress the structuring of thought in line with participation in the realm of history. This is in essence the veil of text. Ricoeur describes the usurpation of the concrete by the abstract as "the emancipation of writing" or "the birth of the text." He observes, "The emancipation of the text from the oral situation entails a veritable upheaval in the relations between language and the world."[19] When someone addresses another person, they say something about something, someone, himself, or the other: "In speech, the interlocutors are present not only to one another but also to the situation, the surroundings and the circumstantial milieu of discourse." In this situation, discourse is only meaningful regarding this "circumstantial milieu." (This is reminiscent of homeostasis as framed by Ong in Chapter 1.) Despite the mentioned intrinsic abstraction in the function of language, "namely the separation of signs from things," Ricoeur argues that all discourse is reconnected to the world: "For if we did not speak of the world, of what should we speak?" Regarding living speech—we could add *textum* and, therefore, the biblical documents—he states that spoken language turns back into the participatory realm of history, that is, the concrete lifeworld of the participants. There is an important difference or transition when autonomous text takes the place of living speech. In living speech, "the *ideal* sense of what is said turns towards the *real* reference, towards that 'about which' we speak" (emphasis original). He does not state

---

19. Ricoeur, "What Is a Text?," 147.

that text is without reference, though the act of reading is to fulfil and look for the reference; it is (inner-historically or uncritically) not self-evident anymore. This changes the nature of the referencing. The relation to the context has changed, it is not anymore necessarily the direct circumstantial milieu. Important to notice is that in the function of language in text he introduces his view on "interpretation":

> The suspense which defers the reference merely leaves the text, as it were, 'in the air', outside or without a world. . . . each text is free to enter into relation with all the other texts which come to take the place of the circumstantial reality referred to by living speech. This relation of text to text, within the effacement of the world about which we speak, engenders the quasi-world of texts or *literature*.[20]

Ricoeur makes clear that in the relation of text to text(s) we come to a specific understanding of them.[21] This understanding ("referentiality") takes place in an independent or extra-historical realm ("in the air"). According to him, interpretation is the process in which we do not allow language to refer to what is self-evidently and clearly "around" the speaker, but lingers in the ever-expanding universe of text.[22]

Especially in a "civilization of writing," the circumstantial milieu or participatory realm of history can become eclipsed by this independent realm: that is to say, "the world itself is no longer what can be shown in speaking but is reduced to a kind of 'aura' which written works unfold."[23] In this respect, he refers to the "Greek" or "Byzantine world" (see discussion

---

20. Ricoeur, "What Is a Text?," 148.

21. Despite a comment that semiotics "deal[s] with various sorts of texts," Eco focuses his attention on "verbal texts" (vii). In this focused limitation, he wants to "examine how the procedures of aesthetic manipulation of language produce the interpretative cooperation of the addressee" (*Role of the Reader*, vii). We can add that Eco distinguishes between "interpretation" as "unforeseeable" and "possible 'aberrant' decodings" as well as the earlier mentioned "cooperative interpretation" as inscribed in the generative process. In his view, the latter kind of interpretation is clearly superior to the former. Both kinds of interpretation, however, are related to "verbal texts."

22. In his semiotics, Eco attributes to the Model Reader an "intertextual competence." Next to "co-textual relations" present in "the linear text manifestation" he speaks of "contextual selections" which "are only virtually present in a given text" (19). The reader is only able to make these selections based on an "encyclopedia"—that is, "the system of codes and subcodes provided by the language in which the text is written" (17). Referring to Julia Kristeva, he concludes that "the encyclopedia also encompasses an *intertextual competence* . . .: every text refers back to previous texts" (19). In section 0.6.1.6. *Inferences by intertextual frames*, he elaborates on this aspect: "No text is read independently of the reader's experience of other texts." (*Role of the Reader*, 21).

23. Ricoeur, "What Is a Text?," 149.

in Introduction to this thesis). The independent media of text prompts its own rather abstracted relation to the "world." The inherently abstracted "world" of representation stands in opposition to the concrete lifeworld to which we relate by our senses, bodies, and primary reflexes. So—on the basis of the element "how"—the agenda of the present study urges to textualizing that the trained reader enters the formal realm or level of text via the physical object in front of him (text). In line with Ricoeur's analysis, we conclude that "text"—in how it functions here-and-now-to-us (text area)—seems to form a physically given portal to an independent realm of extra-historical thought.[24]

Hypervisuality: More Than to "See" and the "Eye"

We have moved away from the opening example of the student sitting in the library. At this stage in our textualization no imagination is involved. As we bring the image into view again, we suggested that actually nothing seems to happen: the student is reading in silence and solitude. When we zoom in, however, we can observe that something is going on: it is rapid movement of the eyes over the words and lines on the page or screen. Instead of limiting our formulation here to the "eye" as such, or defining the activity as "seeing" as such, we will spiral deeper and ask, What is happening to and by our vision when we read?

Let us start by referring to this kind of seeing as the "reading modus." Since we designated the circumstances of silence and solitude as typical,

---

24. This formulation can be seen as contradictory: How can the ultimately abstract can ever be concrete at the same time—or how can the signifier fall together with the signified? This way of structuring thought presupposes an independently existing realm of extra-historical thought. As argued before, in the present study, I see the conceptual matrix of *freischwebendes Denken* located in and determined and governed by the participatory realm of history. I use, however, for the sake of reasoning, both realms. In this respect, we can see a similar movement in Jacques Derrida's *Of Grammatology*. In the first chapter, Derrida calls for the deconstruction of the philosophy of the West or the epoch of the Logos. In deconstruction, there is also a tension. He says, "Perhaps it [the age of the sign] will never *end*. Its historical *closure* is, however, outlined" (14). In short, through his interpretation of, in particular, Nietzsche, the dominance of the Logos in a certain historical period is explicated. Subsequently, he states regarding the economy of the Logos that "it is not a question of 'rejecting' these notions; they are necessary, and, at least, nothing is conceivable for us without them" (13) and "within the closure . . . it is necessary to surround the critical concepts with a careful and thorough discourse—to mark the conditions, the media, and the limits of their effectiveness" (*Role of the Reader*, 14). One could summarize that historicizing the realm of extra-historical thought does not necessarily imply the disqualification of the use of the related thought structures of this realm.

our vision becomes disconnected and isolated from the other senses. To process text, we must exclude sensorial input from our direct context (concrete lifeworld). We have to get confined within the boundaries of the text area. This explains why words such as to "see" and the "eye" remain vague or inadequate in view of the functioning of text. "Seeing" someone walking by, a mouse running, or a photograph posted on social media is explicitly not what we mean. We come to a deeper textualization of this historical activity when we acknowledge that our sight vis-à-vis text transforms in a concentrated kind of attention. Vision transforms into *hypervisuality*: the seeing in itself becomes abstracted—that is, drawn away from the perception of the concrete lifeworld in its primary and naïve sensorial way. Once more, we find another fragment of the answer to the question: How does it function? Dichotomies like "eye"/"ear," "reading"/"hearing," or "literacy"/"aurality," "literacy"/"orality" are lacking depth in the participatory realm of history. In this study the preference is to textualize in light of the understanding that "text means by hypervisuality" or "text perceived as text area." It is not possible to explicate these terms of reference in detail on every occasion because the reading then becomes arduous. For the sake of ease of reading, when the term hypervisuality is used, the damping of all our senses is indicated, and also the daily modus of "seeing."[25] It counters imagination and vice versa. Through hypervisuality—in silence and solitude—we enter the formal realm or level of text.

Context: An Abstracted Context which Comes with "Text"

In addition to this deepening of the question of how, we must consider the elements of "to whom" and "in what state of mind." Once one is caught up in the level of text via hypervisuality, we suggest that "text" is expected to provide its own abstracted context. Similar to text in and of itself, this implied abstracted context is free-standing in nature. With text as the visible counterpart, it seems to float freely around, independent of the dimensions of time and place.

For example, let us recall the reasoning on the circle by Bernhard Oestreich (Chapter 2). Since he does not explicitly differentiate between the composition of text and the composition of oral performance, we can recognize here the presence of this abstracted context. In his reasoning, the

---

25. For an accessible introduction to hypervisuality from a neuroscientific perspective, see Wolf, *Proust and the Squid*, chapter 4, "The Beginnings of Reading Development, or Not," 82–107, and in particular the section, "What's in a Letter's Name?," 90–94.

"circle" exists as abstraction for Paul in the process of composing, as it does as particular experience of a specific circle in the concrete lifeworld of the hearers. In this way, we see that the abstraction of the "circle," as ascribed by Oestreich to Paul, can exist for the apostle because of an abstracted context inherent in autonomous text. We saw the same dynamic in the article by David Rhoads regarding the notions of "hermeneutics," "interpretation," and "composition." Since he does not explicate possible differences between these activities in the realms of history there-and-then-to-them and here-and-now-to-us, their status in his argumentation is free-floating, that is, they function in this implied and abstracted context.

We conclude that in the abstracted context which comes with text we have formulated our deepest answer to the question "How does it function?" *Via hypervisuality—in damping the everyday senses—text means in the abstracted context.* It is a small step to relate or expand this context to the ever-expanding universe of texts. More so, we stated earlier that the communicative dynamic in text and the question, What does it mean? imply that the elements of "how," "to whom," "in what state of mind" and "from whose perspective[s]" have already been filled in. In an uncritical manner, they are determined by the knowing subject *in actu*, that is, the reader. Thus, all these elements are constituted and filled in by this abstracted context. For the present study, this is a crucial observation (see also Introduction: Caution to the reader #3 and 4).

A Meta-perspective on the Perspective: Manifestation of Thought

In this process of textualizing text, attention again needs to be given to the element of "from whose perspective." Earlier, we argued that this perspective for the present-day reader is related and, more importantly, confined to the level of text. But how can we take this perspective on that perspective? A meta-perspective enables us to step back and describe this aspect in the functioning of text. We did so before in the illustration of the student of theology. This meta-perspective is located within the participatory realm of history.[26] In this way, "text" becomes textualized-text-to-us or text-

---

26. When we relate this ultimate location, in the present study, to Derrida's *Of Grammatology*, we might wonder whether or how Derrida relates his approach of deconstruction/differance to the participatory realm of history. An important line of thought is that logocentrism/phonocentrism "merges with the historical determination of the meaning of being in general as *presence*" (12). Presence organizes the related system of the Logos: "presence of the thing to the sight as *eidos*, presence as substance/essence/existence (*ousia*), temporal presence as point (*stigmè*) of the now or the moment (*nun*), . . . and so forth" (12). He consistently, therefore, denies "presence" and

functioning-on-the-level-of-text being pushed beyond that level. It is this meta-perspective that puts solid ground under our feet to ask the governing question: How does the letter (it) function, to whom, in what state of mind, and from whose perspective? In the subsequent section, it is this meta-perspective that enables us to textualize the letter also as performance there-and-then-to-them; namely, from within the realm of history.

Although we have forged (textualized) ourselves a way into the realm of history by this meta-perspective, in a certain manner this meta-perspective also represents the opposite: this textualization is still an abstraction constituted by the abstracted context. We can take this meta-perspective also on the abstracted context of autonomous text: How does the latter become sensorially attainable to us?[27] The answer seems to be simple. When we structure our thoughts on the level of text, then—sensorially speaking—they should also become visible in the text area. The "abstracted context which comes with autonomous text" is, therefore, mirrored in the text area and ripples out in the ever-expanding and ever-available universe of text(s).

'Hail Text and Abstraction!'

At this juncture, we return to the warning given to those who are highly literate in trying to relate to the rather unknown "universe of orality" (Lord and Ong, Chapter 1). We can add now the enormous difficulty of even entering the actually present and overly familiar universe of high literacy. We read all the time without any difficulty—technically speaking—but to critically reflect on and textualize what is happening in this actual process is rather a complicated and demanding intellectual labour.

The "universe of orality" is not only lost to us, but can only come into existence (or perhaps re-emerge) because of our highly developed state of mind and due to the independent media of text. So, on the one hand, we have to critically create a distance between ourselves and our participatory and overly familiar socio-cultural context of academia and on the other, this

---

speaks of the "absence of presence" or, positively, the trace of a presence (18). This represents, in a fundamental way, the deconstruction of the "totality of the ... signified" (18). This enables the "liberation of the signifier" (19). This reasoning seems, however, to be differently related to the interplay of "signifier" and "signified." In this respect, the approach of detextification prompts the question of what will happen when we push the "sign" or the "signifier" ("the signified always already functions as a signifier" [*Of Grammatology*, 7]) beyond the level of text. In other words, What happens when we detextify deconstructionism?

27. In a personal conversation, Prof. Martinus de Boer provided me with this insight.

is only possible on the level of text or because of the operational constituents of autonomous text (media) and high literacy (mindset). In short and once more: we need text to detextify (Introduction).

Subject-object Scheme and the Subject in Actu

After having paid attention to "text," we turn now to the "reader." When the reader *in actu* encounters the "reader" on the level of text, there is a tension between the realm of operation and the formal level. We can take the subject-object scheme into account here. The object (text)—which is perceived and experienced in and as text area—generates and absorbs all critical attention; the subject (reader) *in actu* remains somehow out of sight. This imbalance seems to be inherent in the scheme. Since the subject is the participating (knowing) human being, the latter's attention is directed to the "object." So, in terms of the present study, the reader (subject) is caught up in the text (object). From this, we can draw three conclusions. First, a certain hierarchy is involved: The subject *in actu* pays attention and the object receives or stands in the centre of that specific attention. At the same time though, the subject activates or realizes in real time the object as "object," or lifts it to that level of critical observation. So there is a fundamental difference between them in the participatory realm of history. On the level of text, however, the nouns "subject" and "object" are equals in form and function. In reading these concepts, they both receive the same attention, they are both in the centre of the real-time subject's attention. The reading subject *in actu* realizes the (concept of) "subject" on the level of text—note though that it then functions as an object. The dominance—or spell—of text means that the subject on the level of text persists as the lead actor in structuring our thoughts. In view of the earlier line of thought, the problem is that in the uncritical identification between the actual reader and the subject-on-the-level-of-text, the latter does not adequately represent the former: the structuring of extra-historical thought trumps or eclipses the dynamic of the realm of history.

Second, another conclusion can be drawn on the dampening of our imagination. In this scheme, the subject is framed as the "knowing subject." Since the reader feels called to come to a kind of understanding themselves—especially vis-à-vis text, in an operational way—they resemble the knowing subject *in optima forma*. Thus, one is inclined to fill in oneself in this scheme.[28] At least, this will be the case when the group of actual partic-

---

28. Here we can refer to Eco's *Role of the Reader* as an outstanding concretization of the process in which the reader (Model Reader) participates in the process of coming

ipants, to which the subject refers, automatically identify themselves as the "reader." So we witness here a clash between the "subject" in extra-historical thought and in the realm of history. Readers *in actu*, in their concrete life-world, do not (first) have to textualize their specific realm of history; they do not need any form of justification or explanation among each other: they just read—as they are trained and used to do. Since this intellectual activity is deeply and communally internalized, there is no problem conceived in that community. This critical endeavour to push both the "reader" and "subject" beyond the level of text leads to the opposing stance: we have to debate the consequences of the dominant media and mindset in biblical scholarship for how we come to understand.

In this respect, we come back to the article by Larry Hurtado (Chapter 2). He commences with juxtaposing "oral performance" with "public reading" to disqualify the first regarding the New Testament documents. Subsequently, he does not thematize possible differences between "public reading" and "reading," let alone the differing socio-cultural contexts of these practices. In the end, the element of "public" loses its value in his argumentation. The readers of his article are dealing in "public reading" with the familiar activity of "reading." We concluded that, in this structuring of thought, Hurtado funnels the original functioning of the documents into the one in which we participate ourselves all the time, and there is not even a hint of a problem in this, we are the subject!

Contrarily, the explicit differentiation between media and mindset requires that the original addressees of Paul's letters function as and need textualization as the "subject(s)"—note, in their own realm of history. Once more, we recall the effect of notions such as "performance," "interpretation," and "composition" in the article by David Rhoads (Chapter 2). Regarding the latter, he sidesteps an explicit textualization of "composing" there-and-then-to-them. Instead, he jumps to the level of text from the start of his argumentation. Subsequently, in his advocated praxis of real-time performance of these ancient documents by the biblical scholar, he takes this free-floating version of "composition" as the starting point. As a consequence, he implicitly equates "composition" on the level of text with the uncritically given media and physical artefact, that is, the available edition of the New Testament here-and-now ("text"). So, the *biblical scholar* vocalizes the

---

to understand vis-à-vis text (literature). Several aspects would also apply to the original addressees in the aural event. When we refer to "encyclopedia," we could say that collective memory is a constituent of this notion. We also point to section 0.6.1.7. "Inferences by common frames" (21–22). His description of "frames" is valuable and fitting for our purposes as well. The same applies to the section on "Forecasts and inferential walks" (*Role of the Reader*, 31–39).

documented wording. As a result, the subjects *in actu* and their mindset in the original process of composition—Paul, emissary/public reader, original addressees, and other teachers—become eclipsed and are replaced in his model and praxis by ourselves as (still) highly literate "knowing subjects" asking What does it mean?

Recapitulation

This textualization of text *hic et nunc pro nobis* will be closed by recapitulating and answering the governing question: How does (the letter as) text function to us in our predominantly literate state of mind from the perspective involved? The present-day reader is caught up in the text area of the printed or digital versions available. In this way, the reader relates to the signs, not just by seeing them but by the developed technique of hypervisuality. Since functioning as concrete and available artefact as well as concept, "text" forms the hybrid portal from the participatory realm of history here-and-now, in which the biblical scholar exists in real time, to the realm of *freischwebendes Denken*. At the moment that one passes through this portal, the basic senses by which one relates to the concrete lifeworld are dampened; in a fundamental way, thoughts are abstracted away from the participatory realm of history. The latter realm, as context, has been superseded by an abstracted context which comes with autonomous text. When one thinks in this context, thoughts become mirrored on the level of text. In the abstracted context, all the elements in textualizing history—"how," "to whom," "in what state of mind," and "from whose perspective[s]"—are already fixed and filled in. As long as the readers (and writers) of texts like these do not problematize or engage in debate on the distinctive processing of this media, self-evidently they will have the same text-related perspective and will come to an understanding themselves within the related mindset (interpretation).[29]

---

29. Regarding the textualization of the biblical text here-and-now-to-us—particularly given its functioning—one could ask about the role or phenomenon of *genre*. Historically speaking, genre as qualification emerges from nineteenth-century study of literature. The French term *genre* originates from the Latin term *genus* and means "type," "sort" or "kind." In short, when literary works or texts share specific characteristics, then they can be categorized into one of the existing genres. As characteristics, one can think of form, content, structure, literary technique, style, tone etc. Later when the Bible was studied increasingly as a collection of literary works, this approach became also current in theology. The historical-critical tradition especially has given rise to this literary approach. Instead of a strictly theological reading of a monolithically perceived holy text (singular), it became apparent that there are differences between these biblical documents (plural). One came to distinguish between sorts (genres) of

Textualizing Oral Performance *Illic et Tunc pro Eis*

We will turn now to the distinctive media culture of oral performance there-and-then-to-them. We start with the external perspective once more: we imagine the actual event in which the letter will be delivered—note that this is the perspective of Paul in the process of composition. Since we cannot relate immediately or more self-evidently to our familiar concrete life-world, we will ask questions to activate our imagination: Where does Paul locate these Galatian congregations?[30] Did his converts live in rural areas or cities? Did they come together in modest or palatial Roman houses? Did Paul envision a big gathering at one location, or would his emissary visit all these smaller communities separately? What kind(s) of gathering would be at issue? Did it resemble religious (akin to synagogal), cultic, or political meetings? How lively would it have been? He was familiar with what they did in these gatherings: was there singing, praying, admonition, teaching,

---

texts: historical narrative, law, wisdom, psalms, prophecy, apocalypse, gospel and letter. For the modern academic reader, genre is related to text(s) or literature; through genre, biblical scholars can structure their thoughts on the earlier mentioned plurality and diversity in the Bible. Thus they provide theoretical frameworks to help us study these transmitted texts. When we formulate in this way, we recognize the presented media muddle. In addition, we observe that the present-day reader (to whom) vis-à-vis text (how) is still the one who is coming to an understanding himself (in what state of mind/from whose perspective). The mental dimension—how the originally intended participants would have structured their thoughts regarding these specific sorts of documented wordings in their originally intended operational matrix (genres?)—remains eclipsed (in what state of mind). We can conclude that these "genres of texts" function in an absolute way; how the original addressees would have participated in them is not distinguished from our own (how). In this way, we can textualize genre here-and-now-to-us. We can also formulate the question: How does genre mean to the original addressees—for example, regarding the Letter to the Galatians—in their predominantly oral state of mind from the perspective of Paul? First, regarding the situation in his Galatian congregations, we presuppose that the apostle did not have a choice between different genres, such as gospel, apocalypse, letter etc. In such a situation, the custom was to compose a letter, instruct an emissary, and send that emissary to deliver in the name and spirit of Paul. To the contrary, the choice of this particular genre provided him with the means as such and the range of possibilities involved to regain influence over his former converts. Second, since the apostle wants to change the course in their communal life and regain influence over them, the literary category of genre—as applied by us to come to an appropriate understanding—is to the apostle as a means to an end. So, from this angle, we could recognize and textualize the free-standing category of "genre" in the approach of text here-and-now-to-us as "anticipated participation" there-and-then-by-Paul-in-the-process-of-composition.

30. The exact location of these "communities in Galatia" (Gal 1.1) is beyond the scope of the present study. For information, see Mitchell, *Rise of the Church, Volume 2*; Breytenbach, *Paulus und Barnabas;* the introductions to the commentaries on Galatians as discussed in Chapter 4.

reading Scripture,[31] and so forth? Would Paul have known whether these other teachers would still have been among them in the delivery of his letter? On another level, we can ask: How would Paul have anticipated the general feeling among these converts towards him? The (rather uncritical and self-evident) envisioning of the apostle prompts many questions to us: What kind of experiences would the Galatians have had with emissaries and moments of public reading as *ekklesia*? Would the delivery be a monologue or more dialogical? Since the notions of "letter," "text," and "reading" are important to the present study, we can ask regarding the implied physical artefact: Would the emissary have opened a book roll to start reading it aloud? Or—although the roll was open—would he have looked his audience in the eyes and addressed them directly, extempore to be sure to capture their attention?[32] Or did he hold the rolled-up letter in one hand, or was it even lying somewhere nearby so that he would be able to gesture with both his hands? The present study presupposes that the ultimate goal of Paul was that the emissary would captivate his audience by his bodily presence and performance; in that way, he could reach their hearts and change the course of their communal life.

By means of such questions, we come to the abstracted structure that a group of people is gathered around someone at whom their attention is directed—they are listening (and interacting); this person in the centre is addressing them by reading aloud or speaking directly to them—with the letter as physical artefact in his proximity.

How (1): The Letter as Embodiment of Paul

Let us start with the letter as physical object. The movement of textualizing history overrules the structuring of our thoughts about the letter as free-floating object or product.[33] In this way, we prevent ourselves from

---

31. In Chapter 2, we saw that Joanna Dewey disputes the role of (reading) the Jewish holy scriptures in the Pauline congregations.

32. In Chapter 2, in Section C. Botha: "Letter Writing," I explained the position taken on the possible distinction between an emphasis on free speech by and autonomy of the emissary in the actual moment of delivery, and the limitation to and guidance by the documented wording of the letter as representation of Paul's envisioned delivery.

33. In this respect, one could ask what perspective is taken, for example, by Murphy-O'Connor in his *Paul the Letter-Writer*. Especially, in the first chapter "Putting Pen to Paper," 1–41, it becomes clear that he spirals deep into the realm of history there-and-then: He describes the materials used and technical processes of production into detail. The historical validity of the information is not under dispute here. One could wonder, though, whether the focus and horizon of his book is determined by his own uncritical and self-evident relation to the letter as object or product. Thus, it appears as

jumping to our concrete lifeworld and uncritically fill in aspects or even the structure of the communicative process. In the external perspective on the oral performance there-and-then-to-them, the emissary or public reader is—technically speaking—the one who is reading. Since the latter is a means, the end is formed by the originally intended addressees. In this section, we will textualize the relation between the artefact and the latter. The previous Chapter discussed the strong probability of high rates of non-literacy.[34] The assumption seems justified that most of the Galatian converts could not read (on such a sophisticated level as the letter required, let alone on a level comparable to reading in academia). But even if this assumption were false, then those who were able to read were dependent—in the process of delivery itself—on the emissary to hear the letter in the actuality of vocalization. As mentioned earlier, the same pertains more or less to us when we are exposed to a captivating performance ourselves (a TED Talk, for example). In short, in the aural event, the original addressees were not exposed to the so-called text area (see Introduction).

This confirms the suggestion that the letters of Paul were an "aid to orality" (J. Dewey) and "composed with a view to them being read aloud to groups and experienced aurally" (Hurtado). Contrary to the functioning of autonomous text, the participants are bodily present to each other, that is, body-to-body communication (Introduction). We can fill out, from the

---

if he explains historically the production of the so-called text area and the later dealings with the created artefact. In the approach of detextification, we want to push our understanding beyond the level of the letter as object or text area. We pursue another perspective on the functioning of the letter: to textualize the reciprocity between Paul in the process of composition, on the one hand, and the intended and envisioned emissary and addressees in the process of the oral delivery thereof on the other. For this reason, the perspective of the present study can be seen as an addition to the one as found in Murphy-O'Connor, *Paul the Letter-Writer*; Stirewalt Jr., *Paul, the Letter Writer*; Richards, *Paul and First-Century Letter Writing* and Weima, *Paul the Ancient Letter Writer*.

34. Earlier, we witnessed the broad range of different kinds of literacies and, therefore, the difficulty to define "literacy" (Chapter 1). Note that in a reversed manner this is also valid for "illiteracy." In a similar vein, we can make differences between the intended audiences of Paul's letters. For example, the relation of the apostle to the intended addressees of his Letter to the Romans would have been different from the one to his Galatian converts. Not only because he never visited the communities in Rome before sending his letter, but also because we can imagine a higher level and greater spread of literacy regarding the latter. This exploration is outside the scope of the present study. Nonetheless, based on the differences between the media of oral performance there-and-then-to-them and text here-and-now-to-us (in combination with the implied mental transformations throughout the history of the West) we uphold this distinction regarding the whole collection of Paul's letters. In conclusion, we consequently juxtapose the realm of history *illic et tunc pro eis* with the one *hic et nunc pro nobis*. Therefore the proposed rates of non-literacy remain valuable for this study.

external perspective, that during the delivery one experiences the sphere and the tension: What is happening in (factions of) the group? Crucial in this dynamic is whether the emissary is listened to and gains influence. So, the one who is sent to speak in the name of Paul bodily represents the apostle as sender. Regarding the element of "how," it becomes clear that the letter means as an embodiment of Paul himself. In this way, another dimension can be added to our previous imaginative exploration via the external perspective—as envisioned by Paul: the Galatian converts were relating in the emissary to their spiritual father; Paul himself was addressing them at that moment via the body and voice of his close associate or friend they were relating to.[35] Since their attention was not usurped by the text area, we conclude that the original addressees "saw" the letter from a distance in the hands of the emissary, while the latter attempted to engage them and win their attention in his performance.

How (2): The Letter as Token

How can we deepen this broad perspective on the letter as a thing? First, when we imagine that the emissary travelled with the letter, we might deduce that he could be identified or affirmed in that role because of this specific object. Not only literally but also figuratively, the letter held what Paul wanted to say to the Galatian community as his converts. We can imagine that, before the delivery, they were anxious to know what their spiritual father had to say (From Paul's perspective asked, Were they excited and hopeful? Or anxious because they sensed trouble?). In that way, one could argue that the physical presence of the roll constituted the authority of the emissary. It functioned as a visible mark. The artefact—that which Paul had to say to them—and the emissary—who would perform it—came together in the aural event: the emissary embodied the letter in the delivery.

When reading represented a rather exclusive technology, we can textualize the element "how" in another way. The letter as written media, even if it functioned as *textum,* made non-literate addressees dependent on those who were literate. In this way, the former were faced with their lower social status (e.g., Gal 6.1).[36] So the letter could also have an intimidating effect on (a section of) the addressees. From the perspective of the letter as physical object, a similar effect is advocated by Lee A. Johnson in her article "Paul's Letters as Artifacts: The Value of the Written Text among Non-Literate

---

35. See Richards, *Paul and First-Century Letter Writing,* 13–14: "Letters were in some way a substitute for being there in person"; Funk, "The Apostolic Parousia."

36. Keith, "'In My Own Hand.'"

People."[37] She examines the use of written "texts" by non-literate cultures in the ancient world and beyond. In particular, her analysis of *defixiones*, *lamellae*, and other written magical charms makes her challenge "the long-standing devaluation of Paul's written correspondence."[38] It is her conviction that

> any supposed rhetorical disadvantage that Paul might have suffered by acting as an apostle in absentia was counteracted by the artifact of the written text that endured after the message was first delivered. Instead, one ought to imagine Paul's letters as "gifts" that would bestow a sense of worthiness on his communities... The letters were part of the culture's proclivity to endow illegible markings with the power to provoke results that spoken requests could not produce.[39]

We can broaden this textualization. The *communis opinio* is that the other teachers in Galatia were Jewish. Since reading, debating, and appealing to the Jewish holy scriptures was important to contemporary Jewish religious life, the following questions come to the fore: How had these other teachers with their Judaizing agenda used the Jewish scriptures in their performances? And how did Paul anticipate these possible Scripture proofs in the rhetoric of his opponents? But also, What role did the physical presence of written artefacts play in their performances? Consider the several instances in the letter where Paul uses the introductory formula. One can imagine that this is also an echo from the performances of these teachers: "For it is written!" This kind of appeal grants authority to those who employ it. When framed within this matrix (the letter or another form of "that which is written"), then the "letter" becomes an outward sign of power and authority.[40] For this reason, we will refer to the letter as physical artefact there-and-then-to-them as *token*.

---

37. Johnson, "Paul's Letters as Artifacts."
38. Johnson, "Paul's Letters as Artifacts," 32.
39. Johnson, "Paul's Letters as Artifacts," 33.
40. We recognize statements as found in Chapter 2 as made by Joanna Dewey in Section E.: "In a world in which most were non-literate, writing was both an instrument of power and a symbol of power" ("Textuality," 144), and by David Rhoads in Section H.: "the presence of a scroll, such as a scripture text, could serve as a symbol to enhance oral authority" (Rhoads, "Performance Criticism [Part I]," 122).

To Whom: Subject-Object Becomes Subject-Subject Scheme

When we take once again the external perspective on oral performance, we see that certain persons are together. Note that the present-day reader does not participate themselves in this event. It is in another (also represented) realm of history that this event takes place (and is textualized on that basis). It is, therefore, constituted by different participants. In this way, we can fill in the element of "to whom": in terms of coming to a certain understanding of the letter in the aural event, the Galatian converts—and possibly also these other teachers (see the discussion of Martyn and de Boer in Chapter 4)—are the subjects *in actu*; Paul anticipates them coming to a certain understanding.

When we compare this analysis with the external perspective on the functioning of text, we seem to be dealing here—contrary to the traditional scheme of an object (text) in relation to a subject (reader) –with a subject-subject scheme (emissary and gathered crowd). This communicative process is solely constituted by human beings. Contrary to the subject-object scheme, they all have to be valued as knowing subjects *in actu* or even *in interactu*. Everyone is interlinked and everything is process (becoming). In the present study, the heuristic claim is that in this communicative dynamic there is no product or object (being) comparable to text-as-known-to-us. So, when we bring the letter and a subject-subject scheme together, the implicit equation of "letter" and "product" is excluded from the start.

From Whose Perspective[s] (1): Singular Becomes Plural

After this exploration, we turn to the element of "from whose perspective." As long as the emissary succeeds in holding the attention of his audience, their thoughts will be structured in line with his perspective. We textualize the obvious when we ascribe this perspective to Paul; he is the composer of the letter; we are dealing with the rhetoric and the related agenda of the apostle. Imagining the Galatian converts gathered in the aural event, we can turn our attention to these other teachers as well—if present. Once more, it is obvious that the letter does not represent their perspective. Not without reason, they are commonly described as "opponents" and "adversaries." By their prior performances, they have gained influence over (at least a part of) these Galatian communities. In his article, Louis Martyn comments, "Paul knows that the Galatians will hear his letter with the Teachers' words still ringing in their ears, indeed with the Teachers themselves sitting in their midst, doubtless more than ready to assist them in interpreting the missive."[41] This dynamic in the aural event becomes imaginable.

Therefore, the perspective of these other teachers must have governed the concrete lifeworld of the originally intended addressees when the emissary started his delivery—as envisioned by the apostle. For the process of composition of the letter, this is of greatest importance. In line with the *communis opinio* on their Jewish background, we have to reckon that terms such as "God," "justification/rectification," "law," "to be a Jew," "Abraham," "faith," "Jesus Christ," and so forth resonated amid these Galatian converts in their performances. Paul's hearers are not *tabulae rasae*. Much is going on in their minds, bodies, and hearts: controversial loyalties, associations, feelings, and opposed opinions will cause tension in and among them. (Would Paul imagine them looking anxiously around to other [factions of] hearers or to the other teachers, if indeed they were present?) Therefore, we suggest that the perspective of his opponents comes to the fore in Paul's own perspective. As a result of this spiralling into the realm of history there-and-then, a single and unchanging structuring of thought is broken open. One perspective turns into a plurality: "from whose perspective[s]."

From Whose Perspective[s] (2): Rhetoric and Counter Rhetoric

The two competing perspectives constitutive of the oral delivery lead to the following claim: the rhetoric of these teachers must be countered by Paul's in the aural event.[42] We will refer to this dynamic as *the structure of rhetoric and counter rhetoric*. As a result, when the emissary vocalizes certain terms in the oral performance, Paul—in the process of composition—knows that

---

41. Martyn, "Events in Galatia," 161.

42. Let us presuppose that, in their turn, these teachers gained power in these Galatian communities after Paul had left. We suppose that they did so in relation to the original teaching (performances) of Paul himself. If this is the case, then the framing of these teachers will have been—partially, at least—a reframing of Paul's initial rhetoric itself. As a consequence, we can extend this reasoning further back in time. When Paul arrived in Galatia, besides introducing new themes, figures, and metaphors, he possibly reframed familiar themes in the contemporary worldview of his converts—for example, "Kurios." In the realm of history as such, we will find nobody who is a *tabula rasa* in an absolute way. So the historical rule is that what we frame here as "framing" on the level of text is in fact often (partial) reframing itself. For heuristic purposes, however, we prefer to designate the performances and rhetoric of these teachers as the starting point—"framing" and "rhetoric." As a consequence, the communicative agenda of the apostle is, therefore, understood as "reframing" and "counter rhetoric." Rightly, one could argue here that we use a higher and more self-evident level of abstraction than the participatory realm of history involved allows us to do. Given Baron Munchausen, we can pull ourselves little by little out of the mire but never fully.

his hearers will structure their understanding on those themes, in first instance and self-evidently, in line with this framing of his opponents.

As a first example of this counter rhetoric, we categorize *negative rhetoric* or *rhetoric of denial*. In the next Chapter, we will identify several examples. Here we refer only to Gal 2.16:

> Yet we know that a person is justified *not* by the works of the law but through faith in Jesus Christ. And we have come to believe in Christ Jesus, so that we might be justified by faith in Christ, and *not* by doing the works of the law, because *no* one will be justified by the works of the law (emphasis mine).

A continuously repeated thought structure in which "justification/rectification" "by (the works of) the law" is openly negated and also radically disqualified by "the faith of Christ." (διὰ/ἐκ πίστεως Ἰησοῦ Χριστοῦ). (Would Paul anticipate frowning, bafflement, anger, or relief in this moment of the delivery on the part of the hearers?) Also a *rhetoric of confusion* will be identified regarding Paul's reasoning as found in Gal 2. The apostle creates this confusion on purpose by relating fundamental propositions from the distinctive rhetorics of his opponents and himself. In this way, they short-circuit and the hearer is left in despair to be led into clarity and the truth.

In Chapter 4, we will also see more subtle forms of counter rhetoric. In deepening our understanding from the external perspective, we must reckon with the intended addressee's—or at least, a substantial part of them (Kelber)—loyalty to these teachers. Thus, we conclude that the apostle chooses not to disqualify their teaching as a whole. Conversely, he tries to subtly change or adjust the framing of his opponents on the side of his hearers. We coin this strategy as *Umdeutung* or *reframing*. An example is provided by Martinus de Boer in his commentary on Gal 2.19-21 (see Chapter 4). First, he identifies Gal 2.16a as a fixed missionary formula—"yet we know that a person is justified not by the works of the law but through faith in Jesus Christ." According to de Boer, these teachers had appealed to this formula. Paul uses the formula as well. His framing of the phrases "out of works of the law" and "out of faith" is the same as of his opponents. When it comes to "justification," however, Paul attempts to achieve an apocalyptic redefinition of it. So we have to keep in mind that at the beginning, the framing of "justification" by the other teachers is still ringing in their ears and determining their understanding (collective memory). Regarding the level of text, we should be warned: on that level we do not find indications for such a process. This is a dynamic which is in conflict with the rules of autonomous text. It is rare to read a text that starts regarding a certain term with a specific frame of reference, but later sees that very frame of reference changed without explication on the level of the text.

It is also evident that not every term, theme or reasoning in the performance has to be changed in that way. Paul will assume that his original performances (rhetoric) are also and still part of the Galatian collective memory—although in need of recall and also (partial) reframing (see Chapter 4). Certain themes or reasonings of these teachers will be valid for the apostle as well, for example, the element of "God," "circumcision," and "out of works of law."

Also, the introduction of new terms and topics can be at issue. When Paul envisions that his emissary will be introducing the audience to a new phrase, reasoning, or theme, this implies that he has to introduce and elaborate on it explicitly. So we can formulate that when a sound group is brought in without any explication or introduction, the addressees will have been familiar with a certain understanding; Paul would only need to anticipate on that framing.

In What State of Mind (1): Collective Memory

The introduction of different perspectives in the realm of history there-and-then breaks open the element "in what state of mind." The rhetorical dynamic of *Umdeutung* is constitutive of living speech and, contrariwise, not familiar in the communicative process of autonomous text—especially prosaic and academic ones. So we have to keep this subtle communicative dynamic in mind. But how can we grasp the related process of understanding by the original addressees? Can we distinguish within the realm of history there-and-then a mental context against which background this process or reframing can be textualized by us? We are in search of an alternative for the abstracted context vis-à-vis autonomous text. As a constituent of the element "in what state of mind," we can textualize this process through the implied *collective memory*[43]—as envisioned by Paul. This can be explored in line with questions such as, What had gone before? What was going on? What did they have gone through as a community/communities? How did they see themselves, as "Galatians" (for example, Gal 3.1)? How did they relate to other groups, such as "Jews," "Gentiles," or other converts in Antioch? What was their weakness or need? What was their longing? Regarding the presence and performances of these other teachers, one can ask more specifically, What had impressed the Galatian converts? What terms, themes, or arguments were still ringing in their ears (Martyn)? What role did the

---

43. For the use of this particular term, see note 94.

Jewish holy scriptures play in the performances and presences of Paul and also these teachers?[44] How did they perceive these other teachers? What was their original view of Paul? How did this view develop because of the presence of these teachers—for example, did they only reconsider Paul or was their view of him diminished? Every single word and phrase as documented in the letter was meant by the apostle to resonate with this collective memory of his Galatians audiences. In conclusion, collective memory forms the basis and matrix of the participation as anticipated by Paul.

In the second example in Chapter 4 following, we will see that this perspective will be decisive. Regarding that which is "around" the speaker (Ricoeur) in Gal 2.18–20, we can relate the specific terms "co-crucifixion" and "to die/to live" to the ritual matrix of baptism. In this way, the collective memory of the original addressees frames the phrases of the letter as encountered by the present-day reader. In this way, we start to be able to imagine, although still abstracted to a certain level, their trains of thought.

As a result, we can push our textualization of the oral performance of the letter to the Galatians further into the realm of history there-and-then-to-them. Every specific sound group makes us ask, Through what sensorial experiences and/or lasting memories could they have related to it? Regarding the Letter to the Galatians, we can think in terms of physical artefacts ("letter" as token and/or "law" as book rolls), rites ("baptism," "circumcision"), rhetorical themes ("justification," "sons of Abraham"), experiences ("receiving the Spirit of God," "living as a Jew"), specific human interactions (performances) or ways of wielding power (introductory formula: "For it is written"), thought structures (syllogism), narratives (Jesus's crucifixion, Peter's visit to Antioch) and/or figures ("Abraham," "Cephas/Peter," "Jesus Christ," "Kurios"). In collective memory and concrete thought, sensorial experiences, and for us imagination, comes to the fore.

In What State of Mind (2): Collective Memory and Synonymous and Antonymous Metonymy

In the constituent of collective memory, we can explore how the original addressees were intended to structure their thoughts. In his Theory of Referentiality, Foley explains that in traditional oral poetry meaning is negotiated by structural elements (see Chapter 1). These elements command fields

---

44. As mentioned earlier, one can deny the role of Jewish scriptures in the communal life of the Galatians (see, Chapter 2, Section E. J. Dewey: "Textuality."). However, when these documents are constitutive of the collective memory of the intended addressees, then the study by Hays, *Echoes* is of significant value.

of reference—for the intended audience—that are much larger than the passage in which they occur. They entail "the invoking of a context that is enormously larger and more echoic than the text or work itself, that brings the lifeblood of generations of poems and performances to the individual performance or text."[45] *Metonymy* involves the following mechanism: the part stands for the whole (*pars pro toto*). It forms the subliminal structure through which understanding of the audience is directed by the poet in a live performance. A contemporary example is the *pars* of "9/11" and as *totum* the matrix comprising of images of an airplane crashing into one of the Twin Towers up to the consequence of the War on Terror and fundamentalist forms of Islam. Regarding the envisioned delivery of Paul's letters, the structural elements of terms, themes, thematic matrices, reasonings, narrative fragments, rituals, logia of Jesus, echoes of the Jewish scriptures,[46]

---

45. Foley, *Immanent Art*, 7.

46. In *Echoes*, Hays introduces the notion of echo or *metalepsis*: "When a literary echo links the text in which it occurs to an earlier text, the figurative effect of the echo can lie in the unstated or suppressed (transumed) points of resonance between the two texts" (*Echoes*, 20). In the opening chapter "the Conversion of the Imagination: Scripture and Eschatology in 1 Corinthians," in his *Conversion*, he states: "Metalepsis is a rhetorical and poetic device in which one text alludes to an earlier text in a way that evokes resonances of the earlier text *beyond those explicitly cited*. The result is that the interpretation of a metalepsis requires the reader to recover unstated or suppressed correspondences between the two texts" (*Conversion*, 2) On the one hand, metalepsis is a particular form of metonymy; the *pars*, that is, the allusion or quotation, evokes the *totum*, that is, the passage from Scripture and in, therefore, the authoritative corpus as such. On the other hand, we observe that Hays argues in absolute terms such as "text," "reader," and "interpretation." His definition of metalepsis as well as his intertextual approach seems to be bound to the functioning of the documented words as "text" to the present-day reader, who is asking: What does this echo mean in this text beyond the words explicitly cited? Since the reader relates directly and solely to the words as text, the perspective of Paul's anticipated participation of the originally intended addressees in the moment of delivery seems to be virtually absent. In line with detextification, we prefer to designate these echoes, not as "texts" from the Jewish scriptures as found in the "text" of the letters, but as "sound bites" surrounded by "sound bites" in the body-to-body communication of the oral delivery. When the Jewish scriptures would have played an important role in the presence and performances of Paul himself and, therefore, in the oral performance of his letters, we have to ask: How does the apostle anticipate his addressees to relate to echoes or fragments of stories, prophecies, sayings, etc. to which he alludes from the Jewish scriptures? If they would have been already familiar with these quotations and echoes, the following questions have to be asked: By whom did they get acquainted with these scriptural words? How was it used or What kind of framing was involved? Regarding the presence of introductory formulae ("for it is written"), the question has to be asked how echoes relate to explicit quotations? Detextification implies that we do not relate the "text" as such to the "reader" as such, but that we ask how Paul envisions the "documented wording" as sound bites to affect the originally intended addressees in the moment of delivery.

and so forth, evoke in a certain way the collective memory of the intended addressees as *totum*. Much more is involved in the term to "live," or the "law," then the abstracted definition of the concept, that is, the level of text. Here we can think of the proposal of David Rhoads to locate meaning in the sensorially experienced realm of history (see Chapter 2, Section H. David Rhoads: Biblical Performance Criticism).

In light of this dynamic, Foley's theory can be expanded to *synonymy* and *antonymy*. In this way, the implied structuring of thought comes to the fore. We recognize, in this broadening of the dynamics of metonymy, the oral psychodynamic of redundancy (Chapter 1): *synonymous and antonymous metonymy*.

Given metonymy, we can frame synonymy as *pars pro parte pro toto*. A certain word, sound group, enthymeme, or theme can be replaced by another one, while leaving its framing more or less unchanged. At the same time, a synonym will not be used without a reason; it is used for a certain aspect and/or effect on the hearer. We sense in such an instance the subtleties with which Paul wants to (repeatedly) direct his hearers in the desired direction. In a similar vein, we can grasp antonymy as *pars anti partis pro toto*. The same aspect of the implied whole is used from an opposite stance. Also, here we should be aware that it will be chosen because of a specific anticipated participation on the side of the hearers. We can give some examples from Galatians. In this metonymic structuring, the theme of the "sons of Abraham" is synonymous to the "ones who are righteous" and "Jews" (the first themes are in the first instance in line with the rhetoric of the other teachers). In contrast, the latter functions as an antonym to "sinners" and "Gentiles." We start to imagine—once more compatible with the level of text—how the original addressees were intended and conditioned to understand. We can broaden the dynamic to *thematic matrices*. For example, when the emissary mentions "the law" the hearer will relate this *pars* to the matrix or *totum* of phrases such as "works of the law," "regulations of the fathers" (implying a multitude of rules governing everyday life), "to Judaize," "the faith of Abraham" (at least from the perspective of these other teachers), and the act of circumcision (Gal 2–3). Another kind of example will be provided in Chapter 4: premises and enthymemes of a singular and simple syllogistic reasoning are recalled (Gal 3.10–12). Introduced by these other teachers, Paul is forced to respond to this syllogism. The apostle only needs to mention explicit parts (major/minor terms, major/minor premises, conclusions) to let his intended addressees recall the reasoning as a whole (syllogistic structure as such). In line with the dynamic of synonymous and antonymous metonymy, we will demonstrate that this one syllogism recurs more than twenty times throughout Gal 2–3.

In this way, we may find an answer to the question how we as present-day readers can relate the explicit parts to each other—as they appear to us on the level of text. To use the content-form scheme: collective memory represents the content, whereas synonymous and antonymous metonymy structures the way thought is anticipated by Paul (form). In this way, the elements of "how," "to whom," "in what state of mind," and "from whose perspective[s]" come together in an inner-perspective on the anticipated stream of consciousness of the audience caught up in the performance.

Recapitulation

Now we attempt to answer the governing question: How does the letter (as oral performance) function to the original addressees in their predominantly oral state of mind from the perspective of Paul who is taking the perspective of the other teachers into account? The first key response from the above discussion is that in terms of this question, the letter means as dialogue or living speech. Embodied soundbites invite bodily participation on the side of the original addressees. The emissary somehow resembles the earlier exposure of the Galatian converts to these other teachers; where he now stands and speaks to them, earlier these teachers stood and addressed them more or less in a similar way (in a performance). Their presence and performances form the starting point for Paul, so his rhetoric has to counter the impact of their rhetoric (rhetoric-counter rhetoric scheme). In responding to his opponents, he wants to reach hearts and regain influence so that his spiritual children will change the course of their communal life. By metonymy, we can textualize the intended process of understanding. More precisely, the structure of synonymous and antonymous metonymy connects for us the uttered sound groups (*partes*) and the collective memory of the original addressees (*totum*).[47]

---

47. Given this external perspective, an implication is that this hoped-for change itself lays beyond the moment of delivery itself. This aim of Paul has to be projected in the moments or days following the actual performance. We can imagine debate (during and) after the oral performance, that the emissary would have conversed with individual members, etc. The relation between the actual moments of the intended delivery of the letter and this longed-for future change is found in the original addressees, or—more correctly—has to become manifest in the course of their subsequently lived lives. This sheds another light on the element of "in what state of mind." The goal is that the latter will change (in certain aspects) because of the aural event.

HISTORICIZING TEXT

The proposed approach of detextifying the letters of Paul is constituted by two intellectual movements. The first movement concentrated on the textualizing of context or the realm of history. The second movement of *historizing text* is related to the physical artefact in the realm of history here-and-now, that is, the printed or digitalized versions.

This second movement should overcome the fallacy of a technical and implicit equation in real time: historicizing text implies relating in real time to the text of the letter on the one hand, while not being caught up in the abstracted context of autonomous text on the other. This latter process gives rise to a form of abstraction which is incompatible with how Paul envisioned that his hearers would structure their thoughts. Therefore, we historicize text to be able to textualize history. The latter process takes place in two phases. The first phase has been set out in the first part of this Chapter: this textualization of oral performance *illic et tunc pro eis* was on a higher level of abstraction and provides the basic structure for the second one. This next phase—which is discussed in the following Chapter—is more concrete; it is directed towards specific passages in the letter: Every term that appears to us as on the level of text has to be located in the oral performance which is resounding in the concrete lifeworld of the intended audiences.[48] Their process of coming to understand can be textualized by the dynamic of synonymous and antonymous metonymy. This second intellectual movement is like a crowbar. It has to be applied in the actuality of reading ancient documents such as the Letter to the Galatians. We use this metaphor, because a crowbar implies the activity of forcing oneself a way into a realm that is not normally accessible. The crowbar has to be applied also to the

---

48. From a discourse analytical perspective, David Yoon also identifies and works with "elements" in his study, *Discourse Analysis*. His discourse analysis is governed by Systemic Functional Linguistics (SFL). He distinguishes three components, namely, the field (what is the discourse about?), the tenor (the interpersonal dimensions of the discourse), and the mode (the general outline of the discourse) (88–133). In the mode of discourse, he maps out a general outline by identifying the "thematic" and "prominent elements" of each section. In the next Chapter (Chapter 4), we will recognize many of his elements, such as, "faith," "law," "rectification," "Abraham," "heritage" etc. In the field of discourse, he discerns "processes," "participants," and "circumstance" (33–65). In them, we can recognize constituents of and the explicit terms as used in the approach of detextification. As becomes clear in his chapter 5, however, Yoon identifies these historical constituents on the level of the text of the letter (*Discourse Analysis*, 191–225). Without explanation, he makes the text of the letter the portal and realm of his discourse analysis; the text is granted a *freischwebende* status. In his study, he does not engage in a discussion on the role or interface of the letter functioning as oral performance/public reading/*textum* there-and-then-to-them and as autonomous text here-and-now-to-us.

abstracted context which comes with text through questions in line with the elements of "how," "to whom," "in what state of mind," and "from whose perspective[s]." The aim is not so much to answer the numerous questions, but to break the spell on us of the implied and abstracted context of the letter functioning as autonomous text to us.

INFOGRAPHIC

The previous Sections are brought together now in this Infographic. The intellectual movements of textualizing history (central framework in the middle; see, in this Chapter, Section A), historicizing text (great black arrow; see Section B), together with the key terms constitutive of both (small blue frames), and also the development of the textification of *textum* (small black arrow) are positioned to each other and/or in relation to the realms of history there-and-then-to-them and here-and-now-to-us. The concern is to provide an overview of the presented approach: the detextification of our understanding of the letters of Paul.

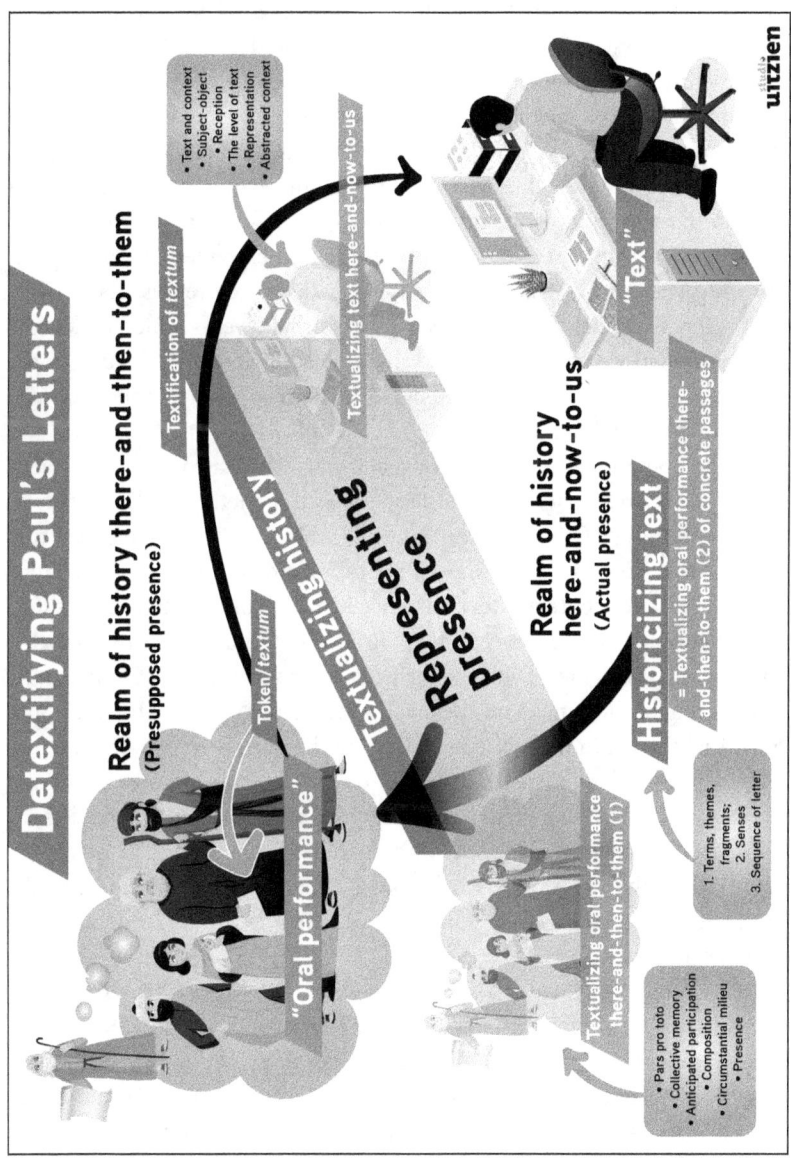

Fig. 1. Infographic to illustrate the process of detextification.

CONCLUSIONS

This Chapter focused on the implicit equation of "letter" and "text" and the related turn from production to product. The leading question was, How can we do justice to the letter as intended aural event there-and-then to the Galatian addressees in accordance with their predominantly oral state of mind, while we are trained and used to perceiving the document as "text" while looking for its meaning in a mindset formed by a predominantly literate context? To find a way out of the media muddle in biblical scholarship, the Chapter contended that we had to relate ourselves to the totality of history on the one hand, while on the other, we need to relate to the letter as artefact through our senses. Bringing these two extremely opposed positions together (extra-historical versus inner-historical; representation versus presence, and level of text versus beyond that level)—which makes the present study into an endeavour in the philosophy of biblical studies—we arrived at the intellectual movements of *textualizing history* and *historicizing text* which lead to *the detextification of Paul's letters*.

The operational dimension of reading in the related mindset—as we are taught, trained, and used to doing[49]—has to penetrate the level of text. The functioning of the text-context and subject-object schemes on that same level hinder us from doing so. Instead of a dichotomous understanding of "text" and "context," "text" also needs to be "contextualized." In short: the functioning of the "level of text" to us has to be pushed beyond that level as well. In a similar vein, we criticized the subject-object scheme: the functioning of the subject on the level of text is uncritically projected onto the actual subject in the realm of history. In this way, extra-historical structuring of thought supresses a more adequate and accurate representation of the dynamics of the concrete lifeworld. Once we grasp how the reader—as technical knowing subject *in actu*—construes meaning in their own typical mindset, the reader can step back to understand (textualize) how the originally intended knowing subjects were intended to understand in the oral performance.

We now turn to the different steps made in this Chapter to draw some more specific conclusions. First, we commenced to textualize text *hic et nunc pro nobis*. Imagining a student in theology sitting in a library, we concluded that reading takes place in silence and solitude. To the reader, text has to speak for itself ("how," "to whom"). When we are reading in real time, we become, bodily or sensorially, abstracted away. We termed this as *hypervisuality*. As an operational result of this reading modus, an implied abstracted context comes with this media. In this context, how, to whom, and in what state of mind certain concepts mean are fixed in advance ("in what state of mind," "from whose perspective"). They are constituted by the

---

49. In a similar way, the original addressees *just* participated in the construal of oral performances in their predominantly oral cultural context.

reader as knowing subject *in actu*. We concluded that in "text"—in the hybrid combination of physical artefact and concept on the level of text—we pass through the inner-historically present portal to the realm of extra-historical representation. Therefore, in the functioning of "text" to us, two realms seem to come together that cannot do so by definition. As a result, the structuring of thought on the level of text supresses or veils the dynamics of the concrete lifeworld.

This led to a major conclusion of the present study: when we—as trained readers in the socio-cultural context of academia—process the letter as autonomous text in an uncritical way, inevitably the abstracted context will govern our understanding. It is, therefore, imperative not only to be aware of this abstracted context, but also to look over the edge into the sensorially determined, circumstantial milieu in which the letter functions/-ed.

Since we give priority to the historian and subject the realm of extra-historical thought to the one of history, the question came to the fore, Where do we sensorially encounter extra-historical thoughts or this abstracted context here-and-now? When hypervisuality is restricted by the text area, the implied structuring of thought is mirrored in the text area.

The second direction in textualizing history related to oral performance there-and-then-to-them. In light of the subject-object scheme, this aural event is constituted by the emissary and his hearers as subjects *in inter-actu* ("how"/"to whom"), thus leading us to better speak of a subject-subject scheme. In this historical situation, the letter as physical artefact is perceived by the original addressees as a *token*, that is, a signal of power and authority. The addressees were not meant to be exposed to the text area as such ("how"). We combined Foley's Theory of Metonymical Referentiality with the crucial notion of *collective memory*: when Paul explicates a theme, term, metaphor, or part of a reasoning (*pars*), the intended hearers recall the implied whole (*totum*). We extended this dynamic to synonyms and antonyms. A crucial conclusion was, therefore, that synonymous and antonymous metonymy provides the mindset in which thought is construed in the moment of delivery ("in what state of mind"). Further, we noted that the presence and performances of these other teachers are crucial in this respect. In their teaching, a different perspective is operative. We argued that this perspective, or their rhetoric, governs the rhetorical situation, that is, the starting point of the aural event. Since the apostle has to undo their influence, his rhetoric is counter rhetoric ("from whose perspective[s]?" [plural]). On this basis, we textualized the final goal of the letter: by countering the influence of these adversaries, the apostle wants his addressees to change their view on and stance in their realm of history according to his will.

In view of the turn from the process of production there-and-then to the available product in front of us, we argued for the need *to historicize text*. In this second movement, we structure our understanding of the documented themes, terms, reasonings, or phrases—to which we are exposed in the moment of reading them in the text of the letter—in line with synonymous and antonymous metonymy. By continuously asking questions that connect the terms and themes (*partes*) to their collective memory (*totum*), our thoughts are bent into the implied historical situation—and the pull of thinking in line with the abstracted context is countered. Our imagination will help us to textualize their collective memory and the way in which they (are intended to) understand. We will embark now on two test cases in which we detextify passages from Gal 2–3.[50]

---

50. At the end of this Conclusion to Chapter 3, we can take a more fundamental or precise stance: when we claim that we can overcome the abstracted context which comes with text, this is relatively or gradually. Since the present study positions itself within the critical tradition and socio-cultural context of academia, it is highly indebted to the technology of reading. More so, the operational media and outcome of this particular research project is "text"—as activated by you in this very moment of reading these words on this page[!]. So the detextification of two concrete passages in Galatians as presented in the next Chapter, functions as autonomous text and comes with a necessarily abstracted context as well. The difference is that, by thematizing this given abstracted context of autonomous text, we can explicitly broaden it. The elements in the governing question push our understanding beyond the isolated level of text into the realm of history itself. In line with the golden rule of Walter Ong, we can scrutinize our abstractions on their level of concreteness. So, like Baron Munchausen, we can pull ourselves further out of the mire—but never fully. For that reason, we repeat that the proposed approach in the present study is heuristically motivated. The goal is to overcome possible confinements—notably the veil of text—and move beyond the functioning of the letter as text to us. This is what the examples in the next Chapter are concerned to demonstrate.

4

Detextification

Test Cases in Galatians 2 and 3

IN THIS CHAPTER, I will present two examples of the proposed procedure of detextifying Paul's letters: Gal 2.19–20 and 3.10–12. Both parts start with a presentation of relevant publications on the passages involved. The evaluation of these academic studies is according to the elements in the question which governs the practice of textualizing history: How does the letter function to whom, in what state of mind, and from whose perspective[s]? Attention is also paid to possible illustrations of the earlier introduced media muddle. Subsequently, we carry out a textualization of the two passages in line with the operational matrix as oral performance there-and-then-to-them.

The first example revolves around how Paul reasons. The point of departure will be formed by a *locus classicus*, Gal 3.10–12:

> For all who rely on the works of the law are under a curse; for it is written, "Cursed is everyone who does not observe and obey all the things written in the book of the law." Now it is evident that no one is justified before God by the law; for "The one who is righteous will live by faith." But the law does not rest on faith; on the contrary, "Whoever does the works of the law will live by them."

In this somewhat laborious passage, one thing is clear: Paul is reasoning. He refers three times to phrases from the Jewish holy scriptures. In the scholarly community, the nature of this reasoning is identified as syllogistic.

The two case studies will show that the coherency of this syllogistic logic, however, is not immediately evident. We will encounter free-floating and rather complicated proposals fleshed out on the level of text. In line with the proposed communicative structure of anticipated participation, we will attempt to textualize the originally intended understanding of this supposedly syllogistic reasoning. We start with this passage from Gal 3 because we will encounter traces of the underlying reasoning throughout Gal 2–3; it implies an overview of the rhetorical situation.

This will be helpful in the second example, where an exposition will be given of Gal 2.19–20:

> For through the law I died to the law, so that I might live to God. I have been crucified with Christ; and it is no longer I who live, but it is Christ who lives in me. And the life I now live in the flesh I live by faith in the Son of God, who loved me and gave himself for me.

In this somewhat mystical passage, several verbs are used referring to "dying" (3) and "living" (5). So a specific thematic matrix can be discerned. One has to look for how the intended audiences were anticipated by Paul to participate in this matrix. Radically, we will relate these terms to their sensorially based collective memory (Chapter 3). As a consequence, new light will be shed on the anticipated construal of thought at the moment of delivery.

EXAMPLE 1: HOW DOES PAUL REASON IN GAL 3.10–12?

As stated before, Gal 3.10–12 is known for its complex or laboured reasoning. In his commentary, Martinus de Boer introduces remarks on the part of the letter to which 3.10–12 belongs as follows:

> Paul's argumentation in this section resists systematization. The precise relation between the reception of the Spirit, believing, justification, and baptism into Christ remains largely inchoate and unarticulated, as does the precise relationship between promise, inheritance, descent from Abraham, and divine sonship. . . . Paul's form of argumentation here is not systematic, but associative.[1]

---

1. Boer, *Galatians*, 168.

This reading experience as described by de Boer can be explained by the mechanism of implicit equation and/or the media muddle in biblical scholarship (Introduction). Thus, we will pursue an explicit differentiation of media and mindsets or the two communicative processes involved: one in which we participate ourselves real-time (text) and one in which the original addressees were intended to participate (oral performance). First, two understandings of this passage will be reviewed.

Moisés Mayordomo: *Argumentiert Paulus logisch?*

In his monograph *Argumentiert Paulus logisch? Eine Analyse vor dem Hintergrund antiker Logik*, Moisés Mayordomo seeks to contribute to the clarification of the logic behind the reasoning of Paul.[2] His reconstruction of Gal 3.10–12 is first presented. According to his procedure of logical analysis, he begins with identifying the possible propositions in the text:[3]

| (6) | Die Nomosmenschen sind unter einem Fluch. (3.10a) | NaK[4] |
| (7) | Jeder, der nicht alle Gebote erfüllt, ist ein Verfluchter. (3.10b) | OaK |

In the first proposition, we recognize the original wording: "For all who rely on the works of the law are under a curse" (Gal 3.10a).[5] As is the case in the second: "for it is written, 'Cursed is everyone who does not observe and obey all the things written in the book of the law'" (3.10b). Given this hotly debated verse, Mayordomo argues: "*Wenn* sich die Aussage in 3.10a aus der Aussage 3.10b *logisch* herleiten soll, dann *muss* eine Zusatzprämisse hinzugedacht werden" (emphasis original).[6] He does not indicate who should supply or add this extra premise: Does he mean the original addressees caught up in the aural event or the present-day reader vis-à-vis the letter as text? "To whom"—as an element of the governing question—is not

2. Mayordomo, *Argumentiert Paulus*.
3. Mayordomo, *Argumentiert Paulus*, 151.
4. Since his attempt is governed by formal logic, Mayordomo uses *term place holders* (capitals) and *infix operators* (lowercase letters). The former designate the middle term, predicate (or major term) and subject (minor term). The latter indicate the categories of universal affirmative (a), universal negative (e), particular affirmative (i) or particular negative (o). In this particular layout, capital O refers to the middle term, N to the subject, and K involves the predicate of the conclusion. Therefore, NaK involves the conclusion, and OaK entails the major premise. As a result, the minor premise would be then implicit in this reasoning of Paul. See Blackburn, "Syllogism."
5. Unless otherwise specified, all biblical quotations are taken from the NRSV.
6. Mayordomo, *Argumentiert Paulus*, 159.

problematized. This observation is in line with the other element of "from whose perspective[s]." We get the impression that, due to the implicit equation of "letter" and "text," he himself is in the process of coming to understand vis-à-vis text. This means that the communicative process *in actu* lays beyond critical awareness.

Let us now focus more closely on the analysis of Mayordomo. First, he notices that Gal 3.10b conveys an explicit quotation (Deut 27.26). He states that, as a consequence, this proposition has to function as a Scripture proof (premise). Thus the implicit presupposition is that when "the Scripture" is used, it has the function and status of a proof. He does not explain or explicate why or how, to whom, in what state of mind or from whose perspective[s] this is the case.[7] In the ever-expanding universe of text—especially in combination with a Christian background—"Scripture" functions as the highest in ranking. This ultimate text among all other texts seems to absolutize the functioning of the media involved. Second, he identifies three terms (O, K, and N) in the two propositions which constitute Gal 3.10. In verse 10b, term K is repeated (to be cursed). Since this term is constitutive of the Scripture proof, K has to be identified as the major term. For that reason, he construes the implicit minor premise as NaO. What is important here is that this premise is not found on the level of the text in the documented wording. He subsequently does not explicate where we could locate this premise, other than it not being present on the level of text, although ideally, this should have been the case.

Mayordomo comes to the following formal reconstruction of the syllogistic reasoning in Gal 3.10 (this is the Barbara model[8]):

---

7. Peter Lampe has the same presupposition: "Ferner nimmt Wunder, inwiefern das Schriftzitat 3.12b den Vordersatz 3.12a zu *begründen* vermag. Offensichtlich soll ein *Begründung*szusammenhang hergestellt werden. Denn warum sonst zitiert Paulus in 3.12b noch einmal *autoritative* Schrift?" ("*Reticentia*," 27–28, emphasis mine). Also, as discussed in the next section, Bachmann values these quotations as "Axiome" ("Zur Argumentation," 537).

8. In this field, the types of syllogistic structures or possible forms are named. Each name indicates a particular syllogistic structure. Barbara involves the structure of AAA-1 and can be seen as the basic structure. These three capitals (A) indicate that the major premise, minor premise and conclusion are all universal affirmative. The number (1) refers to the first of four (or three) figures that provide the possible structures within syllogistic reasoning. Figure one has the following structure. Major premise: middle term—predicate; minor premise: subject—middle term; conclusion: subject—predicate. Therefore, in the layout of Mayordomo, O involves the middle term, K involves the predicate, and N entails the subject.

OaK	(7) Jeder Gesetzesübertreter ist ein Verfluchter.	(3.10b)
<u>NaO</u>	<u>Jeder Nomosmensch ist einer, der nicht alle Gebote erfüllt.</u>	
NaK	(6) Jeder Nomosmensch ist verflucht.	(3.10a)

He then identifies two problems: First, "die Frage *was* diese implizite Prämisse aussagt, ist keine Frage der Logik, sondern der Exegese" (emphasis original).[9] This implicit premise NaO causes a considerable exegetical problem. Regarding the historical or rhetorical situation, it appears to be contradictory: "Die Prämisse in V. 10, dass kein Gesetzesmensch alle Gebote erfüllt, ist gerade im Rahmen allgemeiner jüdischer Vorstellungen über den Bund und den Segen der Vergebung kaum einsichtig."[10] Second, he draws attention to the question of how the first conjunction γάρ in Gal 3.10a functions. In line with his specific procedure he has to reason:

> Wenn es in seiner vollen begründenden Funktion ernst genommen werden soll, dan würde das heißen, dass in 3.10 eine Prämisse gefunden werden muss, die einen Schluss auf 3.9 erlaubt; d.h.: 'Weil alle Gesetzesmenschen unter einem Fluch stehen, sind die Glaubensmenschen gesegnet.' Ein solcher Schluss ist nur sehr schwer zu rekonstruieren.[11]

Notwithstanding this difficulty that the premise in Gal 3.10 is lacking to affirm the conclusion as perceived by him in Gal 3.9, he presents a reconstruction (Camestres model[12]):

KaN	Alle Verfluchten sind Nomosmenschen.	(Das sagt 3.10 nicht aus!)
<u>PeN</u>	<u>Kein Glaubensmensch ist ein Nomosmensch.</u>	(vgl. 3.12a)
PeK	Kein Glaubensmensch ist verflucht.	(3.9 umgewandelt)

Mayordomo remarks that this reconstruction is implausible; in his own words: "Das sagt 3.10 nicht aus!" For him the conjunction γάρ cannot function in this way. He concludes: "Der Übergang von 6–9 zu 10–12 weist

---

9. Mayordomo, *Argumentiert Paulus*, 160.
10. Mayordomo, *Argumentiert Paulus*, 166.
11. Mayordomo, *Argumentiert Paulus*, 160.
12. This syllogism has the structure of AEO-2: The major premise is universal affirmative, the minor premise is universal negative, and the conclusion is particular negative. The second figure has the following structure. Major premise: predicate—middle term; minor premise: subject—middle term; conclusion: subject—predicate. When we compare this layout with the one of Mayordomo, his conclusion seems to be universal instead of particular negative. However, he argues that "beide Verse lässt sich in der zweiten Figur (*Camestres*) mit einer Implikation herstellen" (*Argumentiert Paulus*, 160).

logische Brüche auf,"[13] and later on: "Der Übergang von V. 9 zu V. 10 (mit dem irreführenden einleitenden γάρ in V. 10) ist nicht klar."[14] His proposal also does not explain the disturbed order, which he addresses: the major premise is located in verse 10, the minor premise in verse 12a and the conclusion should be found in verse 9.

Proceeding to Gal 3.11–12, he starts with the following presupposition: "Wieder ist das erste Schriftzitat als Prämisse zu lesen."[15] Once again—without argumentation on "how," "to whom," and "in what mindset"—the words from the Jewish scriptures (Gal 3.11b) are designated as a premise. In search of possible propositions in Gal 3.11–12, he remarks: "Die Formalisierung der beiden Sätze in V. 12 ist deswegen schwer, weil ein Mittelterm kaum auffindbar ist" (152). Five possible propositions are found by him. We notice that the propositions as phrased in lines 11a and 11b are both based on one and the same verse, Gal 3.12b:

(8)	Kein Gesetzesmensch ist ein von Gott Gerechtfertigter. (3.11a)	NeD
(9)	Der Gerecht(fertigt)e ist ein aus Glauben Lebender. (3.11b)	DaP
(10)	Kein Nomos(mensch) ist ein Glaubens(mensch). (3.12a)	NeP
(11a)	Der Nomosmensch ist ein Tatmensch. (3.12b)	NaT
(11b)	Der Tatmensch ist ein Lebender. (3.12b	TaZ

To reach a syllogistic figure, he has to rearrange lines 8, 9 and 10 as 9, 10 and 8 (Camestres):

DaP	(9)	Der Gerechtfertigte ist ein Glaubensmensch.	(11b)
NeP	(10)	Kein Nomosmensch ist ein Glaubensmensch	(vgl. 12a)
NeD	(8)	Kein Nomosmensch ist ein Gerechtfertigter.	(11a)

In a way, Mayordomo feels forced to rearrange the originally documented sequence of verses. Line 11a and 11b—which are both paraphrases of Gal 3.12b—do not fit in this reconstruction. He states: "Die Funktion von 12b ist nicht ganz deutlich." While not elaborating on this obscurity as such, he turns to other scholars and how they understand this verse: "Gerne wird das Zitat als direkte Begründung von 12a gelesen." Thus, this apparent quotation from Scripture is in general conceived as a proof and, therefore, premise for syllogistic reasoning. Contrary to his earlier approach to Deut 27.26 (Gal 3.10b), he argues now—remarkably regarding Gal 3.12b—against this

13. Mayordomo, *Argumentiert Paulus*, 161.
14. Mayordomo, *Argumentiert Paulus*, 165.
15. Mayordomo, *Argumentiert Paulus*, 152.

presupposition: "Dagegen dürfte aber der Anschluss mit ἀλλά (statt γάρ oder ὅτι) sprechen." He draws the following implicit conclusion: Paul's use of this adversative (ἀλλά) instead of causal conjunction (γάρ/ὅτι) excludes the possibility or—at least—plausibility that Gal 3.12b can function as a premise. Asking the relevant parts of the governing question—to whom and from whose perspective does it function?—clarifies the free-floating nature of Mayordomo's line of reasoning. He himself, as reading subject vis-à-vis text here-and-now in academia, attempts to construe a fitting syllogism on the level of text. He continues,

> Das Schriftzitat aus Lev 18.5 [as found in Gal 3.12b] kann vielmehr als 'Definition' dessen verstanden werden, was einen 'Nomosmenschen' ausmacht... Offenbar möchte die Argumentation darauf hinaus, Tun (12b) und Glauben (11b) streng als zwei 'Lebenswege' voneinander zu trennen. Logisch lässt sich jedoch daraus nichts ableiten.

Since these considerations are exegetical in nature, they exceed his original agenda of a strictly logical analysis. Notwithstanding his rejection of Gal 3.12b as premise, his agenda apparently compels him to construe a syllogistic structure. As a result, he concludes "dass hier die logische Analyse an ihre Grenzen gelangt":[16]

TeP		Kein Tatmensch ist ein Glaubensmensch.	(unde?)
NaT	(11a)	Jeder Nomosmensch ist ein Tatmensch.	(3.12b)
NeP	(10)	Kein Nomosmensch ist ein Glaubensmensch.	(12a)

Necessarily, this major premise has to be implied by him in line with his analytical approach. It leads to a separation between "doing" and "believing." He has to conclude, "Die strikte Trennung in V. 12 von Tun und Glauben wird nirgends begründet."

The paraphrase of verse 11b on the one who will live (for example, line 9 "aus Glauben Lebender") has not been integrated in this syllogistic reconstruction of Gal 3.12b. Presupposed by his own agenda, however, all the terms and phrases should have fallen into place. These reconstructions uncover, according to himself, a problematic reasoning: "Nach meiner Wahrnehmung 'rettet' das Kerygma die Argumentation dort, wo sie am schwächsten wird, bzw. wo sie nicht weiter begründet werden kann: Handeln und Glauben sind zwei unterschiedliche Prinzipien."

---

16. Mayordomo, *Argumentiert Paulus*, 161.

In this respect, also another evaluative remark can be made. We observed not only the necessity of rearranging almost all the lines in Gal 3.6–14 (except for verses 6–7), but also this specific procedure as such is not justified. He just does so. Regarding the anticipated participation of the original addressees, this implies that nearly all the time they have to relate the propositions in a different sequence to each other than the one in which these phrases reach their ears in the moment of delivery. More so, while rearranging the position of these propositions, they also have to figure out at the same time whether they function as premise or conclusion in the syllogism. How could they have been able to do so? In this respect, the rule as formulated by David Rhoads is highly relevant: Could the formulations on the level of text, as presented by biblical scholars in their publications, be understandable for the originally intended addressees with their specific mindset in the actual moment of delivery (see Chapter 2, Section H. David Rhoads: Biblical Performance Criticism)? No answer is given by Mayordomo. A fundamental question arises: Why would Paul encode his reasoning in such a laborious way when it should serve the higher end of regaining influence over his hearers? Why pursue such an annoying and alienating path to fulfil such a straightforward rhetorical goal?

This becomes obvious in a concluding consideration on the logic of Gal 3.6–12: "Dass aber Prämissen rekonstruiert werden, die u.U. nicht auf allgemeine Akzeptanz hoffen durften, macht die Argumentation nicht unlogisch, sondern schwächt höchstens im konkreten Kommunikationskontext ihre persuasive Kraft."[17] This comment appears to be a loose end. First, he provides reconstructions of the formal logic on the level of text. A posteriori and secondarily, these extra-historical reconstructions are read into the historical context in which they should have functioned. We recognize—but now in reversed order—the turn from production to product. We can conclude that this final remark reveals that the intended addressees and their specific way of participating in the delivery of the letter do not validate his own decoding process. So, in this approach, the context is subservient to understanding the text as autonomous text (Chapter 3).

At the end, Mayordomo concludes, "Im konkreten Fall von Gal 3.6–12 lässt sich eine logische Argumentation nur mit unausgesprochenen Hilfsprämissen rekonstruieren."[18] Here the adverb *nur* (only) makes clear that Paul's reasoning cannot live up to the expectations of the present-day reader. Mayordomo's intellectual endeavour ends in confusion: "Besonders verwirrend sind die stillschweigende Gleichsetzungen, die hinter der

---

17. Mayordomo, *Argumentiert Paulus*, 166.
18. Mayordomo, *Argumentiert Paulus*, 164–65.

Argumentation immer wieder vorgenommen werden. Die Vertauschung von Subjekt und Objekt wäre zwar ein logischer Fehler, aber es ist ebenso möglich, ein wirkliches Überzeugungssystem (wenn auch ein recht eigensinniges) dahinter zu vermuten." And because of these confusions, he adds, "Gal 3.6–14 zeigt jedoch deutliche Grenzen solcher Konstruktionen."[19]

Two critical issues come to mind. First, what is the reason that Paul does not provide a clear and inevitable reasoning on the level of the text of his letter? How do we know that echoes from the Jewish scriptures must function as a premise for the originally intended addressees? More so, why did the apostle compose a logically inferior "text"? Second, why does Mayordomo not come to the point of critically questioning his own perspective on "formal logic"? Is logical analysis per se bound to the objectified text of the letter? Or—as will be the case in the alternative view below—should the implied logic in the oral performance (media) be placed against the background of a predominantly oral culture (mindset)?[20] A meta-perspective on the media and mindset of his own concrete academic lifeworld is missing; it lays beyond critical awareness. Unintentionally, his approach of the letter suffers from textification (see, Introduction, Caution to the reader #4).

Michael Bachmann: *Zur Argumentation von Galater 3.10–12*

In his article "Zur Argumentation von Galater 3.10–12," Michael Bachmann wants to achieve the following objective:[21] "mit mehr oder weniger formalen Beobachtungen eine These zur Gedankenfolge in Gal 3.10–12 ... zu entwickeln."[22] He puts forward the thesis of a construction (*Ineinanderfügung*) of two syllogisms that commence with their conclusion ("mit jeweils voranstehender *proposition*") so that the following phrases have to offer the proof in reversed order ("von hinten nach vorne"):[23]

> Diese Verkettung, bei der die Prämissen die Korrektheit der *propositio* sozusagen von hinten nach vorne absichern, fußt ... auf vorgegebenen Formulierungen, genauer: auf drei von

---

19. Mayordomo, *Argumentiert Paulus*, 165.

20. In particular, the qualification "besonders verwirrend" illuminates the unreflected relationship of Mayordomo to the letter as text. He does not explicate "to whom" these implicit synonyms (*stillschweigende Gleichsetzungen*) are confusing. This is the case for him as present-day reader. He does not reconstruct how the originally intended addressees would have participated in the event of delivery there-and-then.

21. Bachmann, "Zur Argumentation."

22. Bachmann, "Zur Argumentation," 526.

23. Bachmann, "Zur Argumentation," 537.

> Paulus in recht spezifischer Weise zitierten Schriftworten ... Sie werden vom Apostel ... als wahr eingeschätzt ... Dabei kommt Gal 3.11a eine doppelte Funktion zu: Es handelt sich einerseits um die durch den hinten plazierten Syllogismus V. 11–12 abgesicherte Aussage, um dessen *propositio* ... Andererseits gehört V. 11a nicht allein (als *propositio*) zu diesem Syllogismus ... Vielmehr ist V. 11a auch dem vorangehenden Syllogismus zuzurechnen ... hier indes als Prämisse.[24]

Bachmann presents his thesis in the form of a layout in which he follows the sequence of the originally documented wording, but represents the syllogisms by starting with the conclusion:[25]

Gal. 3.10a:	Jeder, der aus Werken/Einzelregelungen des Gesetzes ist, ist ein Verfluchter.
Gal 3.10b:	Jeder Verletzer von (mindestens einer der) Einzelregelungen des Gesetzes ist ein Verfluchter [s. Dtn 27.26].
Gal 3.11a:	Jeder, der im Gesetz/aus Werken/Einzelregelungen des Gesetzes ist, ist Verletzer von (mindestens einer der) Einzelregelungen des Gesetzes [s. Gal 3.11b–12].
Gal 3.11a:	Jeder, der im Gesetz/aus Werken/Einzelregelungen des Gesetzes ist, ist nicht ein Gerechter
Gal 3.11b:	Jeder Gerechte wird leben/ist aus Glauben [s. Hab 2.4].
Gal 3.12a(–b):	Jeder, der im Gesetz/aus Werken/Einzelregelungen des Gesetzes ist, ist nicht aus Glauben (sondern wird leben in/ist aus Einzelregelungen des Gesetzes) [vgl. Lev 18.5] (539).

Regarding this proposal, we ask once more: How, to whom, in what mindset, and from whose perspective do "*propositio*," "Prämisse," and "doppelte Funktion" function here? First, we must critically scrutinize the reasoning itself. Since a preliminary discussion of the possibly different media functionings of the letter *illic et tunc pro eis* and *hic et nunc pro nobis* is not found (Chapter 3), we take it that the "mehr oder weniger formalen Beobachtungen" seem to be identified by him on the level of the letter approached as text. Also, the formulation "zur Gedankenfolge in Gal 3.10–12" implies that thought is related neither to Paul in the process of composition nor to his addressees in the aural event, but it is located "in Gal 3.10–12"; it seems to

---

24. Bachmann, "Zur Argumentation," 537–38.

25. In the present study, the following abbreviations will be used for the basic structure of syllogistic reasonings: the major premise will be referred to as MajP, the minor premise as MinP, and the conclusion as C.

affirm that the letter as an independent media has to speak for itself—to everyone, everywhere, and every time in the same way.

Second, Bachmann presents both syllogisms as in reversed order. The implied audience, however, does not receive any indication of this reversal. His justification is the following: "Syllogismen werden umgekehrt antiken Menschen recht gut vertraut sein."[26] Although not uncommon in antiquity, we do not hear what the reason is that the apostle has reversed the standard order in these instances.

Not only the reversed orders but, in particular, how the two syllogisms are intertwined requires consideration. In this double function, Gal 3.11a has to serve as closing MinP (not C) of the first syllogism and as opening C (not MajP) of the second one. The situation of the original addressees is even more complex. Bachmann has to rephrase Gal 3.11a (the one who is rectified) as C to make it (transgressor) function as MinP: at one and the same moment, the implied audience has to actively hear in the "(nicht) Gerechter" of Gal 3.11a an echo of the "Verletzer" in Gal 3.10bA. Once more, the criterion of David Rhoads on the comprehensibility of a presented exegesis for the originally intended hearers in the moment of delivery comes to mind (Section H. in Chapter 2).

Since Bachmann needs to flesh out two paraphrases of Gal 3.11a on the level of his text to grasp this particularly intricate reasoning, not only an extremely high level of abstraction is required, but the role of the independently functioning media of text is quintessential in his approach.

Bachmann himself comments in the following way: "Diese These zur Argumentation von 3.10–12 kommt also ohne *die Annahme von impliziten Prämissen* aus und ist insofern von dem Rekonstruktionsversuch P. Lampes deutlich zu unterscheiden, aber auch von dem jüngst durch M. Mayordomo vorgelegten" (emphasis mine).[27] The German adverb *also* (therefore) distinguishes his proposal from those of Moisés Mayordomo and Peter Lampe. The strength of his proposal lies in this lack of implicit premises; all the components of the syllogisms are explicit and are identified on the level of the text. This reflects the fact that the letter has to live up to the expectations typical of an autonomous text.[28]

---

26. Bachmann, "Zur Argumentation," 544.
27. Bachmann, "Zur Argumentation," 538.
28. It is important to note that Bachmann completely passes over the explicit argumentation of Lampe on the reason behind these *Brachylogien*—and, therefore, the absence of certain parts in the reasoning: "Die ausgeführte Syllogismus-Form stand in der Gefahr, sterbenslangweilig zu sein, so daβ sie besonders im polemisch spritzigen Galaterbrief nich paβte" (37) and—with references to Quintilian—"Solange die Beweisführung durchsichtig blieb (*perspicua*), durfte der Schreiber nach Galatiën in

At the end of the article, Bachmann quite unexpectedly turns to the perspective of the intended addressees there-and-then: "Ob das Schriftgelehrte Argument von Gal 3.10–12—und näherem Kontext—seitens der Adressaten als überzeugend empfunden worden ist, lässt sich natürlich schwer sagen."[29] Notwithstanding incidental remarks on the rather abstracted level of "Juden," "Judenchristen," and "Heidenchristen," he does not bring in the originally implied addressees in his own processing of Gal 3.10–12. That the Galatian addressees could have understood in a way that is different from ours is not suggested at any moment; it seems to be excluded from the start. His own *freischwebende* syllogistic reasonings—explicated and made accessible in the presented layouts in his own text—seem to crash like asteroids into the historical realm of the intended addressees there-and-then.

In an illuminating manner, we observe here that the context ("Addresaten") is only invoked after the text itself has been understood by him as such. The approach and product of Bachmann are governed by the text-context scheme. In this reconstruction, the biblical scholar is acting in real time as "knowing subject" in the communicative process as constituted by the letter as autonomous text in the context of the ever-expanding universe of text. Having finished and presented his understanding in text, he turns to the original addressees with his objectified layouts. This is an illuminating observation regarding the goals of this research project. As an example of historicizing text, one can ask, Why does Bachmann not integrate the two syllogisms as such in the whole of Paul's rhetoric? What is the reason for the apostle to use syllogistic reasoning in the first place? Since Bachmann limits the presence of syllogistic reasoning to this passage, we further enquire as to why he uses it all of a sudden and only here in this ongoing and already intricate reasoning, and why this reasoning presents itself to us present-day readers in this laborious way. How would Paul have anticipated the participation of his original addressees?

In recapitulation, neither Mayordomo nor Bachmann relate their search for the syllogistically structured reasoning to the implied audience (to whom) nor do they distinguish between logical reasoning on the level of text and in the participatory realm of history there-and-then-to-them (in what state of mind). Uncritically, "text" is approached as operating autonomously or text in se (how).[30] The following discrepancy is involved:

Brachylogie davonstürmen" (38). In the first part of his article, Lampe concludes on his presentation of the enthymematic reasoning in Gal 3.10–12: "Hat Paulus in 3.10–12 das akzeptable Maß der Auslassung (*detractio/reticentia*) überschritten und seine antiken Leser bereits überfordert?" ("*Reticentia,*" 35).

29. Bachmann, "Zur Argumentation," 543–44.

30. The same can be concluded regarding Lampe's "*Reticentia.*" Notwithstanding the

clearly, their incidental historical considerations are related to historical people other than themselves, that is, Jews, Christian Jews, Gentiles, and the implied Galatian converts (context). It has become clear in the previous analyses, however, that in an unreflected way the "text" (the letter) is related to themselves in the activity of reading (in the present). Once again, the fallacy of implicit equation or unintentional textification is at issue. Since the transmitted document is perceived as autonomous text, how both scholars come to understand it usurps how the implied audience would have understood it in the moment of oral performance. We will now pursue the governing question: How does the reasoning function to the original addressees in their predominantly oral mindset, and from Paul's perspective which incorporates the one of these other teachers?

An Alternative Grasp: Gal 3.10–12 as Enthymematic Reasoning

In line with the intellectual movement of historicizing text, we have to contextualize syllogistic reasoning—from the perspective of Paul in the process of composing: In what way are the originally intended addressees familiar with syllogistic reasoning in general? Who used this kind of reasoning there-and-then? Under what circumstances or on what occasions was this common? Did the Galatian converts reason themselves in that way? Could they have been impressed by this kind of rhetoric? Contrary to the abstracted context which comes with text, we relate this reasoning to their collective memory: What is already known to them of this particular reasoning? In his former performances, had Paul been teaching his Galatian converts with the help of syllogisms, and, perhaps, even specifically the ones mentioned in the letter? What role did this rhetorical device play in the teaching of his opponents? In this respect, we recall the dynamic of metonymy as well (Chapter 3): What did they need to hear (*partes*/structural elements) to construe the *totum*? What is the function of this kind of reasoning in the intended

---

argument on the enthymeme as *oratorius syllogismus* (37), he implicitly equates the letter with "Text," Paul with "der Schreiber nach Galatiën," and the Galatian converts with "die (antike?) Leser." The Galatian converts, their concrete lifeworld, the oral delivery or these other teachers are not mentioned at all by him. The reasoning as a whole remains rather abstracted. We see this in relation to the apparent contradiction between Gal 3.10a en 10b. Namely, it can be solved "[n]ur dann, wenn stillschweigend ein weiterer Gedanke mitgedacht wird: 'Niemand erfüllt alle Gebote faktisch" ("*Reticentia*," 29). From the perspective of the present study, the question of anticipated participation should be asked now: On what basis can Paul reckon his addressees to fill in this typical (Protestant) though implicit premise in the moment of delivery of Gal 3.10? Differently put, how should they—as a community—have come to this premise? When, why, and in what way did this process of internalization take place?

oral performance? An obvious question comes to the fore: Why does Paul want to reason in this way? Regarding the letter as counter rhetoric, we will explore the possibility that the apostle is reacting to his adversaries: When the other teachers used syllogistic reasoning (framing), in what way does Paul counter the impact of this specific rhetoric? How does one reframe an internalized and given syllogism in the setting of an oral performance? As argued before, asking such questions is more important than answering them. We need to historicize text to be able to textualize the oral performance there-and-then-to-them of the documented wording in Gal 3.10–12.

Not Logical but Rhetorical Syllogisms: Enthymeme

When we do not explicitly differentiate the media and mindsets involved, the fundamental differences between participation in the realm of history there-and-then-to-them and the one of extra-historical thought will not become clear. When syllogistic reasoning is located on the level of text and becomes, therefore, equated with *freischwebendes Denken,* the nature of the former is fixed from the start. As a consequence, bound to the media of autonomous text, the common distinction between logical (formal) and rhetorical syllogisms will be out of consideration. Already before the days of Paul this distinction was heard. In *On Rhetoric* 1.2.8–13, Aristotle argued as follows:

> In the case of persuasion through proving or seeming to prove something, just as in dialectic there is . . . the syllogism and the apparent syllogism, so the situation is similar in rhetoric; for . . . the *enthymema* [is] a syllogism . . . Thus it is necessary for an enthymeme . . . to be . . . drawn from few premises and often less than those of the primary syllogism; for if one of these is known, it does not have to be stated, since the hearer supplies it: for example, [to show] that Dorieus has won a contest with a crown it is enough to have said that he has won the Olympic games, and there is no need to add that the Olympic games have a crown as the prize; for everybody knows that (emphasis mine).[31]

The logical syllogism functions in the technical setting of formal logic (as, for example, in the approach of Mayordomo), whereas the rhetorical one functions in the real-time setting of oratory. We recognize different elements from the governing question of textualizing history. Contrary to the implied generalized reader (to whom/in what state of mind) of text (how),

---

31. Aristotle, *On Rhetoric,* 42.

Aristotle relates the enthymeme (how) to "the hearer" as the specifically intended participant (to whom); when premises (explicit parts) are known to the hearer, they should not be expressed "since the hearer supplies it" (in what state of mind). In the explanatory remark that "the Olympic games have a crown as prize; for everybody knows," the dimension of collective memory comes to the fore (in what state of mind)—which implies the dynamic of *pars pro toto*. So enthymematic reasoning is structured by explicit parts presupposing an implied whole (the syllogistic structure), on the one hand, and is meant to persuade the audience on the other.[32]

Given this emphasis on the end of rhetorical syllogistic reasoning, we can turn to the article by David Aune, "The Use and Abuse of the Enthymeme in New Testament Scholarship."[33] He comments on the word "syllogism" in Aristotle's *On Rhetoric*:

> The conventional rendering of συλλογισμός as 'syllogism' . . . is problematic, however, for it obscures the important difference between deduction and syllogism which has led to misunderstandings of Aristotle's logic; συλλογισμός regularly means 'deduction' or 'deductive argument' in Aristotle and almost never 'syllogism' in the technical sense.[34]

Formal syllogisms serve a different purpose than in the context of (oral) rhetoric. Aune remarks, "While dialectical syllogisms are either valid or invalid, rhetorical syllogisms are either convincing or unconvincing."[35] Therefore, the decisive question is whether the presented reasoning is convincing to the participants in the oral performance there-and-then or not—that is, *not* to us here-and-now in our predominantly literate mindset vis-à-vis text.

---

32. Lampe presents the following framing of enthymeme: "Das *Enthymema* stellt eine verkürzte, logisch unvollkommene, aber akzeptable Form des Syllogismus dar. In C. Iulius Victors Ars Rhetorica heißt es: Im Enthymema, 'einen unvollkommenen Syllogismus,' 'ist es nicht nötig, zuerst zu behaupten, dann Beweise anzuführen und endlich zu schließen (*concludere*), sondern er wird gestattet sein, entweder die anfängliche Behauptung auszulassen . . . oder doch wenigstens die Schlußfolgerung (*conclusio*) wegzulassen und es den Sinnen des Richters [also des Hörers] zu überlassen, die Folgerung zusammenzusammeln (*colligere*)'" ("Reticentia," 28).

33. Aune, "Use and Abuse."

34. Aune, "Use and Abuse," 302–3.

35. Aune, "Use and Abuse," 305.

Opponents: "Message" or "Rhetoric"?

When it is of utmost importance that Paul's reasoning is convincing to his audience, according to the structure of rhetoric and counter rhetoric, our attention is drawn to these other teachers once more. In Gal 1.7 and 6.12 we encounter fierce polemic: "not that there is another gospel, but there are some who are confusing you and want to pervert the gospel of Christ" and "It is those who want to make a good showing in the flesh that try to compel you to be circumcised—only that they may not be persecuted for the cross of Christ." In the historical-critical tradition the question on the identity of these teachers has come to the fore: Who were these people?

We step back here. When we textualize the preceding section we can ask, How, to whom, in what state of mind, and from whose perspective does this looked for "identity" function? In all elements, the question is answered in line with the functioning of autonomous text to us. The present-day reader or biblical scholar wants to know and elaborate on this identity through and on the level of text. When we textualize history there-and-then-to-them, contrariwise the original addressees should have been overly familiar with these other teachers. Given their presence and performances, the "knowledge" of the Galatian converts is participatory and uncritical in nature (Chapter 3). For them, there is no need to ask this question; they know them beyond critical awareness. We should keep this explicit differentiation in mind.

In the debate on the identity of Paul's opponents in Pauline scholarship, several proposals have been put forward.[36] This quest has followed the difficult path of mirror-reading the letter. The main problem is that if one perceives the letter—whether in the functioning of a text or in the setting of an oral performance/public reading—as a re-action of Paul to dissociate the Galatian communities from these teachers, the images of these adversaries have to be considered unreliable almost by definition. As a scholar here-and-now one needs an unbiased entrance there-and-then to these teachers.

In his article "Mirror-Reading a Polemical Letter: Galatians as a Test Case," John Barclay structures his thoughts in such a way that we can get more solid ground under our feet in the realm of history there-and-then-to-them:

> We must take into account, that Paul is likely to caricature his opponents... This is not to say that Paul could have *wholly* misrepresented his opponents and their message. If he was attempting to persuade the Galatians to abandon the 'other gospel,' what

---

36. For an overview see Sumney, "Studying Paul's Opponents," 17–24; Elmer, "Paul," 12–37.

he says about it must have been both recognizable and plausible in their ears.[37]

Contrary to providing a caricature of these teachers, Paul cannot completely distort their "message"—as argued before we prefer the notion of "rhetoric."[38] Given the implied dynamic between rhetorician and audience, the emphasis is on the effect by the former on the latter. Traditionally, this effect is constituted by *pathos, ethos,* and *logos*. Therefore, the rhetoric of Paul's opponents includes a logical dimension. At the moment the letter is delivered, this logical, reasonable dimension is dominant. So the apostle has to do justice to the logical dimension in the "rhetoric" of his opponents to counter the impact on his Galatian converts. In this dimension, we find solid ground to portray the identity and teachings of these other teachers there-and-then, which has to be textualized by us: the logos enables us to textualize aspects of their presence and performances.

Criteria to Mirror-read the Letter to the Galatians (Barclay)

In his article, Barclay provides seven criteria to determine the outcome of mirror-reading the Letter to the Galatians. The first five criteria are bound to the level of the documented wording. The first criterion is designated as *type of utterance*. He distinguishes between an assertion, a denial, a command, and a prohibition. Regarding each type of utterance, a scale is presented which ranges from *at least* up to *at most*. For example, concerning the utterance of a denial he writes,

> If Paul makes a *denial*, we may assume that, *at least*, those whom he addresses may be prone to regard what he denies as true, and

---

37. Barclay, "Mirror-Reading," 76.

38. We hold this preference for the following reasons: First, we encounter as a rule the term "message" on the level of text and, therefore, in the ever-expanding universe of text. When this context is not explicated, "message" will also be perceived to function as "text"—recall not only the earlier addressed implicit equation but also the statement of Eco that the message is usually a text (Introduction). Second, on the level of text and the extra-historical, thought as such is also structured by the content-form scheme. According to this scheme, "message" is categorized as "content." As a consequence, the "message" (content) can exist independent from "form," that is, the media *in actu*. Also in this way, "message" tends towards *freischwebendes Denken* and—fleshed out on the level of text—can become an end in itself. Conversely, "rhetoric" is a historical means more than an extra-historical end—that is, an end in itself mirrored and grasped on the level of text. This critical exposé of a term like "message" is once more an example of how decisions on vocabulary or terminology are part of the critical process of textualizing history (Introduction).

at most, someone has explicitly asserted it; again between these two extremes there is a range of other possibilities.

Thus, he textualizes the range of possible scenarios in Paul's anticipated participation of the audience in that specific moment of delivery. The second criterion is *tone*. The range is set between the urgency of a statement and a casual mentioning of an issue. Regarding emphasis, "we may conclude that he [Paul] perceives this to be an important and perhaps central issue." The third criterion is *frequency*: "If Paul repeatedly returns to the same theme it is clearly important for him; conversely, an occasional remark probably signals what he considers to be only a side-issue." The fourth one is *clarity* which is related to reconstructing statements of these teachers. So, reconstructions should neither hinge on ambiguous words or contested textual problems, nor be based on polemically distorted depictions of his adversaries. In this way, these possible sound groups (themes) and phrases (reasonings), which originate from these other teachers, should be clear. The fifth criterion is *unfamiliarity*:

> While taking into account our limited knowledge of Paul's theology, we may be entitled to consider the presence of an unfamiliar motif in Paul's letter as a reflection of a particular feature in the situation he is responding to.[39]

Familiar themes are related to "Paul's theology," but unfamiliar themes are related to "a particular feature in the situation he is responding to." We critically note here that Barclay is apparently structuring "the theology of Paul" (text?) in juxtaposition to "the situation he is responding to" (context). Given his prior presence and performances among his addressees, would Paul's "theology" not be constitutive (already) of that particular situation? As a second remark, we add that the structure of rhetoric and counter rhetoric involves the possibility that the apostle, as well as the teachers, use the same and, therefore, familiar themes.

The last two criteria go beyond the level of the documented wording of the letter and structure our thoughts directly into the realm of history there-and-then-to-them. The sixth criterion is *consistency*: "Thus the results of the previous criteria may be tested to see if they amount to a consistent picture of Paul's opponents." As argued before, we will relate this criterion to the logic of their rhetoric. The last criterion is *historical plausibility*. Once aspects of the realm of history involved are reconstructed, general historical knowledge of that time has to be invoked: "If our results are anachronistic or historically implausible for some reason, we will be obliged to

---

39. Barclay, "Mirror-Reading," 84.

start again."⁴⁰ The criteria offset out by Barclay can regulate attempts to textualize history and put ground under our feet in the realm of history there-and-then-to-them.

John Barclay Meets John Miles Foley

Regarding the *logos* of these teachers, we have to transpose the Theory of Metonymical Referentiality by John Miles Foley (Chapter 1) to this setting of rhetoric and counter rhetoric (Chapter 3). Through explicit parts—argumentative phrases—Paul anticipates and also actively evokes the implied whole—the *logos* of the rhetoric of these teachers. This *logos* forms the governing rationale. On the one hand, explicit parts of the argumentative structure in the aural event can be found by us in the documented wording. On the other, we relate the implied whole of this structure to the collective memory of the Galatian converts. In this way, the present-day reader can get before the functioning of the letter as text to us, that is, enthymemes. We scrutinize the documented wording of the letter for threads of reasoning and ask, What is not fully explicated that the implied hearers would need to have had in mind to grasp the logic of these thoughts?

Historicizing Text: Gal 3.21cd

These introductory considerations should pave the way for textualizing the oral performance there-and-then-to-them of Gal 3.10–12. As a first step, we search for key terms that constitute the laborious reasoning involved: the "law" is mentioned up to four times; the thematic matrix of "curse" is constituted by two explicit parts; the same pertains to the matrices of "rectification,"⁴¹ "l/Life,"⁴² and "faith." The discussion of the studies by

---

40. Barclay, "Mirror-Reading," 85.

41. Especially in view of my Protestant background, the translation "justification"/"to justify" seems to be more appropriate. In this example, however, I will use "rectification"/"to rectify" for two reasons. First, this rather unfamiliar rendering creates a distance to, theologically speaking, a Protestant *Vorverständnis*. This estrangement should prevent the present-day (Protestant?) reader from jumping to the uncritical conclusion that he already knows what Paul means—at least in the attempt to detextify his understanding of the passage. Second, in this preference, I also follow the vocabulary of Louis Martyn in his commentary on Galatians. Since his work has been of great influence on my research project, I can also in this way pay tribute to him.

42. In this test case, I make a distinction between "life/to live" with the opening letter in lowercase and "Life/Alive/to Live" with the same letter capitalized (this pertains also to the synonymous "Blessing"). In this way, I am not only inspired once more

Mayordomo and Bachmann made clear that how these key terms relate to each other is not self-evident to us.

These terms are found throughout the argumentative section of Gal 2–3. When we scrutinize this part of the letter, we touch on a peripheral though interesting passage, Gal 3.21cd. Here three of the crucial terms in Gal 3.10-12 are constitutive of a single argument: "For if a law had been given that could impart life, righteousness would certainly have come by the law." In Pauline scholarship so far, the logic of Gal 3.21cd has not drawn particular attention.[43] In commentaries, the causal conjunction, the key terms ("law," "Life," and "rectification") and the logical relations between them have, in our view, not been sufficiently scrutinized.

Regarding Gal 3.21cd, we will start by historicizing text: What went before in the intended delivery? In the opening of the letter, Paul opposes the teaching of implied adversaries, "a different gospel—not that there is another gospel, but there are some who are confusing you and want to pervert the gospel of Christ" (Gal 1.6-7). What is this teaching about? In the description of his address to Cephas in Antioch (Gal 2.15-21), we find clues. Paul openly refutes here the validity of the "Jewish law" as a means of "rectification" for his "Gentile" converts ("not out of law"). In the same breath, he introduces the only true way of rectification for those who are in Christ ("out of faith"). This juxtaposition is found three times. Because of the frequency (Barclay's third criterion), we can conclude that this topic is important to Paul (Gal 2.14-21; Gal 3.2, 5; 3.10; 3.11). The controversy seems to hinge on how "rectification" for God takes place. Structured by this juxtaposition—in which law functions prominently—his reasoning positively culminates in Gal 3.14b in the theme of the "promise of the Spirit." The theme of the "promise" is elaborated on in Gal 3.15-18.[44] This elaborate train of thought is related to the question who will share and who will not share in the inheritance of Abraham. Since the implied audience could conclude that Paul juxtaposes the "Jewish law" with the "promise," this blunt antithesis needs an explanation. More so—as Louis Martyn comments on this verse—these teachers could pick this up as a loose end and depict Paul

---

by Martyn, but I am also concerned to do justice to the assumed Jewish apocalyptic worldview. That is to say there is an important distinction between the category of "life/to live" in terms of one's deeds on which one will be judged ("living according to the Jewish law" and "living like a sinner"), and the reward and promise of the "Life" in the eschaton which comes with the judgment of the way of living (Day of Judgment).

43. As far as I know, one short article has been published on this passage. The scope of that study, however, is intertextual in nature. See Heckl, "Bezugstext."

44. On word chain, see Harvey, *Listening to the Text*, 103–4.

as juxtaposing the God-given law and the promises of God.[45] Martinus de Boer even proposes that "[v]erse 21b ... most likely conceals in its form the standpoint of the new preachers in Galatia, who are Christian Jews."[46] So the apostle needs to address the exact relation between "law," "promises," and "God."

Here we arrive at Gal 3.21a where Paul frames this standpoint of his opponents as a question: "Is the law, against the promises of God?" An emphatic negation follows (Barclay's second criterion): "Absolutely not!" (3.21b). Here we come to the heart of the matter, namely the function of the "law" for the Galatians who once had converted to Paul's gospel of Jesus Christ. In Gal 3.21cd, Paul substantiates this important negation with a conditional reasoning:

| Because if law had been given that has the power to make Alive, | (c) |
| then would be out of law the rectification. | (d) (translation mine). |

The reasoning of the verse is an interplay of two forms of logic. First, the postpositive γάρ (because) is heard (verse 21c). This conjunction relates this reasoning as a whole to the preceding negation (the juxtaposition of "law" and "promise"). Second, the reasoning as a whole is framed as a conditional: a premise εἰ (if) in verse 21c in combination with a conclusion ἄν (then) in verse 21d. It is a second class or contrary-to-fact conditional clause.[47] The logic is constituted by three terms: "law" (Gal 3.21c and 21d), "to make Alive" (21c), and "rectification" (21d). The vast majority of commentaries do not touch on the logical dimension of this reasoning. This cluster of relations, however, lacks logical self-evidence or clarity vis-à-vis the letter as text: What has rectification to do with the power to make Alive? How is the law related to both these themes? It is also unclear why Paul construes it as contrary-to-fact.

Textualizing Oral Performance
There-and-Then-to-Them: Gal 3.21cd

As a starting-point, we propose that Paul anticipates his intended addressees to be able to follow this layered reasoning without further instruction. Instead of finding this laborious and frustrating, he assumes that they will experience a clear reasoning and that he will be able to reach their hearts.

45. Martyn, *Galatians*, 358.
46. Boer, *Galatians*, 233.
47. See Porter, *Idioms*, 259–61.

On this basis, we will textualize the understanding of the original hearers in five steps. First, the two phrases of this contrary-to-fact conditional will be framed as factual statements. Second, the question about the origin of this implied factual reasoning must be answered. Third, we will scrutinize how the terms of the reasoning are connected. Fourth, the logic behind this interrelatedness will be investigated. Fifth, we will reconstruct this denied reasoning as a logical unity.

If we transpose the contrary-to-fact conditional into a factual statement, the result is the following:

A law has been given that has the power to make Alive
Therefore, out of law is rectification

In this way, we find a logical, self-evident, and characteristically Jewish argument. Since the effect of Paul's conditional is to deny this statement, the intended audience should have heard before about the power of "the" or "a" law to make Alive.[48] Now we can ask: Where does this claim come from?

Once we are aware of this implication of Gal 3.21cd, the answer is rather obvious: Since Paul firmly denies the two statements, he will not be the one who has brought these claims into the Galatian communities. The call to law obedience culminating in the act of circumcision has been brought into the Galatian congregations by these implied adversaries. This outcome is in line with Barclay's first (type of utterance), fourth (clarity), and fifth criteria (unfamiliarity). We can also point to Barclay's criterion of historical plausibility. Therefore, in these two claims, we hear an echo of the teaching of his opponents.[49] This is the first step to understand how the apostle intended his original addressees to process these phrases in the aural event: They had become familiar with and had internalized these statements. Paul leads them in a reasoning which is questioning their validity.

A second step has to be made: How are the terms "law," "rectification," and "the power to make Alive" logically related to each other? Since Paul

---

48. The term that connects the protasis and apodosis of this second-class conditional is the anarthrous substantive νόμος. One could, therefore, translate "law *in se*" or "any given law." The anarthrous substantive can also refer to a specific and already known item. See Porter, *Idioms*, 104; Longenecker, *Galatians*, 143. As we argued above, Paul is counteracting the teaching of his implied opponents. Since he frames the call to circumcision in combination with the law (most often articular) in a Judaistic or Jewish way (for example, Gal 2.14–16, 3.6–18), we suppose that the audience hears in Paul's (anarthrous or articular) "law" a reference to the regulations of the "Jewish law."

49. We repeat that since we take the perspective of Paul, this reasoning is also valid even if he had misunderstood or would have been misinformed about these teachers and their performances or rhetoric.

uses the law in both elements of his reasoning, this term will function as a key in our search. In the protasis (verse 21c) the law is defined by the dependent clause ὁ δυνάμενος ζῳοποιῆσαι. This dependent clause describes a *property* of the law—that is, to make Alive. In other words, the law itself has the ability or power to make human beings Alive.[50]

Now we will proceed with the apodosis (verse 21d). Here the consequence of the condition is constituted by the substantive ἡ δικαιοσύνη. "Rectification" is grammatically related to the law through the preposition ἐκ.[51] The law is a *medium* or *means* through which humanity can be rectified before God.[52] Rectification is, therefore, not a property or power of the law, but is related to a status or quality that is granted to a human being in relation to God because of the relation of that human being to the law. When these considerations on the protasis and apodosis are brought together, the following related reasonings are heard:

| the law is the medium through which one is rectified (Gal 3.21d). |
| the law has the power to make one Alive (Gal 3.21c). |

Two explicit parts have been identified. These parts are like threads, structural elements (Foley), or traces on the level of the documented wording. As a third step, we ask: What is the logic behind the two statements? For the implied audience, the relation between the apodosis and protasis has to be found in the function of the "law." First, humankind is the object and Life is *the end*: the law has the power to make one Alive.[53] We can recognize the thought-pattern of Judaism—for example, Lev 18.5: "You shall keep my statutes and my ordinances; by doing so one shall live: I am the Lord." In this way, Barclay's criteria of historical plausibility and consistency are validated. Second, in the apodosis it becomes clear that the law is a *means* so that rectification can come to humanity. Thus, one hears about the law as a *means* (to rectify before God) and an *end* (to make the one who is rectified

---

50. In oratory, thematic and synonymous relations are decisive. In this respect, the infinitive aorist evokes the theme of "l/Life." Paul has already dealt with this theme in the preceding verses Gal 2.19–20 and 3.11–12. We encounter here an example of amplification. Thus Paul does not express in Gal 3.21cd a new thought. The focus becomes, therefore, how he uses this already familiar and introduced thought in relation to his implied audience at that moment in his oral performance. This is important, especially, in light of the possibility of *Umdeutung* (Chapter 3).

51. We can see that the audience has heard before the theme of rectification concerning the instrumental role of the law: Gal 2.16, 19, 21; 3.2, 5, 10, 11, 18.

52. See Porter, *Idioms*, 154–56.

53. In the light of Paul's preceding reasoning, we assume that this Life-giving power is directed towards humanity. See Martyn, *Galatians*, 359; Beker, *Paul*, 260 and 261.

Alive). If this is valid, a connecting premise is operative in the reasoning of this verse: *the medium through which one becomes rectified before God, has the power to make Alive.* Since it is not expressed on the level of the documented wording, this logical relation is suppressed. We can identify in this argumentative phrase the major premise of a primary syllogism. As a consequence, both earlier reconstructed elements form the minor premise and conclusion. Therefore, we can affirm that the reasoning as implied in Gal 3.21cd is syllogistic in nature.[54] In the following way, the explicit parts form a valid and solid implied whole:

MajP:	The means through which one is rectified before God,	[X]	has the power to make Alive	[Z]
MinP:	The law	[Y]	is the medium through which one is rectified before God	[X]
C:	Therefore, the law	[Y]	has the power to make Alive	[Z]

In the construal of oral performance *in actu*, the original addressees do not process w-o-r-d-s as fixed and visible things in the text area, as we do, but they identify in continuously changing sound groups units of meaning (Chapter 1). For that reason, the terms can also be related to each other in a diverging way while still meaning the same:

MajP:	The one who is rectified before God	[X]	he will Live	[Z]
MinP:	The one who is out of law	[Y]	he is rectified before God	[X]
C:	Therefore, the one who is out of law	[Y]	he will Live	[Z]

We will use now the former layout to frame Paul's incomplete syllogistic conditional as found in Gal 3.21cd. In this way, we will recognize the minor term [Y] twice and the major term [Z] once. In verse 3.21d—the apodosis of Paul's conditional—we encounter the minor premise:

---

54. Regarding this kind of reasoning, a concise explanation will be given now how it is used here: the major premise of a logical or categorical syllogism—in the basic structure of AAA-1 (Barbara)—contains the major term [Z], that is, the predicate of the conclusion. The predicate [Z] refers either to a property of a certain entity or to a relation between entities. The minor premise contains the minor term [Y], that is, the subject of the conclusion. These two premises, that is, major and minor, have the middle term [X] in common. This term [X] conveys the category of things that will be specified in the minor term [Y]. The predicate [Z] and the subject [Y] are related to each other in the conclusion. Subsequently, this conclusion is either true and affirmed, that is, *modus ponens*, or false and denied, that is, *modus tollens*.

MinP:	The law	[Y]	is the medium through which one is rectified before God	[X]
MinP:	"then would be out of law	[Y]	the rectification"	[X]
Gal 3.21d:	Minor Term		Middle Term	

In the protasis (3.21c) the conclusion is heard:

C:	Therefore, the law	[Y]	has the power to make Alive	[Z]
C:	"Because if law had been given	[Y]	that has the power to make Alive"	[Z]
Gal 3.21c:	Minor Term		Major Term	

If the construal by the original addressees is governed by the rationale as reconstructed above, the intended impact of Gal 3.21cd has to be appraised as an example of *negative rhetoric*. Paul uses a contrary-to-fact conditional, because he wants to deny the logos of his opponents ("You have to obey the law [means] so that you will become partaker in the promised Life [end]").[55] The sixth (consistency) and seventh criteria of Barclay (historical plausibility) confirm this understanding.

Once we are aware that this syllogism (which Paul denies) forms the backbone of his adversaries' performances, the conclusion (C) can be regarded as their crucial means of power, namely, "a law has been given that has the power to make Alive." When these teachers would have gained influence over the Galatian communities through this syllogistic argument, it is not surprising that Paul takes the C of their syllogism as his point of departure (Gal 3.21c). He construes his reasoning in such a manner that this negated C functions as premise ("if a law had been given that has the power to make Alive"). In this way, he can draw his own conclusion ("then the rectification would be out of law"). His own C implies the disqualification of their MinP. The apostle is therefore not interested in disqualifying the C of his opponents, but in falsifying the MinP of their implied rhetoric (*logos*). More precisely, his negative rhetoric hinges on the crucial minor term [Y]. Paul wants his audience to recognize that the internalized minor term makes the reasoning a fraud. Simply put, "out of law" has to be rejected by his addressees—in favour of "out of faith" (Gal 2.16; see below).

If this reconstruction of the syllogistic nature of Gal 3.21cd is valid, we can draw three conclusions. First, the structure of the reasoning as a whole is implicit. In the realm of history there-and-then-to-them, the suppressed

---

55. In this, we recognize the structure of the reasoning as described by Beker: "To the Jew, the Torah is the sole means of maintaining righteousness, just as righteousness is the sole means of obtaining life" (*Paul*, 260). See also Boer, *Galatians*, 207.

major premise is part of the collective memory in a self-evident way; while composing his letter, Paul anticipates the familiarity of his audience with this logic. This way, we recognize Barclay's argumentation on the necessity of a reliable representation of the rhetoric of his opponents. Second, by asking for the origin of this reasoning, we as present-day readers spiral into the realm of history there-and-then-to-them. In this way, we move before the letter functioning as text to us. Therefore, if these claims stem from these implied adversaries, the unravelled syllogistic reasoning represents a basic structure in their teaching and preaching—as conceived by Paul. Third, we have to conclude that Paul is not concerned in Gal 3.21cd with the C of his opponents, but with denying and overthrowing the middle term [Y] of their MinP, as illustrated by the high frequency of the dichotomous "out of law" and "out of faith" in Gal 2.16. This is an important insight concerning other threads. The majority of terms in Gal 2.14—3.14 constitute this MinP.

Textualizing Oral Performance There and Then to Them (2): Gal 2.16, 2.21, and 3.11

In keeping with the fundamental oratorial feature of amplification,[56] similar threads of this reasoning will be pursued now. The first syllogistic thread is found in Gal 2.16 (MinP). Here the thread is strong as a twine. The terms of the MinP—"rectification" [X] and "law" [Y]—are mentioned three times. Recall Barclay's criterion of frequency. We also notice that for the first time in the oral performance the explicit utterance of "law"[57] and also "rectification" is heard here.[58] A translation of Gal 2.15 and 16 is presented below in which the terms of the reconstructed MinP are italicized:

> We, Jews by birth, and, not, from the Gentiles, sinners,
> [we] knowing that a human being is not *rectified out of works of law*,
> if not through faith of Jesus Christ, (a)

---

56. Aristotle, *On Rhetoric*, 1.9.35-41, 1.15.23-33, and 3.6.1-7.

57. Note, however, that in the preceding part of the letter we have heard related utterings: "Judaism" (Gal 1.13, 14), "traditions of my fathers" (Gal 1.14), "to eat [as Jews] together with the Gentiles" (Gal 2.12). The same pertains to synonymous themes: "To be/live like a Jew" (Gal 2.13, 14, 15), "circumcision" (Gal 2.3, 7, 8, 9, 12).

58. Furthermore, in comparison with Gal 3.21cd, the instrumental phrase "out of law" is extended to "out of works of law." Since in line with oratory both phrases recollect the broader theme of law, this extension is not considered to be decisive for the present investigation. For this expression, see Bachmann, "4QMMT"; Boer, *Galatians*, excursus 8, 145–48; Yoon, *Discourse Analysis* and his section excursus: The Meaning of ἔργα νόμου: A Response to Dunn Considering Lexical Semantics and Case Semantics, 212–25; Yoon takes a stance against James Dunn's claim that this expression would essentially imply covenantal nomism.

also we have placed our faith in Christ Jesus (b)
so that we might be *rectified* out of faith of Christ,
    and not *out of works of law* (c)
because *out of works of law* shall not be *rectified* all flesh (d)
(translation mine).

The three explicit parts or threads that emerge can now be displayed in tabular format below:

MinP:	The one who is out of law	[Y]		is rectified before God	[X]
[16aB]	"a human being out of works of law	[Y]	[16aA]	is *not* rectified"	[X]
[16dB]	"*not* out of works of law	[Y]	[16dA]	so that we might be rectified"	[X]
[16dB]	"because out of works of law,	[Y]	[idem]	shall *not* be rectified all flesh"	[X]

On the level of the present text, in this tabular format, we, as present-day readers, are able to identify the minor premise. In detextification, the focus is on the way in which Paul anticipated his originally intended addressees to understand. For that reason, we return to the documented wording, as found in the letter, in order to add a plausible way of structuring thought by the addressees in the performance of this specific passage—as envisioned by Paul in the process of composition, and textualized by us here-and-now. The addition of this anticipated participation is necessary in order to understand how the actual hearers would have understood the argumentation. So the explicit parts of the *logos*, which are placed in italics, will be accompanied by the proposed participation, which is underscored and placed between dashes:

We, Jews by birth, and, not, from the Gentiles, sinners,
[we] knowing that a human being is not *rectified out of works of law*,
 – <u>and, therefore, that those who are out of works of law will not Live</u> –
if not through faith of Jesus Christ, (a)
also we
 —<u>those who are Jews by birth, and, therefore,
    rectified on the basis of the law</u>—
have placed our faith in Christ Jesus (b)
so that we might be *rectified* out of faith of Christ,
 —<u>and, therefore, will Live out of faith of Christ</u>—
and not *out of works of law* (c)
because *out of works of law* shall not be *rectified* all flesh (d).
 —<u>and, therefore, it should be clear that no Life will be granted</u>—

Contrary to "What does it mean?," this detextified perspective provides an answer to the question: How does it mean, to whom, in what state of mind, and from whose perspective[s]? In conclusion, Paul is once more labouring in Gal 2.16 to deny the validity of the minor term in the MinP for his implied Gentile audience (*modus tollens*).[59]

We continue to scrutinize the letter for similar threads. In this respect, Gal 2.21b has to draw our attention—the "law" functions here as the means through which (διά[60]) humanity is rectified. The emissary declares (the related terms are italicized),

> I do not nullify the grace of God! (a)
> For if *through law*—there is *rectification*, (b)
> then Christ died for nothing! (c) (translation mine)

Paul feels urged to defend himself: "I do not nullify the grace of God!" In this exclamation, the echo of a possible charge against him can be recognized. Recall Barclay's first (type of utterance) and in particular second criterion (tone). The rhetorical situation becomes intelligible when this allegation is ascribed to his adversaries.[61] Their teaching disqualifies—either explicitly or implicitly, either irenically or pejoratively—Paul and his gospel. They call the Gentile converts to circumcision and make them obey certain rules and, therefore, submit to their authority.

With this context in mind, we proceed to Gal 2.21b. Here the minor [Y], as well as the middle [X] term, can be heard. The postpositive γάρ ("for") introduces an explanatory sentence. It supports and explains Paul's statement of denial.[62] This explanatory phrase—"For if through law there is rectification"—is framed as the protasis of a first-class conditional clause (εἰ, without verb). Grammatically speaking, this means that the condition is either factual or true or construed for the sake of argument.[63] We do not

---

59. Contrary to Gal 3.21cd, however, Paul does not deny here the MinP in an argumentative way. He does so based on knowledge that he shares with Cephas (εἰδότες). Since Peter is the leader of the congregation in Jerusalem (Gal 2.7, 8), this knowledge is charged with his authority and, as a result, rhetorically powerful. Therefore, this is a different rhetorical means of power in comparison with the one under discussion, that is, the syllogistic rationale on and in itself.

60. Porter, *Idioms*, 148–50.

61. Three possibilities can be discerned. First, this charge could have been uttered explicitly by the adversaries. Second, Paul anticipates that this allegation could come to the minds of the hearers when they hear this argumentation based on what his opponents have taught them. Third, the teachers—who would be considered to be still amid his Galatian converts—explain this passage to them in this way (Martyn, Boer).

62. Longenecker, *Galatians*, 95.

63. Porter, *Idioms*, 256–57.

find, however, in Gal 2.21c the apodosis of this conditional. Through the inferential particle ἄρα with aorist verb, a conclusion is drawn. Instead of the expected second part, Paul utters this exclamation in agony: "then Christ died for nothing!" One could argue that the implication of the apodosis suffices here as an example of the element of "in what state of mind." In this disruptive way, the apostle makes clear that the protasis cannot be true. He denies its validity for his Gentile audience who are out of faith.

In the following table, the MinP of the opponents' syllogism becomes clearer:

MinP:	The law is the medium through which	[Y]		one is rectified before God	[X]
[21bB]	"[For if...] through law	[Y]	[21bA]	there is rectification"	[X]

Once the governing rationale is recognized, we as present-day readers can textualize how the implied audience was intended to participate in order to understand:

> I do not nullify the grace of God! (a)
> For if *through law*—there is *rectification*, (b)
> —then the law would have the power to make Alive,
> but this is not the case, and, even worse,—
> then Christ died for nothing! (c)
> And that is blasphemy, because it is through his death
>   only that God makes us Alive!

We conclude once more that the premise of Gal 2.21b has to be constitutive of the realm of history there-and-then-to-them and/or the collective memory of the original addressees ("through the law—there is rectification").

When we continue to hover over the letter, we reach Gal 3.11. In the two phrases, all three terms of the syllogistic reasoning are there. One can recognize the minor term "law" [Y] once in verse 11a. In a similar vein, the middle term "to rectify/rectification" [X] can be identified twice, as a verb in verse 11a and as a noun in 11b. Finally, one can recognize the major term "to Live" [Z] once, as a verb in verse 11b. Regarding the described dynamics of grasping units of meaning, we note that the usage of the verb "to Live" instead of "to make Alive" recalls the same theme. In the following translation, the relevant elements are italicized:

And because no one can *be rectified* before God *in the law*,
it is evident,[64] that *the one who is rectified*[65] out of faith, he will *Live*
(translation mine).

In this rendering, we observe a deviation from the one found in Gal 3.21d and 2.21b. In spite of the usage of ἐκ with genitive in Gal 3.21d, Paul uses in this verse ἐν (dative): "Its [ἐν] basic meaning is 'in' or 'in the realm of.'"[66]

64. For this syntactical understanding of Gal 3.11, see Witherington, *Grace in Galatia*, 234;. Hays, "The Letter to the Galatians," 259; Wakefield, *Where to Live*, 163–67; Boer, *Galatians*, 202–3; Veen, "Staaltje," 51–53.

65. In "Apocalyptic Hermeneutics," as republished in his *Conversion*, Hays suggests that ὁ δίκαιος functioned in those days as a messianic designation. In this way, the reasoning in Gal 3.11 would focus not so much on the addressees themselves but on Christ as "The Righteous One": "When Paul . . . read Hab 2.3–4 in the LXX, a text that already carried apocalyptic/messianic resonances for Jews of his time, how did he understand it? My contention is that he understood it as a messianic prophecy, just as he understood—in a way quite startling to us—Gen 17.8 as messianic prophecy (Gal 3.16). This sort of divinatory reading is a direct and natural consequence of the apostle's apocalyptic hermeneutical perspective: those who have experienced the apocalypse of the Son of God now find the veil taken away from Scripture so that they can perceive its witness to him, including its witness to him as the Coming/Righteous One" (*Conversion*, 141). In line with the approach of detextification, we can explicate a crucial presupposition in this intriguing proposal. Hays's argumentation is based on Paul in relation to the LXX version of Hab 2.3–4 ("reading"). Regarding this perspective on Paul and Scripture, we ask: How do the actual addressees have to participate in this understanding of ὁ δίκαιος as "The Righteous One," while caught up in the moment of delivery of Gal 3.11? First, we remark that these words (sound units) are not explicitly introduced as coming from the Jewish scriptures ("for it is written"); article and noun form an integral part of the documented reasoning. So the addressees should already have been familiar with this specific passage as coming from "Scripture." Second and as a result, in the moment itself—since no indication is found in the stream of sound bites—they should have been aware that the simple notion of ὁ δίκαιος functions as this specific title of Christ. Thus, a minimal anticipation of Paul requires here a maximal participation of his addressees. Third, in the preceding passage, the matrix of "rectification" is consistently related to the Galatian converts themselves. So, when we detextify this intertextual understanding, the conclusion is that Hays's proposal is not self-evident.

66. Porter, *Idioms*, 156. The following commentaries relate this spherical understanding to the citation from Deut 27.26 (Gal 3.10b) and Lev 18.5 (3.12): Betz, *Galatians*, 146; Martyn, *Galatians*, 312; Boer, *Galatians*, 203. Notwithstanding the prevalent locative senses of ἐν, there is also an instrumental one possible. In this way, Gal 3.11a could form a parallel to Gal 3.21bc, i.e. "through the law." This instrumental sense of the dative case in Gal 3.11a, however, seems to be unlikely based on the following observations: First, the sense in which the audience will understand ἐν is plausibly intended to be guided by the twofold usage of the same preposition in the directly preceding verse (Gal 3.10b). Second, in Gal 2.19 the implied audience has already heard the rendering διὰ νόμου νόμῳ. Given this phrase, the instrumental sense of the dative—in comparison to the genitive case of the law—is rendered unintelligible. Since in the oral performance Gal 2.19 precedes 3.11a, the audience has already been brought into the modus of hearing the preposition in the locative sense.

Thus, next to the instrumental relation of the law to humanity, Paul also conceives a spherical one. Humankind can live in the realm or—when the dimension of power is pressed—under the dominion of the law. These different senses of the law together constitute the thematic matrix of the law.

Having said that, we turn to the reasoning of the verse itself. We notice that the intended addressees in Gal 3.11a hear the reasoning as structured by a MinP and in Gal 3.11b as structured by a C. In this table, the usage of the different prepositions will be followed:

MinP:	The one who is in law	[Y]	he will be rectified before God	[X]
[11a]	"because in the law	[Y]	*no* one can be rectified before God,"	[X]
C:	Therefore, the one who is out of law	[Y]	he will Live	[Z]
[11b]	"It is evident that the one who is rectified out of . . .	[Y]	he will Live	[Z]

Regarding the governing rationale, we can reconstruct the original wording of Paul and intimate how the implied addressees would have participated to understand his words-in-the-event-of-delivery:

> And because no one can *be rectified* before God *in the law*,
> —and, therefore, will Live in that way—
> it is evident that *the one who is rectified* out of faith, he will *Live*.

We observe that Paul denies once more the validity of the minor term "law" [Y] for his implied Gentile audience. After this *modus tollens*, we notice a change to the *modus ponens*: in the C of Gal 3.11b, the denied minor term [Y] in verse 11a (the law) is replaced by another one, πίστις (faith). In the preceding reasoning of Gal 2.16, these terms have been introduced more than once in an antithetical way: in the rebuke of Cephas, the "law" is denied up to three times in favour of "faith." So this interchange of minor terms against the background of this syllogistic structure is conceivable and manageable for the implied audience in the aural event.[67]

In this way, we can deepen our textualization of the realm of history there-and-then-for-them. When Paul disqualifies the crucial minor term

---

67. This understanding implies that Paul's allusion to Hab 2.4 in Gal 3.11b [C] neither forms a premise (MajP, MinP) nor a proof per se. These invoked words from Jewish holy scriptures entail the C that opposes the one of these teachers and validates Paul's gospel. As argued, regarding the reconstruction of this working of these words from the Jewish Bible, we have to be able to differentiate between *freischwebendes Denken*—that is, Scripture proof *in se*—and textualization of the distinctive communicative process of the intended oral delivery there-and-then.

"law" of his opponents to put "faith" in its place, we can construe the following counter-syllogistic reasoning:

MajP:	The one who is rectified before God	[X]	he will Live	[Z]
MinP:	The one who is out of faith	[YPaul]	he is rectified before God	[X]
C:	Therefore, the one who is out of faith	[YPaul]	he will Live	[Z][68]

Four conclusions can be drawn regarding Gal 3.11, 2.21b, and 2.16. First, the approach of detextification neither compels one to find complete formal syllogisms on the level of text (so Bachmann) nor to reconstruct incomplete ones (so Mayordomo). We can argue with de Boer that the argumentation is not systematic *on the level of the text*. Once we explicitly differentiate between the letter-functioning-as-text-to-us and textualization in the realm of history involved, however, another kind of systematization becomes possible, namely, textualization of the originally intended understanding of the argumentative threads in the anticipated aural event. Second, the present-day reader encounters up to four instances in which the terms of the crucial MinP are present. In all of the instances, the related terms are clearly—and in Gal 2.16 even redundantly—denied. Between the lines, we hear Paul exclaim, "The law does *not* lead to rectification!" This fourfold observation of denial leads to the conclusion—in line with Barclay's first criterion of type of utterance—that "*at most*, someone has explicitly asserted it." In only one instance, we have identified the structure of the C. Here the minor term "law" [Y] is replaced by the juxtaposed term "faith" [YPaul]. Based on the related amplification in Gal 2.16, this conclusion coincides with Barclay's third as well as fourth criterion, namely frequency and clarity. The structure of rhetoric and counter rhetoric—culminating in the crucial minor term/MinP—becomes more and more visible. Third, the medium through which one is rectified, the law [Y], is crucial to the teaching of Paul's opponents. Law obedience culminates in circumcision. The apostle is taking pains to derail this explicit part of their "bewitching" reasoning (Gal 3.1). In this way, we see Barclay's sixth criterion being met as well (consistency): "Thus the results of the previous criteria may be tested to see if they amount to a consistent picture of Paul's opponents."[69]

---

68. In Gal 2–3, synonymous traces typical of the apostle can be found: as minor term think of [fill in and construe: the one who is] "in Christ" (2.17), "to die in and through the law" (2.19a), "to be co-crucified with Christ" (2.19c), "'I' do not live anymore" (2.20a), and "to be baptized" (3.27a); as major term: [fill in: he will] "(to) l/Live in God" (2.19b), "Christ lives in me" (2.20b), "to clothe oneself with Christ" (3.27b) and "to be one in Christ" (3.28d).

69. Barclay, "Mirror-Reading," 85.

Fourth, we observe that—instead of disqualifying his opponents' reasoning as a whole—Paul follows their logos and even affirms the predicate of their C. The desire which has been awoken in the Galatian converts by these teachers is affirmed by the apostle—that is, "to live" and/or to gain "Life." Therefore, he only denies and reframes their MinP: over against "out of law" he states and points this other way to "l/Life," namely, "out of faith."

Textualizing Oral Performance There-and-Then-to-Them (3): Gal 2.15-17, 3.1-5, and 3.6-14

Since amplification forms a central feature of the predominantly oral state of mind, we now must pursue the identification of synonyms or antonyms of "law," "rectification," and "Life." Contrary to the textualization of text here-and-now-to us, we have to be sensitive to this specific communicative dynamic. We can detect these references to the major, middle, and minor terms through the social memory of his implied addressees, for example, contemporary Graeco-Roman culture and, in particular, Judaism. A textualization on this basis will be strengthened by Barclay's two final criteria, namely, historical plausibility (6) and consistency (7).

From this perspective, we will look into Gal 2-3 once more. We start with Paul's address to Cephas in Gal 2.15-21. The apostle recalls here in a redundant way the thematic matrix related to the minor term: "out of law," "to be a Jew," and "to live like a Jew" [Y].[70]

> If you—who are a Jew with all the privileges involved—(14a)
> live like a Gentile and not like a Jew (14b)
> how can you force the Gentiles to live in a Jewish way (to Judaize)? (14c)
> We, Jews by nature and not, from the Gentiles, sinners, (15)
> (...)
> If we—who seek to be rectified in Christ—(17a)
> have been found ourselves to be sinners, (17b)
> then does that suggest that Christ is a servant of sin? (17c)
> Absolutely not! (17d) (translation mine)

If a thematic equation of "law" and "Judaism" ("to live like/be a Jew") is valid, we should be able to rephrase the MinP in the reconstructed syllogistic structure as follows:

---

70. Paul has already referred to this thematic matrix in Gal 1.13-14 (ἐν τῷ Ἰουδαϊσμῷ).

MajP:	The one who is rectified	[X]	he will Live	[Z]
MinP:	The one who is/lives like a Jew	[Y]	he is rectified before God	[X]
C:	Therefore, the one who lives like a Jew	[Y]	he will Live	[Z]

We can then hone in on the explicit parts in Gal 2.14–15:

MinP:	The one who is/lives like a Jew	[Y]	he is rectified before God	[X]
[14aA]	"you, who are a Jew with all the privileges involved"	[Y]	—and being, therefore, rectified before God—	[X]
[14bB]	"and *not* live like a Jew"	[Y]	—implying that you are not rectified before God—	[X]
[14cB]	"to live in a Jewish way"	[Y]	—to be rectified before God—	[X]
[15A]	"We, Jews by nature"	[Y]	—we are rectified before God—	[X]

We hear four times the MinP of the implied adversaries. Note that in Gal 2.14 and 15 Paul's usage is fully in line with the syllogistic logic of his opponents, but in Gal 2.17 it runs counter to theirs.

The antonymous theme is also present, that is, "to be a Gentile" and "to live like a Gentile" [Y-anti]. Since these antonymous themes are both related to the central question of "rectification" [X], another theme can also be added to the syllogistic structure: "to be a sinner" (Gal 2.15, 17a) and "sin" (2.17b) [X-anti].[71] This theme is the antonym of "to be rectified/rectification." In this way, we can construe the following antonymous syllogism:

MajP:	The one who is sinner	[X-anti]	he will *not* Live	[Z]
MinP:	The one who is/lives like a Gentile	[Y-anti]	he is sinner before God	[X-anti]
C:	Therefore, the one who is/lives like a Gentile	[Y-anti]	he will *not* Live	[Z]

We turn to the documented wording once again:

MinP:	The one who is/lives like a Gentile	[Y-anti]		he is sinner before God	[X-anti]
[14bA]	"[If you . . .] live like a Gentile"	[Y-anti]		—then you are a sinner (not righteous)—	[X-anti]
[15Ba]	"We . . . *not*, from the Gentiles,	[Y-anti]		[not] . . . sinners"	[X-anti]

---

71. See Bachmann, "Zur Argumentation," 534.

| | —When we (Paul and Cephas) have table fellowship with Gentiles/live like Gentiles— | [Y-anti] | [17b] | "we have been found ourselves to be sinners" | [X-anti] |

While reproducing the wording of the letter, we can textualize the anticipated participation of the Galatian addressees—as intended by Paul:

> If you—who are a Jew with all the privileges involved- (14a)
> —and being, therefore, rectified before God—
> live like a Gentile and not like a Jew (14b)
> —and, as a result, are sinner/not rectified before God—
> how can you force the Gentiles to live in a Jewish way (to Judaize) (14c)
> —to become rectified before God—?
> We, Jews by nature
> —who are rectified before God—
> and not, from the Gentiles, sinners, (15)
> (...)
> If we
> —as Jews who have to live accordingly—
> —who seek to be rectified in Christ—(17a)
> have been found ourselves to be sinners, (17b)
> —because we live like Gentiles (for example,
>   have table fellowship with them)—
> then does that suggest that Christ is a servant of sin? (17c)
> —so that we will not Live?—
> Absolutely not! (17d)

Here the MinP of the syllogistic reasoning of the implied opponents is found up to seven times.

In this line of thought, we can scrutinize other passages of the letter as well to find synonymous threads. The first is Gal 3.1–5. In verses 2 and 5, we encounter once again the antithesis between "faith" and "law" (for example, Gal 2.16). This juxtaposition revolves around the theme of the "reception of the Spirit":

> This is the only thing, I want to know of you, (2a)
> out of works of law did you receive the Spirit, (2b)
> or out of hearing faith? (2c)
> ...
> The one granting you the Spirit and working powers among you, (5a)
> [does he do so] out of works of law or out of hearing faith? (5b)
> (translation mine)

Since the "reception of the Spirit" has not been mentioned before in the oral performance of the letter, one has to ask for how the audiences will relate to it when they hear it here for the first time. We recall at this juncture the second intellectual movement of historicizing text (Chapter 3): What is the *Vorgeschichte* of the intended addressees with the "Spirit"? Or—related to experiences/senses and collective memory—what does the "reception of the Spirit" involve? Who introduced them to this theme and in what way? Barclay remarks, "One could also draw up an interesting list of points on which Paul and his opponents would have agreed ... The Spirit has been given to the people of God who believe in the Messiah."[72] Although once introduced and experienced by Paul, this theme is also constitutive of the teachers' rhetoric. If this is the reason that Paul recollects this theme here without any introduction, we can attempt to frame it in terms of the uncovered syllogistic rationale. Given the relation to the minor term "out of law" [X], the possibility comes to the fore that "reception of the Spirit" is synonymous with the major term "to Live" [Z]. Gal 3.1–5 can be reconstructed as follows:

MajP:	The one who is rectified	[X]	he will receive the Spirit	[Z]
MinP:	The one who is out of works of law	[Y]	he is rectified	[X]
C:	Therefore, the one who is out of works of law	[Y]	he will receive the Spirit	[Z]

In these verses, we encounter the C of the implied primary syllogism:

C:	Therefore, the one who is out of works of law	[Y]		he will receive the Spirit	[Z]
[2b]	"out of works of law	[Y]		[did] you receive the Spirit [?]"	[Z]
[5bA]	"out of works of law	[Y]	[5a]	The one granting you the Spirit?"	[Z]

In this reconstruction, two times the two key terms come together, namely the specifying minor term "law" [Y] and the major term "to receive the Spirit" [Z]—synonymous with "Life."

Recalling Gal 2.16, in which "out of law" is consistently opposed and ruled out by "out of faith," we can recognize in this reasoning once more the counter reasoning of Paul: the one who is out of faith, he will receive/has received the Spirit (C). In every juxtaposition of "out of law" and "out of faith," Paul's alternative and—more important—only true syllogistic reasoning is strengthened.

72. Barclay, "Mirror-Reading," 89. See also Martyn, *Galatians*, 284; Boer, *Galatians*, 173.

In the next unit Gal 3.6–9 and 14a the audience is led into another thematic matrix. This is the theme of the patriarch of Israel, "Abraham":

> [It is] as [with] Abraham, (6a)
> he had faith in God and it was reckoned to him as righteousness. (6b)
> You know, therefore, that the ones out of faith,
>   that these are the sons of Abraham. (7)
> And foreseeing that God rectifies the Gentiles out of faith, (8a)
> the Scripture was able to gospel-preach
>   Abraham beforehand [saying]: (8b)
> 'Blessed will be in you all the Gentiles.' (8c)
> So then those out of faith are Blessed together
>   with the faithful Abraham. (9)
> (...) so that the Blessing of Abraham might come
>   to the Gentiles in Christ Jesus (14a) (translation mine)

Before this passage, the theme of "Abraham" is neither introduced nor mentioned in any way. Many commentators argue that this thematic matrix originates from the teaching of the implied opponents.[73] If this is correct, we have to relate the key word πίστις here in the first instance to these teachers and to their performances as well. In a Judaizing context this term—in a particular framing—fits his opponents like a glove: In Judaism, the faithfulness of Abraham is seen in his obedience to the commandments of God. In particular, the act of circumcision illustrates the thematic matrix of "law" and "to live like/be a Jew"—compare Barclay's seventh criterion (historical plausibility).

From the perspective of these teachers, we can perceive the following underlying syllogistic structure. Both synonymous middle terms will be explicated and combined: "Sons of Abraham" is described as X1 and "rectification" as X2:

MajP:	The one who is son of Abraham/	[X1]/	he will be Blessed in Abraham	[Z]
	The one who is rectified before God	[X2]		
MinP:	The one who is faithful as Abraham	[Y]	he is son of Abraham/	[X1]/
			he is rectified	[X2]
C:	Therefore, the one who is faithful as Abraham	[Y]	he will be Blessed in Abraham	[Z]

---

73. See Barrett, "Allegory of Abraham," 6–8; Barclay, "Mirror-Reading," 87, 88; Witt Burton, *Galatians*, 153; Longenecker, *Galatians*, 109–11; Dunn, *Galatians*, 159; Martyn, *Galatians*, 296–98; Boer, *Galatians*, 186–87. Contrariwise, Witherington, *Grace in Galatia*, 218–19.

We encounter the MajP, MinP as well as the C—the MajP with X1 (son of Abraham) in Gal 3.8c, the MinP with X1 in 3.7, the MinP with X2 (rectification before God) twice in 3.6 and 8a and the C in 3.9:

MajP1:	The one who is son of Abraham	[X1]		he will be Blessed in Abraham	[Z]
[8cB]	"'In you (*in your offspring*)	[X1]	[8cA]	will be Blessed [all the Gentiles]'"	[Z]

MinP1:	The one who is faithful as Abraham	[Y]		he is son of Abraham	[X1]
[7]	"You know, therefore, that the ones out of faith	[Y]		that these are the sons of Abraham"	[X1]

MinP2:	The one who is faithful as Abraham	[Y]		he is rectified	[X2]
[6b]	"he [Abraham] had faith in God	[Y]		and it was reckoned to him as righteousness"	[X2]
[8aC]	"out of faith	[Y]	[8aB]	God rectifies [the Gentiles]"	[X2]

C:	Therefore, the one who is faithful as Abraham	[Y]		he will be Blessed in Abraham	[Z]
[9]	"So then those out of faith	[Y]		are Blessed together with the faithful Abraham."	[Z]

Thus, all the terms of the reconstructed syllogism of the implied adversaries are present in Gal 3.6–9. More so, everything is stated in the *modus ponens*. Paul seems to let one of the themes of his opponents resound according to their own reasoning! This time no juxtaposition with "law" or a denial of the reasoning (MinP) is heard. What is Paul doing? Instead of an open refutation (*negative rhetoric*), the apostle follows the rhetorical strategy of *Umdeutung* (Chapter 3). In the intended construal of thought in the aural event, the original addressees should grasp this familiar reasoning on the "faith of Abraham" differently; this should be the moment that one way of structuring thought is transformed into another. The prior juxtapositions of "law" and "faith" and the explicit exclusion of the former should cause them to frame this theme ("faith") not any longer in line with these other teachers—as obedience to "the law"—but solely as Paul's earlier advocated trust in God.

In Gal 3.10 and 13, the theme of "curse" occurs. In Gal 3.13, the matrix is explicitly phrased as the "curse of the law." Thus, according to Paul, the "law" is related to "curse." The present-day reader vis-à-vis the text of the letter encounters "curse" for the first time in Gal 3.10. The term is used by the apostle, however, without any form of introduction or explication. In line with the proposed approach, we may assume that the implied addressees are familiar with this specific theme: so to speak, the threat of curse—which is activated in and by the spoken word—is hanging in the air.

> For all who are out of works of law (10a)
> are under curse, (10b)
> for it is written:
> "Cursed everyone who does not remain in all things written
> in the Book of the law to do them." (10c)
> (...)
> Christ has bought us out from the curse of the law (13a)
> by becoming for us curse, (13b)
> for it is written: "Cursed everyone who is hanged on a tree" (13c)
> (translation mine)

Through the conjunctive γάρ (for), the "curse of the law" is connected with the preceding verses on the "Blessing of Abraham" (with Mayordomo; against Bachmann). Moreover, the "curse of the law" is an antonym of the "Blessing of Abraham" (see also Mayordomo; Bachmann). Therefore, if the reconstructed syllogistic rationale of the opponents' teaching is valid, the theme of the "curse of the law" can be unfolded according to the same pattern:

MajP:	The one who is *not* rectified before God	[X]	he will be cursed by the law	[Z-anti]
MinP:	The one who is *not* out of works of law	[Y]	he is *not* rectified before God	[X]
C:	Therefore, the one who is *not* out of works of law	[Y]	he will be cursed by the law	[Z-anti]

In Paul's own statement of Gal 3.10a, a denial is missing this time. Thus, the implied audience hears the C of the opponents bluntly turned upside down.

C:	Therefore, the one who is *not* out of works of law	[Y]		he will be cursed by the law	[Z-anti]
[10a]	"all who are [*not*] out of works of law	[Y]	[10b]	are under curse"	[Z-anti]

In the following alleged Scripture proof (Gal 3.10c), however, the addressees will recognize once again the unaltered C of these other teachers:

[10cB]	"'everyone who does *not* remain in all things written in the Book of the law to do them,	[Y]	[10cA]	Cursed!'"	[Z]

When the syllogistically structured reasoning governs the implied realm of history, this rationale has to direct the implied addressees in their participation in the construal of the performance at this point. For that reason, the present-day reader is no longer (subliminally) forced to harmonize this laboured argumentation on the level of the text. Just as the original participants understood beyond critical awareness, one is compelled, however, to understand the effect of this blunt contradiction in keeping with the appearance and performances of these other teachers. In Gal 3.10, we can discern the C two times. The first time the C is stated by Paul in the *modus ponens*—in line with the opponents (Gal 3.10c). Another time the C is formulated in the *modus tollens* (Gal 3.10a). How does the audience participate in this clash of bluntly contradicting conclusions? Since these C's are not logically related to each other, the answer to this question is not within the scope of the present study but worth pursuing.[74]

Textualizing Oral Performance There-and-Then-to-Them (4)

The interesting point is that the reconstructed primary syllogism functions as text to us (see the previous tables). Also, this example of textualizing the oral performance there-and-then of Gal 3.10–12 is caught up in layouts of the documented wording. As we have stated before, however, the realm of history of the original addressees lacked these textualized tables. Therefore, detextification aims to bend our thoughts into that specific realm of history in line with the senses. After Paul had left, the Galatian communities became challenged in their convictions, practices, and social hierarchy. The presence and performances of others who claimed leadership (the other "teachers") formed the incentive to a process of change in the communities. Were they able to answer questions which had risen after the apostle had

---

74. In his commentary, Martyn reasons that the implied opponents had already used these words from Deut 27.26. So these soundbites would have had their impact on the Galatian converts prior to the oral performance of the letter. Once this perspective is introduced, this Scripture proof (on the level of text/in se?) cannot be understood anymore as being absolute or *freischwebend*. In this respect, the structure of rhetoric-counter rhetoric seems to be more promising. For a proposal to understand this contradiction in line with anticipated participation, see Veen, "Staaltje."

left? Were convictional or practical loose ends troubling the converts? First, we assume that this specific syllogistic reasoning of these teachers on "law," "rectification," and "l/Life" has been newly introduced in their concrete lifeworld. Second, once a growing number of them had understood and internalized the logos of their reasoning (collective memory), it would have sufficed for the teachers to reaffirm time and again this syllogistic reasoning in an enthymematic way. That is why Paul can relate to it without much preparatory work. Regarding this anticipatory approach of the apostle, Martyn even presents a fully-fledged proposal for one of their sermons. In direct speech, he offers one on the descent of Abraham.[75] Although results will always remain tentative or suggestive, this approach is legitimate and helpful. It directs our thoughts deeper into the realm of history there-and-then-to-them.[76] Third, this repetitive syllogistic reasoning did not only structure their performances (rhetoric), but this emphasis on the "law" was affirmed in their own daily presence among the Galatian converts: the latter became familiar with Jewish religious regulations—consider "works of the law," "circumcision," and "not to have table fellowship with Gentiles." Sociologically speaking, these outstanding practices function as identity markers; they bring hierarchy and distinction in communities. Implicitly, this kind of presence/way of living as Jews reflected their superior status in distinction from "Gentiles" who are "sinners."

---

75. In his Comment #33, Martyn provides an imaginational "The Teachers' Sermon on Descent from Abraham, and Paul's Modulation of that Theme into Descent from God": "Listen Now! It all began with Abraham. Looking beyond the fascinating movements of the heavenly bodies he was the first to discern that there is but one God. Because of that perception, . . ." (*Galatians*, 303–6).

76. In line with the approach of detextification, we can comment that this sermon—as presented to the reader of his commentary on the level of text (media)—resembles a present-day sermon from the pulpit in a traditional Protestant church. Critical analysis of the composition of this proposal prompts the question whether the intricacies of real-time communication in a predominantly oral culture are done justice. Since the present study anticipates a preceding and reversed form of rhetoric by these teachers, the structure of rhetoric and counter rhetoric would then be as follows: Paul's original presence and performances (rhetoric) is countered by the presence and performances of these teachers (counter rhetoric). In conclusion, in how Martyn presents this so-called sermon (singular) of these teachers we miss the explicit differentiation of media and mindset once more. How would this sermon look (hear!) in the light of the teachers' anticipated participation of the Galatians and their prior experiences with Paul? In line with the call to textualize history, we would propose to explicate in the structure of such a "sermon" the oral-aural communicative dynamics of synonymous and antonymous metonymy as well as the specific collective memory of the original addressees at that moment. So the element of anticipated participation and/or metonymical disclosure of the specific collective memory of Paul's Galatian converts seems to be lacking in Martyn's composition.

Conclusions

In Gal 2.14—3.14, we discern up to twenty-one threads of identical, synonymous, and antonymous terms in one syllogistically structured reasoning. In this enthymematic way, a consistent basic issue comes to the fore: that is, the call of these other teachers to live in obedience to the Jewish law, culminating in the act of circumcision. In this way, Barclay's overarching criterion of consistency is met:

> Unless we have strong evidence to suggest that Paul is responding to more than one type of opponent or argument, we should assume that a single object is in view. Thus the results of the previous criteria may be tested to see if they amount to a consistent picture of Paul's opponents.[77]

In line with the proposed approach, we observe that this textualized *totum* reaches also into the realm of history there-and-then-to-them and becomes imaginable in how these teachers must have been active among the Gentile converts in Galatia. From a sociological point of view, one can argue that this syllogistically structured reasoning must have impressed the Galatian converts; as means of power, this reasoning could help to explain how these teachers had gained influence over Paul's addressees. This clear and continuously repeated structuring of thought would have indoctrinated Paul's Galatian converts. We conclude that the apostle does not deny the reasoning as a whole, but he disqualifies and replaces the minor term. We can even explicate the syllogistic counter reasoning which governs his anticipated participation: "Therefore, the one who is out of faith, he will Live" (conclusion; see Gal 3.11b). In sum, in this detextification, we did not so much say new things nor provide an answer to the question, What does the text say? We scrutinized and textualized the distinctive functioning of the documented wording there-and-then-to-them: How do these (documented) phrases in the oral delivery of the letter mean to the originally intended addressees in their predominantly oral state of mind from the perspective of Paul—who has integrated the rhetoric of his opponents?[78] In view of the warnings of

---

77. Barclay, "Mirror-Reading," 85.

78. In light of the critical evaluation of the text-context scheme in Chapter 3, we can observe the following hermeneutical dynamic: since the anticipated whole (*totum*) is constitutive of the communicative process there-and-then *in actu*, this implied collective memory is not explicated on the level of text; it will not, therefore, automatically arise from the *freischwebende* context of the letter functioning as autonomous text here-and-now-to-us. Conversely, it is firmly bound to the originally intended subjects *in actu* there-and-then. These actors exist per se beyond the level of text. Therefore textualizing—in the elements of "to whom" and "in what state of mind"—their participation

Albert Lord and Walter Ong, we conclude that we can textualize—to a considerable extent—the originally intended structuring of thought implied in Gal 2–3. To strengthen our thesis, we will discuss a second example of our approach in the next section.

EXAMPLE 2: *FREISCHWEBENDE* THEOLOGY OR RHETORICAL STRATEGY IN GAL 2.18–20?

The following example of detextification is related to the role ascribed to the senses of the intended addressees. This example deals with Gal 2.18–20:

> For, if I would rebuild anew that which I broke down, (18a)
> I show myself to be a transgressor. (18b)
> For I myself died through law in [the realm of the] law, (19a)
> so that I will Live in God, (19b)
> together with Christ, I have been crucified. (19c)
> Not any longer do I live, (20a)
> but Christ, he Lives in me: (20b)
> And that which I now live in [the realm of the] flesh, (20b)
> I Live in faith, (20cA)
> the faith of the Son of God, who loved me
>   and gave himself for me. (20cB)
> I do not nullify the Grace of God! (21a)
> For if rectification is through law, (21b)
> then Christ died in vain! (21c) (translation mine)

Verse 18 contains an antonymously structured metaphor on "building" and "breaking down" (a wall or a building perhaps?). From verse 19 onward, Paul continues his argumentation with several verbs—which are also related to each other—ἀποθνῄσκω (to die), ζάω (to L/live), συσταυρόομαι (to be co-crucified), and παραδίδωμι (to be handed over; in the implied framing of Christ's voluntary death at the hands of human beings). Perceiving the letter as intended aural event, we can state that this thematic matrix has not been heard before. Since the theme of "life" and "to live" is heard frequently before, an also antonymously structured theme comes to the fore: "dying" and "living/Living."

In this example, the role of the senses by which the originally intended addressees participate in their realm of history cannot be underestimated.

---

is a necessary step so that the biblical scholar comes to an understanding of how the original addressees were intended to understand. In this way, it becomes clear that "context"—that is, textualizing history—has to precede the real-time functioning of the letter as "text" to the present-day reader.

This is, however, not a legitimate for unbridled fantasy. Imagination is structured by historicizing text.

The following steps will be taken. First, an evaluation will be presented of four more recent and influential commentaries.[79] Second, a detextification of Gal 2.19–20 will be undertaken. Although not always congruent with each other, we aim to provide a historical-critical deepening of the dimension of media and mindsets in current understandings of this passage. Again, it is not so much the "what" but the "how" of Paul's rhetoric which is at issue in this example.

Hans Dieter Betz: *Galatians* (Hermeneia)

It has become practically axiomatic since the appearance of the commentary by Hans Dieter Betz that study of the argument and structure of Galatians begins with classical rhetoric.[80] In his introduction, he states,

> Paul's Letter to the Galatians can be analysed according to Greco-Roman rhetoric and epistolography. This possibility raises the whole question of Paul's relationship to the rhetorical and literary disciplines and culture, a question which has not as yet been adequately discussed.

As a historically attested amalgam of the letter-form and the genres of autobiography and apologetic speech, Betz categorizes Galatians into the "apologetic letter genre."[81] This type of letter presupposes the situation of a "court of law." This framework (court) provides a structure for Paul to envision how his addressees will participate in the actualization of his letter. Paul anticipates his Galatian converts to participate as a "jury" who will

---

79. This selection of commentaries is based on the frequency of occurrences in scholarly publications and on the way in which they have left their mark on the scholarly debate. For commentaries published over the last forty years, see Bruce, *Galatians*; Lightfoot, *Galatians*; Mussner, *Galaterbrief*; Fung, *Galatians*; Rohde, *Galater*; Matera, *Galatians*; Ziesler, *Galatians*; McKnight, *Galatians*; Williams, *Galatians*; Esler, *Galatians*; Witherington, *Grace in Galatia*; Becker and Lutz, *Galater*; Hays, "The Letter to the Galatians," 139–348; Cousar, *Galatians*; Lührmann, *Galater*; Nanos, *Irony of Galatians*; Fowler, *Galatians*; Schreiner, *Galatians*; Jervis, *Galatians*; DaSilva, *Galatians*; Keener, *Galatians*; Vanhoye and Williamson, *Galatians*.

80. Betz, *Galatians*. Since this paradigm shift took place more than forty years ago, see for a recent and balanced evaluation Classen, "Theory of Rhetoric."

81. Betz, *Galatians*, 14. Given Greco-Roman epistolography/rhetoric, he determines the following structure: I. Epistolary Prescript (1.1–5); II. *Exordium* (1.6–11); III. *Narratio* (1.12–12.14); IV. *Propositio* (2.15–21); V. *Probatio* (3.1–4.31); VI. *Exhortatio* (5.1–6.10); VII. *Epistolary Postscript/Conclusio* (6.11–18). As a consequence, Betz identifies Gal 2.18–20 as part of the *Propositio*.

"judge" him as a "defendant" because of the "accusations" made by these other teachers.

In view of historicizing text, several questions come to the fore: How do the original addressees know their role (judge) and participate accordingly in the delivery of the letter? And if so, what would the outcome or verdict of the jury imply? In terms of imagination, we ask, What does Paul expect to happen? How does this complicated and layered process look like in the realm of history there-and-then-to-them? No clear directives or indications are encountered on the level of the documented wording of the letter itself. So, in line with the dynamic of anticipated participation and/or metonymic referentiality, we must ask, When absent words should form the *partes*, how can the *totum* (court of law) be reconstructed by the addressees themselves in the moment of delivery?

Betz continues that in this framework of the court the letter becomes "a self-apology, delivered not in person but in a written form." Regarding the original use of the letter, he writes, "Since it is simply a lifeless piece of paper, it eliminates one of the most important weapons of the rhetorician, the oral delivery." Since no further elaboration of the "lifeless piece of paper" is found, the letter seems to function as text there-and-then-to-them as it does here-and-now-to-us (how). The dimension of performance or a real-time event of delivery or public reading seems to be absent. So it becomes even more difficult to imagine the actual functioning of the letter as a "court of law." Regarding the participants who are reading the letter as text, we ask, Do they do so in silence and solitude, all of them at the same time (multiple copies available) or one after another (single autograph)? When, how, and under whose supervision would they discuss that which they have read and come to a verdict in the "court of law"?[82] Betz continues his reasoning by asserting that since the advantages of oral communication are lost, the art of persuasion has to take place through "rational arguments." This leap makes us ask once more: Do these arguments function on the level of text to the generalized reader of the letter? This question seems to be answered in an earlier comment by Betz, namely, that the Letter to the Galatians functions in an ongoing debate: "Because of the fundamental issues under discussion,

82. At the end of his commentary, we find a line of reasoning on the realm of history there-and-then. Betz says that Paul hopes that his letter re-enacts his former apostolic parousia in their midst: "The difference is that at the beginning they were confronted as to whether or not they should accept the 'gospel of Christ,' while now they are asked to remain loyal to it and not bring upon themselves the curse of apostasy" (*Galatians*, 325). Comparable to the evaluation of Bachmann's article, this remark is not only a minimal and still a highly abstracted form of textualizing history there-and-then-to-them, but this context is also explicated independent of and after the processing by him of the letter as text.

the readers do not simply include the Galatian churches but all churches. . . . In principle, therefore, even the present readers of the letter are participants in this debate."[83] The implication is that, historically speaking, Paul—as author and origin of this letter—would have anticipated, in the moment of composition, the whole history of reception (hitherto or perhaps even centuries beyond) of his letters as "text"-functioning-independently-of-time-and-place. Once more we add that we do not state that this "ongoing debate" is not useful or is inadequate (in terms of the question what does it mean), but we want to thematize and discuss two media cultures involved in this process of coming to understand: that is, oral performance there-and-then-to-them over against autonomous text in the later history of Western Christian theology.

Notwithstanding the inherent value of rhetorical analysis, these leaps in his own argumentation, that is, from the setting of a "court of law" there-and-then, via the letter as "lifeless piece of paper," up to the point that he remarks that "all churches . . . even the present-day readers are participants in the debate," make clear that Betz does not take one clear perspective in the realm of history, neither there-and-then-to-them nor here-and-now-for-us.

We turn to the passage under scrutiny. Betz considers Gal 2.18–20 to be composed mainly of "doctrinal abbreviations." He observes that "these abbreviations are difficult to translate. Commenting upon them means that they must be resolved into the doctrinal statements which they intend to abbreviate."[84] Neither it is clear how he comes to this conclusion on the presence of "doctrinal abbreviations" nor who (to whom) relates in what way (how, in what state of mind) to these abbreviations. Nonetheless, we recognize a metonymical structure in his observation. The abbreviations function as the parts that should recall the whole (doctrine).

Here we step back for a moment. Textualizing history implies scrutinizing familiar terminology: What are the consequences of using "doctrine" regarding the collective memory of the original addressees? This notion—like, for example, "theology"—tends towards the frame of a fixed, coherent, and free-standing belief system. This structure is perhaps fitting in our Western theological tradition and predominantly literate state of mind vis-à-vis the letter as text and its reception throughout time, but what about a predominantly oral mindset in the original intended aural event and the purpose to change the communal course of life in these congregations (inner-historical)?

---

83. Betz, *Galatians*, 24.
84. Betz, *Galatians*, 115.

In Gal 2.15–16, Paul elaborates on "the doctrine of justification by faith in Christ." Based on the participle εἰδότες in verse 16 ("we know/knowing"), Betz makes the case that one is a Christian by this "theological conviction"—unlike being a Jew, what a person is by birth.[85] What are the implications of this doctrine for Gentile Christians? In verse 17, Paul constructs a false and vehemently denied argument: Gentiles—even when they have become Christian—are sinners until they come under the Torah. "The question is whether Paul himself has merely invented this idea or whether he has adopted a slogan from his opponents."[86] Here we see that Betz bends his thoughts into the realm of history there-and-then-to-them (from whose perspectives).

In Gal 2.18, Paul continues with an explicit legal critique of this false argument. The terms of "building," "annulling," and "rebuilding" emerge. Betz offers a helpful paraphrase here: "If I want to regard the Gentile Christians as 'transgressors' of the Torah and 'sinners' in the Jewish sense of the term, I have to first reinstate the Torah as the law which then the Gentiles would be obliged to obey." As a consequence, "the doctrine of justification" would collapse. On a logical level, this paraphrase is clarifying and solid to us as readers of his commentary here-and-now—especially when one is (theologically) raised in a Protestant environment. It remains unclear how this reasoning, as explicated on the level of his text, would have functioned in the aural event.

We see this confirmed in Betz' interpretation of Gal 2.19–20 where Paul provides "the basic elements of his own theological position" in four theses. Betz relates the verb "I have died" to "co-crucifixion" without further elaboration or justification. He only mentions that the verb "in a metaphorical way points to some kind of death experience."[87] Neither does he explicate to whom this metaphorical death experience should mean nor how, in what state of mind, and from whose perspective; is it related to the original addressees (collective memory) or the present-day (Christian?) reader (doctrine)?

In the second thesis, Betz relates the abbreviated phrase "I have been crucified together with Christ" (2.19b) to Rom 6.1–10. A majority of the older commentaries also structure their readings in view of this parallel text.[88] However, Betz explicitly denies the ritual of baptism to be a pos-

---

85. Betz, *Galatians*, 115–19.
86. Betz, *Galatians*, 120.
87. Betz, *Galatians*, 121.
88. In this respect, Betz explicitly refers to the commentary by Schlier, *Galater*. In note 636, we briefly discuss his reading of Gal 2.18–20.

sible interpretative framework. His argument is that baptism in Galatians is only mentioned once (3.27): "Strangely, in 3.27 Paul does not mention the dying together with Christ, while in 5.24; 6.14, when he speaks of the death together with Christ he does not mention baptism." The horizon of this argument is as broad as the level of text allows. Betz places the notion of "co-crucifixion" against the background of the abstracted context which comes with text. What would happen if we were to imagine these words sounding in an aural event, that is, when we imagine that Paul is anticipating a specific participation by his Galatian converts there-and-then?

Another argument against the relatedness of Romans 6 is the observation that nowhere in Galatians does Paul mention Christ's resurrection or any other of the concepts as used here. We see this affirmed in another line of reasoning:

> It is only in Romans 6 that Paul interprets the ritual of baptism in terms of death and resurrection together with Christ. That interpretation must be secondary and cannot be tied entirely to baptism in the way Schlier does. In fact, it may be just the other way around; Gal 2.19 may contain the theological principle by which Paul interprets the ritual of baptism in Romans 6.[89]

It is questionable why Betz would limit Paul's activity of "interpretation" to the documented wording in the so-called authentic letters in the corpus Paulinum—for example, "It is only in Romans 6 that Paul interprets the ritual of baptism in terms of death and resurrection together with Christ." What role do the presence and performances (baptisms?) of the apostle play in all the places which he visited on his several journeys? Alternatively, we can ask, On what grounds does Betz relate the Letter to the Romans to the one to the Galatians and vice versa? How would this relation have looked to the original addressees in the realm of history there-and-then, more so, in the event of oral performance? No argument is given. Should we conclude that Betz—as writer of his commentary on Galatians as text—is simply working uncritically in the ever-expanding universe of texts? This small detour leads to a viewpoint from which we see fundamental differences between Betz's perspective on the letter and the approach of detextification.

As commented before, the reconstructed reasoning by Betz is insightful and solid in the abstracted context of text or as *freischwebendes Denken*. However, from the perspective of textualizing history or sensorial manifestation in the participatory realm of history there-and-then-to-them, we must ask, In what way would the Galatian converts (or even Christians here-and-now?) relate to this beneficial death by the Christ? How does this

---

89. Betz, *Galatians*, 123.

death manifest itself to them in their concrete lifeworld? In Betz' interpretation, "[t]he doctrine of justification by faith in Christ" and "the death of the 'I'" remain highly abstract notions. He presents an absolute understanding (being) which does not leave much room for a distinction between the first-century original addressees caught up in the aural event in their concrete lifeworld, and the twentieth or twenty-first-century academic reader vis-à-vis the letter-as-text (becoming). Therefore the governing question—How does it function, to whom, in what state of mind, and from whose perspective[s]?—will be answered to come to a historically more plausible understanding of the issues involved.

EXCURSUS: ANCIENT RHETORICAL SOURCES AND ORAL PERFORMANCE

Since the rhetorical approach of Hans Dieter Betz in his Hermeia commentary has become paradigmatic, we will turn now to some ancient sources on rhetoric to inquire into oral performance: How important is this aspect and what role does it play in ancient rhetoric?

Regarding ancient Greece, it is well-known that Socrates (c. 470–399 BCE) and Plato (c. 427–347 BCE) distrusted the teachings of poets, sophists, and the writers of handbooks.[90] They considered their practices not only morally irresponsible but also unrelated to the search for Truth. Also Aristotle (384–22 BCE) was dismissive of this kind of oratory. In his *On Rhetoric: A Theory of Civic Discourse*,[91] he remarks that "delivery seems a vulgar matter when rightly understood" (3.1.5), "[delivery] has great power . . . because of the corruption of the audience" (3.1.5), and he depicted poets as "speaking sweet nothings" (3.1.9). Nonetheless, he had a different stance in recognizing that "rhetoric as an art of communication was morally neutral, that it could be used for either good or ill."[92] In his lectures on rhetoric, on which *On Rhetoric* is based, he wanted to teach his students to understand the dangers of sophistic rhetoric, on the one hand, but he also wanted them to be able to defend themselves and to be effective in public life, on the other.[93]

---

90. For example, in Plato's dialogue *Gorgias*, Socrates criticizes rhetoric as a form of flattery. In the *Republic*, Plato even identifies it with "poison." In Chapter 1, Section D. Eric Havelock: Birth pangs of a new state of mind, the role of the poets and Plato's reaction to them will be dealt with extensively.

91. Aristotle, *On Rhetoric*, 195.

92. Kennedy, "Prooemion," in *On Rhetoric*, x.

93. Kennedy, "Prooemion," in *On Rhetoric*, xi.

In view of the leading question in this Excursus, we will turn to book three, in which he addresses the theme of delivery (*hypokrisis*). Analysing effective speech, he differentiates between the "facts," the "composition" thereof in "language" (style [*lexis*] and arrangement [*taxis*]), and the last element "that has the greatest force but has not yet been taken in hand, the matter of the delivery [*hypokrisis*]" (3.1.3). Because of this "great power" and the small place in teaching hitherto, he qualifies the delivery of oratory as an *art* (3.1.5). Although comprising almost the whole book, the treatment of style and arrangement functions as a means to the end of delivery. This is important to note. Although the intellectual legacy of Aristotle could last until today because it was recorded in writing and in that way transmitted throughout the ages, we should not uncritically identify the philosopher with this media, even as in writing a speech for effective delivery. As Daniel Melia argues in his article "Orality and Aristotle's Aesthetics and Methods; Take #2": "Unlike many contemporaries and later Classical rhetorical handbooks, Aristotle's Rhetoric is concerned not with how to compose a speech in advance—how to write it down—but with how to access material that is already in one's head exactly when needed." (see Chapter 2, Section E.2. Ancient rhetoric as speech art).[94]

In ancient Rome, Aristotle's book *On Rhetoric* reached Marcus Tullius Cicero (106–43 BCE).[95] He also wrote extensively on rhetoric. Aristotle's emphasis on delivery can be recognized in book three of *De Oratore*.[96] Here Cicero describes the speech of Lucius Licinius Crassus who attempts to persuade the Roman people to replace the Senate with a new council. In this elaborate speech, Cicero makes Crassus at a certain moment comment, "But the effect of all of these oratorical devices depends on how they are delivered. Delivery, I assert, is the dominant factor in oratory; without delivery the best speaker cannot be of any account at all, and a moderate speaker with a trained delivery can often outdo the best of them" (3.56.213). So, Cicero emphasizes the need and impact of training in delivery, even for those who are gifted in speaking.

In his *Institutio Oratoria*, Marcus Fabius Quintilianus (35–100 CE), dealt with *De Oratore* of Cicero.[97] In book nine, he hails the study of artistic structure as conducted by Cicero. He does so by subsequently opposing a number of writers who "contend that language as it chances to present itself

---

94. Melia, "Orality," 122.

95. For example, see the tables and discussion as provided by Rubinelli, *Ars Topica*, 93–109.

96. Cicero, *On the Orator*.

97. Quintilian, *Orator's Education*, 507.

in the rough is more natural and even more manly. If by this they mean that only that is natural which originated with nature and has never received any subsequent cultivation, there is an end to the whole art of oratory" (9.4.4). He describes what these "first men" missed, namely "[t]hey knew nothing of introducing their case by an exordium, of instructing the jury by a statement of facts, of proving by argument or of arousing the emotions" (9.4.4).[98] In this summary, we recognize the approach of Hans Dieter Betz as applied to the Letter to the Galatians (see above) and, more important, see the aptness thereof affirmed. Once more Quintilian lauds Cicero's study of structure by concluding, "And for this reason all the best scholars are convinced that the study of structure is of the utmost value, not merely for charming the ear, but for stirring the soul" (9.4.9). The persuasive power of oratory is constituted by the weaving together of rhythm, melody, and eloquence (9.4.13; see Introduction, Section D.5. Etymology of text: Between *textum* and text-as-known-to-us).[99] The rest of the book is dedicated to a minute study of the artistic structure. Based on the elements of comma, colon, and period and the qualities of order, connexion, and rhythm, the activity of writing becomes implied in his own dealing with artistic structure. Thus, at this stage in his exposé as present-day readers we enter familiar ground. However, it is paramount that writing is utilized by him in view of the oral delivery of rhetoric. So, the documented testimonies to this science—the transmitted handbooks that we can study in the ever-expanding universe of text—did not impair but enhance and served the art of delivery, that is, the specific context of speaking to captivate the heart of the hearers in order to wield power over them. In conclusion, the examined cross section of ancient rhetorical evidence is not only directed towards but also by the dynamics of real-time oral performance.

Richard Longenecker: *Galatians* (WBC)

The second commentary under scrutiny is by Richard Longenecker.[100] It consists of two parts, an introduction and a text and commentary section. In the first part, he describes the reception and historical context of Galatians. Important for the following discussion is that in this section we find an elaborate description of the Galatian addressees and Paul's opponents,

---

98. Quintilian, *Orator's Education*, 509.
99. Quintilian, *Orator's Education*, 512.
100. Longenecker, *Galatians*.

that is, the other teachers.[101] In the second part Longenecker offers his exegesis of the verses, passages, and chapters of the letter.

Regarding Gal 2.19–20, he notes its "highly compressed language."[102] We encounter neither the question of the reason for nor the effect on Paul's implied audience of this kind of compressed language. Since he does not explicitly address the media-dimension, we suppose that he does so as "reader" of this passage framed as "text." In line with Betz, he approaches this passage (Gal 2.19–20) as part of the larger section 2.15–21: "For if the *probatio* contains the proofs or arguments introduced by the *propositio*, we must look to Paul's *probatio* of 3.1—4.11 for an understanding of how to unpack the terms of the *propositio* of 2.15–21."[103] So Gal 3.1—4.11 should disclose the preceding passage 2.15–21. Operationally speaking, this proposal is dependent on the typical fixedness and availability of, and continuous looping back[104] in the letter-as-text to us (how).

Before we hone in on the theme of "dying" and "living"[105] in Longenecker's commentary, we first make some observations in line with the approach of detextification. Regarding Gal 2.19, he comments, "Paul presents in encapsulated form the essence of his own theology vis-à-vis Jewish nomism."[106] The formulations of "Paul's own theology" and "Jewish nomism" imply that we are dealing with two belief systems that can be compared with or even contrasted with each other on that abstracted level. Regarding the original addressees—especially in the aural event of the delivery—one

---

101. Longenecker, *Galatians*, xcvi–viii.

102. Longenecker, *Galatians*, 80.

103. Longenecker, *Galatians*, 81.

104. The meaning of "back looping" is here that the text is physically available to the reader, as book or on a screen, and that, when they have difficulty in following the line of reasoning while reading, they can go back and linger over the preceding lines and parts of that text to find clues to come to an understanding of the difficult or obscure section.

105. First, Paul introduces to his hearers the theme of "dying" and "living." Subsequently, he mentions the "cross of Christ" (Χριστῷ συνεσταύρωμαι). Without further explanation, Longenecker relates, however, this preceding thematic matrix to the crucifixion of Christ. The point we can make here is that the mechanism of synonymy is uncritically operative in his own understanding. As experienced and skilled a Christian commentator with his *Vorverständnis* (Gadamer) or encyclopaedia (Eco) as Longenecker is, he participates in the intended construal of meaning. Hence, we advocate concerning detextification that we should always ask explicitly—if this dynamic is operative—what the prerequisites are on the part of the original addressees and/or their collective memory that would cause this to be the case. In this way, the communicative structure of anticipated participation by Paul in the process of composition becomes constitutive of our understanding.

106. Longenecker, *Galatians*, 91.

can ask whether they were trained for and attuned to such a highly literate or typically "academic" endeavour (what state of mind).

Similarly, some remarks prompt the question for the element "to whom." Longenecker offers the following stipulation of the law: "the law's purpose was to work itself out of a job and point *us* beyond itself to fuller relationship with God," and continuing with a spatial metaphor, this was in order ". . . to bring *us* to a place of being no longer dependent on its jurisdiction . . ." (emphasis mine).[107] Regarding the matrix under scrutiny in this example, he states, "Christ's death on the cross and *our* spiritual identification with his death affects freedom from the jurisdiction of the Mosaic law" (emphasis mine).[108] The pronouns "us" and "our" betray some sort of generalized Christian reading community (to whom).

Now we can focus on the theme of "dying" and "living" itself. According to Longenecker, "Christ's death" is framed as "spiritual identification." He argues,

> The σύν- prefix of the verb συνεσταύρωμαι highlights the *believer's* participation with Christ in his crucifixion. Paul is undoubtedly not here thinking of a literal physical death on the part of *the Christian*, but of his or her spiritual identification with Christ's death on the cross. The perfect tense of the verb signals *the believer's* once-for-all act of commitment, with that act having results and implications for the present (emphasis mine).[109]

Once more we see that possible differences between the original rhetorical situation there-and-then-to-them and the one of the present-day reader are not made explicit. Longenecker's reasoning starts with the crucifixion of Christ—that is, the "participation" in it of the "believer." Since he rejects the thought of "a literal physical death," the suggestion of "his or her spiritual identification with Christ's death on the cross" becomes abstracted to an extremely high degree. It cannot appeal to the senses of the present-day reader here-and-now, let alone to the original Galatian addressees, who must have been familiar with it in their concrete lifeworld. No connection is found anymore to crucifixion as a historically specific and humiliating form of Roman execution or martyrdom.

The exposition of Longenecker is surprising in the light of his own introduction. In this description of the addressees, date, opponents, situation, and epistolary and rhetorical structures we find a clear example of textualizing history (Chapter 3). In the text and commentary part, however,

107. Longenecker, *Galatians*, 90.
108. Longenecker, *Galatians*, 91.
109. Longenecker, *Galatians*, 92.

the original addressees have become generalized and abstracted into free-floating "Christians/believers;" similarly, "co-crucifixion" becomes abstracted (or maybe spiritualized) beyond imagination. This (co-)"crucifixion" is severed from the typically Roman practice of crucifixion. This can be seen as a telling example of the turn from production to product: his commentary starts with this historical exploration of forty pages (process of production); then he turns, also on the level of the text, in the second part, to the "text" of the letter (product); once caught up himself on this level, he offers his own understanding or commentary. In this transition, he somehow loses the perspective of the reconstructive historian and becomes the actual reader who is involved in answering the deeply ingrained question, What does it mean—to me/us (Christians)?

Louis Martyn: *Galatians* (AB)

The third commentary, published in 1997, is written by J. Louis Martyn.[110] He understands the letter against the background of the Jewish-apocalyptic worldview of Paul. The thematization of this worldview touches on aspects of the distinctive mindset and collective memory of the original addressees and forms an example of textualizing history. We will start our discussion with some illustrations of this approach. Martyn ascribes an important role to the other teachers who gained influence over the Galatian converts. Their presence among the gathered addressees in the aural event forms a structural feature in his understanding of the letter: "as they [the Galatians] listen to the speech as he [Paul] addresses the Teachers . . ." So the apostle, Martyn suggests, wants to address these teachers more than the Galatians themselves. Once more, in line with textualizing history, we recognize the structuring elements of "to whom" and "from whose perspective[s]."

As we saw already in Chapter 2, Martyn frames Paul's communicative strategy in terms of "theology"/"theologies"—Paul versus these teachers. We pause here for a moment. On the one hand, we observe a clear intellectual movement into the realm of history there-and-then: Martyn describes an apocalyptic worldview there-and-then contrary to our given present-day one and also the theology of Paul there-and-then in reciprocity to the one of his opponents there-and-then. On the other hand, when these other teachers become the actually intended hearers, the collective memory of the Galatian converts—in their relation to and experiences with Paul's former presence and performances in their midst—becomes superseded. The

---

110. Martyn, *Galatians*.

apostle would then anticipate the participation of these Jewish teachers and their collective memory.

Martyn also provides comments in which he thinks through the participation of the Galatians themselves. We see this in his comments on Gal 2.17c, where Christ is charged to be a servant of sin: "Is 'servant of sin' an expression Paul quotes rather than coins?" He argues that this expression is "coined," it originates from the apostle himself. If "quoted," he would refer to the rhetoric of these other teachers:

> the best route lies in the assumption that Paul can take for granted comprehension on the part of the Galatians (as they listen to the speech he addresses to the Teachers) because he is borrowing several of his expressions from things the Teachers are saying about him.[111]

Martyn's formulation—the apostle has borrowed "several of his expressions from things the Teachers are saying about him"—entails the phenomenon of collective memory of his Galatian converts. Regarding Gal 2.19c, Martyn states that Paul's initial perspective coincides with the one of his opponents. This is affirmed in how he tackles the charge that Christ would increase "sin." Contrary to an unchanging and absolute (theological?) grasp of "sin," Martyn textualizes two opposing ways of understanding "transgression" in the rhetorical situation there-and-then.

> The Law *can* play a role leading not to the defining and vanquishing of transgression, but rather to transgression itself! Specifically, Peter in Antioch and the Teachers in Galatia uphold the food laws in order, they think, to avoid transgression. In fact, however, they follow a new route towards transgression.[112]

Anticipating their own understanding, Paul wants these teachers (as addressees) to participate in the construal of the letter and seduce them, as it were, to follow his reasoning instead of theirs. In this way, they should come to a radically opposite valuation of "sin": the law—framed in how they preach—does not protect against, but leads necessarily into sin. The phrase "to rebuild the wall that one has torn down" (translation by Martyn) should lead to a radical redefinition of "transgression" on the part of his hearers. Now the perspectives of Paul and his adversaries become diametrically opposed. In the implied aural event, this is an example of *Umdeutung* or reframing.

---

111. Martyn, *Galatians*, 254.
112. Martyn, *Galatians*, 256.

Another relevant example set out by Martyn in which we get before the letter functioning as text is found in Gal 3.26–29. Here he locates the crucial theme of "sons of God" in baptismal liturgy.

> If this identification was already part of the baptismal formula, and if Paul had used that formula in his evangelistic work in Galatia, he now knows that the Galatians will recall having been addressed at their own baptism as "sons of God," an address to which they presumably responded by the exclamation: "Abba, Father" (see 4.6 below). Affirming the corporate existence already given to the Galatians, therefore, Paul can boldly say: "You *are* sons of God."[113]

This is a clear example of historicizing text—to let "sons of God" resound in the realm of history there-and-then-to-them—and also textualizing history, when he describes the anticipated participation by the Galatian converts of Gal 3.26–29. We recognize the dynamic of metonymy: the "sons of God" functions to the intended hearers as *pars pro* baptism as *toto*.

We now hone in on the theme of "dying" and "living" in the passage under scrutiny. Martyn comments, "I have died to the Law . . . meaning to be separated from that thing by the event of one's own death,"[114] adding that the (Jewish) "Law" should be seen as existing in its paired existence with the "Not-Law" (living like a Gentile).[115] When we step back now, we critically scrutinize this proposed understanding according to anticipated participation: this argument would mean that the addressees themselves (teachers?) should fill in this whole dichotomous structure of the "paired existence of Law and Not-Law." Questions come to the fore: How would they have become familiar with this typically "Jewish apocalyptic" scheme? By whom would they have been so taught? What does a process look like in their concrete lifeworld in which the original addressees could have internalized such a thought structure? A fundamental implication would be that to Martyn these teachers will think in terms of "Law and Not-Law" when the simple and central term of "law" is heard.

The following phrase "through the Law" makes clear that the law played an independent role in the death of Christ: "It pronounced a curse on Christ, effectively, taking up its own existence and carrying out its own activity apart from God." Paul's dying with Christ on the cross (Gal 2.19c) is "participation in the event in which the Law acted against God's Christ!" It is the "law" that "cursed" Christ:

---

113. Martyn, *Galatians*, 375.
114. Martyn, *Galatians*, 256.
115. Martyn, "Apocalyptic Antinomies."

One can scarcely think of a statement more highly foreign to the theology of the Teachers (and to Jewish and Jewish-Christian theology in general). It is not an exercise in mere fantasy to imagine, that, as Paul's messenger finished reading v 18, the Teachers jumped to their feet, loudly charging Paul with blasphemy![116]

In comment number thirty, Martyn enquires as to the origin of the "participatory language" of "co-crucifixion" (Gal 2.17c). One of his considerations is related to baptism:

> When was this participatory language expanded to include not only Christ's resurrected life but also his death? It is probable that the *thought* of participating in Christ's death and burial was tied to the act of baptism prior to Paul (Rom 6.3–8). It may have been Paul himself, however, who forged an indelible link between the motif of participation in Christ's death and the expressions "with Christ" and "in Christ."[117]

Martyn suggests a possible relation between Paul's participatory language of co-crucifixion and the rite of baptism. Related to the experience of the Galatian converts, it should be reckoned to be part of the social memory in the Jesus movement then and there. How this general assumption relates to the anticipated participation of the addressees (teachers?), however, is left open. In his explication of Gal 2, baptism does not play any role.

Martyn's interpretation of Gal 2.18–21 hinges on the process in which the "old human being" has suffered death and the "eschatological one" has been brought to life. This explains, according to Martyn, the remarkable turn from "we" (Gal 2.15–17) to "I" (2.18–21):

> Using the first person, Paul presents himself as the paradigm of this human being. Crucified with Christ and thus experiencing mortal separation from the Law, this *anthrôpos* does not any longer have an identity given by the Law. He is neither Jew nor Gentile. Thus vis-à-vis the old collectives called Jews and Gentiles, this eschatological human being can no longer say "we," but rather has to say "I," speaking of his own death to these collectives.

From the perspective of detextifying the letter, we have to notice that this thought structure—on "old" and "eschatological human being"—is not found in the documented wording in the passage. As a consequence, Paul must have anticipated the presence and actuality of this specific thought

---

116. Martyn, *Galatians*, 257.
117. Martyn, *Galatians*, 279.

structure on the part of his hearers. Therefore, in terms of metonymy, the two parts of "we" and "I"—as overly common personal pronouns and not introduced in any way—should evoke and carry this fairly abstracted reasoning as a whole in the aural event. Martyn's proposed understanding can be evaluated as an anticipatory minimum and a participatory maximum. In the presented detextified perspective, we will provide a basis in the presupposed concrete lifeworld of the Galatian converts, and in that way strengthen this thought structure.

Martyn then elaborates on the "eschatological human being." He argues that the motif of Gal 2.19-20 is not "union with divine nature, but rather the resurrected Christ's powerful invasion, seen on a personal level."[118] The governing question pushes us to ask, How does this "personal level" look like for the original addressees? Or how does Christ's powerful invasion become personal to them? He does not clarify what this "personal level" means. Martyn also alludes to the famous passage on baptism in Galatians, "neither Jew nor Gentile" (Gal 3.27-28). On a more abstracted level, he relates the expression to "baptism," but in the concrete reasoning on "Jew" and "Gentile" in the passage under scrutiny he does not take this dimension into account. What is the reason that he leaves it out of his reconstruction of the aural event of this passage as anticipated by Paul? The omission leaves us still uncertain as to whether the apostle anticipated the soundbites on "neither Jew nor Gentile" (*pars*) evoke somehow the experiential matrix of "baptism" (*totum*) on the side of his original addressees at that moment in the oral performance or not. We conclude that to Martyn, the "theology" of Paul seems to function here on a different level than his rhetoric does in the aural event. Of course, they do not need to be related in such a direct way. But on all accounts, we think it is important to historicize text in a systematic way, that is, to relate specific (theological?) terms, phrases, and thought structures to the senses and collective memory of the intended addressees.

Evaluating his commentary, we conclude that in several instances Martyn's way of thinking spirals deep into the realm of history there-and-then. The present study is heavily indebted to his understanding of the Letter to the Galatians. However, what was notably lacking, and in terms of this study disappointingly so, the explication of elements such as "how," "to whom," "in what mindset," and "from whose perspective[s]."[119] These elements become explicit only incidentally, not as part of any systematic study.

118. Martyn, *Galatians*, 258.

119. Now a decisive question comes to the fore regarding aspects of the historical situation as textualized by Martyn: Would it have been the rhetorical goal of Paul to win his adversaries for his gospel (as Martyn suggests)? Or—as we will presuppose—is his goal to dissociate his converts from these teachers and discourage them to obey their

Martinus de Boer: *Galatians* (NTL)

The last commentary to be discussed is by Martinus de Boer, published in 2011.[120] De Boer is a doctoral student of Louis Martyn and critically engages with the understanding of his *Doktorvater*.[121] According to de Boer, Gal 2.15-21 can be divided into three units: verses 15-16, 17-18, and 19-21. The second unit consists of a refutation to an accusation—"But if by seeking to be justified in Christ, we ourselves were found also to be sinners, is Christ then a servant of Sin? Of course not!"[122] He places this unit between brackets, because the last unit (19-21) picks up, with the word "law," the argument begun in the first unit (15-16):

> The new preachers are Christian Jews, accepting Jesus as the Messiah but still taking their theological bearings from the law . . . ; on the other hand, Paul has become a Jewish Christian, no longer taking his theological bearings from the law but from Christ, in particular his death on the cross (2.19-21).[123]

In the passage as a whole, Paul aims at a redefinition of "justification." In verses 15-16, this redefinition is still inchoate. The passage ends "with an argument for the absolute incompatibility of the law and the death of Christ in the matter of 'justification' (*dikaiosyne*)."[124]

As mentioned in Chapter 3, de Boer takes verse 16a ("because we know that someone is not justified based on works of the law but through the faith of Jesus Christ," his translation) as "a quotation whose content was known to, and perhaps even given its specific formulation by, the new preachers in Galatia."[125] In this way, this missionary formula becomes severed from the level of the text-for-us and is brought into the realm of history there-and-then-to-them, that is, we hear these teachers say it to the Galatian converts in their prior performances. In line with the element of "from whose perspective[s]," de Boer equates the referential meaning of "rectification," "works of the law," and "faith of Jesus Christ"[126] by the new preachers with the one of Paul himself at this stage of the letter. So, as an example of

---

call to circumcision? We will deal with this aspect later on in this section.

120. Boer, *Galatians*.
121. See Boer, *Defeat of Death*.
122. Boer, *Galatians*, 140.
123. Boer, *Galatians*, 139.
124. Boer, *Galatians*, 140.
125. Boer, *Galatians*, 143. See also Boer, "Paul's Use."
126. Boer, *Galatians*, 145.

detextification, this particular perception should govern the rhetorical situation which Paul confronts in his letter.

Then de Boer focuses on one referential aspect of "justification": Paul and the teachers agree on it as a divine activity. However, "they do disagree on an important point: the reference of the word 'someone' (*anthropos*)."[127] According to the new preachers, the word only refers to a Jew or an Israelite; the formula does apply to Gentiles only to the extent that they also become part of Israel and "live like a Jew." In his train of thought, de Boer now relates "observing the law" to "justification" and explains, "In the apocalyptic Judaism of Paul's time, justification had come to have a distinctly eschatological dimension." Since the new preachers limit the possibility of justification to the Jew, they are telling the Galatian converts to observe the law, beginning with circumcision, in order to be declared righteous at judgment day. De Boer argues that Paul's converts must have internalized this thought structure of the teachers constitutive of the contemporary Jewish worldview:

> In the view of the new preachers, justification is something that will occur for the law-observant believer in the future . . . This faithful death did not put an end to law observance for Jewish believers, but it obligates those so forgiven now to obey it all the more, to reach a level of law-based righteousness . . . surpassing that of other (nonbelieving, non-Christian) Jews.[128]

In hindsight, we note that this whole explanation is based on the implicit reference to "someone." At the end of his discussion of the first unit (Gal 2.15–16), de Boer recapitulates that Paul does not discuss the precise definition of "justification," but for that moment leaves intact the meaning as attributed to it by his adversaries in Galatia: "He contents himself with rhetorically separating 'justification' (however defined) from law observance and binding it instead and exclusively to Christ's faithful death." This observation discloses the structure of *Umdeutung* (Chapter 3).

After the digression in Gal 2.17–18, Paul—in the first-person mode of discourse which he began in verse 18, "I through the law died to the law, that I might live to God"—presents himself "not as an example (as in v. 18) but as a paradigm of the born Jew who has come to believe in Christ (v. 16b)."[129] Similarly, de Boer stresses "[t]he apocalyptic discontinuity between 'then' and 'now.'"[130] Here we note that this structuring scheme of "then" and "now"—which is located on the level of text in his commentary—is

---

127. Boer, *Galatians*, 151.
128. Boer, *Galatians*, 153.
129. Boer, *Galatians*, 156.
130. Boer, *Galatians*, 157.

necessary to structure the understanding on the part of the intended hearers. In the present study, we advocate that the related and decisive question has to be asked, How does this scheme manifest itself to them sensorially or how is it activated by them during the course of the oral performance? Put differently, what participatory basis does Paul anticipate?

Because of the apocalyptic discontinuity, de Boer distinguishes between an old and new identity: "it is thus his nomistic 'I'—the 'I' that finds its identity and its hope of justification (5.5) in (the observance) of the law—that has died."[131] Regarding this exposition, which will be recognized in our detextified perspective, we have to ask about the relation between the explicit parts and the implied whole which is called upon by the apostle. Once again there seems to be minimal anticipation by Paul and maximal participation on the side of the addressees in this scheme of an "old" and "new eschatological human being."

Later in his commentary, de Boer links the line of thought on an old ("nomistic 'I'") and new identity ("coming to believe in Christ") to the theme of "justification/rectification." With regard to the redefinition of "justification" by the apostle, he says,

> God not only justifies (declares right) in the future, but also rectifies (makes right) in the present; God does so concretely by joining believers to the death of Christ, thereby separating them from the powers that enslave: Sin (v. 17; cf. 3.22) and the law (cf. 2.4; 4.1–5).[132]

The novelty in Paul's reasoning is that "justification" is not only related to the future (teachers), but already takes place in the present. This is the paradigmatic eschatological human being. Regarding his transition from "old" to "new," Paul anticipates the participation of his addressees: "Paul refers to himself, but he expects the new preachers and the Galatians also to say it after him and to apply it to themselves."[133] In this way, de Boer pays explicit attention to the dimension of participation ("participationist language").

Now we take a moment to scrutinize de Boer's conclusion that Paul primarily addresses the new preachers. First, similar to Martyn's commentary, we do not find a clear answer to the reason behind this presupposed communicative strategy of the apostle. The implication is that when Paul is able to convince his adversaries and win them over for his interpretation of the missionary formula ("someone," v. 16a), the Galatians will follow.

---

131. Boer, *Galatians*, 159.
132. Boer, *Galatians*, 164.
133. Boer, *Galatians*, 163.

So the apostle wants to wield power, according to de Boer, by focusing on the cognitive level, that is, by seeking to achieve some sort of "theological" consent. However, in the present study, the conviction is that in a process of conversion more seems to be needed—in the concrete lifeworld. Cognitive consent is only one aspect of radical change in the identity, loyalties, and lives of the former Galatian converts (or, as Martyn and de Boer primarily see it, of these new preachers)—even if it would be the most important one.

Second, the association of the Galatian converts with these other teachers is a new situation. Paul—who is their spiritual father and already well-known to them—can better attempt to dissociate his spiritual children from these teachers than first win the theological consent of his adversaries, see them submit to his authority in order that, in their turn, the Galatian converts will follow the now radically new course of these other teachers. (In terms of activating our imagination, we could ask, Had Paul hoped that they would come to some sort of public conversion or repentance among the Galatian converts?) Alternatively, we suggest that the aim is to re-establish and reaffirm the undivided loyalty of the Galatian converts towards Paul and his co-workers by rejecting the authority of these other teachers and their pressing call to circumcision, and to expel them from their midst.

In terms of Paul's participationist language, we continue with de Boer's explanation of the term "co-crucifixion" (Gal 2.19–20):

> Paul's claim to 'have been crucified with Christ' (v. 19b) cannot be taken literally. His language is metaphorical and hyperbolic, yet also realistic and serious (cf. 5.24; 6.14); it is not just a figure of speech, but a vivid interpretation of a truly painful and real experience (. . .) everyone who 'has come to believe in Christ Jesus' (v. 16a) participates in . . . this all-embracing cosmic, apocalyptic event . . . through which human beings are delivered 'from the present evil age' (1.4), after which they can truly 'live to God.'[134]

When one asks how one is to participate in the "dying" and "Living of Christ," de Boer provides a clear answer regarding the apostle himself: "Paul's death to the law was no self-chosen path; it occurred in his being 'crucified with Christ,' an event that took place on the Damascus road." In terms of anticipated participation, we first ask, How should the originally intended hearers relate Paul's co-crucifixion to his conversion on the Damascus road? In the documented wording, no indication in that direction is found. So, regarding his prior performances among his Galatian converts, the term (structural element [Foley]) "co-crucifixion" should bring to mind

---

134. Boer, *Galatians*, 161.

the whole of his conversion story as also documented in the book Acts. The second question is, What about the intended addressees of the letter? How do these teachers and Galatian audiences participate in this "metaphorical and hyperbolic, yet also realistic and serious"[135] death of Christ? How do they die to their nomistic "I" and how is Christ born in them?

This is the moment where de Boer remarks that the new preachers and the Galatians should "say it after him and . . . apply it to themselves."[136] When one presses and employs the intellectual movement of textualizing history, however, the question remains unanswered of how would Paul have envisioned this "saying after him" and "applying it to themselves"? We find a clue neither on the level of the documented wording nor on the level of the text of de Boer's commentary. Should we presume that before the aural event the emissary provided an instruction as to this intended effect? Or—in line with systematically bending our thoughts into the realm of history there-and-then-to-them—should the intended addressees already have been familiar with the notion of such a particular participation in "dying with Christ" (rite)? What, in other words, is the hoped-for consent that Paul anticipates here?

Later in de Boer's commentary, "baptism" is related to receiving this "new identity." On Gal 3.26-28 de Boer argues, "In the formula, as for Paul, being baptized 'into Christ' involves 'putting him on' as if he were an article of clothing . . . The new article of clothing—Christ—bestows a new identity (cf. 2.20)."[137] In this section, however, he subsequently separates this bestowing of a new identity from this rite: "The citation of the baptismal formula thus serves to remind the Galatians of their new identity in Christ . . . the identity bestowed not through the baptismal rite itself but, according to Paul, 'through this faith,' the faithful death of Christ."[138] So "bestowing," "new identity," and "the faith of Christ" become severed from the prior ritual of baptism. What then is the function or value of the baptismal rite itself to Paul, according to de Boer? And how does the apostle anticipate his (baptized?) Galatian converts to frame this rather abstracted transition from "old" to "new" at the moment of delivery? According to the Boer, we have to conclude that apparently two separate historical moments are involved

---

135. Boer, *Galatians*, 160.
136. Boer, *Galatians*, 161.
137. Boer, *Galatians*, 243.
138. Boer, *Galatians*, 245.

regarding "co-crucifixion," namely, the future act of participation "to say it after him [Paul] and apply it to themselves"[139] and past events of baptism.[140]

Moreover, in footnote 241, de Boer states explicitly that baptism and co-crucifixion are not connected here to each other: that "Paul's 'participationist' language is not here sacramental (as for many commentators who read Rom 6.1–10 into Gal 2.19), but informed and shaped by the categories and motifs native to Jewish cosmological apocalyptic eschatology."[141] He juxtaposes the anachronistic category of "sacramental" with the Jewish worldview there-and-then and he also does not explicate this adjective for his intended readers here-and-now. This reveals that his understanding of the letter is uncritically directed to the present-day reader. In view of the originally intended addressees (to whom), we must, therefore, ask, How does "sacramental" mean to them in their concrete lifeworld? How do they relate sensorially to "sacraments"? Thus, de Boer does not structure consistently this "participation language" of Paul into the realm of history. Since the senses do not come into play, "sacrament" seems to function in an extra-historical way or solely on the level of text—in the accompanying abstracted context—to his own readers.

Second, a free-floating structuring of thought ("sacramental") is juxtaposed to a historical one ("Jewish cosmological apocalyptic eschatology"). As the previous questions suggest, detextification urges for a historicization of "sacrament" and "baptism" as well. De Boer's language represents here higher forms of abstracted thinking—that is, for everyone, everywhere, and every time being the same. In detextifying our understanding of Gal 2.19–20, the question comes to the fore: How do the soundbites "through faith of Christ" and "co-crucifixion" mean to the Galatian converts (to whom) against the background of their specific collective memory (in what state of mind), according to Paul, in the process of composition (from whose perspective)? In what sensorial, concrete, or experiential way can the original addressees relate to these terms or to this theme?

So the remark on the participation in the dying of the nomistic I there-and-then-to-them—"to say it after him" and "to apply it to themselves"—seems to be a loose end. Nonetheless, "baptism" as matrix for textualizing history—as proposed in the following section—brings several aspects and lines of thoughts together as encountered in the commentaries by Martyn and de Boer.

---

139. Boer, *Galatians*, 161.
140. Boer, *Galatians*, 243.
141. Boer, *Galatians*, 161.

Detextified Understanding: The Recall of Baptism Countering the Call to Circumcision

We now attempt to get before this part of the letter functioning as autonomous text to us (Gal 2.18–20). We will take the words (sound groups) of the letter as *partes pro toto*. The *totum* of the collective memory of the original addressees will frame our understanding. In accordance with metonymy, redundancy is constituted by synonymy and antonymy (see Chapter 3). As a result, we will attempt to textualize the oral performance there-and-then-to-them of this passage.

When we studied the various commentaries on Galatians, we continuously asked what participation Paul would have anticipated in his characteristic parlance on ἀποθνῄσκω (to die), ζάω (to live), and συσταυρόομαι (to be crucified together).[142] Which parts would have been known by everyone at that time and which were limited to the collective memory of the intended addressees?[143] By whom then were they introduced to these latter themes and arguments? By Paul himself, by the other teachers, or by someone else? Which terms were new to them? Can we identify the related dynamic of explicit introduction and explanation in the intended aural event? These questions open up the intellectual movement of historicizing text. We will start with ἀποθνῄσκω. Gal 2.19 is the first instance in the delivery when this particular soundbite reaches the ears of the addressees. This is also the case with συσταυρόομαι. Moreover, these verbs are immediately and tightly related to the antonym ζάω (to live). This verb has been heard just before in Gal 2.14c: "If you, though a Jew, live [ζῇς] like a Gentile and not like a Jew, how can you compel the Gentiles to live [ζάω] like Jews?" So we see that the theme of ζάω is introduced in the letter as "living according to Jewish religious regulations (law)." This frame is clearly in line with the rhetoric of Paul's adversaries (from whose perspective [singular]). We posit that this framing of "to live" constitutes the reconstructed syllogistic rationale which structures the thoughts of (a section of) the addressees at the start of the

---

142. Regarding Gal 2.20 ("who loved me and gave himself for me") we could also think of the verb παραδίδωμι (to hand over). Since we confine this example to the notion of "co-crucifixion," we will only mention this related term in a later note.

143. As argued regarding the commentary of Martyn and also applicable to the one of Boer, we will adhere to the following formal communicative structure of the letter: in the process of composition, Paul anticipates the participation of the Galatians as his spiritual children in the moment of delivery. As a result, the assumed grasp, presence or reactions of these other teachers in the aural event are subservient to this perspective. In other words, we answer the question of "To whom does it mean?" by pointing at Paul's Galatian converts as intended addressees.

delivery (see the previous example in this Chapter). It forms the pivotal minor term [X].[144]

After this first exploration in historicizing text, we continue by setting out what went on before the mentioning of "to die" and "to co-crucify." In Gal 2.14–16—as argued by Martyn and de Boer—the apostle labours to detach "rectification" from "the works of the law," which is synonymous with "to live like a Jew." His rhetorical aim is to connect it with the antithetical phrase "out of the faithfulness of Christ." This repetitive antithesis has to function as a shibboleth or crowbar. The apostle to the Gentiles posits the two formulae as mutually exclusive. We named the repetitive denial of "out of law" as *negative rhetoric* (Example 1).

We notice that this antithetical reasoning is framed by Paul in direct speech, notably in his address to Cephas in Antioch in Gal 2.16–21. Preparatory to this represented speech—in the process of the aural event—Paul narrates what he observed in Antioch: First, Peter did not "live" in accordance to the Jewish regulations in his fellowship with the Gentile converts there. Later on—at the start of a second phase—"certain people came from James." As a result, Paul comments that the leader of the mother community started to change his attitude and presence—"he drew back and kept himself separate" (Gal 2.12). In this way, as Paul describes it, in the Antioch community, the distinction between those who were Jewish and those who were Gentile became apparent ("even Barnabas was led astray"). So, at the start, all were united and one; this was apparent in table fellowship. Subsequently, Jews isolated themselves from Gentiles.

Presumably, Paul would anticipate his hearers recognizing how he as Jew had lived with them in their midst. When Peter arrived in Antioch, he initially did not present himself (lived) like a "Jew." The leader from Jerusalem was not there as someone who was "circumcised" but—like Paul and the Galatian converts themselves—as a "brother" among "brothers" (Gal 1.2). All were one. In a next phase, however, a clear division became apparent between Jews and non-Jews/Gentiles. Some were circumcised and obeyed the law, others were not/did not. So, in an exemplary way, Peter (in his second phase) embodies "to live out of law."

---

144. In this way, we recognize the thought structure as textualized by Boer (see above): in Jewish apocalyptic eschatology, the distinction is pivotal between "now" and "then." The implied question is the following: How does one live [lower case] in the present evil age (now) to Live [uppercase] in the age to come (then)—Gal 1.3? The answer to this question by the teachers is to live like a Jew, that is, according to the regulations of the Jewish law, to be a partaker in the promises to Abraham and be Blessed with him in the Life to come. We recall that this rhetoric or eschatological vista could explain the impact of the performances and call of these other teachers amid Paul's Galatian converts.

Using Peter's changed behaviour as a warning signal, Paul will have anticipated his addressees recognizing these other teachers. They represent Peter in this second phase. The powerful though conditional promise of "Blessing" and "Life" makes the difference between "haves/winners/those who are saved" and "have-nots/losers/those who are lost" clearer. The social dynamic of this framing is obvious: everyone wants to belong to the former group; the initiation into this group is through receiving circumcision. As a result, this persistent and demonstrative acting (living) of these other teachers brought a fundamental pressure to bear on the everyday life of the communities.

It is given this emerging situation of separation that Paul introduces himself while addressing Peter in Antioch. As direct speech, Gal 2.16–21 culminates in a blunt rebuke of this representative of the mother community in Jerusalem. In terms of the anticipated imagination of the addressees in the moment of delivery, they see Paul standing alone in Antioch over against Peter, who is grouped with the other Jews. Although the addressees know that the apostle is a Jew himself, they see him standing isolated and alone. So, on another level, the Galatian addressees feel how the apostle addresses the teachers and those loyal to them through the figure of Peter.[145]

The rebuke is based on the antithetical reasoning of "out of law" versus "out of faith." Paul commences by appealing to "knowledge" of both him and Peter (εἰδότες, 2.16a). In this framing of the antithesis as shared knowledge, we can recognize a way of wielding power. This public announcement has to function as a clear indication to both Jews and Gentiles that Paul's position is the only true one. Although being a circumcised Jew, Paul did not "live" according to the law concerning Gentile converts. A knowledge shared and (originally) lived out by the leader of the mother community as well. Thus, the primary situation of unity, in which there was as yet no awareness of division or hierarchy and all lived in the same way, embodies the "knowledge" of "not out of law but out of faith."

Paul's vivid description of the Antioch incident is antithetically structured. As a prism, the two phases involved have to shed light on the developments in the community of the Galatian converts. The first phase under the influence of Paul was without distinction. Even as a Jew by birth the apostle himself along with other Jews on the one hand, and Gentiles on the other, lived together and were all one. The second phase which has been caused

---

145. We can press this sensorial dimension and propose the following anticipated participation by Paul in the moment of delivery: as Paul stood alone in Antioch (or formed a minority), so does his emissary in the aural event *in actu*. The latter embodies the apostle. As a consequence, Cephas and the many who joined him in his change of attitude are represented by these other teachers and those who adhere to their call.

by the presence and performances of the other teachers causes a division between those who obey the regulations of the Jewish law and those who do not. In light of his antithetical formula, we must conclude that according to them "out of law" is right—"from what perspectives" (plural). The goal is that everyone should live like Jews. Only then can Gentiles be allowed to eat with them and take part in the "promises to," "Blessing of Abraham," and "Life." This group embodies a new set of criteria for being one/oneness—on the basis of a subtle form of exclusion.

This textualization of the realm of history there-and-then regarding the formula "out of law" can be expanded. In Gal 2.17, Paul uses the notion of "sinner" and "sin" for the first time in the letter (v. 15b; next to the related and pejorative identification of those who are not Jews as "Gentile sinners"). In an antonymous way, we can frame this term in line with the rhetoric of these other teachers: "sin" equals "*not* to live in accordance to the law." Therefore, we can paraphrase the accusation: to have table fellowship with the non-circumcised and to violate other Jewish regulations means "sinning" against the law (that is, *not* to be out of law). Regarding "how does it mean," we textualize that Paul anticipates that at the start of the aural event "sin" as soundbite still echoes in the ears of the intended addressees as framed by the rhetoric of these teachers. Now, as a kind of short circuit, Paul connects the embodiment of the gospel by Peter in Antioch (to have table fellowship/first phase) with this specific condemnatory rhetoric. What Peter did before the arrival of some from James is "sin" (wrong)! He confronts his perspective ("out of faith" [right]) with how his adversaries wield power: When one does not live according to the Jewish law (sin) but in obedience to Christ (to have table fellowship with Gentiles), is Christ then "a servant of sin"? The apostle turns the accusation against himself—"Paul is a servant of sin; he is disobedient to the regulations of the law!"—towards Christ. The apostle puts the one who is above both parties at the centre. All of a sudden, one has not to decide whether Paul or Peter/the teachers are right, but to emphatically deny the conclusion: it is, of course, impossible to condemn the Lord as someone who calls to "sin"![146] We can characterise this intended collision of both reasonings as *rhetoric of confusion*. In an exemplary way, the element of "from whose perspective[s]" is constitutive here of the realm of history as such.

Paul will probably expect his hearers to hold their breath at this point. Based on the antithetical formula, however, the solution is already implied. Paul has to guide his hearers out of this confusion into clarity and "the truth

---

146. As phrased by Fowler: "The character of Christ, as God, is absolute righteousness. Christ was sinless, is sinless, cannot sin, does not sin, and does 2.17 not lead the Christian to sin (cf. James 1:13)" (*Galatians*, 79).

of the Gospel" (Gal 2.5b). As a climax in the aural event, this incongruous conclusion is rejected by an emphatic denial—"Absolutely not!" (2.17d). This is what went on before the passage to which we return now (Gal 2.18-20).

Based on this anticipated confusion, the apostle launches—as we will call it—a three-stage-rocket rhetoric. The aim is to disqualify his opponents' frame of ζάω as "obeying the law." To change the grasp of this theme on the part of his intended hearers, he introduces in Gal 2.18 the metaphor of "building (anew)" and "destroying." As a first phase in his rhetorical strategy, he evaluates the narration on Peter and his actions in Antioch in light of these metaphors. Once the law was "built" with a specific purpose for the Jews (Gal 3.17-20). For the Galatian converts, however, Paul's narration should make clear that the initial unity with Peter—as a circumcised Jew having fellowship with Gentiles—demonstrated that the law had been rightly "destroyed." The law does not count anymore—for example, "there is neither Jew nor Greek" (3.27). Later on—think of the second phase after the coming of some from James—Peter all of a sudden begins to "build up again" this dividing wall; he starts anew to live according to the Jewish regulations (Martyn). So Paul wants his hearers to understand that Cephas contradicts himself in his opposed ways of acting (living).

In this way, we find an answer to the question of manifestation in the concrete lifeworld of the original addressees. Peter in person, in the second phase in Antioch, represents the whole matrix of the teaching of Paul's opponents—consider "circumcision," "out of law," "living like a Jew [not a sinner from the Gentiles]," "being a son of Abraham," amongst other phrases. The actual presence of these teachers constitutes the experiential dimension of the teaching on "out of law." So we assume that these teachers appealed to "Peter" as a Jew who self-evidently lived according to the Jewish regulations (also) among Gentiles. In blunt opposition, Paul condemns this specific behaviour as wrong. More so, he states that Peter's initial behaviour among the Antiochean Gentiles was right: he had table fellowship with them. The apostle turns the world, according to his adversaries, upside down: they call to "build up" the law, whereas Paul states that "destruction," which has already taken place in the death and resurrection of Christ, is the only right thing to do.

We proceed to Gal 2.18b. Earlier we referred to the rhetorical impact of "sin" on the Galatian converts. The previous *Umdeutung* has to reverberate here as well. We will recognize the line of thought as provided by Betz and Martyn in their commentaries. In this verse for the first time, the expression "to be a lawbreaker" (παραβάτης) is heard. Since this term is so perfectly suited to these teachers, Paul anticipates that this pejorative qualification will echo in the ears of his audience as well. In "sin" and "lawbreaker," we recognize the social dynamic by which the Galatian converts are put under pressure: "when you do not live in accordance to the law, you are a παραβάτης!" Paul turns this apotropaic term against these teachers themselves: "you, who qualify the initial fellowship of Peter as Jew with Gentile converts as 'sin' are truly 'sinning' yourselves!" (paraphrase mine).

In this way, we textualize the first phase in the three-stage rhetoric: a process of division is taking place within the communities, at least from Paul's perspective. Through these accusations, the Gentile converts are placed in a field of tension. In terms of the syllogism in the previous example, they have to become "rectified" and "sons of Abraham" to take part in the "promises," "Blessing of Abraham," or "Life." In conclusion, they have to cross the Rubicon of circumcision into the realm of the law.

When we turn to the next verse (2.19), we see that Paul proceeds to counter the rhetoric of his opponents but now more profoundly. The metaphor of "building" and "destroying" is not absolute. One actually can wrongly rebuild what has been rightly destroyed; this is what the leader of the mother community did in Antioch. In reversed order, Peter crossed the line marked by circumcision.

In launching his rhetorical rocket, we witness here the second stage. Now the apostle introduces the more irrevocable metaphor of "dying." Paul ("I") has to oppose the leader of the mother community: ἐγω γάρ διὰ νόμου νόμῳ ἀπέθανον. Echoing his adversaries ("to live"), the apostle invokes the antonymous theme of "dying." Paul turns their rhetoric upside down: contrary to Cephas and those who "live out of law," he presents himself as the one who "died in and through the law."

In line with the governing question, we can recollect here once more the aspect of manifestation: How is this "dying" sensorially mediated there-and-then-to-them? Note that in the statement the sequence of "dying" and "living" is reversed. Normally, one first "lives" and then "dies." In a provocative manner, the apostle starts his rhetoric of *Umdeutung*: he interchanges "living" with "dying" and explicitly states the counter-reasoning—that is, "to die to the regulations of the Jewish law." Now the logic behind the earlier observed reversed order of "dying" and "living" comes to the fore. There is no room for doubt anymore: Paul has separated himself from Peter—embodying in his second phase in Antioch these teachers in Galatia—and this is as radical as "death" and "dying" itself! In one and the same remarkable phrase (verse 19b), the apostle introduces his distinctive and juxtaposed frame on "living": "so that I might l/Live in God" (θεῷ ζήσω).

The following implicit consequences are involved. In a radical way, the apostle tears "law" and "God" apart. Contrary to the given perception hitherto, "living" cannot mean anymore "living by the Jewish law/as a Jew."

Moreover, the "law" cannot be related to "God" positively or constructively anymore. In this respect, we recognize this mutual exclusion in the final exclamation of this passage: "I do not nullify the grace of God; for if justification comes through the law, Christ died for nothing" (Gal 2.21). In conclusion, the world as construed by these other teachers ("law") is annulled ("destroyed").

Second, a radical reframing of "to live" is pronounced. Since the addressees had come under the influence of these teachers and their framing of this term—that is, "to live" is based and dependent on the "law"—disorientation and panic must be the anticipated result on the side of the hearers. All of a sudden, their loyalty to these teachers becomes (all the more) under strain. The apostle has to guide them out of this confusion. When they identify with him ("I"), as Gentiles who have died in and through the law, they will "Live" with him. As an additional observation, we note that "to live (in God)" represents the opposite of "out of works of the law." For the Galatian converts, "to live" should not be to obey a set of rules. To the contrary, "to live [in God]" is per se after the abolishment and outside the dominion of the law, and, therefore, as representatives thereof, these teachers. Thus, the hearers are confronted with a radical and absolute antithesis between two realms, that is, between "the law" (wrong) over against "God" (right).

As a consequence, Paul condemns the social dynamic instigated by his opponents. He attempts to evoke a question on the side of his hearers: When this is the case, how do we get beyond the law so that it becomes possible to "live in God"?[147] Another Rubicon that has to be crossed is involved. The answer is provided in the following synonym of to "die" in verse 20a. In the aural event, this verb has not been heard until now: συσταυρόομαι (to be co-crucified). In light of the question of how to get beyond the dominion of the law, Paul presents himself as the ultimate guide for his addressees (over against Cephas): "I have been crucified together with Christ." In that way, you achieve the required situation of living in God. The two previous stages in Paul's rhetoric aim at this final stage, to lead his hearers to the theme of co-crucifixion/crucifixion.[148]

---

147. A different framing is provided by Keener: "The expression *live to God* (2:19; Rom 6:10–11; cf. Rom 14:8; 2 Cor 5:15) could echo an expression from the Jewish martyr tradition" (*Galatians*, 111). From the perspective of anticipated participation: How does Paul direct the thoughts of his hearers in this direction? How does it constitute the structuring of thought in this specific moment in the delivery?

148. Here we can pay attention to παραδίδωμι as well—another term constitutive of the matrix of "dying" and "living" (Gal 2.20e). This verb can be heard as an echo of the introductory words in Gal 1.4: "our Lord Jesus Christ, who gave [τοῦ δόντος] himself for our sins." Clearly, Paul recalls the narrative of the crucifixion of Christ and the effect on his audience. The participatory and particular verb συσταυρόομαι (being crucified

So, after our exploration of to "live," we turn our attention—note that this is the movement of historicizing text—to "co-crucifixion." We notice that the address to Peter in Gal 2.15–19 is structured and dominated by the thematic matrices of his opponents ("Jew," "to live like a Gentile/Jew," "Jewish customs," "Gentile sinners," "rectification," "law observance," and "sin/sinner/transgressor") and culminates in the collisional conclusion that "Christ" would be "a servant of sin." In the notion of "co-crucifixion" (2.20), however, Paul now shifts the attention to frame "out of faith" more clearly and in view of the present situation.

After this preliminary observation, we ask, "To whom," "in what state of mind," and "from whose perspective" does the soundbite "co-crucifixion" mean? We assume that the original addressees should have been familiar with "Christ," his central role in their conversion and communal religious life and, more specifically, with the narrative of his death on the cross as the ubiquitous Roman form of execution (for example, Gal 1.4 and 3.1). Second, and, more so, they must know about the resurrection of Christ (for example, Gal 1.1). This turn towards Paul's gospel is, however, more complicated than that. Since the verb implies participation (σύν, together with), more is at stake than the crucifixion of Christ himself. The implication of this soundbite is, namely, that the apostle himself has been crucified as well with Christ. We fill in, though, that the intended audience subliminally knows that he is not literally dead at that moment (remember that he is addressing them at that very moment through the emissary). For us, a question comes to mind: How is Paul crucified with Christ? Important to note is that he refers to this participatory process ("I am co-crucified with Christ"), with all these implications regarding an anticipated proper understanding on the part of his intended audience, without any form of introduction. We recall that detextification implies that we attempt to understand how the original addressees were intended to understand in the aural event. In conclusion, the anticipatory minimum by Paul in συσταυρόομαι as soundbite (with an emphasis for us on the prefix)—which comes to the reader of the letter as text very unexpectedly—demands a participatory maximum by the Galatian audiences, namely to recall themselves the experience of and provide the thought structure of to die-with-Christ-on-the-cross-in-order-to-come-to-Life.

We see this affirmed in Gal 3.1. Here Paul rebukes his audience: "You foolish Galatians! Who has bewitched you? It was before your eyes that Jesus Christ was publicly exhibited as crucified!" His former converts hear him accuse them of losing sight of what is most important. Paul summarizes

together with Christ) frames ἀποθνῄσκω, ζάω, and παραδίδωμι for the intended addressees—as anticipated by Paul. Since not structural to the implied reasoning, we will not elaborate on the role and framing of the particular notion of παραδίδωμι here.

his former presence and performances among them in the picture of Christ crucified. Implied in this exclamation, he anticipates the presence of this knowledge. For us it is important to consider that co-crucifixion, which is mentioned without any form of introduction, has to be related. So, in the process of composition, Paul envisions that this specific single part ("co-crucifixion") recalls the thematic and experiential matrix of his gospel as a whole (*totum*).[149] The question remains now as to what the nature and form of this anticipated participation is.

We will turn to the culmination of this passage as a whole. Our attention is attracted by the explicit mentioning of "baptism" on the level of the text in Gal 3.27: "you who have been baptized (ἐβαπτίσθητε) into Christ." Different from the two previous and elaborate sections in Gal 3.1–25, this final and concise passage is dominated by terms of Paul's gospel: "Sons of God," "faith in Jesus Christ," "to be baptized into Christ," "to be clothed with Christ," "neither Jew nor Greek," and "to be all one in Christ" (3.26–28). More so, in the last verse of this passage, the apostle formulates a conclusion in which his gospel provides the ultimate warrant for the themes central to his adversaries which govern the previous passages of argumentation ("seed of Abraham" and "heirs according to the promise").

What role does baptism play in this final passage of Gal 3? The explanatory or causal conjunction of γάρ will help us to understand how the apostle intends his addressees to understand in the moment of delivery:

> For (γάρ) in Christ Jesus you are all children of God through faith. As many of you as were baptized into Christ have clothed yourselves with Christ. There is no longer Jew or Greek, there is no longer slave or free, there is no longer male and female; for (γάρ) all of you are one in Christ Jesus. And if you belong to Christ, you are Abraham's offspring, heirs according to the promise.

We recognize a double synonymous structure. First, the status of "being a son of God" (26a) is mediated by (διά) "faith in Christ Jesus" (26b). In Gal 3.27, subsequently, this status of being "son of God" is based on another and synonymous medium, namely, baptism ("for all of you who were baptized into Christ," 27a). So both media of "faith in Jesus Christ" and "being baptized into Christ" result in "being sons of God" and "clothing oneself with Christ." As an explication of the latter, Paul formulates his famous dictum: when you have clothed yourself with Christ—that is, when you are baptized into/have faith in Christ, there is "neither Jew nor Greek, slave nor free, male nor female, for you are all one in Christ" (3.28). In contradistinction to

---

149. This rhetorical effect is strengthened by the antithetical structure implied in "not out of law, but out of faith."

the divisive rhetoric of his opponents, therefore, the apostle attempts to redefine the newly won status and identity of his addressees as "sons of God." These teachers have introduced the question and shibboleth of the sonship of Abraham. In addition to his *Umdeutung* in the previous section (3.6–14), Paul firmly states in this final passage that they are all "sons of God." In this ultimate sonship in which all distinction and hierarchy is excluded, they are united and one—"there is neither Jew nor Greek" (3.28). Here we touch on the ultimate goal of the three-stage rhetoric: they are all included, saved, and one because of their prior baptism, which they—as I suppose—received by the hands of Paul.

When we get beyond the level of the text in our way of structuring thought, this theme of oneness can become transparent to us as present-day readers: by the recalling of baptism and through that all-uniting ritual, Paul wants his audiences to revalue the original situation as right and appropriate; what they had prior to the divisive presence and performances of these teachers is the ultimate goal to strive for.

As present-day readers, we notice that in Gal 3.27 baptism, on the level of the text, is only mentioned very briefly. This anticipatory minimum on the side of Paul asks for a participatory maximum on the side of his addressees. The whole reasoning of the apostle hinges on this ritual of "dying" and "living" (rising) with Christ in referring to "co + crucifixion."[150] So the

---

150. From another perspective, we can also find a substantiation of this understanding of "co-crucifixion." We distinguish terms and themes which are typical of these teachers. Similarly, we relate other terms to Paul's gospel. When the latter is thematically consistent in his rhetoric throughout his letters and, more importantly, throughout endless (undocumented) other performances in real time, we can turn to Rom 6.1–10 as well. Contrary to his letter to the Galatians, we encounter here an elaborate explanation of how he relates "co-crucifixion" to the senses of his hearers. This part of Romans is on the function of the "law." Paul has argued that "sin" (the impression is that in this letter this term is differently framed) entered the world through "one man," "Adam." Through "Christ," however, "grace" and "righteousness" have become abundant. The law was added so that sin would increase. And where sin increased grace increased all the more. So now he asks whether the hearers are called to sin more so that grace will overflow. At that point, Paul introduces the matrix on "dying" and "living": "What then are we to say? Should we continue in sin in order that grace may abound? By no means! How can we who died to sin go on living in it? Do you not know that all of us who have been baptized into Christ Jesus were baptized into his death? Therefore we have been buried with him by baptism into death, so that, just as Christ was raised from the dead by the glory of the Father, so we too might walk in newness of life. For if we have been united with him in a death like his, we will certainly be united with him in a resurrection like his. We know that our old self was *crucified with* him so that the body of sin might be destroyed, and we might no longer be enslaved to sin. For whoever has died is freed from sin. But if we have died with Christ, we believe that we will also live with him. We know that Christ, being raised from the dead, will never die again; death no longer has dominion over him. The death he died, he died to sin, once for all;

DETEXTIFICATION

third and final stage of his rhetoric is aimed at the recollection, reframing, and reaffirmation of this ritual by his addressees.[151]

---

but the life he lives, he lives to God" (emphasis mine). We see the resemblance of the textualized understanding in the main body of the text above—which is anticipated by Paul: the Gentile converts have to get beyond the realm of the law. Also in Romans 6, the governing structure is one of transition—to move from one realm or dominion to another, to die to live. According to Paul, this transition becomes manifest in the ritual of "baptism," explicated by him in terms of "co-crucifixion." In this respect, we observe that, in his commentary, Keener calls in the help of Romans 6, however, without thematizing the role of baptism: "Paul's more detailed elaboration of this idea in Romans helps us understand the premises of his argument: Christ died to sin (Rom 6:10) so that those identified with him died with him (6:3-8, 11). Believers died to the law through Christ's body (Rom 7:4); the old person (in Adam) thus died (Rom 6:6) and a new person lives in Christ (Gal 2:20)" (*Galatians*, 110/111). In a similar way, Fowler argues similarly with a reference to Romans 6, without addressing the link to baptism (see his *Galatians*, 82).

151. In several studies, Gal 2.19-20 has been related to baptism. As a typical approach, we can refer to *Paul and the Crucified*. In this study, Cummins already ties 2.16 closely to baptism. Based on linguistic and conceptual parallels, he states that a correlation is operative between believing in/to Christ (faith parlance) and baptism. Regarding Gal 2.16b, he comments, "In echoing what appears to be baptismal language, Paul reminds errant Jewish Christians—in Antioch, Galatia, and elsewhere—that their belief/baptism into Christ entails dying and rising with him" (*Paul and the Crucified*, 204). In this statement, we recognize the communicative structure of anticipation on the side of the composer of participation by the intended addressees. We can also point to the commentary by Schlier. His view is structured by several partially synonymous key concepts. In an intricate way, he differentiates between *Gerechtsprechen* (to rectify), *Gerechtigkeit erweisen*—as related to God (to justify)—and *Gerecht werden aus den Glauben* (to be rectified out of faith). In a similar vein, he differentiates between *Zum-Glauben-Kommen* (to come to believe) and *Glauben* as a way of life (faith). According to him, all these different concepts come together in the theme of baptism: "Dieses πιστεῦσαι hatte zum Ziel das δικαιωθῆναι ἐκ πίστεως Χριστοῦ καὶ οὐκ ἐξ ἔργων νόμου, so dass das Zum-Glauben-Gekommensein das aus Glauben Gerechtfertigt werden ermöglicht. Solche Aussage ist nur sinnvoll, wenn das πιστεῦσαι die Taufe in sich begreift" (*Galater*, 98). We can critically state that the concepts used remain highly abstracted. In no way are these terms and their nuances related to the senses—neither in terms of the original addressees nor of us as present-day readers. Now we could argue that the original addressees must have been familiar with a concrete baptismal ritual—cf., Gal 3.27. The same pertains to us. No differentiation between these groups of participants-in-process-of-coming-to-understand is found. Baptism encompasses the initiation rite for new adult converts there-and-then as well as a centuries old ritual of infant baptism in traditional churches up until today. In no way does he relate his thoughts on the role of baptism to the realm of history in general—think of "how," "to whom," or "from whose perspective[s]." In conclusion, "baptism" is introduced on and, as a consequence, confined to the level of text. For a comparable approach, see Schnackenburg, *Das Heilsgeschehen*, 64-65. A blunt denial can be found, however, in James Dunn's *Baptism*. No baptism in relation to water is at issue, according to him, but a clearly and radically different one with the Spirit. When we turn to the compendium on the ritual of baptism in early Christianity, *Baptism*, we see that Everett Ferguson

Recalling their baptism becomes a powerful rhetorical tool. Two effects are aimed at. First, the final exclamation of verse 21 entails the impossibility of obeying the law any longer: "I do not nullify the grace of God; for if justification comes through the law, Christ died for nothing." So his addressees have to make a radical decision: either they will undergo future circumcision or they will reaffirm their past baptism in the light of this reframing of the dying of Christ (co-crucifixion [dying] with Christ).

Second, when his original addressees are caught by his argumentation and reaffirm their own baptism, they become assured, as a result, that they—like Paul—"have died in and through the law." They can no longer follow the call of these other teachers, that is, "to live out of/in the law."[152] Another conclusion is that baptism must have been central to Paul's (former) presence and performances among them; his gospel of Christ crucified must have come with this ritual, that is, of "co-crucifixion."

Third, these other teachers wielded power and put inner pressure on the members of these communities by introducing a dynamic of exclusion. Paul's reframing of their past baptism brings relief, it makes his converts conclude that they were already included by God. In short, *circumcision excludes* (in line with the performances and presence of these teachers), *whereas baptism includes and unites* (Paul).

When we turn to the perspective of the present-day reader vis-à-vis the letter as text, the counter rhetoric of Paul opens up a new horizon. Autonomous text summons the implied abstracted context. When our thought is structured in and constrained to that communicative process, it is impossible to identify the role of "baptism" and "circumcision" and the counter framing of "living" in the passage under scrutiny.[153] In line with

---

does not mention Gal 2.19-20. Regarding this specific letter, he only elaborates on Gal 3.27 (see *Baptism*, 106-7, 115, 150). From the perspective of the present study, we may not be surprised; it strengthens the general assumption of implicit equation, since only in this passage "baptism" is explicitly present on the level of the text.

152. In line with the mental structure as presented by Boer, we can recognize in his formulation the contours of "to live" (now) in distinction from "to Live" (then). The promised Life which is related to the coming age would reverberate in the phrase, "I no longer live, but Christ Lives in me" (Gal 2.20bc). The question of how one should live in the present evil age (now) would be answered then in the subsequent exclamation: "The life I live in the body, I l[L?]ive by faith in the Son of God, who loved me and gave himself for me" (20d-f; based on NRSV). In combining the normal and the capital l/L, we can indicate the fusion of the "now" and "then" or the age to come and the present evil age in Paul's rhetoric. This is, however, not the focus of the present exemplification.

153. Regarding this passage, we find in one remark the combination of a literary constraint and a grasp of the intended thought structure by Tom Wright: "Paul is not speaking of baptism here, he does a chapter later, but his thinking in these verses is exactly in line with his view of baptism in Romans 6" (*Paul: A Biography*, 160).

the Cautions to the reader in the Introduction, detextification infringes on the communicative process inherent in autonomous text. We have to push terms and themes beyond the level of text (as it functions to us) to gain this perspective on the intended understanding (as it functioned to the Galatians). An *argumentum e sensoriis* comes to the fore.[154] In this way, we can come to a deepened grasp of the letter here-and-now—namely, in line with the intended functioning as oral performance there-and-then-to-them.

CONCLUSIONS

The present Chapter aimed to demonstrate the approach of detextification. In the first example, we turned to the logic as heard in Gal 3.10–12. First, the studies by Moisés Mayordomo and Michael Bachmann were discussed. In both cases, we concluded that the attempt to grasp the syllogistic structure of the reasoning takes place on the level of the text. Bachmann states that, contrary to other proposals, his reconstruction does not require implicit premises; he can identify all the parts on the level of the text. Mayordomo, who keeps strictly to the rules of formal syllogizing, admits that no clear rationale can be found in the laboured reasoning. On both proposals, we commented that these studies as texts themselves degrade or supervene the documented wording as text. The sub-questions of "how" (text), "to whom" (Bachmann and Mayordomo themselves or the present-day reader), "in what state of mind" (highly literate), and "from whose perspective" (the academic writer and reader of the article and study) have already been filled in before the whole enterprise started. In this analysis, we recognize an important restriction of the subject-object scheme (Chapter 3): at the moment that the "subject" functions on the level of text (hypervisuality/"eye to text area"), the whole participatory matrix in which this subject *in actu* (Mayordomo and Bachmann themselves) functions is eclipsed.

We provided an alternative understanding of the syllogistic structure of this documented reasoning. In line with the distinctive media cultures, we differentiated between formal and rhetorical syllogizing. By nature, the rhetorical syllogism manifests itself in an *enthymematic* way: only the necessary parts are explicated since the implied reasoning as a whole is constitutive of the collective memory involved. In the enthymemes, we recognized the dynamic of (synonymous and antonymous) metonymy. Following the procedure of historicizing text, the central terms in the reasoning of Gal

---

154. Interestingly, the role of baptism in the realm of history there-and-then-to-them prompts the question of how these other teachers would have positioned themselves in relation to this ritual.

3.10–12 ("law," "rectification," and to "l/Live") shed new light on Gal 3.21. We textualized the following syllogistic structure: The one who is rectified, he will Live (major premise); the one who is/lives out of works of law, he will be rectified (minor premise); therefore, the one who is/lives out of law, he will Live (conclusion). This reasoning must have governed the performances of these other teachers in such a way that they gained influence over the Galatian converts and prepared them for a life "out of law" marked by circumcision.

Given Gal 2.16–17 and 3.11b, Paul's counter logos can be identified as well: the one who is rectified, he will Live (major premise); the one who is/lives out of faith, he will be rectified (minor premise); therefore the one who is/lives out of faith, he will Live (conclusion). In line with the predominantly oral state of mind, we could scrutinize the documented wording for synonymous and antonymous parts as well. We identified up to twenty-one threads in approximately eleven enthymemes. We also saw that this single and self-evident logos meets the criteria as formulated by John Barclay.

Based on this example, we can draw several conclusions: First, this detextification does not answer the traditional question of "What does it mean?". More so, in the moment that we structure our thoughts in line with this question, the original operational matrix in which the letter functioned suddenly and totally disappears. Notwithstanding the acknowledgment of the differences between *what did it mean* and *what does it mean*,[155] how this kind of meaning is constituted is fixed from the start. The functioning of text and the constitution of meaning in the related mindset usurp the unfamiliar one of oral performance and the accompanying state of mind. Second, the detextified presentation of the passage is directed by the question guiding the historian: "What is happening there and then to them?" In this way, we get an impression of the oral-aurally determined communicative and rhetorical strategies of the apostle: in using the syllogistic rationale of his adversaries, Paul acknowledges his hearers in their longing for to "Live"/"Living." Subsequently, by disqualifying the minor term of these teachers ("out of law") and putting forward his own gospel ("out of faith"), he forces his addressees to take a stance: either they dissociate from these teachers and (re)associate with him or vice versa. Not so much the question "What does it mean?" is at issue—on the level of text, but "What are you going to do?"—beyond that level. Third, in this detextificatory identification

---

155. See the description of exegesis as provided by Porter and Clarke in their essay "What Is Exegesis?," 11, 12: "Exegesis that seeks to answer what the text *means* at present is usually based upon the synchronic condition of the text, that is, *what it is*. On the other hand, exegesis that concerns itself with what the text *meant* relies more heavily upon the diachronic condition of the text, that is, *how it came to be what it is*."

of not only this complex of syn- and antonyms but also in the underlying metonymical or enthymematic structure, we can recognize the treatment of *lexis* (style) and *taxis* (structure) as provided by Aristotle in his *On Rhetoric: A Theory of Civic Discourse*[156] and the emphasis on the artistic structure as found in Cicero and Quintilian (see Excursus: Ancient rhetorical sources and oral performances). Fourth, we get more clarity in how detextification has to be applied. From a historical-critical point of view, it is imperative first to textualize the envisioned oral performance of Gal 3.10–12 there-and-then-to-them. The outcomes of this intellectual activity precede any endeavor in fleshing out any meaning of the text for the present-day reader (such as the gospel of Paul in Galatians or the theology of the apostle in this letter or in general on the level of text). Fifth, this search for meaning should not only progress from this media-specific historical reconstruction, but it could also be transformed by the intellectual movements of textualizing history and historizing text. When different media imply distinctive mindsets (Introduction), there has to be more at stake than differences in what it meant and what it means or contemporary differences in ascribed meanings to the text. The central question would be: How do these soundbites function to the original participants *in actu*? This vista is paramount so that the reader does give priority to the historian.

In the second example, we detextified our grasp of Gal 2.18–20. In the commentaries that were discussed, some illustrations of the media muddle came to the fore. On the sub-question regarding the element of "how," Betz argues first that the letter should be seen as a "court of law": Paul is the accused, these teachers are the accusers, and the Galatians themselves function as the jury or judges. Subsequently, he states that the letter is no more than a "lifeless piece of paper," that is to say stripped of all benefits of oral communication or bodily presence. These two concrete perspectives on the realm of history there-and-then-to-them are, however, not brought together; they remain contradictory loose ends in his text. More so, he finally adds that Paul did not only write for his Galatian converts but all the generations of Christians after them. How can we unite all these perspectives? In the commentary by Longenecker, we touched on another discrepancy. He starts with a forty-page introduction to the letter—with amongst others, questions on date, identity of original addressees, opponents—to exegete the passage under scrutiny with regard to "us" (without further specification), "believers" (idem), and "Christians" (idem). All of a sudden, there is no difference anymore between the original addressees there-and-then and his own readers here-and-now. This transition has to be ascribed to the implicit equation

---

156. Aristotle, *On Rhetoric*, 3.2–12 and 3.13–19.

of "letter" and "text" in combination with the turn from describing the process of production to the product in real time. The next two commentaries discussed both took the other teachers as their focal point and intentionally concentrated their thinking on the realm of history-there-and-then. Martyn bends his thoughts into the realm of history there-and-then. He structures his understanding of the passage according to the transition from the "old" to the "eschatological human being." De Boer argues along the same lines. The latter even suggests that Paul—given his turn from "we" to the "I" who has "died in and through the law"—expects these teachers and the Galatians "to say it after him and to apply it to themselves." Although still rather abstract and inchoate, de Boer locates this "saying after" and "applying to themselves" in the realm of history there-and-then. Since he denies that Gal 2.18–20 involves "sacramental" language, we asked how this saying after him would have looked like there-and-then.

In our own detextification of Gal 2.16–20, we honed in on the documented thematic matrix in the passage of ἀποθνῄσκω (to die), ζάω (to live), and συσταυρόομαι (to be co-crucified). Since the sequence of the letter structures the intended aural event, we set out to scrutinize Gal 2.14–17 for these terms. We touched on ζάω. Based on his account of Peter's changing attitude in Antioch, Paul anticipates the frame of reference of his opponents ("to *live* like a Jew"). Instead of forcing his audience to choose between the teachers ("law") and himself ("faith"), he puts Christ in the centre of attention by the disturbing accusation that when you *live* out of faith (think of Jews having table fellowship with Gentiles) then Christ would be "a servant of sin." Paul solves this *rhetoric of confusion* with the metaphor of "to build," "to destroy," and "to build anew the law" (Gal 2.18–20). He explains why Peter first "lived" rightly in Antioch (to destroy the law/have table fellowship) and then later acted wrongly (to rebuild it/separate himself). In the blunt rebuke of Peter, Paul disqualifies the way in which these other Jewish teachers "live" with the Galatian converts. In this light, we also textualized the *Umdeutung* of notions of his adversaries, such as "sin/sinner" and "lawbreaker." Because of Peter's changed attitude in Antioch, Paul makes clear that there is no more "we." In opposition to the leader from Jerusalem—who once again started "to live according to the regulations of the law" (rebuild)—the apostle confesses that "'I' died in and through" that same "law." After having hitherto followed the frame of his opponents concerning to "live," we touch on the radical turn that the apostle intends his hearers to make: when you "die" to the law, you "live" in God. The normal sequence of to "die" and to "live" is being reversed. In this turning around, the apostle further explores his reframing of "living." In verse 19, he specifies the sequence of "to die" and "to live" as "co-crucifixion with Christ." This term forms the culmination of his rhetoric in Gal 2.14–20. When we value "dying" and "living" as preparatory, Paul wants to recall—consider here his prior presence and performances—the matrix of his own rhetoric by this single notion. Especially, the participatory dimension in the prefix σύν- (together with) led to the argument that Paul expects his audience to frame "co-crucifixion with Christ" in a self-evident way: they structure this reasoning by the ritual of baptism. We saw this affirmed in the only briefly mentioned verb "to be baptized" at the end of this part of the letter (Gal 3.27). The counter rhetoric of Paul—which he commenced in the rebuke of Peter in Antioch—comes to a climax: over against the newly experienced and appealing call to circumcision, to become "sons of Abraham," the apostle recalls the ritual of baptism. In his reframing of this liminal experience, they are already "sons of God," that is, the true "sons of Abraham." Precisely because of the experiential nature of baptism we valued this as a powerful example of Paul's counter rhetoric: baptism annuls and trumps circumcision. There is no distinction between Jew and Greek. Baptized into Christ, they are united and one as "sons of God" (also with those who are Jew by birth).

Two conclusions can be drawn: First, in detextifying the passage in this way, an *argumentum e sensoriis* comes to the fore that deepens the proposed—rather abstracted and more theological—understandings as provided by Martyn and de Boer. Second, this detextified understanding transforms meaning there-and-then-to-them as proposed by David Rhoads (Chapter 2, Section H.): the involved recalling of baptism penetrates the concrete lifeworld of the Galatians. Thus, Paul is reframing (re-"mean"-ing?) a liminal experience being stored in their bodies in order to prevent them to answer the call to another ritual. It is the ritual that marks (baptism) or will mark (circumcision) their identity, loyalty, and course in life.

Conclusions

In the Introduction, it was stated that in biblical scholarship one reads the Bible in silence and solitude asking questions such as, What does it mean? and What does the text say? We phrased this process as "eye to text area." Regarding the corpus Paulinum, this procedure implies an implicit equation of "letter" and "text." At the same time, however, an emerging *communis opinio* is found in this community: the original addressees of Paul's letters were exposed—in the distinctive context of predominant orality—to an emissary or public reader (lector) who is addressing them in real time. We encapsulated this procedure in the phrase "body to body." This rather unfamiliar (at least to us!) communicative situation prompted the question: What is happening there-and-then-to-them? Thus, two different media functionings and also mindsets regarding the letters—in which two distinct subjects *in actu* are implied (biblical scholar here-and-now and original addressees there-and-then)—came to the fore. On this basis, the leading question of the present study could be formulated: How can we—as present-day readers in the predominantly literate context of academia—relate here-and-now to Paul's letters mediated by the available versions as "text" in order to understand how the original addressees in their predominantly oral state of mind would have grasped these documented words while being embodied by the emissary in the oral delivery, as envisioned by Paul in the moment of composition?

A NEW PERSPECTIVE ON "TEXT"

The history of research showed, indicative of the emerging *communis opinio*, that many studies accept the notion of oral performance as significant for understanding Paul's letters (Chapter 2). Several of these studies could be categorized as individual intellectual explorations into the field of orality studies, and it was observed that it is with the movement of Biblical Performance Criticism, in which a practice of live performances of the biblical texts here-and-now by the contemporary scholar is advocated, that debate more widely in biblical scholarship starts to be generated. In all the studies discussed in the history of research, however, even in David Rhoads's proposal on performances in real time,[1] the role and status of "text" as such remain implicit. The present study does not question the fact that there was a physical artefact from the start (Introduction; Chapter 3). Instead of exploring the orally determined context there-and-then or vocalizing these documents here-and-now, the contribution of the present study is to investigate the distinctive framing of these presupposed artefacts as "text" and/ or as a means to "oral performance." As indicated in the Introduction, the third and more fundamental question as to how the dominant media of autonomous text and the related mindset in academia influences our grasp of the functioning of oral performance there-and-then-to-them, has governed and structured the present study. From this perspective, we come to the more general conclusion that there is an intellectual challenge at issue here: in biblical scholarship, one has to explicitly textualize the functioning of the letter as "text" here-and-now-to-us. When we have identified how this specific media determines our own understanding, we can attempt to grasp the "oral performance"/"public reading" of the letter there-and-then-to-them, as good as possible, on its own terms. Unfortunately, this specific intellectual endeavour is virtually absent in Pauline or New Testament studies. Detextification provides a program to meet that challenge.

Detextification *avant la Lettre*: Louis Martyn and David Rhoads

In two studies in the history of research, however, these two media were indeed related to each other (Chapter 2). In one particular consideration, Rhoads provides the following criterion/question: Would the original addressees have been able to grasp and structure the oral delivery of the actually documented wording of the letter in line with the represented reasoning in text here-and-now (commentaries, articles, monographs, and so forth)?[2] Regarding the reconstructed syllogisms by Michael Bachmann

---

1. Rhoads, "Performance Criticism (Part I and II)."
2. Rhoads, "Performance Criticism (Part I)," 179. While acknowledging the usefulness of live performances of the biblical text for better understanding of the original functioning, there is an important difference between the Biblical Performance Criticism as advocated by Rhoads and the approach of detextification. In Chapter 2,

and Moisés Mayordomo (Chapter 4), the conclusion was that these layouts are too difficult to follow in an actual oral delivery; training in the method of abstraction, the aid of fixation-in-text, and the possibility of rereading is a prerequisite here.

From a different angle, we observed a crucial structure in the article "Events in Galatia" by Louis Martyn.[3] He locates the gospel neither in the transmitted document nor on the level of text as such, but postulates it as an invasion in the concrete lifeworld of the Galatian converts as anticipated by Paul: "the aural event" (Chapter 2). In a specific realm of history or beyond the level of text, Martyn envisions a communicative process between the emissary and the audience; in particular, the presence and performances of these other teachers is anticipated by the apostle in the process of composition. In this way, Martyn introduces a different matrix for grasping the implied "theology" of the letter. His reasoning led to the assumption that two "theologies" must have been operative in this rhetorical situation, specifically, that of the other teachers, and that of Paul himself. We found several examples of how these theologies inform the actual reasoning of the apostle as recorded in the letter. Martyn's approach on the "aural event" intimates the detextification of Paul's Letter to the Galatians.

We concluded that both in the work of Rhoads and Martyn the dimensions of media and mindset remain implicit. On the level of these texts, "text" itself—in the vagueness of concept and/or physical artefact—remains an unquestioned given. The operational result is an implicit and, in our view, unjustified equation of "letter" and "text." This works like a veil over the understanding of the present-day reader vis-à-vis the biblical document as "text."

Section H. David Rhoads: Biblical Performance Criticism, we observed that he uses in his grounding articles the term "text" indiscriminately, that is, it floats freely from the realm of history there-and-then-to-them to the one here-and-now-to-us and back. Subsequently, we argued that his praxis of present-day performances is also based on and dependent on the given "text" of the documents; his performances are like vocalizations of the text learned by heart. We also observed that in his argumentation the term "performance" has an extra-historical status. As a result, he interchanges his own experiences of vocalizing the biblical text for present-day audiences with the originally intended performances of these biblical documents. These observations led us to conclude that he is somehow still stuck in the media muddle (Introduction). Since he takes his stance in the actual event of delivery, Rhoads is not only the *performer*, but also the *audience* and *interpreter* at the same time. This is the main difference with detextification. Since we take the perspective of Paul in the process of composition, we become neither performer, nor audience, nor interpreter, but historian. We are called then to textualize (describe) how the apostle anticipated his intended addressees to participate in the envisioned event of delivery; in terms of style and arrangement, we attempt to understand how Paul intended his hearers to understand.

3. Martyn, "Events in Galatia."

Implicit Equation of "Letter" and "Text": Larry Hurtado and Joanna Dewey

The clearest instance of this implicit equation of "letter" and "text" was encountered in Larry Hurtado's polemical article on "Oral Fixation and New Testament Studies" (Chapter 2).[4] A critical evaluation of Hurtado's reasoning led to the conclusion that he had effectively engaged in a circular argument: from the start of his essay, he implies "texts" to be a given in the realm of history there-and-then. Similarly, he draws his conclusions on the New Testament documents, despite his acknowledgment of the *communis opinio*, in terms of the uncritical use of notions such as "reader," "writer," "manuscript," and "text." Neither the ancient practice of nor the recent attention to oral performance seems to lead him to re-evaluate his conclusions. He declares the New Testament to be "text," that is, he *textifies* these ancient documents.

We also discussed Joanna Dewey's article and found there an implicit equation and explicit differentiation in one and the same conclusion: "while texts were produced that later became very important within Christianity *as texts*, these texts began as aids to orality, and seemingly had little importance in themselves."[5] So although *text* later on and text originally do not function in the same way beyond the level of text, they are equated on the level of text and one and the same term is used for both. This illustrates the complexity of being reader and historian at the same time. In a more general way, we conclude that when the word "text" is used uncritically, the reader fills in the related operational dimension to which they are used themselves beyond critical awareness. At that moment, the originally intended media functioning and anticipated mindset are overruled and eclipsed. Despite good intentions, the media muddle infringes on the processes of coming to understand the realm of history there-and-then-to-them.

The Turn from Production to Product: Paul Achtemeier and Richard Longenecker

In Chapter 2, we identified a leap from process to product: given the process of production, the participants were explicitly discussed (Paul, emissary, addressees, and teachers); once the scholars discussed started to "read" the "text" themselves, they then became the sole and actual participants in the communicative process *in actu*—the result of textification. A sudden

---

4. Hurtado, "Oral Fixation."
5. J. Dewey, "Textuality," 51 (emphasis original).

role reversal takes place from historian to reader.[6] Paul Achtemeier, for example, started with a detailed exploration of the oral environment of late Western antiquity.[7] However, when he comes to the formulation of what he sees as a central problem on the original functioning of the New Testament documents, his reasoning seems to break down. He observes that the visual format of the manuscripts conveys virtually no information about the organization of the content. First, he argues that this problem is absent when an emissary or public reader is instructed on the delivery thereof. After this exploration, he restates the problem of "the visual format" but from then on, the emissary is no longer constitutive of his reasoning. Suddenly, it is we ourselves who are dealing with this apparently problematic "visual format" and "the content it [the manuscript] intended to convey." Without explanation, Achtemeier frames his own experience—as reader of the letter as text here-and-now—as a "problem." The setting of the original functioning is lost; he as reader fills in uncritically his own overly familiar praxis. Finally, he solves the problem by looking for the oral overlay in the available version of these documents (text).[8] Thus we concluded that his own processing of the letter as text lays as a veil over the realm of history there-and-then or the originally intended functioning of the letter.

In a similar vein, we touched on a rather confusing contradiction in the discussion of the commentary by Richard Longenecker in Chapter 4.[9] In his introduction, he describes the realm of history there-and-then-to-them profoundly and systematically (also the originally intended addressees), that is, he is acting as a historian. In his text and commentary part, however, his understanding of Gal 2.18–21 is structured consistently towards the realm of *freischwebendes Denken*. Notions such as "Christians" or "Christian belief" float around freely, meaning—as a consequence—the same everywhere, every time, and to everyone. Contrary to his introduction, Longenecker fails to differentiate between the two distinctive realms of history and his roles as historian and (Christian) reader. When the letter is processed as autonomous text in real time, abstraction trumps historicization or concretization.

---

6. Regarding this tendency, one could ask—for the sake of debate—whether this deeply ingrained reflex vis-à-vis the biblical text as "text" searching for (the) "meaning" reveals in biblical scholarship uncritical remnants of practicing traditional theology, setting out universally valid prepositions on "God," "humanity," "world" etc. Despite omnipresent relativism as well in academia, this provocative question remains valid because of the unquestioned media and mindset on which this search for meaning is based.

7. Achtemeier, "*OMNE VERBUM.*"

8. We came to the same conclusion in Chapter 2 regarding Davis, *Oral Biblical Criticism*.

9. Longenecker, *Galatians*.

"TEXT": THE PRESENT PORTAL TO REPRESENTATION

Looking for a way out of the media muddle, we explicitly related both media processes to each other (Chapter 3). We argued for the need to bring them together on one and the same level, that is, on the level of text. In this way, we could become historian of oral performances there-and-then *and* of our overly familiar activity of reading, according with the question What is happening there-and-then and also here-and-now? We designated this as the intellectual movement of *textualizing history*. Within this endeavour, two directions were distinguished: *textualizing text here-and-now-to-us* and *textualizing oral performance there-and-then-to-them*.

Regarding the first textualization, it was Walter Ong who helped us to approach text from the perspective of the spoken and heard word. In essence, spoken and heard words are combinations of identifiable and shared sound units. Sound is an evanescent process caused by the one who vocalizes and experienced by the one who hears. Spoken words are therefore bound fundamentally to the realm of history and to those who bodily and actually participate in this (live) communicative process. As a rule, ancient documents (*texta*) were subservient to such historical events (Introduction, Section D.5.; Chapter 2, Excursus: Silent reading in antiquity?). Later on, the product of writing became independent of someone who is vocalizing and the time and place in which the performance took place. Paul Ricoeur refers to this process as the emancipation of *textum* into the birth of text (Introduction; Chapter 3). In search of the originally intended functioning of ancient documents like the corpus Paulinum, we marked this observation as a turning point from ancient oral discourse to modern textual discourse. Since the text area compels the eye not to notice anymore that which is concretely present outside that frame, we contended that the implied effect is *hypervisuality*. This encompasses one to process specific codes printed or reflected on a flat surface that represent reality. We distinguished, therefore, a realm of extra-historical thought or *freischwebendes Denken*, characterized by the constituents of oneness, unchangingness, and, in particular, "being"—or, being everywhere, every time, and for everyone the same. In line with the subject-object scheme, the reader becomes an outsider defined by his cognitive capacities. The inner-historical realm is in itself the opposite, that is, it is diverse, complex, and changing ("becoming"). We exist bodily and uncritically in this realm (*totum*). Once representation starts, one somehow withdraws from naïve participation in that presence. From an uncritical participant, we become a critical observer. Text is a motor to do so. The prerequisite is, though, that this motor or "text" is physically available. For that reason, we concluded that "text" is a hybrid combination: it functions at the same time in two opposed realms that cannot come together. By means of the text as inner-historical artefact or thing (that is, beyond the level of text), the reader is enabled to enter or activate the level of text (realm of extra-historical thought). Hence, this media accomplishes the impossible, that is, the turn or leap from the operational/inner-historical realm to the formal/extra-historical level. We argued, therefore, that "text" is the given and operational portal (presence) to the realm of *freischwebendes Denken* (representation).

Abstraction and the Abstracted Context which Comes with Autonomous Text

So, when sound turns into record, then event, flux, immediacy, and presence turn into thing, fixedness, mediacy, and representation. We viewed this intellectual effect of text as *abstraction*. At this point in our argumentation, we explicitly acknowledged that in the present study we ourselves also work in real time with text and, as a result, with abstraction. In abstraction-by-means-of-text, we cross the line between presence and representation. As an intellectual activity, this way of structuring is inevitable and fruitful. The golden rule of Walter Ong is crucial with respect to this. He asserts that we can be critical on the level of concretization in our abstractions (Chapter 1). In this respect, we can think of the earlier described dynamic in the usage of vocabulary such as "text" and "reading" regarding the New Testament. So, if we want to do justice to the rule to get beyond the biblical documents while they function as "text" to us, we have to bend our thoughts into the realms of history, in which they function, there-and-then and here-and-now, as adequately as possible.

In the textualization of text here-and-now-to-us, we could concretize this tendency to abstraction vis-à-vis text. Since, technically speaking, "text" can travel freely throughout times and places, we argued that the proper way to come to understand must be independent as well of the concrete context in which the actual reader is processing. For that reason, the crucial insight is that the processing of autonomous text requires an equally free-floating context. This is a context that furthers abstraction or this kind of structuring thought away from the concrete situation in which one actually participates when one reads. This *freischwebende* context as constituent of the implied participatory realm of history—the bodily and intellectual activity of reading—is implicit in the given functioning of "text." So, as long as "letter" and "text" are equated, the abstracted context can or will dominate and govern the process of coming to understand the letter-as-text. This is essential to the media muddle in biblical scholarship; it becomes difficult for us to do justice here-and-now to this other and distinctive realm of history in which the letters of Paul originally had to function.

"Interpretation," "Performance," and "Hermeneutics": *Freischwebend* or Historical?

In the foundational articles of the movement of Biblical Performance Criticism (Chapter 2), Rhoads intricately describes several constitutive elements in composition and oral performance there-and-then. Subsequently, he proposes real-time performances of these same documents by the present-day biblical scholar so that one may gain a new entrance to them. This new entrance is consistently framed by Rhoads as "interpretation." We do not find any explication of what he means by this. As a result, concretization of possible differences between this activity here-and-now-by-us and there-and-then-by-them is lacking (consider the explicit differentiation of media and mindsets involved). Thus the abstracted context of text directs his reasoning and governs his praxis. Since it is neither explained nor explicated, we structure this activity of "interpretation" somehow uncritically in line with the familiar one in biblical scholarship, namely, the present-day reader processing the Bible as "text" asking, What does it mean?

This tendency to default to the familiar question of what does it mean similarly emerged in our critical scrutiny of Rhoads's approach to "performance." He jumps from represented performance there-and-then-to-them in their specific situation to his advocated present vocalizations of the given text here-and-now in schools, prisons, hospitals, universities, and so forth. Based on these present experiences, he reads these documents as autonomous texts here-and-now in order to come to a new understanding of them in that double-bound movement. So "performance"—alongside "interpretation"—receives an extra-historical status. This represented activity floats freely and uncritically back and forth between there-and-then and here-and-now due to the abstracted context of text. In the end, Rhoads's own practice of "performances" here-and-now dominates his understanding of the operational matrix of "performance" there-and-then-to-them. As if "performance" is everywhere, every time, and for everyone the same. Given Rhoads's agenda, we asked the following crucial question: Does the biblical scholar become Paul (composer), emissary (performer), or audience (interpreter?), or all of them at the same time? We noted that these consequences are not systematically elaborated. They all seem to come together in one and the same knowing subject *in actu*, that is, the biblical scholar in an attempt to come to a new understanding of these documents still conceived as "texts" (objects).

The problem involved is that the perspective on the originally intended aural event of Paul is eclipsed. Historically speaking, the original addressees whom Paul had in mind would not themselves have been exposed to the documented wording in their written form (eye-to-text-area) in any moment in the intended communicative process but to an embodiment by the emissary in the moment of delivery. Since we emphasize their predominantly oral state of mind and the composition of the letter from the perspective of the aural event (body-to-body), we were compelled to conclude that this distinctive process of composition does not only precede the moment of, but, more important, determines the nature of the intended oral performance of the letter there-and-then-to-them. The functioning of terms like "interpretation," "text," and "performance" on the level of Rhoads's text itself precludes this kind of exploration.

A similar tendency was found in the study by Werner Kelber.[10] We observed that when he engages with orality and literacy, a *Fundgrube* of insights is offered. But when it comes to his usage of the matrix of "reader," "hearer," "writer," "letter," and "text," a monolithic and highly abstracted framing seems to structure his thoughts away from the realm of history. The contribution of his book is to develop an "oral hermeneutics." Since he does not explain what he mains by "hermeneutics," we argued that, technically speaking, a similar leap to our presence and practice is involved. Therefore, despite his intention to correct "a disproportionately print-oriented hermeneutics" in biblical scholarship, his own approach is still based on the biblical documents as "text."[11] In conclusion, "hermeneutics" in his argumentation is caught up in the abstracted context which comes with autonomous text. So, given the third and more fundamental governing question, we argue that unthematized, abstracted, and free-floating concepts on the level of text, such as "text," "reading," "performance," "composition," "interpretation," and "hermeneutics," lie as a veil over these attempts to understand distinctive communicative processes beyond that level.

"TEXT" AND "CONTEXT"

Despite this critique, it is Rhoads's call to perform the biblical documents here-and-now that enabled us to explicate this uncritical turn from the

---

10. Kelber, *Oral and Written Gospel*; for a discussion, see Section A. in Chapter 2.

11. In a similar vein, we scrutinized the use of "composition" in the argumentation of Oestreich, *Performanzkritik*.

formal level (representation) to the operational realm (presence). As long as we do not distinguish between the functioning of "text," "oral performance," "interpretation," and so forth on the level of text and beyond that level, representation and presence continually become muddled or implicitly equated. We argued that this is due to *the scheme of text and context* (Chapter 3).

Relating Presence and Representation: Textualizing History

On the level of text, both nouns function as pair or equals, spelled as: t-e-x-t and c-o-n-t-e-x-t. Beyond that level, "text" (product/*pars*/being) and "context" (process/*totum*/becoming) represent presence in totally different ways. In biblical scholarship, one speaks of the "context" when one wants to understand the "biblical text" involved. So context is subservient to and follows (the givenness and processing of) text. Therefore, it was argued that a price is paid when we use "text" and "context" as a pair or scheme on the level of text without thematising the intricate relation between representation (as that level) and presence (beyond that level).

In this respect, we can turn to our treatment of the Letter to the Galatians and ask how the original addressees were expected to understand the letter: Is this related to the "context" or the "text"? At the moment that we turn to the latter in real time, however, the former is called in only if it is necessary in our process of understanding the text by reading. The actual functioning of "text" will supervene the distinctive media functioning and structuring of thought of the "context" beforehand (oral performance and predominantly oral mindset). So, in this procedure or approach, "context" cannot determine "text."

We found a notable exception in Joanna Dewey's article "Textuality in an Oral Culture." As we saw earlier, she explicates the role of "text" in the realm of history there-and-then-to-them: distinguishing between a later phase in which "*text*" (sic) becomes important in itself and the original setting in which "text" (sic) is only an aid to orality (*textum*). Thus she locates "text" in the "context." In terms of the present study, she textualizes text. So we argued that Dewey has provided the incentive to subvert the relation between "text" and "context." In conclusion, the general modus of doing biblical scholarship, however, remains dominated by an uncritical and fixed hierarchy between "text" and "context."

We saw this illustrated in our first test case. In their search for syllogistic reasonings in Gal 3.10–12, Mayordomo and Bachmann work within the confinement of text. Both go back and forth between the recorded wording of the letter as text and their own reconstructed representation as layouts in text, that is, in the ever-expanding universe of text. We recognize this same mechanism in the earlier mentioned studies in Chapter 2. At the moment that one jumps in real time to the letter as product here-and-now (exposure to the text-area of the printed version of the biblical document), the structuring of the original process in which the letter was intended to function (context) is bypassed. When we want to understand how the Galatian converts were expected to structure their thoughts in the aural event, we need to penetrate the specific operational dimension of that "context." Thus, we need to do justice to "context" beyond the given functioning to us of this concept in the abstracted context of text.

In Our Presence Coming to Representation of Their Presence: Historicizing Text

Therefore—in addition to *textualizing history*—a second intellectual movement was needed. We argued that the veil of text can be taken away—at least, partially—in the actual moment of turning to the letter as a physical artefact in real time (available versions here-and-now and/or text area). This was designated *historicizing text* and led to an answer to the first part of the leading question of the present study: How to operate in the realm of history here-and-now vis-à-vis these letters as "text" in which the present-day reader participates himself beyond critical awareness? This intellectual movement implies that the present-day reader relates every term, theme, thematic matrix, reasoning, metaphor, or narrative in a systematic way to these other knowing subjects *in actu*—in the realm of history there-and-then, that is, in the case of the present study, the Galatian converts—who participate in a distinct media (oral performance) and in a distinct mindset (predominantly oral). In this way, justice was done to the fact that there was a physical artefact from the start, but also to the claim that the structuring in the free-standing context of autonomous text can be overcome. These terms and reasonings have to resound, so to speak, in that specific inner-historical realm. Instead of "text" as the present portal to representation, we proposed an alternative opening to represented presence. On that basis, we can attempt to textualize (put into words) how the originally intended participants would or could have structured their thoughts in the event of delivery. We concluded that this intellectual movement is an antidote to the turn from the represented process there-and-then to the present product as product, or to the implicit equation of "letter" and "text" through which the abstracted context can take over our structuring of thought.

DETEXTIFICATION: HOW, TO WHOM, WHAT MINDSET, AND WHOSE PERSPECTIVE[S]?

In the movements of textualizing history and historicizing text, the leading question of the present study turned into a path to pursue. Since text is a motor of abstraction, a reader vis-à-vis the text area tends to think away from the concrete realm of history in which they participate in real time. This explains the value of John Miles Foley's critique of the question, What does it mean? Since in this question the actual media (text), mindset (predominantly literate), and subject *in actu* (I/we) are not explicated, these aspects seem to be determined in advance. Moreover, these elements constitute that concrete situation of reading from which thoughts are structured away. Foley transforms this deeply internalized question into "How does it mean?" and this helped him to formulate the Theory of Metonymical or Traditional Referentiality (Chapter 1). We preferred to speak of "to function" instead of "to mean" and were able to extend this question in our attempt to textualize oral performance there-and-then-to-them (Chapter 3). In the research of Milman Parry and Albert Lord, the original participants in the performances of Homer remain generalized. The Letter to the Galatians is composed with a view to Christian-Jewish teachers who had gained influence over (a section of) the Galatian communities by their presence and performances. Since Paul attempts to counter the influence of these teachers, there is a more specific situation related to the Letter to the Galatians—also to the corpus Paulinum in general—than in the case of Homer. According to this reasoning, we identified—in line with Foley's question of "how"—other elements such as "to whom," "in what state of mind," and "from whose perspective(s)." As a result, the governing question in detextification of ancient documents such as Paul's letters is the following: How does it function to whom, in what state of mind, and from whose perspective[s]?

In this way, we could formulate an approach to the second part of the leading question of the present study: How can we understand the way in which the original addressees in their predominantly oral mindset would have grasped these documented words in the moment of delivery as envisioned by Paul while composing? We identified this structure as *anticipated participation*: in the moment of composition, Paul anticipates a specific participation in the oral performance of the letter on the part of his original addressees caught up in their specific lifeworld (collective memory) in line with their predominantly oral mindset.

Anticipated Participation and Abstraction

For heuristic purposes, this communicative structure in real time spoken discourse—especially against the predominantly oral background of the first-century Mediterranean world—can be contrasted with the intellectual movement of abstraction vis-à-vis text. In anticipated participation, the structuring of thought is made subservient by the sender to the specific addressees in the realm of history in which they are addressed. It is based on the shared history, relation, and dialogue in which both sender and receiver somehow participate. More so, this kind of communication aims at how the addressees frame, act in, or even change that specific situation. Thus, the communicative process is dominated by and is aiming at presence.

Abstraction is an intellectual movement away from the concrete situation. The aim of this activity is related to the knowing subject—for the subject wants to understand (aspects of) reality. In text, presence is overruled by representation. Even when the lines of thought offered deal with the concrete situation in which readers find themselves, they are being cognitively caught in the process of abstraction, somehow bodily severed from, or critical outsiders to this realm of history/other human beings as persons of flesh and blood. It is not based on the dialogical structure of subject-subject but the relation between subject-object. In this latter scheme, the subject is in the process of getting to know. This is a monological or one-way structure. As a result, abstraction creates distance and isolates the knowing subject. Instead of immediate action, it enables a mode of observance and distant consideration on which basis possible and multiple future plans can be formed. This contrast would lead us to conclude that abstraction defines and determines the knowing subject as a *spectator* of reality. Anticipated participation wants to involve the participant in the communicative event as an *actor* in a concrete situation (Kelber). Necessarily, this goal lies beyond the level of text.

Explicit Parts and Implicit Whole: Metonymy and Collective Memory

With the help of Foley, we textualized the governing dynamic of *metonymy* (how), on the one hand, as well as the decisive role of *collective memory* of the actual audiences on the other (to whom/in what state of mind; Chapter 3). We observed how both are related to each other. In the actual performance of the letters, the apostle provides from his side the explicit parts—terms, themes, fragments of reasoning, narrative elements, and metaphors—while

CONCLUSIONS 289

he anticipates his hearers to fill in or supply the implied whole, which he anticipates as familiar to them. The latter refers to collective memory.

In this way, we textualized the enthymematic structure in the reasoning of Gal 3.10–12 (Chapter 4). Contrary to Bachmann and Mayordomo, we concluded that Paul only explicates those elements (*partes*) of the underlying syllogism (*totum*) that are necessary to enable his hearers to recall this already familiar reasoning. Based on Gal 3.21, we identified three constitutive terms of the somewhat laborious reasoning involved: "Law," "the one who is rectified," and "to l/Live." These three terms led to the reconstruction of a single, simple, and self-evident syllogism: the one who is rectified/righteous before God, he will Live (major premise). The one who is out of law, he will be rectified/righteous (minor premise). Therefore, the one who is out of law, he will Live (conclusion). Based on this anticipated participation, we could identify the logos of his opponent's rhetoric. A majority of the enthymemes thus identified in the letter, relate to the minor premise. Since they are crucial in this type of reasoning, they are consistently and openly denied by the apostle.

Since redundancy is characteristic of oral-aural communication, we argued that this also works for similar and opposed parts, that is, *synonymy* and *antonymy*. In the first example of Gal 3.10–12, we noticed that "the Blessing of Abraham" (3.8, 9, 14) is synonymous to the promise of "to Live" (3.11) and "to receive the Spirit" (3.2, 3, 5, 14). At the same time, they are antonymous to "the curse of the law" (3.10). The same pertains to "to be rectified/righteous" (2.16a, 16c, 16d, 17, 21b; 3.6, 8a, 11, 21d) and "to live like a Jew" (2.14c, 14d, 15). Given this synonym, we also encountered the antonym "to be/live like a sinner" and "sin" (2.15, 17), or "to be/live like a Gentile" (2.14c, 15). As a result, we noticed that the same syllogistic reasoning is at work in the thematic matrix of "Abraham" and "Blessing" (Gal 3.6–9): the one who is son of Abraham, he will be Blessed in Abraham (major premise). The one who is faithful as Abraham, he is son of Abraham (minor premise). Therefore, the one who is faithful as Abraham, he will be Blessed in Abraham (conclusion). In a similar vein, we could textualize the antonymous version on "law" and "curse" (Gal 3.10): the one who is not rectified before God, he will be cursed by the law (major premise). The one who is not out of works of law, he is not rectified before God (minor premise). Therefore, the one who is not out of works of law, he will be cursed by the law (conclusion). We construed a similar syllogism regarding the key terms of "sinner" and "to live like a Gentile" (Gal 2.14–15, 17) as well as "to receive the Spirit" (Gal 3.1–5). We drew the conclusion that a metonymical network of synonymous and antonymous terms and themes was integral to this section of the letter. Therefore, the approach of detextification does not cause differences on the level of the meaning of these specific words or sentences, but it enables the identification and textualization of the distinctive way in which they were intended to function and to structure thought in the envisioned oral delivery. We identified up to twenty-one parts of this one and simple syllogistic reasoning in Gal 2–3. This detextified understanding satisfied all seven criteria developed by John Barclay in his article on mirror-reading the Letter to the Galatians.[12]

A Reversed Example: Reading the Letter as Autonomous Text

Contrary to the structure provided by metonymy and collective memory, in Chapter 4 we found examples of how the presupposed autonomy of text and the abstracted context determine the understanding of the present-day reader. In the first example on the reasoning in Gal 3.10–12, Bachmann implicitly argues for the superiority of his reconstructions. Contrary to Mayordomo,[13] he can identify all the elements in his syllogisms on the level of the text of the letter. Since supplying implicit premises is apparently inferior, we highlighted the implied literate bias. Since Bachmann himself is the reading subject *in actu*, his syllogistic reconstructions of this passage function as "text" (media), "to him" (knowing subject) in his "predominantly literate state of mind" (mindset). Similarly, we saw that in all studies consulted in the first example references to the Jewish holy scriptures function necessarily as premise in the letter. Without explanation, this presupposition is maintained consistently. In the ever-expanding universe of text, "Scripture"—as the primal and ultimate "text"—seems to supersede other texts as text.

Paul and Other Teachers: Rhetoric and Counter Rhetoric

The third element, "from whose perspective[s]" (plural), is based on the article by Louis Martyn. Due to his reasoning on the invasion of God in the aural event, he pushes his understanding of the gospel beyond the level of text. The structure of his commentary brings our imagination to life. In the light of the crucial role of these other teachers, we arrived at the following line of thinking: Paul felt urged to compose this letter because he is

---

12. Barclay, "Mirror-Reading."

13. In Chapter 4, we also discussed, in several footnotes, the article by Peter Lampe, "*Reticentia*." Bachmann also refers to the article by Lampe as an example of an explanation in need of implicit premises (see, in Chapter 4, Section A.2. Textualizing oral performance *illic et tunc pro eis*).

CONCLUSIONS

displeased with developments in his Galatian congregations. The presence and performances of these other teachers had changed the course in (parts of) the communal life there. In this way, these teachers had gained influence over the Galatian converts.

When we relate this insight to how text works for us, a crucial insight emerges: the letter as intended aural event anticipates but does not explicate this preceding and even partially opposed ethos and rhetoric (collective memory). When one approaches the letter uncritically by reading, an explicit elaboration of how these conflicting opinions or interests determined the realm of history there-and-then is not found on the level of the text. In particular, in the commentaries by Martyn and Martin de Boer,[14] we found several examples in which this dimension is taken into account. We observed, however, that these instances are incidental. We argued that these conflicting presences and performances—Paul versus these teachers—determine the intended communicative process from start to finish. For that reason, we developed the systematic approach of detextification.

In that respect, turning to the vocabulary used, we argued for the utilization of the notion of "rhetoric" over "theology." The latter tends to extra-historical thought, fixation-in-text, and is governed by related expectations of oneness, unchangingness, fixedness, and "being" (God-centred). In general, "theology" is related to cognitive capacities and thriving in the ever-expanding universe of text, disconnected from our bodies.[15] "Rhetoric" implies situation, purpose, change, conflict of interests, body, and "becoming" (flux of history). It aims at moving people and making them into actors. Therefore, instead of two "theologies" in Galatia (Martyn), we structured our understanding by two "rhetorics." As a result of taking into account the anticipated performances of these other teachers on Paul's part (collective memory), we distinguished a structure of *rhetoric and counter rhetoric*.

---

14. Martyn, *Galatians*; Boer, *Galatians*.

15. In this respect, we can refer to Jacques Derrida's *Of Grammatology*. In line with his claim of the "epoch of the Logos" or the "age of the sign" is his analysis of the alleged secondariness or exteriorization of "writing" (in the narrow sense): based on Aristotle, it starts with "mental experiences" that are symbolized in "spoken words" that are, in their turn, symbolized in "written words" (11). Since the Logos originates from God, the latter is in essence separated from or has to be mediated to the body, senses, and the realm of history (*Of Grammatology*, 14/15).

Counter Rhetoric: Negative Rhetoric, Rhetoric of Confusion, and *Umdeutung*

As a next step, the complicated way in which these rhetorics interact in the realm of history there-and-then was textualized. We distinguished different forms. First in the first example, we noticed the explicitly denied minor premises of the logos of these other teachers (Chapter 4). Besides Gal 3.21cd, we encountered five other examples of this blunt denial (Gal 2.16a, 16c, 16d, 21b, 3.11a). We classified them as *rhetoric of denial* or *negative rhetoric*.

Second, Paul aims to regain the hearts of his addressees, since he wants to discourage circumcision and dissociate the Galatian converts from these teachers ("to live out of law"). From this perspective, he picks up the themes, terms, and reasonings of his opponents in the course of his own rhetoric. We saw this in the verb to "live" in Gal 2. In the delivery of the letter, the first mention of the term is related by Paul to living "out of law" (2.16a). In Gal 2.20, however, the apostle relates his actual reasoning on "living" to his earlier introduced antithetical formulation of "out of faith" (2.16b). As a result, both teachings collide: when you "live out of law," living in obedience to Christ (Jews having table fellowship with Gentiles) will turn you into a "sinner." In the central term of "living," the apostle creates a short circuit between two ways of thinking. We categorized this as *rhetoric of confusion*.

We argued that with this rhetoric he aims at a specific reaction: How do you have to "live" and avoid to become a "sinner"? First, he openly disqualifies the referential framing of his adversaries, that is, "to live out of law." Second, he turns to the antonym to "die": he states that he has "died in and through that law" (19a). The goal and claim are the possibility to "live in/for God." Through "co-crucifixion" with Christ, a different kind of to "live" is realized. In this train of thought, to "live" is not only disconnected from but even becomes opposed to the "law," and in a surprising way connected to Paul's gospel of the cross. We argued that, first, by reversing the natural sequence of "living" and "dying," and then by introducing the theme of "co-crucifixion," Paul wants to lead his hearers through a restructuring of their thoughts: their past baptism has already made them participants in this "Life in God"—just like Paul himself. We classified this counter-rhetorical strategy on the theme of "I/Life" as the structure of *framing and reframing* or *rhetoric of Umdeutung*.

In the preceding passage, the apostle applies the same strategy to the notion of "sin"/"sinner" (Gal 2.17). In the envisioned delivery of the letter, he commences with the framing of his opponents: "sin" is living in violation of Jewish regulations. At the end of this passage, he leads his addressees by means of an exclamation to decide on the opposite frame (2.18): the one who knows of the crucifixion of Christ (2.20; to have died in and through the law) and, nonetheless, still dares to claim that disobeying the law is "sin," he is the only true "transgressor"!

Regarding his gospel, another level of framing and reframing was identified. In an attempt to counter the influence of his opponents, Paul has to deal with typically Jewish issues such as the "law," "Jews and Gentiles," "sin," and "Abraham." In Gal 2.19–21, we observed that he reframes the past baptism of his Galatian converts in the light of this thematic matrix. This *Umdeutung* should make clear that baptism disqualifies circumcision and, therefore, the whole rhetoric and authority of these other teachers (Chapter 4).

Based on this dynamic of reframing, we can conclude that another fundamental difference comes to the fore in comparison to autonomous text. In composing text, one cannot implicitly change the referential meaning of a used term during one's reasoning. Apart from being extraordinary, this would also only be possible under the conditions of explication and justification on that same level. The second test case, however, showed that this is the case in the Letter to the Galatians and, in that way, disclosed the distinctive nature of the originally intended communicative process involved.

IN THE END: THERE IS ALWAYS MANIFESTATION IN THE REALM OF HISTORY

As a consequence of the approach of detextification, we structure our thoughts as adequately as possible into the realm of history involved. Therefore, when the present study is valued as a contribution in the philosophy of biblical studies as set out in the Introduction, it is imperative that, in the end, some sort of manifestation or embodiment can be discerned. Because of the textualization of text here-and-now-to-us, we also asked for the manifestation of our typical "thoughts" or "structuring of thought." We contended that they are mirrored in the text area by hypervisuality (Chapter 3). Similarly, we asked this question regarding the originally intended structuring of the single and simple syllogistic reasoning on the "law," "rectification," and "Life" in Gal 3.10–12 (Chapter 4). We suggested that this reasoning would have become manifest in the performances and presence of these other teachers. Besides their preaching being governed by the specific logos of law obedience leading to the promised Life (performances), they also lived according to those legal regulations themselves (presence). The syllogistic reasoning lends authority to their performances and their living according to these rules makes their teaching accessible and appealing to the

Galatian communities: by receiving the mark of circumcision, they (fully) will become partakers in that Life.

In the second example of Gal 2.18–21, we saw that Martyn and de Boer both argue that Paul is juxtaposing the "old" with the "eschatological human being." Here we encountered an example illustrating that the implied structurings of thought—in processing the letter as text by the present-day reader and the anticipated participation by Paul in the aural event—can overlap (Introduction). We noted, though, that this specific formulation is not taken from the explicitly documented wording. Historically speaking, the formulation is anachronistic and abstracted. Therefore, we asked, In what sensorial way does Paul anticipate the original addressees in the aural event relating to this transition from the "old" to the "eschatological human being"? In our detextification, we pointed to the typical way in which Paul uses the sequence of "to die"/"to live" and the matrix of "co-crucifixion." We suggested manifestation in the ritual of "baptism." The "eschatological human being" becomes visible in their memory of those who rise out of the water; baptism reaches into the presence of their bodies. So, in this detextification, it becomes clear that the addressees could relate sensorially—in terms of "memory" and "experiences"—to that which Martyn and de Boer express in this abstracted and anachronistically "theological" way.

Since in Gal 3.27 "baptism" is found on the level of the text, we noted that all the commentaries involved acknowledge and discuss the relevance of "baptism" regarding the Letter to the Galatians. None of them asks, however, the question of how this ritual—as constitutive of their identity as converts vis-à-vis Paul (collective memory)—functions in the structuring of thought by the original addressees in the oral performance of the letter from start to finish. Through "baptism," we could structure our understanding of Gal 2.18–21 beyond the level of text. Thus, we concluded that detextification enables us to deepen our grasp here-and-now of the letter in its originally intended media functioning there-and-then. In this way, it was the concern of the present research project to validate the hypothesis as presented in the Introduction. That is to say, to demonstrate the difference between searching for meaning based on the uncritical functioning of the letters as "text" here-and-now-to-us and an understanding based on the approach of detextification.

Bibliography

Achtemeier, Paul J. "*OMNE VERBUM SONAT*: The New Testament and the Oral Environment of Late Western Antiquity." *Journal of Biblical Literature* 109 (1990) 3–27.

Aland, Barbara, and Kurt Aland. *The Text of the New Testament: An Introduction to the Critical Editions and to the Theory and Practice of Modern Textual Criticism.* Translated by Errol F. Rhodes. 2nd rev. ed. Grand Rapids: Eerdmans, 1995.

Aland, Barbara, et al. *Novum Testamentum Graece.* 28th rev. ed. Stuttgart: Deutsche Bibelgesellschaft, 2012.

Aland, Barbara, et al. *Novum Testamentum Graecum, Editio Critica Maior: IV/I Die Katholischen Briefen, Text.* 2nd rev. ed. Stuttgart: Deutsche Bibelgesellschaft, 2013.

Aland, Barbara, et al. *The Greek New Testament.* 5th ed. Stuttgart: Deutsche Bibelgesellschaft, 2014.

Aristotle. *On Rhetoric: A Theory of Civic Discourse.* Translated with Introduction, Notes and appendices by George A. Kennedy. 2nd ed. New York: Oxford University Press, 2007.

———. *Prior Analytics.* Translated with Introduction, Commentary, and Notes by Robin Smith. Indianapolis: Hackett, 1989.

Assmann, Jan. *Religion and Cultural Memory.* Translated by Rodney Livingstone. Stanford: Stanford University Press, 2006.

Aune, David E. "The Use and Abuse of the Enthymeme in New Testament Scholarship." *New Testament Studies* 49 (2003) 299–320.

Bachmann, Michael. "4QMMT und Galaterbrief, מעשה תורה und ΕΡΓΑ ΝΟΜΟΥ." *Zeitschrift für die Neutestamentliche Wissenschaft* 89 (1998) 91–113.

———. "Zur Argumentation von Galater 3.10–12." *New Testament Studies* 53 (2007) 524–44.

Barclay, John M. G. "Mirror-Reading a Polemical Letter: Galatians as a Test Case." *Journal for the Study of the New Testament* 31 (1987) 73–93.

Bagnall, Roger. *Everyday Writing in the Graeco-Roman East.* Berkeley: University of California, 2011.

Balogh, Joseph. "*Voces Paginarum*: Beiträge zur Geschichte des Lauten Lesens und Schreibens." *Philologus* 82 (1927) 85–109, 202–40.

Barrett, Charles K. "The Allegory of Abraham, Sarah, and Hagar in the Argumentation of Galatians." In *Rechtfertigung: Festschrift für Ernst Käsemann*, edited by Johannes Friedrich et al., 1–16. Tübingen: Mohr Siebeck, 1976.

Bauer, Thomas J. *Paulus und die kaiserzeitliche Epistolographie: Kontextualisiering und Analyse der Briefe an Philemon und an die Galater*. Wissenschaftliche Untersuchungen zum Neuen Testament 276. Tübingen: Mohr Siebeck, 2011.

Becker, Jürgen, and Ulrich Lutz, *Die Briefe an die Galater, Epheser und Kolosser*. Das Neue Testament Deutsch 8/1. Göttingen: Vandenhoeck & Ruprecht, 1998.

Beker, J. Christiaan. *Paul the Apostle: The Triumph of God in Life and Thought*. Edinburgh: T. & T. Clark, 1980.

Betz, Hans Dieter. *Galatians: A Commentary on Paul's Letter to the Churches in Galatia*. Hermeneia. Philadelphia: Fortress, 1979.

Bitzer, Lloyd F. "The Rhetorical Situation." *Philosophy and Rhetoric* 1 (1968) 1–14.

Blackburn, Simon. "Syllogism." In *Oxford Dictionary of Philosophy*, edited by Simon Blackburn, 278–79. 2nd ed. Oxford: Oxford University Press, 1996.

Blass, Friedrich, et al. *Grammatik des neutestamentlichen Griechisch*. 18th ed. Göttingen: Vandenhoeck & Ruprecht, 2001.

Blomberg Craig L., and Jennifer F. Markley. *A Handbook of New Testament Exegesis*. Grand Rapids: Baker Academic, 2010.

Boer, Martinus C. de. *The Defeat of Death: Apocalyptic Eschatology in 1 Corinthians and Romans 5*. Journal for the Study of the New Testament Supplement Series 22. Sheffield: JSOT Press, 1988.

———. *Galatians: A Commentary*. New Testament Library. Louisville: Westminster John Knox, 2011.

———. *Paul, Theologian of God's Apocalypse: Essays on Paul and Apocalyptic*. Eugene, OR: Cascade Books, 2020.

———. "Paul's Use and Interpretation of a Justification Tradition in Galatians 2.15–21." *Journal for the Study of the New Testament* 28 (2005) 189–216.

Boomershine, Thomas E. "Peter's Denial as Polemic or Confession: The Implications of Media Criticism for Biblical Hermeneutics." *Semeia* 39 (1987) 47–68.

Botha, Pieter J.J. "Letter Writing and Oral Communication in Antiquity: Suggested Implications for the Interpretation of Paul's Letter to the Galatians." *Scriptura* 42 (1992) 17–34. Reprinted in *Orality and Literacy in Early Christianity*, 193–211. Biblical Performance Criticism Series 5. Eugene, OR: Cascade Books, 2012.

———. *Orality and Literacy in Early Christianity*. Biblical Performance Criticism Series 5. Eugene, OR: Cascade Books, 2012.

Bowman, Alan K., and J. David Thomas. "New Texts from Vindolanda." *Britannia* 18 (1987) 125–42.

———. "Vindolanda 1985: The New Writing-Tablets." *Journal of Roman Studies* 76 (1986) 120–23.

Breytenbach, Cilliers. *Paulus und Barnabas in der Provinz Galatien: Studien zu Apostelgeschichte 13f.; 16.6; 18.23 und den Adressaten des Galaterbriefes*. Arbeiten zur Geschichte des antiken Judentums und des Urchristentums 38. Leiden: Brill, 1996.

Bruce, F. F. *Galatians*. The New International Greek Commentary Series. Grand Rapids: Eerdmans, 1982.

Bühler, Karl. *Sprachtheorie: Die Darstellungsfunktion der Sprache*. Jena: Fischer, 1934.

Burton, Ernest de Witt. *A Critical and Exegetical Commentary on the Epistle to the Galatians*. International Critical Commentary. Edinburgh: T. & T. Clark, 1921. Reprinted 1971.

Byrskog, Samuel. "Co-Senders, Co-Authors, and Paul's Use of the First Person Plural." *Zeitschrift für die Neutestamentliche Wissenschaft* 87 (1996) 230–50.

———. "Epistolography, Rhetoric, and Letter Prescript: Romans 1.1–7 as a Test Case." *Journal for the Study of the New Testament* 65 (1997) 27–46.

———. "History and Story in Acts—A Middle Way? The 'We' Passages, Historical Intertexture, and Oral History." In *Contextualizing Acts: Lukan Narrative and Greco-Roman Discourse*, edited by Todd Penner et al., 257–83. Society of Biblical Literature Symposium Series 20. Atlanta: Society of Biblical Literature, 2003.

———. *Story as History—History as Story: The Gospel Tradition in the Context of Ancient Oral History*. Wissenschaftliche Untersuchungen zum Neuen Testament 123. Tübingen: Mohr Siebeck, 2000.

Cicero, *On the Orator: Book 3, On Fate, Stoic Paradoxes, Divisions of Oratory*. Loeb Classical Library 349. Translated by Harris Rackham.

Classen, Carl Joachim. "Can the Theory of Rhetoric Help Us to Understand the New Testament, and in Particular the Letters of Paul?" In *Paul and Ancient Rhetoric: Theory and Practice in the Hellenistic Context*, edited by Stanley E. Porter et al., 13–39. New York: Cambridge University Press, 2016.

Clayton, Jay and Eric Rothstein. "Figures in the Corpus: Theories of Influence and Intertextuality." In *Influence and Intertextuality in Literary History*, edited by Jay Clayton, 3–36. Madison: University of Wisconsin Press, 1991.

Cousar, Charles B. *Reading Galatians, Philippians, and 1 Thessalonians*. A Literary and Theological Commentary. Macon: Smyth & Helwys, 2001.

Cribiori, Raffaella. *Gymnastics of the Mind: Greek Education in Hellenistic and Roman Egypt*. Princeton: Princeton University Press, 2001.

Culler, Jonathan. *The Pursuit of Signs: Semiotics, Literature, Deconstruction*. Ithaca: Cornell University Press, 1981.

Culley, Robert C. "Oral Tradition and Biblical Studies." *Oral Tradition* 1 (1986) 30–85.

Cummins, Stephan Anthony. *Paul and the Crucified Christ in Antioch: Maccabean Martyrdom and Galatians 2*. Society for New Testament Studies Monograph Series 114. Cambridge: Cambridge University Press, 2001.

DaSilva, David A. *The Letter to the Galatians*. New International Commentary on the New Testament. Grand Rapids: Eerdmans, 2018.

Davis, Casey W. "Hebrews 6.4–6 from an Oral Critical Perspective." *Journal of the Evangelical Theological Society* 51 (2008) 753–68.

———. *Oral Biblical Criticism: The Influence of the Principles of Orality on the Literary Structure of Paul's Epistle to the Philippians*. Journal for the Study of the New Testament Supplement Series 172. Sheffield: Sheffield Academic, 1999.

Deissmann, Adolf G. *Bibelstudien: Beiträge, aus den Papyri und Inschriften, zur Geschichte der Sprache, des Schrifttums und der Religion des hellenistischen Judentums und des Urchristentums*. Marburg: Elwert, 1885.

———. *Licht vom Osten: Das Neue Testament und die neuentdeckten Texte der hellenistisch-römischen Welt*. Tübingen: Mohr Siebeck, 1923.

———. *Light from the Ancient East: The New Testament Illustrated by Recently Discovered Texts of the Graeco-Roman World*. Rev. ed. Translated by Lionel R. M. Strachan. 1927. Reprint, Eugene, OR: Wipf & Stock, 2004.

Derrida, Jacques. *Of Grammatology*. Translated and Preface by Gayatri Chakravorty Spivak. Rev. ed. Baltimore: Johns Hopkins University Press, 1997. Translation of *De la Grammatologie*. Paris: Minuit, 1967.

Dewey, Arthur J. "A Re-Hearing of Romans 10.1–15." *Semeia* 65 (1994) 109–27.

———. *Spirit and Letter in Paul*. Studies in Bible and Early Christianity 33. Lewiston, NY: Mellen, 1996.

Dewey, Joanna D. "Textuality in an Oral Culture: A Survey of Pauline Traditions." *Semeia* 65 (1994) 139–68.

Doty, William G. *Letters in Primitive Christianity*. Guides to Biblical Scholarship: New Testament. Philadelphia: Fortress, 1973.

Dunn, James D. G. "Altering the Default Setting: Re-envisaging the Early Transmission of the Jesus Tradition." *New Testament Studies* 49 (2003) 139–75.

———. *Baptism in the Holy Spirit: A Re-examination of the New Testament Teaching of the Gift of the Spirit in Relation to Pentecostalism Today*. 2nd ed. London: SCM, 2010.

———. *The Epistle to the Galatians*. Black's New Testament Commentary. London: Black, 1993.

———. *Jesus Remembered: Christianity in the Making*. Vol. 1. Grand Rapids: Eerdmans, 2009.

———. "The Theology of Galatians." In *Pauline Theology*. Vol. 1, *Thessalonians, Philippians, Galatians, Philemon*, edited by Jouette M. Bassler, 125–46. 4 vols. Minneapolis: Fortress, 1991.

———. *The Theology of Paul the Apostle*. Grand Rapids: Eerdmans, 1998.

———. *The Theology of Paul's Letter to the Galatians*. New Testament Theology. Cambridge: Cambridge University Press, 1993.

Eco, Umberto, *The Role of the Reader: Explorations in the Semiotics of Texts*. Advances in Semiotics. Bloomington: Indiana University Press, 1979.

Elmer, Ian J. "Paul, Jerusalem, and the Judaisers: The Galatian Crises in its Broader Historical Context." PhD diss., Australian Catholic University, 2007.

Esler, Philip F. *Galatians*. New Testament Readings. London: Routledge, 1998.

Evans, Paul S. "Creating a New 'Great Divide': The Exoticization of Ancient Culture in Some Recent Applications of Orality Studies to the Bible." *Journal of Biblical Literature* 136 (2017) 749–64.

Fee, Gordon, D. *New Testament Exegesis: A Handbook for Students and Pastors*. 3rd ed. Louisville: Westminster John Knox, 2002.

Ferguson, Everett. *Baptism in the Early Church: History, Theology, and Liturgy in the First Five Centuries*. Grand Rapids: Eerdmans, 2009.

Finnigan, Ruth. *Literacy and Orality: Studies of Communication*. 2nd ed. Preface to 2014 edition by the author. Old Bletchley: Callender, 2014.

———. "What Is Orality—if Anything?" *Byzantine and Modern Greek Studies* 41 (1990) 130–49.

Fisch, Yael. "The Origins of Oral Torah: A New Pauline Perspective." *Journal for the Study of Judaism* 51 (2020) 43–66.

Fischer, Steven R. *A History of Writing*. London: Reaktion, 2001.

Foley, John M. ed. *Comparative Research on Oral Traditions: A Memorial for Milman Parry*. Columbus: Slavica, 1987.

———. "Editing Oral Epic Texts: Theory and Practice." *Textus* (1981) 77–78.

———. *How to Read an Oral Poem*. Urbana: University of Illinois Press, 2002.

———. *Immanent Art: From Structure to Meaning in Traditional Oral Epic*. Bloomington: Indiana University Press, 1991.

———. "Introduction: The Oral Theory in Context." In *Oral Traditional Literature: A Festschrift for Albert Bates Lord*, edited by John M. Foley, 27–122. Columbus, OH: Slavica, 1981.

———. *Oral Formulaic Theory and Research: An Introduction and Annotated Bibliography*. New York: Garland, 1985. Reprinted, 1989.

———. *Oral Tradition and the Internet: Pathways of the Mind*. Champaign: University of Illinois Press, 2012. Centre for eResearch. Cited date June 3 2019. http://www.pathwaysproject.org.

———. *The Singer of Tales in Performance*. Bloomington: Indiana University Press, 1995.

———. *The Theory of Oral Composition: History and Methodology*. Bloomington: Indiana University Press, 1988.

———. *Traditional Oral Epic: The Odyssey, Beowulf, and the Serbo-Croatian Return Song*. Berkeley: University of California, 1990.

Fowler, James A. *A Commentary on the Epistle to the Galatians: The Gospel versus Religion*. Christocentric Commentary Series. Fallbrook, CA: CIY, 2006.

Franklin James L., Jr. "Literacy and the Parietal Inscriptions of Pompeii." In *Literacy in the Roman World*, edited by Mary Beard, et al., 77–98. Ann Arbor, MI: Journal of Roman Archaeology, 1991.

Fung, Ronald Y. K. *The Letter to the Galatians*. New International Commentary on the New Testament. Grand Rapids: Eerdmans, 1988.

Funk, Robert W. "The Apostolic Parousia: Form and Significance." In *Christian History and Interpretation: Studies Presented to John Knox*, edited by William R. Farmer, et al., 249–68. Cambridge: Cambridge University Press, 1967.

Garner, R. Scott. "Annotated Bibliography of Works by John Miles Foley." *Oral Tradition* 26 (2011) 677–724.

Gamble, Harry Y. *Books and Readers in the Early Church: A History of Early Christian Texts*. New Haven: Yale University Press, 1995.

Gaventa, Beverly Roberts. "The Singularity of the Gospel: A Reading of Galatians." In *Pauline Theology*. Vol. 1, *Thessalonians, Philippians, Galatians, Philemon*, edited by Jouette M. Bassler, 147–59. 4 vols. Minneapolis: Fortress, 1991.

Georgi, Dietrich. *The Opponents of Paul in Second Corinthians: A Study of Religious Propaganda in Late Antiquity*. Philadelphia: Fortress, 1986.

Gerhardson, Birger. *Memory and Manuscript*. Acta Seminarii Neotestamentici Upsaliensis 22. Translated by Eric J. Sharpe. Lund: Gleerup, 1961.

Gill, David W. J. "The Roman Empire as a Context for the New Testament." In *Handbook to Exegesis of the New Testament*, edited by Stanley E. Porter, 389–406. 3rd ed. Boston: Brill Academic, 2002.

Gilliard, Frank D. "More Silent Reading in Antiquity: *Non Omne Verbum Sonabat*." *Journal of Biblical Literature* 112 (1993) 689–94.

Goody, John R. *The Domestication of the Savage Mind*. Themes in the Social Sciences. Cambridge: Cambridge University Press, 1977.

———. *The Logic of Writing and the Organization of Society*. Studies in Literacy, the Family, Culture and the State. Cambridge: Cambridge University Press, 1986.

Goody, John R., and Ian Watt. "The Consequences of Literacy." In *Literacy in Traditional Societies*, edited by Jack Goody, 27–84. Cambridge: Cambridge University Press, 1968.

Gravilov, Andrei K. "Reading Techniques in Classical Antiquity." *Catholic Quarterly* 47 (1997) 56–73.

Guthrie, George H. "Cohesion, Shifts and Stitches in Philippians." In *Discourse Analysis and Other Topics in Biblical Greek*, edited by Stanley E. Porter et al., 36–59. Sheffield: Sheffield Academic, 1995.

The Hamburg Declaration on Adult Learning and the Agenda for the Future. Hamburg: UNESCO, 1997. UNESDOC Digital library, https://unesdoc.unesco.org/ark:/48223/pf0000116114.

Halverson, John. "Goody and the Implosion of the Literacy Thesis." *Man*, new ser., 27.2 (1992).

Harris, William V. *Ancient Literacy.* Cambridge: Harvard University Press, 1989.

Harvey, John D. *Listening to the Text: Oral Patterning in Paul's Letters.* Evangelical Theological Society Studies 1. Grand Rapids: Baker, 1998.

Havelock, Eric A. *The Liberal Temper in Greek Politics.* New Haven: Yale University Press, 1957.

———. *The Muse Learns to Write: Reflections on Orality and Literacy from Antiquity to the Present.* New Haven: Yale University Press, 1986. Reprinted, 2005.

———. *Preface to Plato.* Cambridge, Mass.: Harvard University Press, 1982.

———. Review of *Preface to Plato*, by Robert G. Hoerber. *Classical Philology* 59 (1964) 70–71.

———. Review of *Preface to Plato*, by Stacia Dunn Neeley, et al. *Rhetoric Review* 17 (1998) 201–3.

Hays, Richard B. *Echoes of Scripture in the Letters of Paul.* New Haven: Yale University Press, 1989. Revised and reprinted, 1993.

———. *The Conversion of the Imagination: Paul as Interpreter of Israel's Scripture.* Grand Rapids: Eerdmans, 2005.

———. *The Faith of Jesus Christ: The Narrative Substructure of Galatians 3.1—4.11.* Revised and enlarged ed. Biblical Resource Series. Grand Rapids: Eerdmans, 2002.

———. "The Letter to the Galatians." In *2 Corinthians, Galatians, Ephesians, Philippians, Colossians, 1 & 2 Thessalonians, 1 & 2 Timothy, Titus, Philemon.* Vol. 11 of *The New Interpreter's Bible*, edited by Leander E. Keck, 139–348. Nashville: Abingdon, 2000.

Hearon, Holly, and Philip Ruge Jones, eds. *The Bible in Ancient and Modern Media: Story and Performance.* Biblical Performance Criticism Series 1. Eugene, OR: Cascade Books, 2009.

———. "The Story of 'the Woman Who Anointed Jesus' as Social Memory: A Methodological Proposal for the Study of Tradition as Memory." *Semeia* 52 (2005) 99–118.

Heckl, Raik. "Ein Bezugstext für Gal 3.21B." *Novum Testamentum* 65 (2003) 260–64.

Heidegger, Martin. "Die Frage nach der Technik." In *Vorträge und Aufsätze*, 13–44. Pfullingen: Günther Neske, 1954.

———. *Sein und Zeit.* 17th ed. Tübingen: Max Niemeyer, 1993.

Henten, Jan Willem van, and Luuk Huitink. "The Publication of Flavius Josephus's Works and their Audiences." *Zutot: Perspectives on Jewish Culture* 6 (2009) 49–60.

Holland, Glenn S. "'Delivery, Delivery, Delivery.' Accounting for Performance in the Rhetoric of Paul's Letters." In *Paul and Ancient Rhetoric Theory and Practice in the Hellenistic Context*, edited by Stanley S. Porter et al., 119–40. New York: Cambridge University Press, 2016.

———. "Playing to the Groundlings: Shakespeare Performance Criticism and Performance Criticism of the Biblical Texts." *Neotestamentica* 41 (2007) 317–40.

Horsley, Richard A. "Prominent Patterns in the Social Memory of Jesus and Friends." *Semeia* 52 (2005) 57–78.

Hurtado, Larry W. "Correcting Iverson's 'Correction'." *New Testament Studies* 62 (2016) 201–6.

———. *The Earliest Christian Artefacts: Manuscripts and Christian Origins.* Grand Rapids: 2006.

———. "Greco-Roman Textuality and the Gospel of Mark A Critical Assessment of Werner Kelber's The Oral and the Written Gospel." *Bulletin for Biblical Research* 7 (1997) 91–106.

———. "Manuscripts and the Sociology of Early Christian Reading." In *The Early Text of the New Testament,* edited by Charles E. Hill et al., 49–62. Oxford: Oxford University Press, 2012.

———. "Oral Fixation and New Testament Studies? 'Orality,' 'Performance' and Reading Texts in Early Christianity." *New Testament Studies* 60 (2014) 321–40.

———. "What Do the Earliest Christian Manuscripts Tell Us about their Readers?" In *The World of Jesus and the Earliest Church,* edited by Craig A. Evans, 179–92. Peabody: Hendrickson, 2011.

Ito, Akio. "The written Torah and the Oral Gospel: Romans 10.5–13 in the Dynamic Tension between Orality and Literacy." *Novum Testamentum* 3 (2006) 234–60.

Iverson, Kelly R. "Oral Fixation or Oral Corrective? A Response to Larry Hurtado." *New Testament Studies* 62 (2016) 183–200.

Jaffee, Martin S. "The Oral-Cultural Matrix of the Talmud Yerushalmi: Comparative Perspectives on Rhetorical Paideia, Discipleship, and the Concept of Oral Torah." In *The Talmud Yerushalmi and Graeco-Roman Culture, Volume 1,* edited by Peter Schäfer, 7–61. Texte und Studien zum antiken Judentum 71. Tübingen: Mohr Siebeck, 1998.

———. "A Rabbinic Ontology of the Written and Spoken Word: On Discipleship. Transformative Knowledge, and the Living Texts of Oral Torah." *Journal of the American Academy of Religion* 65 (1997) 525–49.

Jakobson, Roman. "Closing Statements: Linguistics and Poetics." In *Style in Language,* edited by Thomas A. Sebeok, 350–77. Cambridge: MIT, 1960.

Jervis, L. Ann. *Galatians.* Understanding the Bible Commentary Series. Grand Rapids: Baker, 2011.

Jewett, Robert. "The Agitators and the Galatian Congregations." *New Testament Studies* 17 (1971) 198–212.

Johnson, Lee A. "Pauls Letters as Artifacts: The Value of the Written Text among Non-Literate People." *Biblical Theology Bulletin* 46 (2016) 25–34.

Johnson, William A., and Holt N. Parker, eds. *Ancient Literacies: The Culture of Reading in Greece and Rome.* Oxford: Oxford University Press, 2009.

———. Introduction. In *Ancient Literacies: The Culture of Reading in Greece and Rome,* edited by William A. Johnson et al., 3–12. Oxford: Oxford University Press, 2009.

———. *Readers and Reading Culture in the High Roman Empire.* Oxford: Oxford University Press, 2010.

———. "Toward a Sociology of Reading in Classical Antiquity." *American Journal of Philology* 121 (2000) 593–627.

Keener, Craig S. *Galatians*. New Cambridge Bible Commentary. Cambridge: Cambridge University Press, 2018.

Keith, Chris. *Jesus against the Scribal Elite: The Origins of Conflict*. Grand Rapids: Baker, 2014.

———. *Jesus' Literacy: Scribal Culture and the Teacher from Galilee*. Library of New Testament Studies 8. London: T. & T. Clark, 2011.

———. "'In My Own Hand': Grapho-Literacy and the Apostle Paul." *Biblica* 89 (2008) 39–58.

Keith, Chris, and Larry W. Hurtado. "Writing and Book Production in the Hellenistic and Roman Period." In *The New Cambridge History of the Bible: From the Beginnings to 600*, edited by James C. Paget et al., 63–80. Cambridge: Cambridge University Press, 2013.

Kelber, Werner H. "The Case of the Gospels: Memory's Desire and the Limits of Historical Criticism." *Oral Tradition* 17 (2002) 55–86.

———. "In the Beginning Were the Words: The Apotheosis and Narrative Displacement of the Logos." *Journal of the American Academy of Religion* 58.1 (1990) 68–98.

———. "The Generative Force of Memory: Early Christian Traditions as Processes of Remembering." *Biblical Theology Bulletin* 36 (2016) 15–22.

———. "Jesus and Tradition: Words in Time, Words in Space." *Semeia* 65 (1994) 139–67.

———. "Modality of Communication, Cognition and Physiology of Perception: Orality, Rhetoric, and Scribality." *Semeia* 65 (1994) 193–212.

———. *The Oral and the Written Gospel: The Hermeneutics of Speaking and Writing in the Synoptic Tradition, Mark, Paul, and Q*. Philadelphia: Fortress, 1983. Reprinted with a new introduction by the author. Bloomington: Indiana University Press, 1997.

———. "The Works of Memory: Christian Origins as MnemoHistory—A Response." *Semeia* 52 (2005) 221–48.

Kennedy, George A. *A New History of Classical Rhetoric*. Princeton: Princeton University Press, 1994.

———. *New Testament Interpretation through Rhetorical Criticism*. Chapel Hill: University of North Carolina Press, 1984.

———. "Prooemion." In *On Rhetoric: A Theory of Civic Discourse*, by Aristotle, ix–xiii. Translated with Introduction, Notes, and Appendices by George A. Kennedy. 2nd ed. New York: Oxford University Press, 2007.

Kern, Philip H. *Rhetoric and Galatians: Assessing an Approach to Paul's Epistle*. Society for New Testament Studies Monograph Series 101. Cambridge: Cambridge University Press, 1998.

Kim, Seon Yong. *Curse Motifs in Galatians: An Investigation into Paul's Rhetorical Strategies*. Wissenschaftliche Untersuchungen zum Neuen Testament 531. Tübingen: Mohr Siebeck, 2019.

Kirk, Alan, and Tom Thatcher. "Jesus Tradition as Social Memory." *Semeia* 52 (2005) 25–42.

———. "Social and Cultural Memory." *Semeia* 52 (2005) 1–24.

Klauck, Hans-Josef. *Ancient Letters and the New Testament: A Guide to Context and Exegesis*. Translated, revised, and elaborated with the collaboration of Daniel P. Bailey. Waco: Baylor University Press, 2006.

Knox, Bernard M. W. "Silent Reading in Antiquity." *Greek, Roman, and Byzantine Studies* 9 (1968) 421–35.

Koch, Alex-Dietrich. *Die Schrift als Zeuge des Evangeliums: Untersuchungen zur Verwendung und zum Verständnis der Schrift bei Paulus*. Beiträge zur historischen Theologie 69. Tübingen: Mohr Siebeck, 1986.

Kristeva, Julia. "Le mot, le dialogue et le roman." In Σημειωτικὴ: *Reserches pour une sémanalyse*, 82–112. Paris: Seuil, 1969.

———. "Word, Dialogue, and Novel." In *Desire in Language: A Semiotic Approach to Literature and Art*, edited by Leon S. Roudiez, 64–91. New York: Columbia University Press, 1980.

Lampe, Peter. "*Reticentia* in der Argumentation: Gal 3.10–12 als *Stipatio Enthymematum*." In *Das Urchristentum in seiner literarischen Geschichte: Festschrift für Jürgen Becker zum 65 Geburtstag*, edited by Ulrich Mell et al., 27–39. Beihefte zur Zeitschrift für die neutestamentliche Wissenschaft 100. Berlin: de Gruyter, 1999.

Lewis, Charlton T., and Charles Short. *A Latin Dictionary*. Oxford: Oxford University Press, 1879. Reprinted, 1980.

Lietaert Peerbolte, Bert Jan. "Pauline Christianity as an Urban Phenomenon." In *Early Christian Encounters with Town and Countryside: Essays on the Urban and Rural Worlds of Early Christianity*, edited by Markus Tiwald et al., 195–209. Novum Testamentum et Orbis Antiquus. Göttingen: Vandenhoeck and Ruprecht, 2021.

———. *Paulus en de rest. Van farizeeër tot profeet van Jezus*. Meinema: Zoetermeer, 2010.

Lietzmann, Hans. *An die Galater*. Handbuch zum Neuen Testament 10. 4th rev. ed. Tübingen: Mohr Siebeck, 1971.

Lightfoot, Joseph B. *Saint Paul's Epistle to the Galatians*. 10th ed. London: MacMillan, 1986.

Long, Frederic J., and T. Michael W. Halcomb. *Speak Koinè Greek: A Conversational Phrasebook*. Accessible Greek Resources and Online Studies 1. Wilmore: Glossa-House, 2014.

Longenecker, Richard N. *Galatians*. World Biblical Commentary 41. Dallas: Word, 1990.

Lord, Albert B. "Homer as Oral Poet." *Harvard Studies in Classical Philology* 72 (1968) 1–46.

———. *The Singer of Tales*. 2nd ed. Edited by Stephen Mitchell, et al. Cambridge: Harvard University Press, [1960] 2000.

Lührmann, Dieter. *Der Brief an die Galater*. 3rd ed. Zürcher Bibelkommentare Neues Testament 7. Zürich: Theologischer Verein Zürich, 2001.

Luther, Martin. *Erklärung des Briefes St. Pauli an die Galater*. 2nd ed. Stuttgart: Calwer, 1925.

Macdonald, Michael C. A. "Literacy in an Oral Environment." In *Writing and Ancient Near Eastern Society: Papers in Honor of Alan R. Miljard*, edited by Piotr Bienkowski et al., 49–118. London: T. & T. Clark, 2005.

MacMullen, Ramsay. *Christianizing the Roman Empire (AD 100–400)*. New Haven: Yale University Press, 1984.

Martyn, J. Louis. "Apocalyptic Antinomies in Paul's Letter to the Galatians." *New Testament Studies* 31 (1985) 410–24.

———. "Events in Galatia: Modified Covenantal Nomism versus God's Invasion of the Cosmos in the Singular Gospel: A Response to J. D. G. Dunn and B. R. Gaventa." In *Pauline Theology*. Vol. 1: *Thessalonians, Philippians, Galatians, Philemon*, edited by Jouette M. Bassler, 160–79. Minneapolis: Fortress, 1991.

———. *Galatians: A New Translation with Introduction and Commentary*. Anchor Bible 33A. New York: Doubleday, 1997.

Mayordomo, Moisés. *Argumentiert Paulus logisch? Eine Analyse vor dem Hintergrund antiker Logik*. Wissenschaftliche Untersuchungen zum Neuen Testament 188. Tübingen: Mohr Siebeck, 2005.

Matera, Frank J. *Galatians*. Sacra Pagina Series 9. Collegeville, MN: Liturgical, 1992.

McKnight, Scot. *Galatians*. NIV Application Commentary. Grand Rapids: Zondervan, 1995.

McLuhan, Marshall. *The Gutenberg Galaxy: The Making of Typographical Man*. Toronto: University of Toronto Press, 1962. Reprinted, 2011.

McLuhan, Marshall, et al. *The Medium is the Message: An Inventory of Effects*. London: Penguin Books, 1967. Reprinted, Berkeley: Gingko, 2001.

Meeks, Wayne A. *The First Urban Christians: The Social World of the Apostle Paul*. 2nd ed. New Haven: Yale University Press, 1983. Reprinted, 200

Meider, Thomas, et al. *Materiale Textkulturen: Konzepte—Materialien—Praktiken*. Materiale Textkulturen 1. Berlin: de Gruyter, 2015.

Melia, Daniel F. "Orality and Aristotle's Aesthetics and Methods: Take #2." In *Oral Performance and Its Context*, edited by Chris Mackie, 117–28. Mnemosyne Supplements 248. Boston: Brill Academic, 2003.

Michel, Otto. *Paulus und seine Bibel*. Beiträge zur Förderung christlicher Theologie 2/18. Gütersloh: Bertelsmann, 1929. Reprinted, Darmstadt: Wissenschaftlicher Buchgesellschaft, 1972.

Milnor, Kristina. "Literary Literacy in Roman Pompeii: The Case of Vergil's *Aeneid*." In *Ancient Literacies: The Culture of Reading in Greece and Rome*, edited by William A. Johnson, et al., 288–319. Oxford: Oxford University Press, 2009.

Mink, Gerd. "Eine umfassende Genealogie der neutestamentlichen Überlieferung." *New Testament Studies* 39 (1993) 481–99.

Mitchell, Margaret. "New Testament Envoys in the Context of Greco-Roman Diplomatic and Epistolary Conventions: The Example of Timothy and Titus." *Journal of Biblical Literature* 111 (1992) 641–92.

Mitchell, Stephen, ed. *The Rise of the Church*, Vol. 2 of *Anatolia: Land, Men, and Gods in Asia Minor*. Oxford: Clarendon, 1993.

Moo, Douglas J. *Galatians*. Baker Exegetical Commentary on the New Testament. Grand Rapids: Baker Academic, 2013.

Morgan, Teresa. *Literate Education in the Hellenistic and Roman Worlds*. Cambridge: Cambridge University Press, 1998.

Murphy O'Connor, Jerome. *Paul the Letter-Writer: His World, His Options, His Skills*. Good News Studies 41. Collegeville, MN: Liturgical, 1995.

Mussner, Franz. *Der Galaterbrief; Auslegung*. 5th ed. Herders Theologischer Kommentar zum Neuen Testament 9. Freiburg: Herder, 1974.

———. *Paul a Critical Life*. Oxford and New York: Oxford University Press, 1996.

Nässelqvist, Dan. *Public Reading in Early Christianity: Lectors, Manuscripts, and Sound in the Oral Delivery of John 1–4*. Novum Testamentum Supplements 163. Leiden: Brill, 2016.

Nanos, Mark D. *The Irony of Galatians: Paul's Letter in First-Century Context*. Minneapolis: Fortress, 2002.

Niditch, Susan. *Oral World and Written Word: Ancient Israelite Literature*. Library of Ancient Israel. Louisville: Westminster John Knox, 1996.

Norden, Eduard. *Die antike Kunstprosa, Volume 1–2*. 4th ed. Leipzig: Teubner, 1923.

Oestreich, Bernhard. *Performanzkritik der Paulusbriefe*. Wissenschaftliche Untersuchungen zum Neuen Testament 296. Tübingen: Mohr Siebeck, 2012.

———. *Performance Criticism of the Pauline Letters*. Translated by Lindsay Elias and Brent Blum. Biblical Performance Criticism Series 14. Eugene, OR: Cascade Books, 2016.

Ong, Walter J. *Language as Hermeneutic: A Primer on the Word and Digitization*. Edited and with Commentaries by Thomas D. Zlatic and Sara van den Berg. Ithaca: Cornell University Press, 2018.

———. *Orality and Literacy: The Technologizing of the Word*. London: Methuen, 1982. Reprinted, New York: Routledge, 2002.

———. *The Presence of the Word: Some Prolegomena for Cultural and Religious History*. New Haven: Yale University Press, 1967, Reprinted, Binghamton: Global, 2000.

———. "The Psychodynamics of Oral Memory and Narrative: Some Implications for Biblical Studies." In *The Pedagogy of God's Image: Essays on Symbol and the Religious Imagination*, edited by Robert Masson, 55–73. Catholic Theological Society of America Proceedings. Chico, CA: Scholars, 1981.

———. *Rhetoric, Romance, and Technology: Studies in the Interaction of Expression and Culture*. Ithaca: Cornell University Press, 1971.

Parker, Holt N. "Books and Reading Latin Poetry." In *Ancient Literacies: The Culture of Reading in Greece and Rome*, edited by William A. Johnson, et al., 186–229. Oxford: Oxford University Press, 2009.

Parry, Milman. "Homeric Formulae and Homeric Metre." In *The Making of Homeric Verse: The Collected Papers by Milman Parry*, edited by Adam Parry, 191–239. New York: Oxford University Press, 1971. Translation of *Les Formules et la métrique d'Homère*. Paris: 1928.

———. "The Homeric Gloss: A Study in Word-sense." *Transactions of the American Philological Association* 59 (1928) 233–47. Reprinted in *The Making of Homeric Verse: The Collected Papers by Milman Parry*, edited by Adam Parry, 240–50. New York: Oxford University Press, 1971.

———. "Studies in the Epic Technique of Oral Verse-Making I: Homer and Homeric Style." *Harvard Studies in Classical Philology* 41 (1930) 73–147.

———. "Studies in the Epic Technique of Oral Verse-Making II: Homeric Language as the Language of an Oral Poetry." *Harvard Studies in Classical Philology* 43 (1932) 1–50.

———. "The Traditional Epithet in Homer." In *The Making of Homeric Verse: The Collected Papers by Milman Parry*, edited by Adam Parry, 1–190. New York: Oxford University Press, 1971. Translation of *L'Épithet traditionnelle dans Homère: Essai sur un problème de style homérique*. Revue de Philologie de Littérature et d'Histoire Anciennes 3. Paris: Klincksieck, 1929.

The Persepolis Declaration. Paris: UNESCO, 1975.

Person, Raymond F., Jr. "The Ancient Israelite Scribe as Performer." *Journal of Biblical Literature* 117 (1998) 601–9.

Popović, Mladen. "Reading, Writing, and Memorizing Together: Reading Culture in Ancient Judaism and the Dead Sea Scrolls in a Mediterranean Context." *Dead Sea Discoveries* 24 (2017) 447–70.

Porter, Stanley E. *Idioms of the Greek New Testament*. 2nd ed. Biblical Languages: Greek 2. Sheffield: Sheffield Academic, 1992.

Porter, Stanley E., and Kent D. Clarke. "What Is Exegesis? An Analysis of Various Definitions." In *Handbook to Exegesis of the New Testament*, edited by Stanley E. Porter, 3–23. 3rd ed. Boston: Brill Academic, 2002.

Powell, Barry B. "Text, Orality, Literacy, Tradition, Dictation, Education, and Other Paradigms of Explication in Greek Literary Studies." *Oral Tradition* 15 (2000) 96–125.

———. *Writing: Theory and History of the Technology of Civilization*. Oxford: Wiley Blackwell, 2009.

Prager, Jeffrey. *Presenting the Past and the Sociology of Misremembering*. Cambridge: Harvard University Press, 1998.

Quintilian. *Orator's Education, Volume IV: Books 9–10*. Loeb Classical Library 127. Edited and translated by Donald A. Russel. Cambridge: Harvard University Press, 2002.

Rhoads, David M. "Performance Criticism: An Emerging Discipline (Part I and II)." *Biblical Theology Bulletin* 36 (2006) 118–33, 164–84. https://biblicalperformancecriticism.org/index.php.

Richards, E. Randolph. *Paul and First-Century Letter Writing: Secretaries, Composition, and Collection*. Downers Grove, IL: InterVarsity, 2004.

———. *Secretary in the Letters of Paul*. Wissenschaftliche Untersuchungen zum Neuen Testament 2/42. Tübingen: Mohr Siebeck, 1991.

Ricoeur, Paul. *From Text to Action: Essays in Hermeneutics II. Studies in Phenomenology and Existential Philosophy*. Translated by Kathleen Blamey, et al., with a foreword by Richard Kearney. London: Athlone, 1991.

———. "What Is a Text? Explanation and Understanding" In *Hermeneutics and the Human Sciences: Essays on Language, Action, and Interpretation*, edited, translated, and introduced by John B. Thompson, 145–64. Cambridge: Cambridge University Press, 1981.

Roberts, Colin H. "Books in the Graeco-Roman World in the New Testament." In *From the Beginnings to Jerome*, edited by Peter R. Ackroyd, et al., 48–66. *The Cambridge History of the Bible*, vol. 1. Cambridge: Cambridge University Press, 1970.

Rohde, Joachim. *Der Brief des Paulus an die Galater*. Theologischer Handkommentar zum Neuen Testament 9. Berlin: Evangelische Verlagsanstalt 1989.

Rodríguez, Rafael. *Oral Tradition and the New Testament: A Guide for the Perplexed*. London: Bloomsbury, 2014.

———. "Reading and Hearing in Ancient Contexts." *Journal for the Study of the New Testament* 32 (2009) 151–78.

———. *Structuring Early Christian Memory: Jesus in Tradition, Performance, and Text*. Library of New Testament Studies. London: T. & T. Clark, 2010.

Rubinelli, Sara. *Ars Topica: The Classical Technique of Constructing Arguments from Aristotle to Cicero*. Argumentation Library. Dordrecht: Springer, 2009.

Ruf, Martin G. *Die Heiligen Propheten, Eure Apostel und Ich: Metatextuelle Studien zum zweiten Petrusbrief*. Wissenschaftlichen Untersuchungen zum Neuen Testament 300. Tübingen: Mohr Siebeck, 2011.

Sanders, E. P. *Paul and Palestinian Judaism: A Comparison of Patterns of Religion*. Philadelphia: Fortress, 1977.

———. *Paul, the Law, and the Jewish People*. Minneapolis: Augsburg Fortress, 1983.

Scheid, John, and Jesper Svenbro. *The Craft of Zeus: Myths of Weaving and Fabric*. Cambridge, Mass.: Harvard University Press, 1996. Reprinted, 2006. Translation of *Le métier de Zeus: Mythe de tissage et du tissu dans le monde gréco-romain*. Paris: Découverte, 1994.

Schlier, Heinrich. *Der Brief an die Galater*. 6th rev. ed. Kritisch-Exegetischer Kommentar über das Neue Testament 7. Göttingen: Vandenhoeck & Ruprecht, 1989.

Schnackenburg, Rudolf. *Das Heilsgeschehen bei der Taufe nach dem Apostel Paulus*. München: Zink, 1950.

Schreiner, Thomas R. *Galatians*. Zondervan Exegetical Commentary on the New Testament. Grand Rapids: Zondervan, 2010.

Schwartz, Barry. *Abraham Lincoln and the Forge of National Memory*. Chicago: University of Chicago Press, 2000.

———. "Christian Origins: Historical Truth and Social Memory." *Semeia* 52 (2005) 43–58.

———. "Jesus in First-Century Memory—A Response." *Semeia* 52 (2005) 249–62.

Shiell, William D. *Reading Acts: the Lector and the Early Christian Audience*. Leiden: Brill, 2004.

Shiner, Whitney. *Proclaiming the Gospel: First-century Performance of Mark*. Harrisburg: Trinity, 2003.

Stanley, Christopher D. *Arguing with Scripture: The Rhetoric of Quotations in the Letters of Paul*. London: T. & T. Clark, 2004.

Starr, Raymond. "*Lectores* and Book Reading." *Classical Journal* 86 (1990–91) 337–43.

Stirewalt, M. Luther, Jr. *Paul: the Letter Writer*. Grand Rapids: Eerdmans, 2003.

Street, Brian V. *Literacy in Theory and Practice*. Cambridge Studies in Oral and Literate Culture 9. Cambridge: Cambridge University Press, 1984. Reprinted, 1993, 1995.

Sumney, Jerry L. "Studying Paul's Opponents: Advances and Challenges." In *Paul and His Opponents*, edited by Stanley E. Porter, 17–24. Pauline Studies 2. Leiden: Brill, 2005.

Thomas, Rosalind. *Literacy and Orality in Ancient Greece*. Cambridge: Cambridge University Press, 1992.

———. "Writing, Reading, Public and Private 'Literacies': Functional Literacy and Democratic Literacy in Greece." In *Ancient Literacies: The Culture of Reading in Greece and Rome*, edited by William A. Johnson, et al., 13–45. Oxford: Oxford University Press, 2009.

Tov, Emanuel. *Textual Criticism of the Hebrew Bible*. 3rd ed. Minneapolis: Fortress, 2012.

Trebilco, Paul R., "Jewish Background." In *Handbook to Exegesis of the New Testament*, edited by Stanley E. Porter, 359–88. 3rd ed. Boston: Brill Academic, 2002.

Valette-Cagnac, Emmanuelle. *La lecture à Rome: rites et pratiques*. Paris: Bellin, 1997.

Vanhoye, Cardinal A., and Peter S. Williamson. *Galatians*. Catholic Commentary on Sacred Scripture. Grand Rapids: Baker Academic, 2019.

Veen, Ben F. van. "Een staaltje van paulinische hermeneutiek: Een onderzoek naar het gebruik van de Heilige Schriften door Paulus in Gal 3.6–14." MTh thesis, Vrije Universiteit, 2001.

Vos, Johan S. "Die Hermeneutische Antinomie bei Paulus. Galater 3.11–12 und Römer 10.5–10." *New Testament Studies* 38 (1992) 245–70.

Vouga, François. *An die Galater*. Handbuch zum Neuen Testament 10. Tübingen: Mohr Siebeck, 1998.

Wakefield, Andrew H. *Where to Live: The Hermeneutical Significance of Paul's Citations from Scripture in Galatians 3:1–14*. Society of Biblical Literature Academia Biblica 14. Atlanta: Society of Biblical Literature, 2003.

Ward, Richard F. "Pauline Voice and Presence as a Strategic Communication." *Semeia* 65 (1994) 95–107.

Weima, Jeffrey A. D. *Paul the Ancient Letter Writer: An Introduction to Epistolary Analysis*. Grand Rapids: Baker, 2016.

West, Travis. *The Art of Biblical Performance: Performance Criticism and the Genre of the Biblical Narratives*. PhD thesis, Vrije Universiteit, 2018.

Williams, Sam K. *Galatians*. Abingdon New Testament Commentary. Nashville: Abingdon, 1997.

Wischmeyer, Oda. ed. *Lexikon der Bibelhermeneutik: Begriffe, Methoden, Theorien, Konzepte*. Berlin: de Gruyter, 2005.

———. "Texte, Text und Rezeption: Das Paradigma der Tekst-Rezeptions-Hermeneutik des Neuen Testaments." In *Die Bibel als Tekst: Beiträge zu einer textbezogenen Bibelhermeneutik*, edited by Oda Wischmeyer, et al., 155–92. Neutestamentliche Entwürfe zur Theologie 14. Tübingen: Francke, 2008.

Witherington, Ben, III. *Grace in Galatia: A Commentary on St Paul's Letter to the Galatians*. Edinburgh: T. & T. Clark, 1998.

Wittgenstein, Ludwig. *Philosophische Untersuchungen*. 9th ed. Berlin: Suhrkamp, 2003.

Wolf, Maryanne. *Proust and the Squid: The Story and Science of the Reading Brain*. New York: Harper, 2007.

Wright, Brian J. "Ancient Literacy in New Testament Research: Incorporating a Few More Lines of Enquiry." *Trinity Journal* 36 n.s. (2015) 161–89.

———. *Communal Reading in the Time of Jesus: A Window into Early Christian Reading Practices*. Minneapolis: Fortress, 2017.

Wright, N. T. *The Climax of the Covenant: Christ and the Law in Pauline Theology*. Minneapolis: Fortress, 1991.

———. *Paul, A Biography*. San Francisco: HarperOne, 2018.

Yoon, David I. *A Discourse Analysis of Galatians and the New Perspective on Paul*. Linguistic Biblical Studies 17. Leiden: Brill, 2019.

Ziesler, John. *Galatians*. Epworth Commentary Series. London: Epworth, 1992.

Zwiep, Arie W. *Jairus's Daughter and the Haemorrhaging Woman: Tradition and Interpretation of an Early Christian Miracle Story*. Wissenschaftliche Untersuchungen zum Neuen Testament 421. Tübingen: Mohr Siebeck, 2019.

———. "Traditie, oraliteit en schriftelijkheid in de perikoop *haemorrhoisa et filia Jairi* (Mar. 5:21–43 parr.): Een tussentijdse bestandopname." *Kerk en Theologie* 69 (2018) 239–54.

———. *Tussen tekst en lezer: Een historische inleiding in de bijbelse hermeneutiek*. 2 vols. Amsterdam: VU University Press, 2009–13.

www.ingramcontent.com/pod-product-compliance
Lightning Source LLC
Chambersburg PA
CBHW071232230426
43668CB00011B/1402